Reform and Regicide

REFORM AND REGICIDE

The Reign of Peter III of Russia

CAROL S. LEONARD

INDIANA UNIVERSITY PRESS

Bloomington and Indianapolis

The paper used in this publication meets the minimum requirements of American
National Standard for Information Sciences—Permanence of Paper for Printed
Library Materials, ANSI Z39.48-1984.
∞™

Manufactured in the United States of America

Library of Congress Cataloging-in-Publication Data
Leonard. Carol S.
Reform and regicide : the reign of Peter III of Russia / Carol S.
Leonard.
p.   cm.—(Indiana-Michigan series in Russian and East
European studies)
Includes bibliographical references and index.
ISBN 0-253-33322-9 (cloth : alk. paper)
1. Peter III, Emperor of Russia, 1728–1762.   2. Soviet Union—
History—Peter III, 1762.   I. Title.   II. Series.
DK166.L64 1992
947'.062—dc20   92–5176
1 2 3 4 5   97 96 95 94 93

CONTENTS

ACKNOWLEDGMENTS

Among the organizations and institutions which made my research possible, I am especially grateful to the International Research and Exchanges Board, the American Council of Learned Societies, the Department of History at Indiana University, the Russian Research Center at Harvard University, and the administration at the State University of New York at Plattsburgh. I would also like to express appreciation for the invaluable assistance of archival authorities in Russia and Western Europe, particularly Svetlana Romanovna Dolgova and other members of the staff at the Central State Archive of Ancient Acts, Liudmila Evgenievna Selivanova at the Foreign Sector of the Main Archival Administration, and the staff of the manuscript divisions of the Lenin Library in Moscow and the Saltykov-Shchedrin Library in St. Petersburg, the Archives of the Ministry of Foreign Affairs in Paris, France, the State Archive at Oldenburg, Germany, and the Slavonic Division of the Helsinki University Library. Bent Madsen at the State Archive in Copenhagen, Denmark, was extremely generous in his assistance.

I have a special debt of gratitude to Michael Metcalf, professor of Scandinavian history at the University of Minnesota, who assisted me in the early 1970s in my archival work in Stockholm and again in 1990 in patiently reading the chapters of my revised manuscript. All the translations of Swedish material are his.

I am indebted for many of my ideas about Peter III and eighteenth-century Russia to those who have read and commented on my manuscript. Daniel Field must receive heartfelt thanks for his many insights and for his encouragement. David Griffiths, Herbert Kaplan, Nancy Leonard, Boris Mironov, Marc Raeff, David Ransel, and Douglas Skopp gave me criticism and guidance. Anonymous comments by readers for the press were useful. Richard Wortman was especially helpful at a critical final stage. I greatly appreciated comments on particular chapters by Mikhail Timofeevich Beliavskii and Gregory Freeze. Robert Gallman, who read the manuscript with care, gave me invaluable advice.

Two years ago in St. Petersburg, it was a pleasure to discuss the ideas in this book with A. S. Myl'nikov, who began work on the reign of Peter III, as I did, in the early 1970s, and who drew much the same general conclusion from studying the archival and published sources. His book about the legend of Peter III has enriched my understanding.

During my work, I have been grateful to my close associates and friends for their cheerfulness and support. I am especially thankful to Nancy Condee, Suzanne Massie, and Nina Tumarkin, whose personal and professional support was important to me. I would also like to express enormous gratitude to Donald Bogle, Leonid Borodkin, John and Christine Bushnell, Ben Eklof, Heidi Kroll, Hiroaki Kuromiya, Alan Olmstead, Christine Porto, Amy Randall, Adam Ulam, and Mary Zirin. To Richard Sutch, who helped me think more broadly and more clearly, I owe a great deal.

I have followed the Library of Congress system of transliteration, with some modifications.

INTRODUCTION
INTERPRETING THE REIGN OF PETER III

After a reign of scarcely six months, on June 28, 1762, Peter III, Emperor of Russia, was deposed. His wife and successor, Catherine II, issued manifestoes that imparted a revolutionary significance to the carnival atmosphere in the capital, St. Petersburg, where imperial regiments massed in her support. Peter was overthrown, Catherine announced, because he threatened the institutions of state and society with arbitrary laws and alien customs.[1] In a second manifesto of July 6, Catherine elaborated her accusation with a list of alleged abuses of power.[2] Her appeal was as successful as her political victory, and her own image emerged as the representation of authority, the classical feminine allegorization of justice.[3] The coup d'état, with its augustan imagery, gave to the victors an exhilarating experience with a "mythic present."[4] Their writings, taken together with Catherine's manifestoes, can be seen to constitute a text. Implicitly the coup was a turning point, when new leadership emerged to redefine government and separate it from the legacy of irresponsible and foolish rulers of the past.

The victors' justifications have influenced historians, who present the coup as elite resistance to excessively authoritarian rule. The outcome, the liberal era that followed, has been seen as a vehicle of political modernization. This book argues that such a view of the significance of the coup is misleading.[5] The record shows no evidence of especially arbitrary rule. Peter III closely adhered to the traditional legislative process and took great interest in European liberal ideas. Indeed, his reign was an astonishing achievement of the pre-Catherinian Enlightenment, a witness to the force of the Petrine imperial idea between 1725 and 1762. Peter III left Catherine a legacy of reforms that make the first few years of her reign seem but a link in the chain between origins and outcomes.

This book attempts to shed new light on pre-Catherinian political culture. Peter's reign has provoked almost no empirical research, but it is the natural foundation for the study of Enlightenment absolutism in Russia. His rationalist vision reflected the fundamental aspirations of post-seventeenth-century secular rulers, mobilization of the economy and expansion of the powers of the state, with awareness that this entailed increasing the ability of the population to pay taxes. He transferred Church lands to the state, completing the Petrine ecclesiastical reforms. He improved revenues, eliminated overlapping functions of the central organs of power, and liberalized commercial regulations to encourage the grain trade in the south. He and his advisors raked over past laws trying to produce a more efficient government. His emancipation of nobles from obligatory state service overturned the unintended and undesired results of Petrine legislation binding the nobility to lifetime service. He had an active conception of the functions of government. Everywhere in the laws, one finds evidence of a government at work on technical problems relevant to such tasks as the production of munitions, the improvement of conditions of commerce and agricultural productivity, the building of canals, the making of maps, and the design of mental hospitals.[6] The harshest components of the Petrine legal system were subjected to an unmistakable Enlightenment critique. The medieval judicial procedure that extracted testimony by torture was overturned;[7] the idea of religious tolerance was introduced in an edict welcoming back to Russia the formerly persecuted Old Believers.[8] Peter III issued an amnesty for peasants who participated in revolts on monastic estates and extended a pardon to political exiles from the previous reign.

After the turmoil of rebellion in 1762 had subsided, Catherine implicitly recognized the new foundation of law by bringing the entire program of reforms to fruition in new enactments. She completed the Church reform in 1764. She allowed the emancipation of nobles to remain in effect and used it as the basis for her later Charter of Nobility of 1785. She repromulgated Peter's liberal commercial regulations. Even in foreign affairs, after castigating the peace with Prussia as proof of her predecessor's betrayal of the national interest, Catherine maintained the peace and renegotiated the alliance with Russia's former enemy, Prussia. Catherine shared with Peter an understanding of the vital importance of Prussia to the expansion of Russian interests in the Baltic.[9] Thus the claims of Catherine's manifestoes have little substance, even in some ways in regard to foreign policy.

Peter's rule was characterized by a combination of ongoing imperial reform tradition and Enlightenment thought. By the time of the coup d'état, Russians had tasted the reality, or the promise, of certain freedoms and welcomed the demise of certain traditions. Catherine's formulaic assertions can best be read as a guarantee that these achievements would not be lost and that reform would continue.

Continuity in reform revealed the powerful impact of Enlightenment ideas on the entire cohort that reached maturity in the 1750s. Although modern fiscal and political thinking was imported from the West in the reign of Elizabeth by scholars and publicists such as Vasilii Tatishchev (1686–1750) and Mikhail Lomonosov (1711–1765) and by statesmen such as Senator Peter Shuvalov (1711–1762), reformers failed to develop let alone weld together a consensus until the late 1750s. The impetus for the initiation of reform was the constraint on spending during the campaigns of the Seven Years' War (1756–1763). As a consequence of not meeting payrolls, the government became more willing to consider decisive changes to improve revenues. Planning for war reaped a rich harvest of economic and political ideas. The ablest of the reformers in Elizabeth's government was the physiocrat Dmitrii Volkov (1718–1785), a man with a speculative spirit, intellectually convinced in the value of free labor and the importance of trade for agriculture.

In January 1762, the proposals by Volkov and Aleksandr Glebov (1719–1790) attracted the new autocrat. Peter III announced a new program of reforms to the Senate and restructured the government to give his sponsorship to those who would carry it out. He appointed Glebov as general procurator of the Senate. He made Volkov, a noble insufficiently distinguished to be senator, imperial privy secretary and president of the College of Foreign Affairs. As the reform coalition grew stronger, Volkov acquired nearly ministerial powers which he channeled largely into domestic affairs.

Although Peter allowed Volkov's authority to grow at the expense of the Senate, as he initiated sweeping reforms, he also gave considerable authority to the Senate to carry them out. Peter thus strengthened the Senate's command over the ecclesiastical domain of power, over nobles' rights, and over the secret police and the courts. That is, he granted more authority to the Senate than it had wielded since the early 1740s. To be sure, the ruler diminished the Senate's role of initiation by his style of issuing personal manifestoes. In this way he tightened the line of imperial command over decision-making in state institutions. Whatever the long-term ramifications for the Senate of such political adjustments, a number of immediate consequences were significant—the reduction of conflict over policy and the control gained over the financial crisis. The unbudgeted needs of an aggressive foreign policy were met, while noble senators gained a fresh supply of loans from newly minted money and some short-term credit was extended to lower-ranking servitors.

Peter III and Catherine II secured their sovereign authority in the traditional way, by conferring state lands and peasants or, alternately, threatening confiscation. For example, Peter imposed his authority in Church affairs decisively and forcibly. He seized ecclesiastical lands and denied the Church's asserted rights and claims. Although the main short-term effect was to increase state revenues from new taxes and the long-term effect was to strengthen the economy of the former ecclesiastical sector by encouraging a more market-oriented agriculture, the central authority was also strengthened by this blow to ecclesiastical rights.

Meanwhile, the rights of the nobility were reaffirmed and their property secured: their estates, Peter declared, were no longer subject to confiscation for evasion of service. By freeing them from the service obligation, Peter gave nobles more political autonomy and economic independence. The impulse to ground social transformaton in legal rights marked the adaptation of the closely monitored statism of the Petrine model to the incentive orientation of the physiocrats.[10] These two reforms affecting the Church and the nobility constituted a fundamental redirection of policy, and they powerfully contributed to the political atmosphere of the time.[11]

This book is about the transformation of law. Why did autocrats seek new laws? What constraints or intellectual movements led to the development of a new ethic by which the governing Petrine principles were changed or enforced? The answer lies in the history of ideas, contracts, prices, property, politics, crime, and punishment. In this period, as the power of the post-Petrine mercantilist state increased, concern with efficiency and tax revenues was probably the single greatest part of administration, yet it by no means alone accounted for the interpenetration of Western European and Russian ideas of statecraft.[12]

. Before these larger issues can be addressed, it is necessary to explore the reputation of Peter III. The influence of the traditional derogatory portrait has prevented the substantive achievements of Peter's reign from emerging; historians are convinced that little of significance could have been enacted by him. V. A. Bil'basov's attack on Peter III in his biography of Catherine shows how deeply Catherine's writings could color perceptions of Peter's reign:

> It was Catherine's good fortune that Peter had no understanding of his position. After acquiring unlimited autocratic powers, convinced that everything was possible and that he would be forgiven everything, he gave free will to his whims. Poorly raised and badly educated, from his very first day on the throne, believing that it would be degrading even to think that his views might be challengeable, he pushed away all advisors. Self-confident in the manner of those who are uneducated, he determined to "spoil everything and overturn what had been established"; straightforward in the manner of adolescents, he shut his eyes to obstacles and did not want to listen to opinions contrary to his own. He even failed to understand that there, where his lowly subjects were—that was nothing, that power depended entirely on the educated elements of society, which, at the time, were the clergy and the military: he decreased the price of salt, and meanwhile offended the clergy and degraded the military.[13]

Bil'basov's description cannot be trusted, but to flesh out a new portrait or to show that Peter was perceived differently in his time one would need to use sources that no longer exist, and to disregard some of those that do. Personal details in diplomatic sources are particularly vulnerable to bias and rumor. One can indicate fairly easily on the basis of the laws, as some historians have done, that his leadership was not by any means destitute of coherence and rationality.[14] It is a more difficult matter to assess his direct role in state affairs on the basis of personal papers and correspondence.

Among rulers of the Enlightenment, we know almost nothing about Peter III apart from what was written down by the conspirators who deposed him. Not one of his closest advisors, Dmitrii Volkov, Aleksandr Glebov, Lev Naryshkin (1733–1799), or Aleksei Mel'gunov (1722–1788), left memoirs. The rich archival materials of Mikhail (1714–1767) and Roman Vorontsov (1707–1783) pertain to other years and contain no information of great value about Peter III or Dmitrii Volkov. Ivan Shuvalov's (1727–1797) papers date to the 1750s, before he withdrew from public life. In general, available correspondence from 1762 is meager. Little of importance, including the record of discussion preceding reforms, survived the evident eradications of Catherine after she ascended the throne. Peter's cabinet papers have almost entirely disappeared. The archives of his advisors and of diplomats, who disposed of incriminating evidence, have been purged. Given both the distortions and the gaps in the record, how can the historian hope to rightly reassess Peter's role and achievements?

Institutional records offer a place to begin a political biography. In looking at these records, piecing together a chronology, and attributing ideas to groups and individuals, I have had to draw on deduction, implication, and association. Each chapter of this book constitutes a study of a separate reform. Each is also a partial portrait of Peter III's government. Taken together, the chapters present a plausible alternative to the traditional interpretation.

The personal biography of Peter III offered below proceeds from a similar reconstruction. I have used selected sources, mainly the memoirs of his tutor, Jakob von Staehlin (1709–1785), and diplomatic dispatches by two diplomats not involved in the conspiracy (the British envoy Robert Keith and the Danish special envoy Gregors Christian von Haxthausen) dated from before his fall from power. I screened the hostile dispatches by diplomats such as Baron Breteuil of France and Mercy d'Argenteau of Austria, who were frustrated by their inability either to reverse Peter III's foreign policy or to get the conspirators to act. I have ignored much of the anecdotal material that entered the record after the coup. The observers I relied upon were not apologists. They did not discount the importance of Peter's rush into foreign policy decisions or his too close involvement in Holstein politics, which had a bearing on their assessment of his character. Yet they did provide confirmation that a narrow and dismissive view is incorrect. The typical description of Peter as "a sickly simpleton" who could be characterized by alleged "Lutheran proclivities," "blatantly provocative" steps, "contempt for things Russian," and "drunken antics" can properly be set in a semiological context as a veil of language drawn from the writings of the conspirators and the memoirs of Catherine, who concealed her competition for power by demeaning an able opponent.[15]

Karl Peter Ulrich, later Peter III, was born on February 10 (21), 1728, in Kiel, Holstein, where he was raised until the age of thirteen. His father, Karl Friedrich, Duke of Holstein-Gottorp, married Anna, the elder daughter of Peter I of Russia, in 1724. Through the house of Holstein, as a descendant of Charles XII's elder sister, Karl Peter Ulrich was in line to inherit the Swedish throne, and, as a descendent of Peter I, the Russian throne. After Peter I's death and his parents' expulsion from court, and particularly after the loss of his mother in infancy, the Holstein prince's ties to Russia were temporarily severed. His education nevertheless included instruction in the Russian language and Orthodox religion, but Swedish notebooks also appeared in his library along with instruction books in the Lutheran faith.

Peter's first tutors were among the university educated elite of Holstein, including an officer named Adlerfeld, the author of a history of Charles XII of Sweden. Peter learned French from a special tutor and—unwillingly—Latin from the Rector of the Kiel Latin school. Among his studies, the German language and Lutheran theology attracted his special interest, and he habitually read from his German Bible.[16] Because of the Holstein background of his tutors, pietism, the dominant strain of thought in the education of German princes, can assuredly be assigned a central place in the background of Peter III. According to German pietists, classical languages and literature were not important for their own sake. This may be the reason Peter did not acquire more than conversational fluency in foreign languages. His writing was graceless, hesitant, and forced.[17] Language, according to pietists, was a medium for instruction in theology. Peter's absorption of educational principles was revealed in his anticlericalism and hostility to ritual; at the same time he upheld values of faith.[18] German rulers shared with pietists a sense of the distinction between institutionalized forms of worship (ritual) and a spiritual essence. The Enlightenment in Germany may have been fundamentally protestant, as Ernst Troeltsch has demonstrated, but it still engendered a spirit of questioning and redefinition which made those who professed it relatively tolerant of other faiths (except perhaps Roman Catholicism) and anticlerical.

A Holstein education would also have accorded a central place to legal thought and to the history of Peter's ancestral lands. His seventeenth-century ancestor Christian Albrecht had been one of the first Enlightenment rulers in Europe. Albrecht considered the reform of institutions as the key to expanding human possibilities in a "historically determined political and social world."[19] His profound faith in natural law and dedication to the elimination of social abuse led him to examine the disjunction of institutions and the ideas they were meant to serve. German thinkers, more like the anti-Cartesian French philosophes than the followers of Christian Wolff, were wary of overspeculation. They dealt with realms of action and perception.

This was the intellectual tradition of the university culture from which Peter's tutors were chosen.[20] If he easily lost his concentration and did not read extensively, he was, it seems, imbued with a respect for learning. Later, in Russia, he sent for his father's large library from Holstein, and he continued throughout his life to supervise the purchase of new books for his library.[21]

In Holstein he acquired a military outlook. Through military advancement, he strained to transcend his youth and isolation at his father's court. He took exceptional pride in achieving the rank of lieutenant by the age of nine. His father's mission—to restore the greatness of the Duchy of Holstein—accounted for the strict regimen to which the young prince was subjected and for Peter's preoccupation with this goal. Peter often told his friends of a dream in which, with a handful of other officers, he routed an army of Danes, and sometimes, showing the emotional effect of the despair of his father's last years, he told the story as if it had actually happened.[22]

Peter arrived in Russia on February 5, 1742. His mother's sister, Empress Elizabeth, designated him her heir to the throne.[23] Left on his own at the Russian court and suffering from frequent illness, he nevertheless acquired an education. He was formally educated from 1742 to 1746. The Swedish officer, Marshall of the Court O. Brummer, who had cared for him since 1739, when his father died, was dismissed when he came of age as Duke of Holstein in August 1745.[24] He dismissed his court-appointed tutor, Jakob von Staehlin, in 1747 when he was eighteen.[25]

Staehlin, professor of elocution and poetry and member of the Russian Academy of Sciences, tutored him in, among other subjects, Russian and Orthodox theology,[26] which he studied with apparent success. At the ceremony where he accepted the Orthodox faith, on November 7, 1742, Peter was serious, well-versed, and composed.[27] Staehlin gave him lessons twice a week in each of three categories of knowledge: history and geography (Peter's best subject), mathematics and physics, and morals and politics. In the areas of moral philosophy and politics, Staehlin focused on the reform tradition in Russia, "the state as it is now and as it should be—what is still necessary to accomplish."[28] Using the common Enlightenment approach to education, Staehlin taught history from coins, botany from walks through the parks, geography from globes, current events from newspapers, and military strategy from models of fortifications. An adherent of the theories of Leibniz and Wolff, the tutor believed that knowledge began with the senses; visual experiences were more important than books. Staehlin tried to become the kind of friend with whom one shared confidences; he allowed Peter to define his own interests."[29] Staehlin thought the result was successful. At least in the beginning, Peter was a serious student. He became interested in the arts.[30] He came to love music and painting. He listened to opera and played the violin.[31] Peter demonstrated a good memory: "his memory was excellent to the smallest details," wrote Staehlin. "He willingly read travel accounts and military books." Staehlin described his pupil as assertive and easily distracted, but logical and thoughtful. Peter emerged from Staehlin's care with a good knowledge of geography, Russian history, and the accomplishments of the reign of Peter I.[32]

Elizabeth's few demands gave the Grand Duke free time for walks around Moscow, which he enjoyed. Peter socialized with the Russian and German officers,[33] and formed a special regiment for his friends—he appointed himself captain and Prince Repnin his adjutant.[34] He enjoyed the out-of-doors and the physical discipline of being a soldier.[35] Like Peter I, he was fond of company of soldiers, servants, and foreigners. Wrote one observer, "Like Peter the Great, he . . . is familiar without choice or nuance."[36] He and his friends smoked cigars and drank beer. They formed a freemason organization, where they could enjoy a relaxed environment away from the formal ceremonies of the court routine.[37] The behavior of these officers apparently evoked criticism at court, at least according to diplomats' testimony. Criticism of Peter was similar to that leveled at the freemasons in Germany and England, whose smoking and drinking offended the burger culture of the eighteenth century.[38] In Russia in the 1750s and early 1760s there were apparently three lodges. Although freemasonry was relatively new, there was little official prohibition and an open forum for freemason treatises and it may be that diplomats misjudged the atmosphere. Tatiana Bakounine described freemasonry of the 1750s as "a diverse and multiple organization, which, if not under any central direction, was still very powerful."[39] Peter's lodge, "Permanence," was a gathering place for his friends (see chapter 1), and it may have been his only sanctuary in the tense atmosphere as Elizabeth was dying and the throne was being contested.[40]

In 1744 Princess Sophia, daughter of Christian August of Anhalt-Zerbst, was brought to Russia as a possible wife for the Grand Duke. Elizabeth took a liking to her, and on June 28 Sophia was received into the Orthodox Church and renamed Catherine. The next day she and Peter were formally betrothed, but they did not marry until August 21, 1745. The two had much in common. They were both German and only a year apart in age—he was seventeen, she was sixteen. Evidence of dislike and dissatisfaction does not appear until roughly the time of their marriage, which suggests that Peter was an incompatible rather than an unsuitable mate.

In the critical years of 1760 and 1761, when Elizabeth was near death, their rivalry had become so intense that the succession itself was threatened. Peter was the heir, but his wife could be the regent of their son, Paul, if Elizabeth should change her mind. Catherine was building alliances with foreign diplomats and friendships with Russian statesmen who wished to change the succession. Her memoirs do not go up to 1761, and her other writings provide no reliable account of the alignment at court at the end of Elizabeth's life. Her writing does, however, attest to a broken marriage, affairs by both spouses, and intense rivalry over the succession.[41] "The length of the Empress's illness," wrote Gregors von Haxthausen, "helped him prepare—which included promises to some Senators and the most important and necessary lords."[42] A coalition consisting of the Shuvalov and Vorontsov families and their allies, Dmitrii Volkov, Aleksei Mel'gunov, Nikita Trubetskoi (1699–1767), and Aleksandr Glebov, rallied to defend his succession to the throne.[43] The situation was filled with uncertainty. "Even the Grand Duke does not appear to be entirely at ease," wrote the French ambassador. "On the eve of the Empress' death, he had his own regiment ready to march."[44] His succession, it turned out, was unchallenged.

After Peter came to the throne, he acquired a false sense of security as a result of having protected himself against a potential bid for power. Believing that he had succeeded in the struggle against his rivals, he let down his guard. He moved Catherine's rooms to the opposite end of the Winter Palace. He paid her debts and gave her an annual pension.[45] He openly tolerated her affair with a guards officer, Grigorii Orlov, and openly conducted several of his own, including a stormy relationship with Elizaveta, the daughter of Roman Vorontsov, and a new affair with the sixteen-year-old stepdaughter of the general procurator, Glebov.[46] Both of these relationships implicitly threatened Catherine's position. It was rumored that Peter was considering elevating the status of Prince Ivan VI, the other claimant, who was kept imprisoned in the fortress of Schlüsselburg, disinheriting Paul (thought not to be Peter's son), and sending Catherine to a monastery.[47] Yet he failed to have Catherine watched or arrested. He saw her in his chamber every day and dined with her on formal occasions. His apparent sense of security helps explain why he rid the court of the Secret Chancery and returned political exiles from Siberia.[48] This in turn may have fed his sense of his own popularity. Although uncertainties persisted and he was warned of a conspiracy, he failed to move against the opposition. "The Emperor fears Panin and Shakhovskoi,[49] because of their closeness to Catherine, but he cannot yet remove them," wrote Breteuil.[50] Even toward the end of his reign, he was still insufficiently wary.[51]

Peter was liked by some, while to others he appeared contentious and difficult, direct and confrontational.[52] "If I can form any judgement of the Emperor's Temper," wrote Robert Keith, "it is not proper to cross or thwart him [at] first . . . but rather to appear to enter into his Views." Nevertheless, he was approachable. "His Imperial Majesty is really open to Reason, especially when it comes from his friends."[53] Nearly all diplomatic accounts show him to have been exceptionally conscientious during the first few months of intense reform effort. On January 4/15, Gregors von Haxthausen, the Danish envoy, wrote of Peter's "great concern" for internal affairs and the "astonishing rapidity" of his acts by comparison with the previous regime.[54] "With Respect to the Interior of the Empire," Robert Keith wrote on January 1/12, "it was impossible for his Imperial Majesty to conduct himself more wisely or with more dignity than he has done in every step of his government; the Favours he has bestowed have been, in general, upon very worthy Subjects."[55] On January 11/22 Keith commented again, "business of all kinds goes on with more celerity than formerly, the Emperor entering into every branch of it; in home affairs he gives the necessary orders, according to the Representations brought to him from the several Colleges, or the Petitions of the Parlys, who have a very easy access to his Person."[56] On February 1/12, Breteuil, the French ambassador, wrote that "the Emperor is really something quite different than he has appeared to be to the whole world." He was both "wise in his interior administration" and "enlightened."[57] For a while Peter was immensely popular, judging by the response to his edicts. The abolition of the Secret Chancery was "the greatest Blessing that could have happened to the Nation," wrote Keith.[58] "His Imperial Majesty marks each day of his reign with some event or edict, useful and advantageous to his Subjects," commented Haxthausen.[59]

In most instances Peter himself played a minor role in the actual composition of the laws he enacted. However, he was not detached from the process. Staehin provided a portrait of the Emperor consistent with his substantive involvement. The Emperor was up at seven, in consultation with the general procurator of the Senate, Aleksandr Glebov, and the presidents of the first three colleges from eight until eleven, at the Holy Synod and ruling Senate some mornings, and on the parade ground in the afternoon.[60] Haxthausen wrote, "Since the beginning of his reign . . . the Emperor's own mind is the only council; it is the inspiration of everything. As soon as an idea which he wants to execute occurs to him, he calls to him the State Chancellor Volkov, who sets down his order. . . ."[61] In sum, Peter was active, and in his reforms he built a large capital of political assets upon which he believed he could rely.[62]

The issue that launched the conspiracy was a proposed campaign to begin in June. As duke of Holstein, he sought to realize a dynastic claim in northern Germany and, as emperor of Russia, by expanding his territory on the Baltic, enhance the commercial and political position of both Holstein and Russia. The Russian military elite, on the whole, did not support the campaign. This was Catherine's opening. "Catherine courts the guards and soldiers and bides her time," wrote the French ambassador in mid-March from St. Petersburg."[63] Peter was warned of the conspiracy.[64] He responded. A military committee was formed to keep order in the capital when he went to the front. Barricades went up in St. Petersburg to protect the center of his government. Nevertheless, the devaluation of currency and delay of the government payroll contributed to the further spread of discontent in the army.

Peter counted on loyalty at least in his personal regiments. He had proceeded methodically, drilling the troops and dressing the guards according to the Prussian style in order to change their look and improve their readiness for combat. The intensified drills provoked fears that the easy and privileged life of young noble officers would be drastically changed. One guards corps was abruptly dissolved.[65] The seemingly trivial introduction of new uniforms was used by the conspirators as a symbol that Russian custom was yielding to foreign domination.[66] From what happened afterward, it would seem that Peter's constant presence on the parade ground improved the discipline but had no effect in cementing the loyalty of the Russian and Baltic guards (see chapter 6).

The critical moment came when Peter actually mobilized the Izmailovsk regiment. The government was on the alert for sedition but was ineffective once it was discovered. On the afternoon of June 27, 1762, in the Izmailovsk barracks near St. Petersburg, an officer named Passek was asked, "When will the Emperor be overthrown?" When he failed to respond, he was arrested, and the plot was exposed, but before Peter could return to St. Petersburg from his provincial palace of Oranienbaum (now Lomonosov), on the morning of June 28, Catherine succeeded in leading the discontented among the Izmailovtsy to the Winter Palace, where the Senate and Synod were in session. Other regiments under the charge of the other members of the conspiracy—Peter's long-time rivals—contributed to the large number of troops that surrounded the government. Peter's government quickly fell. This brief biography is all the direct information about Peter III that the sources reveal.

Catherine employed two conscious strategies in seizing power and imposing her authority over the government of Russia. The first was a direct assault on Peter's reputation in her manifestoes and memoirs. The second and more subtle involved the use of language to persuade public opinion that the events of June 28 were revolutionary in their implications. From her manifestoes, contemporaries understood a sense of the coup d'état of June 28 as a moment of passage in state and society. Language was the instrument by which Catherine simultaneously laid claim to imperial authority and broke with the past. The practice of politics in the absolutist regime remained the same but the political discourse was altered. The monarch declared her intent to observe the institutional boundaries of her power, a declaration which historians later used as evidence of a political accomplishment. To V. O. Kliuchevsky, for example, Catherine's promise of July 6 to observe the laws of the empire was the beginning of a role for the Russian people in their government. Catherine was not just an incidental figure elevated to the throne by the guards, but an independent "revolutionary political force."[67]

The key to understanding the confirmation and sanctification of a self-proclaimed legend in pre-modern Europe is study of how the political elite, the main transmitter of culture, was affected. Coups d'état, like revolutions, are vertiginous. This one resolved a sense of discontent and aroused new expectations among a well-defined group at court. None of the beneficiaries of Catherine's patronage, either the participants in the coup or her supporters at court—writers such as Andrei Bolotov—had anything to gain by challenging the substance of her accusations against Peter. Her manifestoes provided a political mapping with which they identified because it gave them a sense of place in the historical process as those who brought an end to an allegedly despised regime.[68] The coup of 1762 linked a faction at court to the "sacred center" of a new representation of political culture.

Catherine's self-justification thus gave rich meaning for her supporters to the intent of her coup d'état. The symbols of monarchy, the mystical and quasi-divine representations of absolute power, acquired romantic and liberal attributes.[69] The political community she represented was held to have a dramatically new political understanding, a new attachment to law and legalism. The autocracy remained the "center" of the Russian culture frame. No new "master fiction" replaced the traditional authority but its representation acquired romantic resonance in the image of a single invented personality who embodied tradition, law, and culture.[70] Romanticism heightened an ambiguity already present in the Russian imperial succession—its Byzantine aspect, where power rested both on inheritance and popular acclaim.[71]

In this sense, the coup d'état in Russia virtually always approximated an event with revolutionary significance.[72] The military force which enabled Catherine to seize the civilian center of government did not pose a military threat to dominate civil society. The officers and soldiers emerged instead as a kind of public. Their acclaim and the Byzantine-style succession gave Catherine the cultural authority to manipulate the malleable symbols of her victory.

Catherine used the derogatory portrait of Peter III as the political content and symbolic representation of what her victory overcame. Peter's new image was as integral to the rhetorical matrix of Catherine's political strategy as was her own. A pitiful renunciation by Peter was appended to the manifesto of July 6, which invented and broadly diffused the ridiculed image of the previous ruler. Caricature was thus taken up in official fashion:

> During my brief reign in Russia, experience itself made me aware that my abilities were not equal to the task; that I was not fit to govern the Russian state either as autocrat or in any other capacity. And so even I became aware that there were changes of my own doing that would have led to the utter ruin of the state and to its eternal disgrace.[73]

Once invented and used as a device in a political strategy, Catherine's contrived image of Peter III evoked resistance. In immediate defiance, discontented members of the regiments wore the uniforms Peter III had given them, instead of discarding them as Catherine commanded. Emelian Pugachev, the Cossack rebel, moved against Catherine in 1774—one of numerous peasant pretenders who claimed to be Peter III—and he resurrected in his "court" all the symbols of the degraded ruler: the ugly mistress, the Prussian uniform, and the foreign advisors.[74] Among the elite, however, the reverse occurred. Incentives to show loyalty to the new regime encouraged the elaboration of the skeletal image provided officially in his renunciation.

Anecdotes acquired the force of simple demonstration of political conviction. After the coup, Catherine and her supporters—Grigorii Orlov, Grigorii Potemkin, and Ekaterina Dashkova—regaled the court and salved their consciences with anecdotes about Peter's dissolute and frivolous behavior.[75] The popular biography of

Peter III has been constructed upon these anecdotes, which passed into memoirs and from there into historical literature. There were stories about Peter's cruelty and violent temper, his drunkenness, childish behavior, and love of practical jokes. Andrei Bolotov and Ekaterina Dashkova, both writing many years afterwards, described his pranks and unpleasant appearance.[76] Even the writings of sober statesmen like Mikhail Shcherbatov and Iakov Shakhovskoi offered little besides anecdotes.[77] The distinguished government official Nikita Panin, another of Catherine's accomplices, maintained that he felt "revulsion" because Peter's mistress was "ugly, stupid, annoying."[78]

Such observations cannot be entirely rejected, nor can they be trusted. Dashkova and Panin had a leading role in the coup. Shakhovskoi regained prominence after his disgrace under Peter III. None of these eyewitnesses is impartial; none is well informed.[79] Nowhere in these writings, for example, do we find reference to the ruling Senate, although Peter's supposedly high-handed treatment of established institutions caused offense. Secularization of Church lands is not mentioned. No serious study could draw uncritically on these writings, yet they have been influential in perpetuating the unfavorable image of Peter III. Particular credence, for example, has been placed in the account of the powerful and intelligent Panin.[80]

In Panin's and Dashkova's memoirs there is a note of contempt; but in Catherine's, savage, gloating revenge prevails. Written between 1771 and 1791, her memoirs dealt exclusively with the young Grand Duke. She described his drunkenness, his fits of rage, his irrational hostility to her and her son, his "interminable" military drills, and his brutal treatment of animals, whose cries aroused her pity. While she debased his image, she emphasized her own piety, charity, and wisdom.[81]

Catherine's unremitting attack, at once contemptuous and fervid, powerfully affected historians' views of Peter III, beginning in the nineteenth century, when her memoirs circulated in manuscript. After Karamzin read them, for example, the times about which Catherine wrote underwent "an astonishing transformation."[82] The effect of her memoirs on the depiction of Peter III can be seen in the writings of Solov'ev, Kliuchevskii, and even N. N. Firsov, who was generally sympathetic to Peter III's program.

On the basis of Russian accounts, in other words, it is virtually impossible to reconstruct a satisfactory biography of Peter III. For lack of neutral observers or statesmen unaffected by Catherine's demand for loyalty after the coup, the derogatory portrait cannot be validated. Catherine's suppression of the publication of anything positive about Peter III contributed to the remarkable conformity of the literary record with the official point of view.[83] Her reach even occasionally extended abroad, as in, for example, the French ban on the publication of Claude Rulhière's *Revolution 1762*, a light, unreliable account of the conspiracy. This work appeared in France after her death and in Russia only in 1909.

Foreigners' writings help identify the distortion in the sources. These writings are no less anecdotal than the hostile Russian memoirs. However, since they have been overlooked, they warrant a review. Foreigners objected in their writings mainly to the mantle of censorship, to the extremes of opinion, and to the derogatory portrait. The comment by a German officer at court, C. F. Schwan, is characteristic:

As soon as Peter III ascended the throne, he became great and wise in all respects . . . everyone talked about his superb spirit; he was credited, in fact, with virtues he did not possess. . . . After all, was he not the grandson of Peter the Great? No sooner had his misfortune [the deposition] occurred, than . . . he was nothing but a traitor, unworthy of occupying his ancestral throne.[84]

Foreigners saw the inventions of the manifestoes as the source of the distortion. Schwan, for literary effect, used an epistolary form of memoir which allowed him to speculate and argue, as if convincing a reader already influenced by Catherine's manifestoes. According to Schwan, Peter III was an energetic monarch, concerned with education, law, and the courts. Despite his consuming interest in military affairs, Peter consulted frequently with his advisors; one letter described an exchange of views on parish schools with the archbishop of Novgorod.[85] Writing after the coup, Schwan was not free of bias. As a German, he was resentful of the anti-foreign proclamations. However, he provided a relatively objective account. Indeed, the sum of his writings does not constitute an entirely revisionist view of Peter III, although it casts doubt on the validity of the extremes of the official description.

Caspar von Saldern, Peter's Holstein advisor and a close friend of the Emperor, similarly criticized the official attack on Peter III. In contrast to Schwan, he flatly denied Catherine's allegations. The laws themselves "suffice for [Peter's] apology, confounding the calumnies of his enemies and undermining the false assertions contained in Catherine's manifestoes." Saldern was writing many years later and in the spirit of resentment against Catherine for his own fall from favor at her court. Nevertheless, his protest over the distortion of the record must be registered. His personal correspondence from the time of Peter's reign reveals a continuity in his political conviction. He wrote in 1762 that "Peter acquired the love of his people and the attachment of the nobles of the empire."[86]

Similarly, memoirs (published in 1799) by Charles T. de Laveaux, the French commercial consul in St. Petersburg from 1761 through 1773, showed a sense of outrage at the derogatory portrait. According to Laveaux, Peter was intelligent; although he suffered from "nervous irritability" and was impatient, he was "generous and open."[87] Like Saldern and Schwan, Laveaux denied the substance of some though not all of the allegations, claiming that Peter was falsely represented "practically everywhere as an imbecile and a ridiculous figure because of the manifestoes of his treacherous wife."[88]

Two other commentaries can be mentioned. Staehlin's notes about his pupil, used above, praised Peter's intellectual gifts.[89] Staehlin naturally believed Peter's education had been adequate. Staehlin's recollectons do not directly contradict the traditional view, but they fail to uphold it. Georg Helbig's biography based on interviews with Russian statesmen in the 1770s and 1780s adds confirmation to the general notion that the derogatory portrait is not correct.[90] He characterized Peter as a reformer, whose particular interest in education permeated his projects. He hinted that Peter's role in reform was more than minor. "His advisors did not act independently of the monarch's will."[91] The lack of specificity or identification of sources greatly inhibits the usefulness of Helbig's work, although it is one more challenge to tradition.

Not all foreigners' accounts were revisionist. The unflattering description of Peter from Claude Carloman de Rulhière's history of the coup d'état found its way to a large audience in the mostly plagiarized life of Catherine by Jean Castera, a minor author of fiction and translator who never set foot in Russia.[92] Castera described Peter as manic, violent, and always inebriated, even though he also wrote that a sober Peter could be found each day on the parade ground, drilling his regiments.[93]

The distortion in the sources sets a premium on anything written before the coup d'état, particularly by observers who were neither involved in the conspiracy nor, like Schwan and Saldern, part of Peter's entourage. Diplomatic dispatches would seem at first to fit this description. On the whole, during Peter's youth, reporters tended to provide a positive portrait.[94] As Peter's reign progressed, however, diplomatic dispatches become less and less a yardstick by which the controversial sources can be measured. Their substance was influenced by the state of relations between their country and Russia and by their personal situations vis-à-vis the Russian court and their own. In the first months of 1762, diplomats commented warmly about Peter's administration, with praise for his intelligence. After a Holstein campaign—a threat to all of northern Europe—was announced in March, diplomats began to contradict their earlier assessments. The Austrian ambassador, Mercy d'Argenteau, whose scorn and disgust, deriving from profound resentment of Peter's peace with Prussia and new plans for a campaign, can be felt in all major treatments of Peter's reign, offered what has become a commonplace, that the Emperor's intelligence was "little exercised in serious occupations."[95] The Swedish diplomat Mauritz Posse, who repeatedly referred to Peter's "bad" qualities and Catherine's "sympathy with the nation," described with regret the court revolt that had been planned before Peter's ascent to the throne but had not had time to mature, preventing the reversal of Russian policy.[96] Diplomats were relieved by the coup not because of anything to do with Peter's domestic policy, but because Catherine was amenable to compromise in foreign policy, and Peter, they believed, was not.

A new portrait of Peter III can be drawn from the writings of Schwan, Saldern, and Staehlin. Idiosyncrasies of personality remain, attributes of incompetence and cruelty do not. New features emerge to fill out a more complex personality. My book is not the first attempt at revisionism. Suffice it to say that the argument for a stronger, more competent Peter III has worked against the writers who have attempted it—the revised portrait differs too significantly from the one in the history books. It should be noted that foreigners' works on Peter III have suffered particularly from the fact of non-Russian authorship. The question that has always concerned historians is what Russians thought.

For Russians, over the years Catherine succeeded by sheer repetition in reducing the complexity of historical experience to a few simple lines of interpretation with a ritualized content.[97] By the end of the eighteenth century, a consensus formed, as Aleksandr Vorontsov expressed it to Alexander I, that Peter was "a ruler who aroused the general distaste of the country" by a careless attitude, offense to the faith, and a disastrous foreign policy.[98] In the nineteenth and twentieth centuries, the essential understanding did not change. New generations found different ways of representing the signficance of the coup d'état, but each used Catherine as mediator. In the early and mid-nineteenth century in an era of nationalism, Catherine's romantic image as a ruler who promised to restore a golden age (sometimes Old Russia, sometimes Petrine Russia) and to enhance the future glory of Russia had virtually universal appeal. Drawing conclusions from her memoirs, which were now available in manuscript, nineteenth-century historians sympathized with what she and, by her account, the country suffered under Peter III.[99] In the twentieth century, the symbols of her authority were transformed by liberal historians into the "spirit" of the rule of law which they claimed she introduced into the history of the Russian autocracy by overthrowing the arbitrary rule of Peter III.[100] In sum, Catherine's personal appeal, admiration for her character and intellect, and the appeal of her creativity led nineteenth- and twentieth-century historians to place confidence in self-serving sources.

The consequence of fixed convention is that research on sources of social cohesion has been encumbered by a lack of accurate information. Interpretions about pre-Catherinian reform have construed an almost leaderless autocracy. The critical example, because of its influence on scholarship, is the pioneering study by N. L. Rubinshtein of the activities of lawmakers in the 1750s.[101] Rubinshtein gathered considerable new evidence about reform. Without alternative explanations resting on a stronger autocratic figure, however, he invested the entire reform process with intra-class conflict, "underlying" economic and social interests. In particular, conflict between Peter Shuvalov and Iakov Shakhovskoi, two powerful Elizabethan statesmen, became the expression of pro-merchant and pro-aristocratic interests (see chapter 2). In an interpretation upheld in nearly all subsequent monographs, Rubinshtein claimed that this conflict broadly determined the outcome of policy decisions, Elizabeth and Peter III notwithstanding.[102] His massive source work has to be reexamined. His allocation of the unsigned 1750s policy projects to separate camps is without coherence or justification at a court where nobles' landholding privileges were steadily advancing without opposition. Apart from the physiocrats Volkov and Teplov and the "liberal" rulers Peter and Catherine, few at court were interested in any restraints on nobles' economic activity. Yet few statesmen went so far as to support Roman Vorontsov's and Peter Shuvalov's codification project, designed virtually to eliminate the merchants' place in manufacturing. The Senate overwhelmingly rejected it. Therefore, interests conflicted, but Rubinshtein has raised a question about policy formation that he cannot answer by identifying lines of social and economic stratification within the nobility. Why under Peter III, even if interests had not hardened into pro-merchant and pro-aristocratic factions, did the Shuvalovs and Vorontsovs act together in a single coalition behind a physiocratic program? This is a question explored in my book. Partly the answer lies in the stakes and rewards, partly in the appeal of physiocracy, and partly in the politics of Peter's rise to power. To a very large extent, conflict in the 1750s was driven by a personal contest. A major fissure opened up at court over the role of the Senate in legislation, but the cause of conflict cannot be separated from personality. The Senate's advocate was the idiosyncratic and testy general procurator Iakov Shakhovskoi, his opponents, Volkov and Shuvalov.[103] With Peter Shuvalov's death and Shakhovskoi's removal in January 1762, the way was made clear for a strong ruling coalition under Volkov, who pushed through action on fiscal reform as demanded by Peter III.

The sheer mass of work Peter III shouldered in six months crushes the frivolous figure of the contemptuous portrait. "This prince was filled with life," wrote Burkhard von Münnich.[104] In foreign plicy, it was his very energy that led to his demise, his unrelenting pursuit of a foreign campaign which had disastrous domestic implications. Stripped of the extreme features and ridiculous behavior that are described in the writings of Catherine and her associates in his deposition, Peter III emerges as a serious monarch.

I

ORIGINS OF REFORM

The strategic evolution of Peter III's foreign policy—his withdrawal of Russian forces from the Seven Years' War, the treaty of peace with Prussia, the drafted treaty of alliance with Frederick of Prussia, and the projected military campaign against Denmark—was linked to the recovery of Russia from the war. In response to the crumbling of his army in Europe, Peter grounded politics in a search for revenues. He secularized ecclesiastical property, reducing labor services and excess payments so that the former ecclesiastical peasants could pay more to the state. He lifted restrictions on grain exports and redirected foreign trade away from ill-defined frontiers toward the Baltic, White Sea, and Caspian ports, where customs were collectible. He announced an issue of assignats and devalued the currency. Peter's vigorous efforts served to mark off the magnitude of the financial constraints that bound his policy.

The political innovation of Peter III and his advisors, however, was to look beyond finances toward the agricultural sector and to emphasize economic expansion in his taxation policy. Turning to French economic ideas that prescribed a new model for the agricultural economy, he and his advisors took steps to allow more commercial penetration of the backward rural areas, ease the severe shortage of personnel in provincial government and law enforcement, and reduce the use of forced labor in rural manufacturing. In his most important reform, he released nobles from the service obligation in order to encourage their entrepreneurial ambition and investment in agriculture, while granting them a fundamental right of choice. Beginning with finances, the ambit of state initiative widened enormously, and a new course was set in the history of reform in eighteenth-century Russia.

Mobilization of the country's resources did bring some financial relief. Savings during the six months of Peter's rule were substantial. After strenuously objecting, the senators (members of the highest organ of civil power) finally agreed in June to support Peter's military campaign against Denmark. The military elite was considerably more reluctant. The social costs of the Seven Years' War (including delayed furloughs for a large part of the officer corps and urban and rural disorder) were borne largely by the military. The interpenetration of military and civilian elites meant that acting without a broad consensus could have repercussions. Thus the campaign against Denmark, the culmination of Peter's laborious efforts in foreign affairs and extensive domestic programs, was, in fact, infeasible. For several months Peter hesitated. Then, in early summer, the season of war, for reasons that are not entirely clear, he abandoned his course of caution and began intensive preparations for war. Certainly he was weighing the domestic risk against the overwhelming military advantage of beginning the campaign—his troops were ready, in contrast to the western European forces, which were exhausted and unable to resist the attack; fresh reserves from Prussia had joined his troops; the Swedish government had agreed in principle to help provision his new ships in case of war. At the end of May, in a serious miscalculation, he announced his intended departure. On June 28 he was overthrown, and eight days later he was killed.

The period of transition following the coup did not lead to a break with the past. Peter's coalition was dispersed, but most of his advisors retained their influence. As a consequence of this continuity, reforms that Catherine initially rescinded were soon restored. Their lasting effect emphasizes the power of the informal consensus that led to their initial passage.[1] Peter III's reforms represented measures carefully conceived and long sought within the bureaucracy. Despite the chaos, lawlessness, and revolt with which Peter III's reign ended, the reforms did not come to a stop. The impact of the diverse and generally enlightened measures undertaken under Peter lasted well into the nineteenth century.

The Major Reforms

The chief landmark in legislation was the edict of emancipation of the nobles (February 18). It granted nobles personal freedom and greater political autonomy by abolishing the necessity of appearing for service at the age of twenty and spending the next twenty-five years in the army. In its broadest implication, the act relaxed the enforcement of service and thus eliminated the threat of confiscation of estates, the heavy penalty evaders had paid. By making retirement and reentry into service attractive and flexible by rank adjustments, the decree also encouraged the process of ennoblement of non-noble servitors, a largely landless civil service elite which the Petrine concept of service helped foster in early modern Russia.

The main precedent for the enactment was the permission granted to nobles in 1736 by Anna Ivanovna to retire after twenty-five years of service and, if there were two or more sons, to keep one on the estate. The enactment went considerably beyond Anna's acknowledgment of the importance of nobles' home needs, however. In its broader purposes, it reflected a struggle by a group within the service class to create a new foundation of estate rights. More ambitious than the sum of its purposes—to promote nobles' agricultural enterprise, demobilize officers, cut staff, and professionalize the service—it granted to this now corporate estate certain permanent fundamental rights and privileges.[2] Nobles could travel abroad, participate in local assemblies (of unspecified function), and, in theory, elect representatives to central institutions. Some nobles wanted more. Nobles' dominance over manufacturing, for example, which some of his advisors sought, was denied. In a separate enactment, moreover, Peter abolished nobles' commercial monopolies on the grounds that they posed a barrier to trade. In yet another enactment, he passively allowed the ruling Senate to deny non-nobles the right to purchase serf villages for factories, a permission Peter I had granted in a more even-handed fashion to merchant and noble manufacturers. However, serf manufacturing was becoming less common, at least in textiles, and reformers in the Senate argued that the bar on merchant serf-ownership would encourage hired labor, reputed to be efficient. Furthermore, those great merchants who perceived their interests as disadvantaged by this law were ennobled in 1762 and afterward, when Catherine kept the law in effect.[3] The political power of the nobility in this instance curbed the effect of opportunities that the non-noble entrepreneurial elite enjoyed, but both the intentions and the consequences of the new law are ambiguous.

In a second act, distancing himself once again from his indecisive predecessors, Peter fully repudiated the Church's right to own extensive land and maintain peasants. Not content with imitating the emergency measures of Peter the Great, who sent troops to the ecclesiastical villages and confiscated horses and supplies, he staked legal claim to the Church's land, capitalizing on long bureaucratic planning: the accumulation of clerical work can be seen in the text of the enactment, which showed the encumbering weight of precedent. Its terms imposed a monetary tax on the former ecclesiastical, now called "economic," peasants. The tax was to be collected by officers of the College of Economy who were to give economic peasants their allotment land and rent out the rest. Here, as elsewhere, new French physiocratic theories exercised a decisive influence over reform. The so-called economic domain constituted an experiment in agricultural policy. The enactment encouraged incentives in agriculture while launching a rationalist assault upon the Church. It also pushed forward the land survey, stalled by the question of Church property since the 1750s. Its main effects enhanced the state's base of taxation by introducing a single tax and encouraging the gathering of tax estimates. The state also attempted to expand its power within the ecclesiastical domain.

The success of the two measures, secularization of Church estates and emancipation of nobles from obligatory service, can be measured by the determination of the subsequent regime to maintain them. Over the next ten years the parish clergy were transformed even more into a closed caste, and the ecclesiastical hierarchy, reduced in size, came to be maintained on the government payroll. The economic peasants were released from labor services and other constraints on non-agricultural activities. Although deprived in future enactments of their quasi-legal right to land, the economic peasants nevertheless maintained a special status in state law. This may have inspired jealousy and revolt on nobles' estates and helped created a following for countless pretenders, including Pugachev, who led a peasant war from 1774–1775 in the name of Peter III. His symbolic representation showed that the expectations produced by reform had been far greater than the satisfaction.

The success of emancipation was not as a model for the granting of rights to other groups but as an administrative act. It created uniform norms and regulations on entry, retirement, and performance in service, although these were difficult to enforce. More significantly, it provided the means to expedite the hiring of provincial servitors. The exodus of nobles from the capital cities at the end of the Seven Years' War was to positions of prestige and responsibility in provincial capitals, a development facilitated by emancipation.[4] Noble status was tied to service rank well into the nineteenth century, and for that reason service as well as nobility retained attributes of caste despite the counter efforts of nineteenth-century reform to break up nobles' monopoly of land and labor.[5] Nobles' dominance of provincial government, for example, with merchants and *meschane* [townspeople] less well represented in provincial politics, shaped the social and political milieu of rural life.[6] The strengthening of the existing social order, elaborated in the reform of local government of 1774, was the overwhelming legacy of this reform.

Other Reforms

Peter's minor reforms were to a great extent devices to meet the demands of state finance and to reduce inefficiencies in the bureaucracy. He renewed tax-farms, called in overdue loans, devalued the coinage, experimented with an assignat bank, and attempted to cut staff.[7] He centralized legislative work in the Senate, following up on a proposal of 1761 to divide tasks between an appellate and legislative branch.[8] He demobilized many officers, reduced civilian personnel, and eliminated an entire corps of guards. In part to economize and in part to streamline the chain of command, he abolished the Commerce Commission, which had duplicated the work of the College of Commerce. Similarly, at least initially, he restored the powers of the Senate and the College of Foreign Affairs by abolishing the Conference at the Imperial Court.[9] After several months he had second thoughts.[10] With the effect of diminishing the Senate, he created a council called the General Direktorium, suggesting its origins in the councils of Frederick William and Frederick II.[11] Despite the largely military composition of his Direktorium, however, it cannot necessarily be inferred that it was limited exclusively to military affairs.[12] It was designed to serve as temporary command in the capital while he was at the front.[13] In any case, the Senate now experienced the same ambiguous decline of status that had occurred under Elizabeth.

Peter did not recast government. He wielded power in a manner characteristic of the autocracy in the eighteenth century. Peter like Catherine was a forerunner of the autocrats of the nineteenth century, whose social message as spelled out in the formula of Official Nationalism had little in common with the liberal principles of the Enlightenment. Peter and Catherine wrestled with the conflict between welfare and power, and the outcome, different from what occurred in the West, brought little relaxation of the pattern of autocratic supremacy.[14] Yet the extension of supreme authority, while preparing the way for improved bureaucratic centralism of the next century, also opened a wider field for experimentation by the central agencies of the sovereign. The appearance of decisive legislative initiative introduced into the autocracy an essentially innovative force. In Russian history there is an almost unbroken record of the expansion of central power by the elaboration of statutes that created within highly defined bounds new powers and privileges, sometimes new social groups, as in the law by which the Russian government in 1861 finally, in its most important act, ended the social and economic system of serfdom.

Under Peter, as under Catherine, rationalism, anticlericalism, and ideas of judicial reform found expression in policy. Peter issued an edict of religious tolerance for schismatic Old Believers [*raskol'niki*], challenging the Church's prerogative to enforce uniformity of the faith. This edict responded to a petition by a raskol community and sought to repatriate over 70,000 fugitives who had fled to Poland to escape persecution. Old Believers were encouraged to settle in Siberia and were promised protection from the hierarchy.[15] The edict also responded to merchant interests, since Old Believers were numerous among the merchantry,[16] a fact which may have led under Catherine to further relaxation of regulations, including the removal of double taxation and other penalties.[17] Peter, a freemason, promoted noble and non-noble technical education by increasing funds, planning to send students abroad, and establishing new institutions.[18] He sought to expand primary education and remove it from clerical supervision.[19] He eliminated the unregulated and independent activities of the Secret Investigatory Chancery, which conducted interrogations of high officials, by transferring its functions to the Senate, and he abolished the sections of the criminal code which permitted, among other medieval customs, the torture of witnesses.[20] He attempted to hasten the codification of the law, including its fundamental provision of rights to the service nobility.[21] The proposed codification was to serve the need for a single simplified code of law, the first step in the philosophes' program of reform.

Commerce and Foreign Policy

Russian grain "could feed the world," the physiocrat Dmitrii Volkov wrote in 1761.[22] Hoping to stimulate grain exports, Peter III and Volkov enacted a measure liberating the grain trade from mercantilist restrictions (see chapter 4). Customs fees were reduced to encourage foreign purchases. Although hemp and flax were already vital to Russian commerce, grain exports had always been discouraged because of fear of shortages. For the sake of stimulating long-run production, Peter was willing to risk the resulting increase in domestic prices. After Peter was overthrown, the state again became cautious. Catherine's government regulated prices by police controls and controlled exports by means of temporary prohibitions. At least in theory, however, Catherine never restored absolute prohibition of the grain trade or other agricultural exports. In this area of policy, as in social and ecclesiastical affairs, the influence of Peter's policy was decisive in the eighteenth century.

Peter's opening up of trade encouraged Russia's economic position just as the tide in European diplomacy turned to Russia's advantage after its victories in the Seven Years' War. Following Russia's withdrawal from the Seven Years' War, Peter went on to conclude a separate peace and draw up plans for an alliance with Prussia (see chapter 5). This was a resounding defeat to the war aims of the allied powers, France and Austria, whose ministers had hoped for territorial adjustments at the expense of Prussia. At a stroke Peter restored the balance of power in Europe and strengthened his position. His rapprochement with Prussia ended the possibility that England or France would be a powerful force in northern, central, or eastern Europe, where French ministers had sought hegemony since the seventeenth century. Relations between European states after the war took the form largely imposed upon them by Peter's peace, signifying that the sacrifice of territory to

Prussia, by which the peace was bought, had long-term strategic benefits. The main benefit Peter, as Duke of Holstein, hoped to achieve was the conquest with Prussian troops of a part of his ducal lands ceded to Denmark by the treaty of Nystadt which ended the Great Northern War in 1721. His intended campaign against Denmark played a large role in his overthrow, threatening renewed financial insolvency and further warfare. To the end Peter left open the avenue of negotiation, but this fact is buried in cabinet papers and was not obvious at court.[23] Seemingly unwilling to yield his strategic advantage without the outcome he sought, Peter emerges as inflexible and intolerant. Yet his decisiveness left as a vital legacy independence from Austria and France and peace with Prussia, the framework of future Russian foreign policy.

The Comparative Political Context

To summarize, by the time of the coup d'état, a sweeping program of social, economic, and administrative reform was in progress. After the coup, Catherine II ordered a review of all of his laws and rescinded the Church reform which her manifestoes had implicitly condemned. She by no means halted the reform movement, however, and for many years she even maintained Peter's orientation in foreign affairs. In domestic affairs, after her coronation in September, Catherine took slow steps to reenact secularization and the other laws with new prefaces whose tone and content conveyed a political testament of her own enlightened views.[24] These reforms can be attributed to her philosophic position. However, they should also be seen as the outcome of an established direction of reform. Despite her rescission, secularization essentially went into effect in 1762. Similarly, Peter's commercial regulation was a guide for her own, promulgated in July.[25] Emancipation of nobles remained in effect without needing repromulgation, since Peter had issued it as irrevocable. Catherine announced her displeasure with its "hasty composition" and withheld any new pronouncement on nobles' rights until her Charter of Nobility of 1785, but she implemented it nonetheless.[26]

Continuity in policy, linking reform proposals of the 1750s, laws enacted in 1762, and their embodiment in Catherine's legislation, demonstrates that there could not have been a stock of ideas more familiar to contemporaries and less threatening to the state.[27] The problems the Russian government faced in the 1750s were severe and typical. A new fiscal policy was demanded to support the vast expenditure of arms and men demanded by the Seven Years' War (1756–1763). The war demonstrated the scarcity of financial resources in overwhelmingly agrarian countries and exacerbated it, threatening insolvency. The debasement of coinage was widespread in Europe, where finance ministers found few resources to add to the ad hoc levies by which pre-modern states usually paid for their wars.[28] The first lesson of the philosophes was that sound finances were the basis of efficient government. Governments developed a passion for fiscal experiments.

The reforms in Russia resemble the economies introduced both in Prussia and in Austria by the Retablissements of Maria Theresa, initiated in the 1740s by the Council of State and its chancellor, Count Wenzel Anton Kaunitz. Defeat by Prussia in 1745 provided the impetus and the military/fiscal object of reform by which Maria Theresa controlled Church finances and created a new bureaucratic system. She imposed a strict regime of collections and expenditure in the provinces, revamped education, trained servitors, and subordinated provinces more closely to the center. However, the rout of the Austrians at the battle of Leuthen (1757) in the Seven Years' War showed how a country with superior military and material resources needed further reforms to compete with its powerful neighbor, and reforms intensified, especially after 1780 during the rule of Joseph II, who suppressed the monasteries, abolished serfdom, curbed the particularism of the estates, and created a unitary state in his search for revenues. Jansenist advisors had enormous impact in creating an atmosphere conducive to reform. But Joseph and Maria Theresa had no use for heretical attacks on the Church. Joseph's opposition to serfdom came from a kind of iconoclasm common to Enlightenment rulers, and from fiscal reasoning.[29]

In Russia, the doubling of the Russian military budget over the decade of the 1750s to as much as 43 percent of revenues and the periodic deficit in the treasury contributed powerfully to pragmatic arguments in favor of foreign loans and of permanent augmentation of resources: the state could not pay salaries of officers, prevent desertion, or raise the price of salt and spirits any further.[30] The starkly narrow limits of political choice in the eighteenth century were an important factor in making weak institutions like the Orthodox Church increasingly vulnerable. Secularization, sometimes construed as an illustration of Peter's Lutheran sympathies, reflected fiscal concerns beginning in the fifteenth century. It was planned by Elizabeth, whose piety was unquestioned but whose inability to finance a war led to serious reconsideration of the base of taxation. The state in the 1750s depended too closely upon the already heavy tax burden imposed upon the peasants and upon incidental contributions from various sources—monopolies, tax-farming, loans and gifts from the Church. Numerous solutions to fiscal constraints were proposed in 1762—from physiocratic ideas about a single tax on the peasants and the abolition of commercial monopolies to the slashing of expenditures on personnel, institutions, and guards regiments. These were Enlightenment solutions to a shortfall of revenue rather than the idiosyncratic ideas of a ruler hostile to Russian tradition.

Why was Peter overthrown? General discontent, contributing to the spread of disaffection, cannot be ruled out. After six years of war, burdened with huge deficits, the government had repeatedly devalued the currency and delayed its payroll. It was not domestic disturbance, however, that opened the way to conspiracy. Peter's major reforms were widely acclaimed and commanded new loyalty. Their popularity made them difficult to repeal.

The reason for his fall from power was his intended campaign against Denmark, which was opposed by the military elite and by a well-established opposition to his succession. Peter placed enormous weight on the simple dogma of legitimate rights, and these rights (to ducal Schleswig and Holstein) were recognized by the European powers over Danish counter-claims. Because of European recognition, Peter was able to acquire important promises of neutrality from England and Sweden in case war should break out, and this encouraged him further. Austria and

France sought by any means to prevent the campaign. Their envoys in Russia paid lavish sums to Catherine to assist her to the throne.[31] With remarkable insensitivity and a certain recklessness, Peter maintained his Germanic confidence in the justice and force of his legitimate rights, and although he attempted to maintain power by bribing and arresting known conspirators, ultimately he counted as insignificant the antagonism of a circle of statesmen who had long been antagonistic to him and to his ruling coalition.

This chapter sets the political and cultural milieu of pre-Catherinian Russia (1750s–1762), which forms a background to the policies that lay at the heart of the reforms. It concludes with the political divisions that surfaced in struggles for position and power at court. In the 1750s, institutional authority was greatly affected by new agendas for financial reform to meet the demands of war. Tied to institutional authority was the vital question of the succession to the throne. A power vacuum, created by the slow death of the autocrat, was being filled in the early 1760s by a vicious rivalry between Peter and Catherine. The formation of intensely partisan politics thus coincided with the aspiration to expand autocratic authority into new territory and new fields of action at a time when considerations of power and plenty were being formulated as a rational scheme of economic life and as guidelines for more intervention by the state in social and economic life.

Economic Thought

The principles that informed both thought and policy for most of the eighteenth century and, in some sense, the nineteenth century are loosely called mercantilist, or in their German form, cameralist (*Kameralwissenschaft*). Cameralist policy and thought were not distinct activities; "no body of economic literature was ever more closely related to interest and policy than the writings of the mercantilists."[32] Behind policy lay a single set of assumptions, based on a rigid understanding of what contributed to the power and wealth of the state and what did not. Gains through international trade were virtually the sole determinant of mercantilist thought: what promoted gains from trade was in the interest of monarchs, what did not detracted from the primary object, power. As Thomas Mun wrote,

> The ordinary means . . . to encrease our wealth and treasury is by Forraign Trade. . . . This ought to be encouraged, for upon it hangs the great revenue of the king, the honor of the kingdom, the noble profession of the merchant, the school of our arts, the supply of our poor, the improvements of our lands, the nursery of our mariners, the walls of the kingdom, the means of our treasury, the sinews of our wars, the terror of our enemies.[33]

This was an orientation based on "political arithmetic."

The German cameralists preserved this essential core of mercantilism with some differences. Including those who had influence in Russia, mainly J. H. G. von Justi and Jacob von Bielfeld, the cameralists were more academic. They emphasized the importance of treasure, sometimes considered the same as money, to be obtained through trade, and they were concerned with popoulation growth; hence they encouraged immigration, religious tolerance, and all regulations that affected the technical aspects of agricultural production. They placed great confidence in government regulation, especially restrictions on the exporting of agricultural products, which were to be kept at home to feed the populace.[34] Joseph von Sonnenfels and others anticipated some of the theoretical advances of the physiocrats. They made much of the evil of monopoly and of restrictions on movement of peasants and traders. Retaining emphasis on foreign trade, they downplayed population and showed a balanced concern for agriculture and industry.

The later cameralists' assault on outmoded institutions accounts in part for the longevity of their influence in Russia in a period when mercantilism in general was subjected to philosophic attack. As a guide to ruling well, cameralism encouraged rulers to believe that the natural order, a conception of society common to mercantilism and laissez-faire, could only be achieved by "the dextrous management of a skilful politician." Eli Heckscher writes:

> the result was remarkable. . . . it was precisely this general mercantilist conception of society which led statesmen to even greater ruthlessness than would have been possible without the help of such a conception; . . . they believed themselves justified in their interference and, in addition, believed in its necessity, without being held back by a respect for such irrational forces as tradition, ethics, and religion.[35]

Physiocrats were the exception at mid-century in placing some faith in natural law. Few Enlightenment thinkers believed in the inevitability of progress: they believed that a rational approach to social and political problems would bring progress. Cameralism demanded constant intervention, and in Russia it remained a guide to that intervention throughout the eighteenth century.

One reason mercantilism was attacked in France was that it had been greatly discredited by the bankruptcies and extravagances of Louis XIV. By contrast, Petrine policies—the centralization of government, exploitation of new resources, search for bullion, gains in trade and manufacturing, and income from regalias—were associated in the minds of leading officials with the increased power he exercised at home and abroad. "He is your God, he was your God, Russia," S. M. Solov'ev wrote about the image of Peter the Great in the eighteenth century.[36] Thus, while mercantilism was undermined in France by a radical social and intellectual movement, cameralist theory had prolonged appeal in Russia due to the sanctified image of its main practitioner. There is some lack of clarity about the extent of Western influence in Russia but none about the debt of mid-century reformers to Petrine examples.

Just as cameralism changed with the times, however, Petrine ideas were critically reevaluated and modified. Cameralism became the subject of lengthy tomes in German that emphasized not only finance, but freedom, estate rights, and safety of property rights, by which noble officials now sought to escape from Petrine constraints.[37] This transformation distinguishes the program of Peter III and Catherine II from Petrine precedent, although not from cameralism. The dimensions of reform grew, showing a shift in thinking brought about by the individualistic and didactic writings of mid-century. There was more emphasis on the release of un-tapped human and material resources and on duty and obligation, and less on the necessity for social constraints. There was emphasis on the obsolescence of out-dated institutions. Less was done piecemeal for the sake of immediate purposes; reform was intended to be the keystone of a new order.

Among the factors affecting this shift was new economic thinking. Physiocracy as practiced in France attacked the entire mercantilist structure of privilege and reg-ulation as well as the specific assumptions about trade. It may be that physiocrats "have attracted a degree of attention," T. C. W. Blanning begins, "disproportion-ate to their influence on contemporary rulers,"[38] since policies regarded as char-acteristic of "enlightened despotism" are just as easily explained in terms of raison d'état. Centuries before the Enlightenment, an identifiable movement had attacked the privileges of the Church, granted religious toleration, and reformed the admin-istration. The "enlightened" in enlightened despotism, however, was significant, particularly in central and eastern Europe, as in the reforms of Joseph II.[39] The impact of physiocracy in Russia was ambiguous; even at the height of its influ-ence—the 1760s—it led neither to the total relaxation of agricultural exports nor to the abolition of serfdom. Nevertheless, it posed new questions about the source of wealth. As Sergei Troitskii has written, officials began to seek "expansion of state revenues in the development of the productive forces of Russia and in changes in economic policies of the government."[40]

The ideas that lay behind physiocracy emerged from publicistic writings of seventeenth-century England, whose example proved that increased spending and consumption of luxuries were not necessarily accompanied by impoverishment but rather by an evident, growing wealth, improvement in agriculture, capital invest-ments, imports, and range and quality in manufacturing. Such a development starkly contradicted concepts of limited wealth which underlay mercantilism. The focus of these early thinkers, as for the physiocrats, was on internal market rela-tionships and stimulating output in a larger, more varied market—at whatever cost to cameralist sources of revenue. Physiocrats developed these notions into a sys-tematic account of economic life. Inspired by rationalism, they conducted scientific investigation of capital flows, positing an equilibrium which stemmed from the output of the only productive class, the *fermiers,* the investment of the landlords, and the purchases of the sterile class, the merchantry. Their thinking, because of its rationalist, scientific base, attracted immediate and widespread interest among both philosophes and rulers of agrarian countries, and both their publicistic and scientific writings went through numerous editions in a short while.[41] François Quesnay (1694–1774) was the leader of the movement. His chief writings were an article on "Fermiers" (1756) and one on "Grains" (1757), published in Diderot and D'Alembert's *Encyclopédie,* and the *Tableau Economique* (1753–1758), which went through three editions between 1758 and 1759. Mirabeau's *Theory of Taxation* (1760) and *Rural Philosophy* (1763) also had influence.

The key to their thinking was *produit net,* or agricultural surplus. This taxable surplus was to be maintained by high prices, which dictated the unrestricted export of grain and the elimination of all the cumbersome overland duties put in place by treasury-conscious mercantilists, who had never chalked up what the cost of these duties was to the farmers and merchants. The vital element in the theory was agriculture rather than manufacturing. Emphasis was on the domestic market and not the balance of foreign trade. Power flows from wealth, and wealth from prices for agricultural goods: "Valuelessness plus abundance does not at all equal wealth. Dearness plus dearth equals poverty. Abundance plus dearness equals opulence," wrote Quesnay.[42] This logic constituted the first real school of economic thought.

The enormous influence of this thinking on Peter III and his advisors, whose interest in agriculture infused every reform with double purpose, now seems marginal and short-lived, because physiocracy never became more than an admixture in cameralist policy.[43] Even in small doses, however, it created rifts at court, challenged accepted notions, and in general had such great appeal in a world dominated by state regulation that its popular influence endured, as in the writings of members of the Free Economic Society in the late 1760s.

The quest for wealth and greater imperial power was not tied to advanced theories about human potential. Contemporaries believed that Catherine was unusual at the Russian court in her familiarity with European ideas. "That coherent thought of any kind should emanate from Russia was startling enough, that it should bear strong signs of enlightened influence sent the philosophes into a veritable ecstasy of delight."[44] Without making exaggerated claims for widespread Western influence, the Russian court was not as backward as the philosophes believed.[45] The elimination of Russia's political and cultural isolation from the rest of Europe was gradual, rather than sudden.[46]

The Court under Elizabeth

The hallmark of urban culture before the age of Catherine was possession of a library with literature in foreign languages; the privilege most sought by courtiers was travel abroad. In Anna's reign, Artemii Petrovich Volynskii and most of the leading officials were educated abroad.[47] By the 1750s French had become the language of the court; the Russian theater and Academy of Arts were founded and the Academy of Sciences began to hold regular meetings at which treatises were presented. There can be no doubt of the penetration of European thought before the 1760s. Pavel Miliukov wrote, "We know that from the 1750s on, the influence of bookish morality and social theory ceased to be confined to individuals and embraced an entire social circle, to be sure a very limited one, the circle of the aristocratic youth who has passed through higher education."[48] The institutions of higher education, apart from the university, included the Cadet Corps (Sukhoputnyi Shliakhetskii korpus), founded in 1731, the Naval Cadet Corps (Morskoi Shliakhetskii korpus) at the Naval Academy (1752), and the Page Corps (Pazheskii korpus) (1759).[49] Between 1732 and 1760, 2,056 students entered and 1,295 graduated, a small fraction of the educated elite of Russia. The number of nobles exposed to Western literature was much larger, since a majority received education at home rather than in the Cadet Corps.[50]

By mid-century, education had a larger role than technical training for the elite officer corps. Peter III, who had carried out his aunt's education policy as director of the Cadet Corps in the 1750s, formulated a far-reaching policy for his own regime in a decree of April 24, 1762, where he declared that the aim of nobles' education was enlightenment. Education was "for their own welfare."[51] The broadening effects of education were widely felt in various spheres of government at mid-century. Commissioners who worked on the law code tended to have a background in foreign languages. The draft law code repeated in separate chapters that it was important to apply European ideas to Russian law. Miliukov continued,

> Thus, the Empress Catherine had the good fortune to ascend the throne at a time when the ground was already cleared for the acceptance of the last word in modern European literature, for the assimilation of the basic notion propagandized by that literature—that the social order, in the interests of "humanity," can and must be rebuilt according to 'rational' principles.[52]

Rational principles of law led to the curtailment of so-called abuses of the Church. Mikhail Lomonosov, who infused Russian journalism with concern for the development of manufacturing and trade, science and secularism, powerfully contributed to the attack on ecclesiastical authority; the university he founded in Moscow was the first in Europe to abandon instruction in theology.[53] A. P. Sumarokov, in an essay published in his private journal, *Trudoliubivaia pchela* (The Busy Bee) (1759), wrote that the Church should not interfere in secular affairs, and enlightenment thought should be considered the "science of piety."[54]

Rationalism led to an attack on censorship. Sumarokov wrote essays on Locke and on the Enlightenment which he published in his non-government journal. His breakthrough from censorship, the publication of a private journal, was a turning point in the history of Enlightenment journalism. *Prazdnoe vremia* (Leisure Time) (1759–1760), another of Sumarokov's private journals, published his critical essays and translations of French and German moralistic and didactic works "About Honor," "About Consciousness." M. M. Kheraskov's journal, *Poleznoe uveselenie* (Useful Pleasures) (Moscow University, 1760–1762), translated philosophic literature for "young Russians" to whom Kheraskov hoped to appeal in political writings. *Sobranie luchshikh sochinenii* (Collection of the Best Works) (Moscow University, 1762), published by the historian I. G. Reikhel', exposed readers to the contemporary critique of mercantilist thought. Reikhel' advocated freedom of trade; money was to be valued for its utility as well as for a store of wealth.[55] Anticlerical and antimercantile elements were inscribed in clear strokes in the landscape of courtly culture.

The line was drawn at serfdom, the basis of the social and economic power that court life preserved.[56] There was no sweeping social criticism in Russia in the 1750s or early 1760s like that of a Rousseau or a Mably in France in the same era. Yet to Russians in the 1750s the Enlightenment was more than an intellectual abstraction. Beginning in the war years interest in science, progress, and reform was characteristic not merely of an individual like Mikhail Lomonosov but of a milieu and a culture.[57]

Freemasonry

The emergence of a critical cultural milieu in eighteenth-century Russia can be examined more closely through informal associations, whose most visible example was freemasonry.[58] Freemasonry appeared in Russia possibly as early as the seventeenth century when an English lodge seems to have been founded at roughly the same time as in England. French and German lodges appeared in Russia after the death of Peter I. Initially, grand masters and most of the masons were foreigners, but names of members representing some of the most distinguished noble families (Counts Andrei and Ivan Chernyshev, Count N. N. Golovin, Counts Peter and Ivan Shuvalov, Prince M. Shcherbatov), officers of the guard (including Grigorii Orlov, Sergei Saltykov, I. Boltin), writers (such as A. Sumarokov), and court officials (Adam Olsuf'ev and Ivan Elagin), can be found in freemason organizations of the 1740s and 1750s. In 1762, the master of the chair in the lodge at St. Petersburg was Roman Vorontsov, one of Peter's advisors.[59] The expansion of membership in the 1750s and 1760s was probably due to the residence of Russian officers in Germany during the Seven Years' war. Among members of Prussian lodges were Catherine's lover, Grigorii Orlov, and Aleksandr Suvorov, the memoirist Andrei Bolotov, the poet Gavril Derzhavin, and statesmen Peter Panin and Nicholas Korff.[60]

Under Peter III, one branch of the St. Petersburg masons, which included some of his advisors, met at a new lodge near the imperial palace at Oranienbaum [Lomonosov].[61] This lodge was substantial in size. The secrecy and "spiritual closeness," as one eyewitness put it, drew these imperial statesmen together in an organization that was known for its irreverence and anticlericalism.

It is difficult to offer any single general description of freemasonry that would help explain the significance of its appearance in Russia at this time. In eighteenth-century Europe and America, freemasonry represented a diversity of tendencies but in general it did acquire a reputation for radical ideas. Western European masons, especially late in the century, could be described as agents "for the spread throughout Europe of 'the most radical ideas of the Enlightenment: republicanism, anticlericalism, materialism.' "[62] Yet Frederick II was a mason, showing that despotic rule and masonic throught were complementary. In Boston, freemasonry was so widely accepted in elite circles that it seemed a kind of club. Indeed, Boston freemasons were mocked by radicals for their complacent optimism.

In Russia, freemasonry was a mixed informal organization consisting of numerous lodges. Although in some lodges the eighteenth-century masons focused on "the deadly business of world changing" and were important in the transfusion of romantic individualism to Russia,[63] in general, they probably provided a more moderate milieu where the faith of masons in the power of education was cemented by new social interactions between court aristocrats and leading merchants and townsmen, whose social position and rights became a main concern of legislators.[64] This milieu was possibly where the political support for Peter's reforms was won.

Politics: Peter III's Coalition

Vital to the brilliant and complex legacy of this neglected reign was a political process based on new understanding and compromise. Peter III's reign gave brief life to a new kind of coordinated political action and power to a new generation of reformers. Replacing the elder statesmen who had acquired their position by help- ing Elizabeth to the throne in 1741 were younger men, now in their forties and fifties, whose expertise had been acquired during the Seven Years' War. This younger cohort had not experienced the isolation, frustrations, and failures of the 1720s and 1730s. Their optimism, boldness, and sense of shared interests made this reign uniquely the transition between the highly constrained efforts of a handful of Petrine-style reformers between 1725 and 1761 and the streamlined administration put in place by Catherine II to accommodate her more ambitious program.

The key figures of the 1750s had been Count Peter Ivanovich Shuvalov, senator and Conference member, who died at the beginning of Peter's reign, and his ally, the liberal general procurator of the Senate, Prince Nikita Iur'evich Trubetskoi, who lost this post in 1760. The appointments of Peter's reign replaced Prince Iakov Petrovich Shakhovskoi (1705–1777), general procurator since 1760, and removed from the Senate Iakov Lukich Khitrovo (1700–1777), Vasilii Ivanovich Suvorov (1705–1776), Martyn Karlovich Skavronskii (1717–1776), and Petr Borisovich Sheremetev (1713–1788), who had chalked up a barren record of leadership during the worst years of war from 1760 to 1762. Karl Efimovich Sivers (1710–1774), marshall of the court, lost his post and was threatened with exile.

Vacancies were filled in a way that benefited a new coalition of Vorontsovs, Ivan Shuvalov and his associates, and the Trubetskoi family. I. G. Chernyshev, a close friend of Ivan Shuvalov, congratulated him with glee about the fortunes of "our party": "the different promotions which [Peter III] has made announce the good- ness of his reign."[65] Mikhail Vorontsov retained the key post in foreign policy. The second (vice chancellor) was offered to Ivan Ivanovich Shuvalov, who turned it down.[66] The key post in the Senate went to Peter Shuvalov's personal friend and heir to much of his fortune, Aleksandr Ivanovich Glebov, the former commissar of war. The second post, first secretary of the Senate, went to Trubetskoi's son, Prince Peter Nikitich (1721–1764). Another important appointment—privy secretary— was given to Dmitrii Vasilievich Volkov, the former secretary of Elizabeth's con- ference, a noble without aristocratic lineage but with considerable experience in state affairs and knowledge of foreign languages. He was sponsored by the senior Vorontsovs, uncle and father of Peter III's mistress, respectively, Mikhail and Ro- man, who remained in the Senate as head of its most important commission on codification; the third Vorontsov, Ivan (1719–1786), retained his post in the Mos- cow branch of the Senate as its first secretary. The following were also among the prominent figures of Peter's reign: Aleksei Petrovich Mel'gunov, Peter's former ad- jutant and education advisor, now colonel of the Ingermanland guard corps and member of Peter's Direktorium; Aleksei Semenovich Kozlovskii (1720–1785), first procurator of the Holy Synod and the architect of secularization; Aleksandr

Nikitich Villebois (d. 1781), chief of the infantry corps; Lev Aleksandrovich Naryshkin; and Aleksandr Ivanovich Bressan (1719–1779), ennobled under Peter III and made director of the Gobelin factory in St. Petersburg.

The group of statesmen gathered together by Peter III were influenced by the accomplishments in the 1750s of Peter Shuvalov: important commercial reforms, including the removal of internal tariffs in 1753 and the founding of a merchants' bank in 1754, two isolated measures followed up by more minor reforms in the remaining years of Elizabeth's rule. In the late 1750s, Shuvalov's influence waned, largely due to his loss of imperial support. In 1757 secularization was enacted but not implemented. The Senate's ledgers recorded budgetary deficits and unresolved social disturbances. Without Shuvalov's leadership, the senators engaged in intense and unresolved debate.

Among Peter's advisors, two were particularly influenced by Shuvalov. The first was Aleksandr Glebov, who was Shuvalov's protege. The oldest son of General and Senator Ivan Fedorovich Glebov, Aleksandr Glebov entered civilian service in 1749 and six years later in 1756 became first secretary of the Senate, a swift rise due to Shuvalov's patronage. Chief of the War Commissariat and general procurator of the Senate with charge of the budget, under Peter III he became one of the most powerful figures in the government, a leader of the ruling coalition. His main work was in two areas, Church reform and management of the Senate. His most significant contribution was probably the element of agricultural reform in secularization. He also served an important function as an intermediary for Peter III with European bankers; his understanding of finances probably surpassed that of Shuvalov. By 1762, in other words, Glebov could no longer be called, as he has been, a follower of Shuvalov, even though the lack of sources precludes any elaboration of his political views.

The second official who owed many of his ideas to Shuvalov was Dmitrii Volkov, a statesman whose main expertise, at least initially, was in foreign affairs.[67] Volkov's patron, Aleksei Petrovich Bestuzhev-Riumin (1693–1766), gave him his first appointment, secretary to the Conference at the Imperial Court. In this capacity, he read all reports about the war against Prussia and prepared all the summaries of discussions.[68] By 1761, despite his lack of aristocratic lineage, his influence over decision-making at the Conference had grown. One diplomat even observed that the outcome of the Conference "is ordinarily based more on the opinion of this secretary than on that of the ministers."[69] After 1758, he acquired a new patron, Mikhail Vorontsov, and in 1762 he acquired two posts, head of the College of Foreign Affairs and secretary of the imperial privy chancellery, a post from which he wielded control over domestic policy.[70] Well educated, fluent in several languages, and a forceful writer, Volkov developed ability in domestic affairs that matched his understanding of foreign affairs. Because of the letters that he wrote after the coup d'état, the process of reform under Peter III can be followed.[71]

In determining why this cohort and these political figures were so successful in initiating reform under Peter III, the first step is to examine the preceding period more closely. The administrative inefficiencies under Elizabeth, who held back the reform process, were possibly induced by imperial ambivalence over the issues.[72]

Most historians find Elizabeth a weak autocrat. They argue unconvincingly that Elizabeth, who succeeded in placing herself on the throne and then lasting in power from 1741 to 1762 despite several attempted coups, had an entirely frivolous nature.[73] Nikita Panin attributed the general sense of stagnation to the stultifying effect of powerful favorites, who ruled, while Elizabeth did little. Curiously, however, some of the favorites were reformers, and it was their projects that were blocked. Developing Panin's thesis with a more elaborate explanation, N. L. Rubinshtein removed the weakness in the interpretation by attributing the delay in policy to conflicts between groups of powerful statesmen. He saw interest groups forming within the nobility along lines of social and economic position. However, the alignments he posits are not sufficiently coherent or systematic to make such fine-grained distinctions, nor were the gradations in wealth so striking. A missing element in both lines of speculation is the autocrat herself. To be sure, there is general agreement that Elizabeth had few firm convictions. Even where her convictions may have played some role—for example, on the issue of capital punishment, which she opposed—historians cannot find any clear evidence that her opposition was the reason that judicial reform was stalled. Latkin, a historian of Russian law, despaired of finding an answer. "The reasons Elizabeth failed to sanction the project remain unknown."[74] Assuming that Elizabeth was ambivalent about domestic policy, is this a sufficient explanation for why she began but did not complete any major work of reform?[75]

The key to understanding government, even the Russian government of the eighteenth century, is in identifying coalitions and institutional loyalties. Even under autocracy, authoritative decisions on allocations of value were those made by groups and by conscious processes, rather than those made by individuals or by groups in a quasi-mechanical way.[76] After Rubinshtein, the major thesis that has been developed about this process is by David Ransel. His writings about Catherine's reign have delineated patronage networks—"personal and family clientele networks"—that "formed the basis for political action."[77] The considerable difficulty in applying this thesis to the pre-Catherinian period, however, is that alignments crossed family lines and focused sharply on political issues. Moreover, loyalty could not be secured. Groups shifted in their composition, especially toward the late 1750s.

In the last years of the reign of Elizabeth, as she neared death, political discourse was centered around issues of power and the succession. On Catherine's side, according to her own testimony, there existed a group interested in assisting her to the throne. The inspiration was probably the grand chancellor, Aleksei Petrovich Bestuzhev-Riumin, who helped her enlist other supporters, including some foreign diplomats and military leaders, along with a number of courtiers. Opposing her, and sponsoring Grand Duke Peter, were powerful government figures whose main fear, apart from disruption of the succession, was clearly Bestuzhev himself. Their orientation was not limited to the succession; they caucused and planned reform agendas for the time when they hoped to be in power. However, contrary to what historians have argued, adherence to this group was not determined by political attitudes, the aspirations of the nobility, or loyalty to a family patronage network.

This was a court that confronted a critical transition. How profoundly Catherine's opponents feared the grand chancellor's ambitions was demonstrated by their success in having him arrested and put on trial in 1758 on suspicion of treason. It was this moment that actually generated much tighter coalitions. The fear of further arrests and general terror at court, discussed below, explains the extraordinary coalescence and effective actions of the younger cohort that came together in defense of Grand Duke Peter after 1758.

Coalitions under Elizabeth

Still, the gradual emergence of coalitions should have expedited the reform process, rather than halting it. The process of reform in the 1750s remains unclear. The answer is probably that Elizabeth consciously attempted to prevent the emergence of ruling coalitions, given that the leaders sought the luster of the imperial power itself. In a monarchy, power was measured by proximity to a monarch's person. The fulfilment of political responsibility depended upon the ability to approach the Empress. S. O. Shmidt offers the following insightful observation about Elizabeth's style of rule:

> Endowed with intelligence, although little informed about the course of state affairs, Elizabeth frequently entrusted similar matters to different people with different points of view. These high officials, involuntarily controlling each other, kept her impartial, but, mainly, prevented her from arousing the dissatisfaction of competing groups at court.[78]

To draw out the implication of this description, because of a fear of losing control, Elizabeth created overlapping institutions and encouraged futile competition so that no single statesman and no single institution could impose policy.

Her treatment of the ruling Senate is the most important illustration. Created by Peter I and enhanced in its authority by Elizabeth, the Senate became the supreme organ of government with both judicial and legislative responsibilities. Its control extended over the colleges (except the Synod) and over local administration. In law, it had preeminence of place even during periods when rulers resorted to imperial councils for military and financial advice.[79] But no eighteenth-century ruler, not even Elizabeth, who issued a special proclamation on its political authority on December 12, 1741, gave the Senate full powers. Elizabeth rarely made ceremonial appearances at its sessions: "it did not find itself at the heart of the most important governmental affairs."[80] In 1741 she convened a small advisory council called "the highest council," or the "council of the eleven."[81] After a few weeks, she abandoned the council in favor of restoring the collegial principle and granted the Senate considerably more powers than it had before. She nevertheless kept her cabinet, and in another, more decisive undermining of Senate authority, on the advice of Aleksei Petrovich Bestuzhev-Riumin, grand chancellor for foreign affairs, in 1756 she established an imperial council called the Conference at the Imperial Court.[82]

The Conference at the Imperial Court, consisting of ten members including some senators, was convened in order to raise revenues and manage the campaigns of the anti-Prussian war. By the end of the war, the Conference had also assumed considerable authority in domestic affairs—that is, finances, internal trade, even ecclesiastical revenues.[83] Bestuzhev-Riumin had wanted "an extraordinary functioning organ of supreme authority, deriving its strength from closeness to the Empress," and in the first two years under his aegis this conference acquired that character. "It could issue decrees that other institutions would have immediately to fulfill," A. Presniakov wrote, and it could make appointments to the Senate.[84] Its authority led Elizabeth to a form of command by which rulers gave the weight of law to verbal orders issued in their name, a cameralist mechanism called *Machtspruch*.[85] The Conference in theory now represented the autocratic will, powers which overstepped all other prerogatives. There was one critical weakness, however, which increased over time: the inability of the Conference to overcome opposition from the Senate. *Machtspruch* was designed to strengthen the central authority, but it failed to have that effect.[86]

Cameralist theory itself was to some extent responsible for the proliferation of institutions with overlapping powers. As illustrated in Bielfeld's *Political Institutes* (1762), cameralism set up rights and privileges for social groups and institutions and then established mechanisms to undercut their importance.[87] The conference members who were also senators expressed their sense of frustration in a report of 1760, entitled "How a Circumstance Has Come Up Which Impedes the Progress of Great Affairs and Many Useful Accomplishments":

> In fulfilment of your command to accept verbal decrees, the Senate processes commands you declare through the Conference, although it objects and sends Your Imperial Highness a special report [complaining of its demoted status—CSL]; however, when the Conference conceives of an order of service to your Imperial Highness, with your approval, and in fulfillment of your intentions, the Senate blocks its execution.

Why, they complained, should this "struggle over the preeminence of place" continue?[88]

Lack of procedural clarity was at the heart of institutional failure in the last years of Elizabeth's reign. This was not a case where coalitions, as Rubinshtein argued, came to compromise positions. The nature of reform proposals which were defeated has no particular consistency especially on issues of merchants' and nobles' privileges. The expansion of provincial government, debasement of currency, property rights—for one reason or another rifts occurred with apparently shifting alliances. There was a hard fight from 1760 to 1762 for nobles' rights over land and labor at the expense of both the serfs and the merchants. This issue seems to have achieved Senate approval in 1761, but full enactment of an aristocratic program did not follow.[89] Another difficult issue was treasury monopolies, which some senators sought to reduce to improve payment of direct taxes. Peter Shuvalov, both senator and Conference member, failed to gain his own legislation but succeeded in blocking almost everything else.[90] The net result was a stalemate.

The situation was not helped by Elizabeth's attempt in January 1760 to attack the problem of corruption in office by enlarging the Senate to include men of good reputation and to appoint her most scrupulous bureaucrat, Iakov Shakhovskoi, as general procurator in the Senate and member of the Conference.[91] If this was a move against Shuvalov, which seems unlikely, it did not succeed. Although Shuvalov was replaced as head of the Senate's prestigious codification commission by a friend of Shakhovskoi, Senator Roman Vorontsov, a freemason, an ally of Grand Duke Peter, the father of Peter's mistress, and the brother of the new chancellor, the new appointment did not bring an end to Shuvalov's career. Shuvalov continued to accumulate powerful posts, that of land commissar and treasurer of the artillery, and he continued to be allowed to create commissions (the Commerce Commission, 1760–1762).[92] His closest ally, Nikita Trubetskoi, although removed from the post of general procurator, was not retired but elevated to president of the Military College; Shuvalov's friend Glebov became military commissar, a post powerful enough to lead in two years to the general procuratorship. To the Senate were added Shuvalov's brother, Aleksandr, who, according to the French ambassador, had no opinion of his own,[93] and, as first secretary, Ivan Grigorievich Chernyshev, "a man who enjoys greatest friendship and credit with Shuvalov,"[94] and four others, who were related or politically allied to Shuvalov.[95] But the Senate now also included Shuvalov's personal rival, Shakhovskoi, and Shakhovskoi's cousin, Mikhail, as president of the Finance College.

The path for a successful coalition is, in general, numerical superiority and capturing the agenda. The general procurator was in a good position to control the agenda. However, Shakhovskoi's appointment did not have that effect. He should have been able to construct his own program, but what the Senate succeeded in doing did not spell victory for any identifiable faction: the Holy Synod resisted secularization; the judicial code recommended by the Senate failed to gain imperial signature; of numerous projects submitted to the Commerce Commission, headed by Nepliuev and Chernyshev, not one was enacted into law. The net result was a stalled agenda and extensive absenteeism, which provoked a last sigh and imperial reprimand from the Empress on November 29, 1761, that "the Senators either do not want to or do not know how to make decisions, and they rarely attend meetings."[96]

Peter III's Coalition

The formation of a single powerful coalition and a policy consensus under Peter III resolved these problems, as is shown in the chapters below. It seems clear that initially the key figure in his group was an outsider, Elizabeth's favorite, Ivan Shuvalov. Shuvalov forged a new "party" under Elizabeth in part to guide foreign policy and in part to set up a broader base of power in preparation for her death. His bid for sharing influence was made to the Vorontsovs, especially Mikhail Vorontsov, with whom he held a common foreign policy orientation. He also shared with the Vorontsovs support for Peter's succession, which was in jeopardy because of a rivalry that was growing more intense as Elizabeth's health began to fail.[97] The coalition's first accomplishment under Elizabeth was to bring about the fall of one of the most powerful statesmen of his age, Aleksei Petrovich Bestuzhev-Riumin, and thus set back Catherine's struggle for power.

Bestuzhev-Riumin directed Russian foreign policy from 1744, when he was appointed grand chancellor, to 1758.[98] He sought three main rapprochements: with England and Holland for the purpose of expanding trade, with Austria in order to balance the power of Prussia in Europe, and with Saxony in order to influence the succession in Poland.[99] Bestuzhev-Riumin built an anti-Prussian party in the 1740s to counter the pro-French Shuvalovs, and he emerged on top in the 1750s with the declaration of war against Frederick II—a Pyrrhic victory, since war with Prussia entailed distance from England and alliance with France.[100] By 1757 Bestuzhev's power had already slipped; he had few supporters at the Conference except for his protege, Dmitrii Volkov. Volkov rose from a secretary in the College of Foreign Affairs with Bestuzhev-Riumin's patronage to Conference secretary.[101] Power had passed at the Conference to Elizabeth's new favorite, Ivan Shuvalov.

The records of subsequent events provide no entirely trustworthy guide either to Shuvalov's connivance or to one of the most critical events at court in the 1750s, the trial of Bestuzhev-Riumin for treason. The Bestuzhev-Riumin affair began with the disastrous retreat of General Apraksin in 1757 after the Russian victory over Prussia at Gross-Jaegersdorf. The court presumed that Apraksin had refused to advance after his victory because events in Russia—that is, the drastic decline in the Empress's health—made him desire to return to the capital. Because of the friendship between Apraksin and Bestuzhev-Riumin, who was directing the war, the consequence of his retreat from the front was to arouse suspicion of a conspiracy at the highest level over the succession. Apraksin was accused of treason and conspiracy, deprived of his command, and placed in prison, where he died the following year. That the fall of his friend Bestuzhev-Riumin did not immediately follow suggests that the case for collusion was actually very weak. Nevertheless, with the machinations of the Shuvalov group, in 1758, Bestuzhev-Riumin was convicted of treason and exiled to his country estate. Along with Bestuzhev-Riumin, Catherine was also implicated in a supposed plot to carry out a military coup and seize power for herself or her son at the moment of Elizabeth's death. There is no support for any of these suspicions, possibly because Catherine, after ascending the throne, allowed Bestuzhev-Riumin to purge the records of his interrogation.[102] Catherine's own account in her memoirs of her presumed bid for power is unrevealing. The memoirs end with her own interrogation and release.[103]

Catherine and the others accused avoided the fate of Bestuzhev-Riumin, probably because of the intervention of another man, the still powerful former favorite, the Hetman of Ukraine, Kyril Razumovskii. Razumovskii, possibly unofficially married to the Empress, was jealous of his replacement by Ivan Shuvalov. Attracted by Catherine, he apparently helped mobilize some members of court against the Shuvalov/Vorontsov group.[104] Because of his position at court, not even Bestuzhev-Riumin's exile could affect Razumovskii, and Catherine and Razumovskii suffered no estrangement after the interrogations. The fall of Bestuzhev-Riumin was definitely not a decisive victory for the new Shuvalov/Vorontsov coalition. Indeed, it sharpened the sense of political division. Peter's ascent to the throne was the victory that they sought. But it proved hollow because of Peter's generosity to his determined opponents. After his accession to the throne, the celebration of the

Shuvalov group was muted by fear. Chernyshev wrote to Ivan Shuvalov in 1762, "May the Good God . . . have pity on part of the world and prolong his [Peter III's] life."[105]

In many ways, however, the fall of Bestuzhev-Riumin had far-ranging consequences. The trial forged a new coalition of diverse statesmen. It helped launch the career of Dmitrii Volkov, Bestuzhev-Riumin's former protege. Volkov assumed leadership of the coalition after Peter Shuvalov's death and Ivan's retirement from active service after the death of Elizabeth. Volkov's close association with the Shuvalovs dates to the investigation of Bestuzhev, which he conducted as secretary at the interrogation. At these closed hearings, the accusers of the former grand chancellor included the Senate leaders of the Shuvalov group, Nikita Trubetskoi, Aleksandr Buturlin, and Aleksandr Shuvalov. By his shift of loyalty away from Bestuzhev to this new group, Volkov cemented his place among the Shuvalovs and also apparently strengthened his relationship with Peter. His new credentials as a friend to the Shuvalovs and a loyal supporter of the heir to the throne were sufficiently strong to erase the effect of once having been close to Bestuzhev-Riumin: this can be the only explanation for the absolute trust Peter later placed in his judgment. Volkov's spectacular rise under Peter III bears comparison to the careers of Elagin, Teplov, and Adadurov under Catherine and of Mikhail Speransky under Alexander I. His talents remained the best advocate for his continuing place in government, and under Catherine he was appointed to a governorship and presidency of the College of Manufactures. Volkov was never personally disliked by those who opposed him, the way Peter Shuvalov had been; when in 1762 the elder Shuvalov died and the younger, brilliant Ivan Shuvalov retired from an active role in politics, he had the extraordinary ability to forge a consensus among politicians as diverse as Roman Vorontsov and Aleksandr Glebov behind the policies that he largely shaped.

The Shuvalov/Vorontsov group, which acquired virtually unchallenged influence over Peter by their loyalty at the time of Elizabeth's death, had devised a plan to assure his succession. On December 25, 1761, at the moment of the Empress's death, Aleksandr Glebov, Nikita Trubetskoi, Aleksei Mel'gunov, and Roman Vorontsov convened the court, read a prepared manifesto announcing Peter's succession, and gathered the imperial bodyguard around him. They led the guards in an oath of loyalty to the new ruler:[106] "At the moment the Empress had taken her last breath, the entire court threw itself at his feet and, at the same time, the 300 nobles, those who had put the former ruler on the throne, took the oath. The guards regiments followed . . . [they] distributed ducats to officers and soldiers in considerable amount to encourage their demonstration."[107]

Peter rewarded them well. On December 25, 1761, Glebov replaced Shakhovskoi as general procurator of the Senate, Trubetskoi and Aleksandr Shuvalov were promoted to the rank of field marshall, and Mel'gunov was promoted in rank. Trubetskoi was made colonel of the Preobrazhenskii guards regiment, Roman Vorontsov was given the rank of general, and Aleksandr Bressan was ennobled and given 1,904 serfs. Of those in the opposing Bestuzhev-Riumin group, only Catherine, whose debts were paid, and Aleksei and Kiril Razumovskii, two brothers, the latter of whom, out of respect for Peter's aunt, received "all the lands he wants," were favored on Peter's accession. "The Emperor," wrote Keith in February, "goes on in doing good to particular persons."[108]

The rise of a powerful coalition does not necessarily imply that the supreme authority yielded to aristocratic rule, even briefly. By abolishing the Conference at the Imperial Court, Peter III would have discouraged oligarchic ambitions, had they existed. Peter ruled by the force of his leadership. These statesmen regarded him highly and served him loyally, even at the time of the coup d'état (see chapter 6).[109]

The Imperial Power

Elizabeth had mediated conflict in a disfunctional way, resulting in competitors' annulling of each other's influence. Peter created a cooperative atmosphere. His appointments were rooted in political loyalties, but his choice showed careful decisions. The rigid and bureaucratic Shakhovskoi was removed from power.[110] The new procurator general, Aleksandr Glebov, was a man whose rapid career advancement spoke of diplomatic and financial ability, as reviewed above. In 1762 he secured the four million rubles Peter requested for his campaign which could not be found from Russian resources or foreign loans.[111] Glebov's control in the Senate complemented the new powers of Volkov, mentioned above, the privy secretary to the Emperor. In Elizabeth's reign Volkov was already an influential member of the Conference, over which he presided.[112] These two appointments show Peter III's choices; he also benefited from chance—the unpopular Peter Shuvalov's death allowed the younger, more liberal men greater freedom to act.[113]

Where Peter showed greatest ability, however, was in clarifying the chain of command. A British observer writing from Denmark described Peter's style of rule: "His Imperial Majesty applies himself very much to the affairs of government; For which purpose he has, out of every college, taken a secretary whom he makes use of to give orders, according as he finds good."[114] Later, by not relinquishing his imperial authority, he undercut opposition in the Senate—as Catherine also would—by relying on the general procurator to resolve conflict and by in effect giving ministerial authority to Volkov.[115] "More and more power is falling into the hands of Volkov, who is really and truly first Minister of Russia at present," wrote Keith.[116] Peter infused his own enormous power into the structure of decision-making, while not inhibiting his coalition of supporters from acting in support of their own interests.

To be sure, interest groups continued to block legislation. The stalling of commercial reform in May and June was a reminder of the significance of the occasional splintering of his coalition. This problem would soon be resolved by the further enhancement of autocratic will under Catherine.

The lessons of Peter's rule were of decisive importance to Catherine. Her first impression of the highest institution of state was of its " 'internal disagreements, enmity and hatred' leading to the formation of parties seeking to hurt each other, and to behavior unworthy of sensible respectable people desirous of doing good.''[117] Catherine responded by demoting the Senate to a consultative body and by the use of *Machtspruch,* making her verbal commands law. She also used Elizabeth's practice of granting ad hoc authority to special commissions. As a climax to the long evolution of the idea of an imperial council, instead of the imperial council her advisors proposed, she created in 1763 a temporary commission on the nobility's freedom where she controlled the agenda and brought the discussions to an end.[118]

Catherine relied on her own coalition, consisting of the victors in the coup d'état, Grigorii Orlov, Nikita Panin, Grigorii Teplov, and others. That the course of policy remained the same implies that although Peter's coalition certainly fell apart, some of the appointments survived. After the coup d'état, Volkov, forced to leave the capital temporarily, became governor general of the province of Orenburg. Glebov remained in his position, however, until 1764, and Roman Vorontsov remained powerful in the Senate. Mikhail Vorontsov was appointed to Catherine's prestigious commission on nobles' freedom; Mel'gunov was exiled for two years, but returned to prominence later as president of the Finance College. A single small governmental elite thus persisted in power for key years in the eighteenth century. The insecurity of its loyalty to Catherine's coalition helped perpetuate her essentially solitary rule, tempered by small group preferences. The larger dialogue between government and society that had seemed possible in the early 1760s grew remote, especially after the Pugachev revolt. For social policy, the main consequence of the increasingly limited dialogue and streamlined imperial command was that the Russian government failed to develop a system of property rights that encouraged the redistribution of economic power, even as education created the aspiration for power and influence on the part of a larger group.

Under Peter III, the distribution of political and economic authority was under study. His reign marked a vital transition, removing important constraints on economic and social development. Resettling many nobles from the capitals to the provinces by emancipating them from obligatory service gave the central government the manpower to create in the provinces a political and physical infrastructure that had largely been missing in the seventeenth and early eighteenth century. Similarly, the resolution of the centuries-long dispute over ecclesiastical property rights gave a large segment of the peasantry new economic incentives and laid the basis for a stronger network of local markets. In the contradictory legacy of his reign, however, reflecting a contradiction implicit in combining physiocracy with cameralism, even as his reforms encouraged rural and urban growth, they strengthened both the nobility's voice in government and its control over social development. The strengthening of the nobility's status was a priority in the economic plans of the physiocrat Dmitrii Volkov and the autocratic ambitions of Peter III. A strong sense of continuity emerges from a study of the policies of the later part of the eighteenth century. The reforms of this era were based on a broad reconsideration of traditional policy and experimentation with new foreign trade opportunities, which had considerable economic and social impact over many years. These policies nevertheless gave new life to the manorial economy and to local institutions that stood in the way of structural change.

II

EMANCIPATION OF THE
RUSSIAN NOBILITY

Peter I accelerated the formation of a powerful state apparatus in Russia by creating a new service ladder (the Table of Ranks, 1722) and rigidly enforcing a requirement that nobles remain in service for life. The strains on nobles' lives in the course of the next half century undermined this great stroke of central administrative policy. It removed from the already barren countryside the limited governance and estate management that nobles had previously provided.[1] The pursuit of those who refused to serve generated insecurity and resistance.[2] In 1736, the autocracy partially yielded and reduced the term of service to twenty-five years, but compromise had little effect. In the 1750s, nobles' continuing political dissatisfaction was compounded by new lax credit arrangements and the estate's economic behavior. To pay their mounting debts, they hedged against the state's irregular payroll, inflated currency, and arrears on serfs' dues by borrowing hundreds of thousands of rubles using serfs as security.[3] Peter III, who acknowledged the weight of these social consequences in the formation of his financial and social policy, yielded entirely to the advice that the service obligation be ended. Contriving to give his reversal an Enlightenment appearance, Peter issued a manifesto on February 18, 1762, on the ''freedom'' of the Russian nobility and the now voluntary nature of service.[4] Almost immediately, the decree took effect. Within a decade, numerous new organizations, including, for example, the Free Economic Society, emerged to the further encouragement of the economic aspirations of the landholding elite.

The removal of the service obligation was thus the result of forty years of experience. Petrine policy with its short-sighted, exclusively administrative approach to estate definition was discredited. The manifesto essentially responded to the argument that had been made as early as the 1730s by the service elite that nobles were needed on their estates. It also emerged from fiscal thinking, that closer supervision of estates would generate revenues by improving collection of the poll tax.[5] In a related way Peter III's government was made to see the significance of limited local governance by nobles. The long pattern of service in the capital had frustrated the emergence of regionally based networks of authority. The absence of nobles from their estates meant that neither the state nor the nobility could derive benefit from regional investment.

Landlords' absenteeism was an enormous obstacle to the development of provincial services. Most landlords had unconsolidated estates, and they left scattered holdings to the care of the serfs—the state tended to grant to the service noble small parcels of land in distant provinces or the frontier area—while obliging them to live in the capital. The insecurity of nobles' tenure of land, due to the threat of confiscation, was a further disincentive to live on the estate, and meanwhile the untended estate was then subjected to local risks due to the lack of law enforcement.[6] The removal of obstacles to local development was gradual and took several centuries. Emancipation was the first of the major legislative initiatives that laid the foundation. Its impact was so powerful, affecting the residence pattern of nobles, that by the 1770s and 1780s, the development of provincial government and regionally based social services had visibly begun.

A perhaps narrowly conceived but decisive act, the manifesto allowed nobles to serve as long as they wished or to retire. A limitation excluded military servitors, who were prohibited from retiring within three months of the beginning of a campaign. Nobles could travel abroad and enter the service of foreign governments, although they would be obliged to return when recalled on penalty of confiscation of their estates. Nobles were also obliged to educate their children; failure to comply was punishable by confiscation of estates. The remainder of the manifesto consisted of adjustments to the Table of Ranks. Among provisions on retirement and reentry into service, the manifesto forbade nobles who had served twelve years without promotion to apply for reentry into service after retirement. Hiring standards were encouraged, so that lower level bureaus and central offices could in principle show preference to qualified non-noble applicants over those who were unqualified, noble or not.

In its impact on the state, the manifesto secured the newly gained position of non-nobles in the state bureaucracy. By confirming promotions based on "capacity" and by issuing new regulations on retirement and reentry, the act in principle allowed the state to respond more flexibly than it had in the past to staffing needs and to the financial strain of nearly continual warfare. In this sense, but only in this sense, the act was thoroughly Petrine.

Legislative Background

The nobility traditionally served the state; the very word for the first estate, *dvorianstvo,* denoted the military service corps of Muscovite times.[7] By the end of the seventeenth century, however, for many landholders the service obligation meant only a liability to serve for a while on summer campaigns, and evasion was easy. In 1722, to meet new needs of the expanded military and civilian service corps, Peter I penalized evasion more severely and promulgated a Table of Ranks in order to establish a system of precedence based solely upon rank attained in service.[8] He intended nobles to enroll in the Cadet Corps when they were very young, or gain an education by other means, and to devote the rest of their lives to the military service. After 1722, nobles could still evade service, but less easily than before.

Some consequences of compulsory service, as suggested above, were unintended and undesired.[9] As nobles were drawn away from their domains, the significance of the land and serfs in their daily lives diminished, although not the allure of the idealized life of the country squire.[10] Affecting their status as well as their personal lives, the larger bureaucracy and increased opportunities for promotion also incidentally led to the considerable ennoblement of commoners and to the sharing of power by families of ancient lineage, families that had previously held rank by the order of aristocratic precedence called *mestnichestvo*.[11] Finally, compulsory service and the ranking system strengthened the voice of the new civil service elite, some of whom came to feel that they represented the nobility at large since they had control over ongoing adjustments to procedural law relative to the Table of Ranks. From the commission on laws affecting the nobility came new proposals to end the service obligation altogether and to grant to nobles more exclusive rights in agriculture, commerce, and industry.

The necessity of revising the Table of Ranks from time to time was the means by which the civil service elite developed more of a corporate identity. The frequent revisions of the table were used to review its essential principles. In the 1750s, the work of revision was given to the Senate's Codification Commission, which used the excuse of adjusting ranks and salaries to launch a more broadly conceived codification of estate prerogatives than the Table of Ranks. Among its proposals, the commissioners argued from an Enlightenment position that education, rather than compulsion, was the proper means to persuade nobles of their duty to serve the state. Their approach and Peter's acceptance of it suggests how effectively the argument from a value-oriented position could be used to advance a variety of political purposes.

In the Table of Ranks, Peter I's priority had been to create a highly centralized bureaucracy with loyal and competent personnel in the highest ranks of military and civilian service.[12] After forty years, in a different age, Peter III and a new elite sought to affirm the traditional prestige and security of land tenure. The central goals of the elite, to secure the welfare of their hereditary or acquired estates and to reduce risk of their confiscation and seizure by neighbors, were achieved.

The Historical Interpretations

The peculiarity of this manifesto—it granted a preliminary charter of rights without immunities from corporate punishment and other privileges that nobles clearly sought—has made it an object of speculation about the relationship between the nobility and the autocracy in the eighteenth century. The literature on the emancipation is extensive; a few major works deserve mention. The most thorough study was that of the Soviet scholar N. L. Rubinshtein, who looked at emancipation as an example of internal conflict within the nobility.[13] He discovered that two drafts preceded the reform, and that these drafts diverged. The manifesto, he argued, was a compromise. By elaborate dating of the two documents, he claimed to identify two groups in the nobility, one with a pro-merchant and the other a pro-aristocratic position, a divergence deduced from social conflict and social identity. The compromise represented by emancipation was only a partial victory, he argued, for the aristocrats. The state, the mediator of conflict, prevented the aristocrats from gaining everything they sought. Thus Rubinshtein found support for the classic Marxist position on the absolutist state that during the formative process the state was not exclusively a tool of the ruling class. Only later, after the experience of peasant revolt from 1773 to 1775, did class power and economic interest gain against the apparatus of state, which had to provide a stronger defense for the land-holding system. To Rubinshtein and other Soviet scholars, emancipation was key, along with the strengthening of serfdom, in the increasing power of the nobility.[14]

Acceptance, with reservations, of Rubinshtein's dating[15] does not necessarily lend support to the Marxist paradigm. The manifesto was the result of some sort of compromise. However, Rubinshtein's view of the compromise and attribution of political positions according to type and extent of wealth-holding is based on arbitrary assumptions. Essentially, he freezes nobles' ambitions at a moment in time on the basis of wealth-holding data for the late 1750s and on the basis of the deterministic understanding of social and economic identity. His exacting and thorough textual analysis is thus accompanied by a rigid and inaccurate framework which, for lack of alternate interpretations, has served since the 1950s as the basis of almost every Soviet and Western work on the political history of the mid-eighteenth century.

Marc Raeff examined emancipation in order to explore aspects of institutional history, and he accepted Rubinshtein's dating of manuscripts and division of the court, although he reversed the implications. In his view, emancipation was not the work of a pro-aristocratic faction; it benefited nobles very little. It expressed the thinking of the pro-merchant group which, he argued, was chiefly concerned with the expansion of the bureaucracy. Raeff found support for this point in a work by Troitskii, who showed that the manifesto encouraged a process begun much earlier in the eighteenth century of accommodating non-nobles in the bureaucracy.[16]

Robert Jones, the only scholar to reject entirely Rubinshtein's polarization of the court, concurred with Raeff in one respect, that the state's policy was not determined in response to nobles' aspirations to expand their rights. Jones argued that the manifesto was not "a bribe to win the support of the nobility or . . . an alternative to the economic privileges sought by the Vorontsovs."[17] He assumed the government had exclusively administrative purposes.

> The coming peace foretold a sharp decline in the demand for service which would mean an excess of noble servitors in the employ of the state unless some action were taken to eliminate it. The acute financial difficulties created by the Seven Years' War demanded the removal of excess noblemen from the payrolls for simple economic reasons. Arising out of that situation, the Manifesto tried to deal with the problem of demobilization and effect a smooth transition from a wartime to a peacetime service.[18]

Had this been the exclusive motive for emancipation, however, no manifesto or fundamental privileges would have been needed; relief could have been obtained more efficiently by a temporary measure, as Jones indeed concluded. He faulted Peter III's government for its "tactless, haphazard, and reckless" manner of pursuing reform.[19] This interpretation ignores the fact that the emancipation manifesto made full provision for hiring as well as retirement. One of the state's needs to which the manifesto responded was to improve standards used in hiring and to open up jobs to all qualified personnel rather than restricting service to the nobles. It is difficult to agree that the state was negatively affected, since there was no interruption in the bureaucracy's steady expansion in the eighteenth century.

Emancipation and demobilization may seem to some historians like abandonment of the nobility by the state, separation from the sacred center of monarchical authority, but the wording of the manifesto gives expression to a different conceptualization. The manifesto was firm about the continuing moral obligation of nobles to serve. To overlook literal wording is to ignore the political content of language that contains a key to its meaning. In this chapter, I explore how the edict originated in order to determine what the decree meant from context. Much remains unclear. There are no dates or signatures on drafts of the manifesto and no preface giving the circumstances of its origin. A narrative, however, can still be gleaned from the writings of Peter's advisors and from the text itself. As Roman Vorontsov, the author of the manifesto, urged, the state granted the nobility a particular limited privilege with anticipation of its multiform uses and benefits to both the state and the nobility.

Like the causes, the consequences of reform plunge historians into a question of critical importance to social history. Historians including Raeff and Jones tend to defer to the nineteenth-century historian S.A. Korf, who argued that nobles failed to utilize their freedom not to serve.[20] Korf wrote that it was "a very interesting psychological fact, that the noble loved to declare his freedom not to serve, while service remained the ideal activity." Nobles may have spent a few years in the provinces, but then "they almost all returned to service." In the tradition established by Korf, Catherine's hesitance and nobles' continuing service orientation meant that emancipation was neither confirmed nor implemented after Peter III's death. Service remained the definition of their status.[21]

Indeed, as Raeff argued, the decree was not intended to give nobles the kind of functions in provincial life that the German Junkers, for example, enjoyed—responsibilities for police, justice, and administration.[22] There can be no doubt that this was true. Raeff went on to write that those who went back to the provinces after 1762 were "forced" to by government policy and experienced "a sense of frustration and rejection." To Raeff, the meaning of the decree was obliquely indicated in its ultimate result: by not encouraging the development of a real gentry, which would enjoy extensive local privileges and rights, it helped perpetuate autocracy.[23]

There is much that remains unclear about the history of the Russian elite and the reasons for its support of autocracy, but the residence patterns of nobles after emancipation confirm that nobles were neither reluctant to retire nor forced out of service. In the long term, as the state invested more and more in local government, the resident nobility came to constitute a kind of gentry with a significant stake in local concerns. The last part of this chapter sets forth the evidence and arguments in support of that conclusion. Korf relied extensively on laws and narrative evidence about nobles' residence because of the scarcity of systematic statistical data. For this reason his contention—that nobles wanted to and did remain in service after emancipation—remains no more than that. Narrative evidence and legal sources can equally easily be used to demonstrate the contrary. Romanovich-Slavatinskii wrote that voluntary retirement was a response to systematic disobedience by recalcitrant nobles who, after emancipation, were free of an unwanted obligation. In the mid-years of the eighteenth century, he continued, "the service element in nobility weakened against the landholding element."[24] "Finally, under Peter III, the nobles were dispersed in permanent retirement to their homes."[25] From exhaustive study of questionnaires as well as memoir literature, Michael Confino powerfully argued in somewhat the same vein that our understanding of the social history of the nobility drawn on the kind of evidence that Korf provided falls short of historical reality.[26] It is impossible to fully describe what nobles wanted or how they responded to emancipation. For one thing, the 1760s marked the first decade when nobles' residency was traced by official agencies and when noble families were counted. This means that a comparison with the previous period is difficult. For another, the numbers of nobles personally involved in estate management in the second half of the eighteenth century do not necessarily indicate how many of those were eligible for service or retired. Nevertheless, whatever the drawbacks of using the available data, a study of the post–1762 residency of nobles, even without close detail or information about prior residency, indicates, above all, that the complaint giving rise to emancipation no longer had any foundation.

Residence in the countryside did not immediately transform nobles into a leisured gentry or civic-minded rural elite. Many nobles who left in 1762 reentered service in the provincial towns, where after the 1770s they became a powerful force in local government.[27] Some nobles did not retire at all. The ambiguous response to retirement raises a question of how status had actually come to be defined in response to the Table of Ranks, and the answer is by no means clear. Yet even if the manifesto failed immediately to create an articulate landed gentry, it still must be considered one of the most important reforms of the eighteenth century. After 1762, freedom to retire from service encouraged generations of nobles to grow up in the provinces, where, once the Pugachev revolt shattered their illusions about a peaceful, retiring life in the countryside, they then left their mark upon political life. After the 1770s, because of the key role envisioned for nobles in the expansion of governmental authority in the provinces and in the sparsely settled frontiers, the weight of corporate interests in the formation of policy increased.

Implementation of the Table of Ranks

Peter's Table of Ranks of 1722 established an order of fourteen ranks for servitors, the fourteenth *chin* (rank) in military service and eighth in the civilian service conferred hereditary nobility, providing that the service obligation continued to be met. Former boyars (the term boyar was dropped) were downgraded by the same leveling process by which many who had never been nobles would rise through the ranks to acquire the right to own land and serfs. Most successful bureaucrats in the nineteenth century acquired few serfs, if any, and by far the majority of wealthy serf-owners in the eighteenth century were military servitors. Nevertheless, even landless servitors benefited from advancement by gains in salary and status.

The Table of Ranks was enacted in the last phase of Peter I's reforms. Simultaneously building the administrative apparatus of the new capital in St. Petersburg and imposing a new form of taxation, he needed officers loyal to the autocrat and competent to manage affairs of state. More important, he had to staff the officer corps of the enormous army which was constantly in the field. This he did partially by incorporating foreigners into the command and partially by imposing stricter standards for entry into the officer corps and promotion within the seniority system. His law of single inheritance (1714) was implicitly designed to enlarge the officer corps and the bureaucracy: while mitigating the effects of splintering of estates, the act cast younger sons permanently off the land and brought them into the service corps as career officials. In a critical provision, it also eliminated the concept of land grants for service (*pomest'ia*) by establishing permanent salaries in remuneration for service.[28] The incremental cost to the treasury was expected to be a tolerable burden: Peter's officers and regiments already took up one-half to three-fourths of the state budget. Competence, however, was to improve. The benefits—expertise, loyalty, and Westernization—were to outweigh the costs, some of them conceivably unexpected, such as the squires' utter desertion of the countryside.[29]

In the years that followed, much was repealed, including the law on single inheritance. The enforcement of the Table of Ranks revealed the reform to be only a qualified improvement on *mestnichestvo*. Though the Table of Ranks achieved its main purposes, it imposed an unwanted burden on the nobility and a constraint on estate supervision. At the time, Peter I had recognized the necessity for nobles to be released from time to time to tend to the management of their estates. "Military servitors . . . who are landowners will be freed on leave for two or three years because of their domestic needs," Peter I had decreed in 1724.[30] In the reign of Catherine I, nobles were given the right to take extensive leaves. After her death, Peter II hardly ever enforced service. Anna Ivanovna tightened the regime by enforcing registration of young nobles (*iavki*) more effectively. She kept the education requirement in place, and she strengthened general procedures of entry into service by increasing the periodically required iavki. However, in an act of leniency on December 31, 1736, she revised the length of the military service requirement "so that the nobles can tend more closely to their home needs and estates." She reduced the term of service beginning at twenty years of age to twenty-five years, after which a noble could voluntarily retire with the increase of one rank.[31] To reduce the requirement still further, some parents were able to enroll their children at birth. More frequently a male noble entered service as a youngster or teenager, and he could expect to be his own master by the age of forty.[32]

The impact of this legislation was delayed. Anna Ivanovna's limitation on the length of service was not observed until long after the Turkish War. Civil servitors still remained in service their whole lives, and military servitors stayed in the capital cities.[33] As a rule, magnates left their estates under the administration of stewards, lesser proprietors relied on their own wives or on peasant elders, and nobles remained in service until too ill or too advanced in age to work. The condition of permanence was a principle cause for the nobles' resentment of service obligations. The proposals of the assembled nobility during the political crisis of 1730 reflected their demand that the term of service be reduced or eliminated and that the service requirements be relaxed. Resentment was manifest in evasion of service and in discontent at the Russian court.[34] In 1759, senators discussed particularly harsh circumstances as war continued. Nobles were unable to get leaves of absence from the front, which profoundly affected their financial concerns, the monitoring of their estates, payment of sums to the bank, and the defense of boundaries from predatory neighbors.[35]

Another cause of resentment was the increased share of non-nobles in administration, the means by which non-nobles acquired land and serfs. In 1719, Peter I had decreed that people of all ranks could purchase land; in 1723, he extended the application of the law to factories and serf villages.[36] Alarmed over many years by the threat to their monopoly of power and privileges, in 1758 the senators enacted a law to confiscate within a half year all property belonging to those servitors who did not possess hereditary standing.[37] The measure of 1758 and others like it had little effect. Non-noble ownership of property had become too widespread and the enforcement agencies of the state were too meagerly staffed. Service had rapidly expanded the numbers of nobles in Russian society: in the 1750s, roughly 25 percent of those who had reached at least the ennobling eighth rank in central agencies were of non-noble origin.[38]

Among the consequences of the service obligation, beginning in Peter's reign, the frequent summons of officers to war and the subsequent imposition of compulsory service meant a shortage of local personnel, a problem that was only resolved by Catherine II's reform in 1775. In a report of 1732, the governor general of Moscow province—the most settled area with some of the wealthiest estates—complained about the small number of competent officials. Governance consisted virtually of the governor himself. "Without assistants," he complained, "I cannot manage affairs."[39] For collecting the poll tax, army officers were sent to the provinces.[40] But aside from this scattered force, governor generals were left with no resources to deal with fugitive serfs, road repairs, judicial review, and land disputes. Governor Ivan Nepliuev, who transformed Orenburg into a *guberniia* (province) in 1745, brought his son to Orenburg to help direct military operations, foreign expeditions, and civil affairs as dictated by the Senate. There was no other source of assistance.[41]

In the 1750s, a decade filled with peasant revolt, the problems became more acute. The report by a commission established to study revolts on monastic lands decried increasing lawlessness, a condition caused, it was believed, by the leniency of the overburdened courts.[42] A review of provincial police in 1759 disclosed that in thirty-seven provinces there were no police at all.[43] In 1761 and 1762 there was not even a sufficient supply of officers to proceed with the general land survey beyond the borders of Moscow guberniia,[44] nor the geographic investigations ordered by Peter III.[45] The number of troops that could be spared to keep the roads near Moscow and St. Petersburg safe from bandits was shrinking, pointing up the necessity of a local police.[46] Questionnaires sent out in 1758 seeking information about provincial chancelleries and available personnel revealed, in the words of one respondent from the northern guberniia of Novgorod:

> extreme insufficiency; that is, for all state matters and receipts there is one unit from Velikaia Luka consisting of 150 soldiers of all ranks . . . and although there are some chancellery servitors, there are no retired nobles available for assignment; to stand guard on bridges there are only invalid soldiers.[47]

The implementation of the Table of Ranks had developed a pattern of service that left no possibility for the survival of Petrine local government reforms.

The nobility maintained its control over local government despite staffing problems. A law of 1761, for example, reserved the post of secretary, or head of the provincial chancellery, for retired military servitors.[48] The Senate's Codification Commission under Elizabeth (1754–1766) deliberated through 1762 on laws designed to preserve and expand nobles' prerogatives in the countryside. Historians sometimes describe the entire post-Petrine era as an amorphous interlude between the reigns of two great monarchs, Peter I and Catherine II, when no action was taken on critical issues of reform. Got'e wrote about the lack of creative reform in the area of local government, the repetition of proposals which offered "nothing interesting" and nothing "new," and he traces a number to their final place of rest, "burial in the Senate," after their "return by the Empress [Elizabeth]" with suggestions for review.[49] The results indeed showed little concrete accomplishment. However, summaries of discussions and proposals in the archives of the Codification Commission showed that lawmakers were fully engaged in attempting to rectify the consequences of various contradictions of Petrine legislation. They had instructions to "update the law" with the single prohibition against making determinations about local government. The commissioners paid scant heed to the boundaries of their authorization. Under the rubric of estate rights and property law the commissioners found possibilities of remaking key segments of Petrine legislation that had some bearing on local government.

Preparation for Reform under Elizabeth

According to Rubinshtein, the Senate's Codification Commission went through two phases: the first, from 1754 to 1760, dominated by its founder, Peter Shuvalov and his protege Glebov, who actually served on the commission, and the second after 1760, differently guided by new heads of the commission, senators Roman Vorontsov and Mikhail Shakhovskoi. However, Roman Vorontsov explained in a note dated 1761 that the task of the "new" Commission was the same as it had been before, to compile a register of existing laws, "to create one decree on each topic," and to solicit "articles" from central and local institutions. He explained that the work on a code of laws had proceeded steadily throughout the century, beginning with the Council of Nobles (1730–1738) convened in Anna Ivanovna's reign to review the laws.[50] Now, he wrote, was the time to speed up the work, which had virtually come to a halt during the Seven Years' War. This, he claimed, was the reason for the enlargement of the commission (Glebov was not removed, though he ceased to attend its meetings in 1761).[51]

The Shuvalov commission had drawn up one section, a criminal code, and begun another on fundamental rights belonging to different estates, which was the most important work the commission was to do. The Vorontsov commission finished the estate rights section, with some significant revisions, and produced it in separate items of legislation in 1760 and 1761 in a new legislative agenda for the Senate. In 1761, the most important of these proposals was to deprive merchants of the right to petition for ownership of land and villages for their factories. However, by 1762, neither this proposal nor the code itself had been passed by the Senate. The law on merchant property rights, for example, had been sent back to commission. Emancipation, in all likelihood, was the next such item under preparation for proposal to the Senate for separate consideration. It can be seen as part of a plan to construct item by item a new code comprising property and estate rights.

The Vorontsov Version

There can be no question that the February 18 manifesto of emancipation came from the Vorontsov version of the law code from chapter 22, "About Nobles and Their Privileges," section III, "On the General Status of Subjects." Rubinshtein's dating was exact.

How did chapter 22 justify its challenge to existing law? It began not with Petrine precedents as was usually the case in Russian reforms, but with estate rights in western Europe. "In every state governed by enlightened rulers," nobility has certain privileges. In Russia, the privileges ought to distinguish, according to Vorontsov, an elite among nobles with hereditary status and access to land and lifetime holders of nobility. Nevertheless, to Vorontsov, hereditary and lifetime nobility should confer rights and immunities: all nobles should be free of compulsory regulations, arbitrary arrest, confiscation of property, corporal punishment, "forced labor," interrogation, and exile (article 15). Nobles should have the fundamental right "to serve or not serve at will" (article 7). Compulsory service had been motivated by circumstances "of former times" and was no longer necessary. This right was based on the "freedom and liberty" (*svoboda i vol'nost'*) of the first estate.[52]

The Vorontsov version thus saw emancipation as part of a larger agenda. Vorontsov wrote that a forthcoming chapter would elaborate on nobles' rights (it was never written). We can guess what this chapter might have contained from scattered items in chapter 22 and elsewhere. Vorontsov's notion of "freedom and liberty" emphasized personal freedom although it also embraced a notion of local representation. He sought the election to central government of provincial nobles, for example. He envisioned the assignment of thirty nobles to the Senate in St. Petersburg and twenty to the Senate branch office (*kontor*) in Moscow with right of consultation on local (not national) affairs.[53] He sought provincial assemblies with elected rather than appointed officers (article 11).

The electoral principle was far from new. It had been advanced under Peter I and again in the 1730s. "Practically in every project [of 1730] is a clear reference to the electoral principle which should lie at the basis of appointments to the highest positions in government institutions," wrote Got'e.[54] In 1740, A. P. Volynskii sought to improve local government by the principle of elections; in 1744, A. B. Buturlin made a similar proposal in the Senate; and in 1754, Peter Shuvalov either submitted or supported a project in the Senate for local government reform involving elections and the expansion of noble prerogatives. Of all of these, Shuvalov's was the most significant. It called for a decisive control by locally elected noble officials— land commissars—over appointed officials. Shuvalov's project, however, like all others before it, did not get imperial approval.[55]

Either due to caution or lack of concern, Vorontsov used chapter 22 neither to clarify the functions of the assemblies he proposed nor to establish the relationship between central and provincial government. In another project, "About the Nobility," (undated, but by chronological sequence in the manuscript folio written between 1761 and 1763), he provided a better idea of what may have been behind his thinking. "For the sake of discussion of cameralist ideas and other matters of local concern," there should be district meetings, and every two years, two representatives should be elected to consult with the Senate. This suggests something on the order of a regularly convened large assembly with consultative voice in the making of laws—a procedure already set in motion in 1761 with a call for provincial representatives to come to St. Petersburg to review the new code of laws. Moreover, there should be permanent district information centers for the distribution of "cameralist" literature (presumably on land improvement and local government) and for the conservation of legal records (births and deaths and landholding).[56] Vorontsov's idea was to revitalize provincial life by educating nobles and spreading information about agricultural techniques.

He had his own perception of privileged life. Nobles, he wrote, should be "freed of all local burdens and responsibilities." This key phrase shows resistance to the established reciprocal relationship between the nobility and the state, where the state demanded that nobles collect taxes and provide recruits and in return gave the nobility control over land and labor. Vorontsov sought to free nobles from that contract and from all compulsion: nobles should be concerned mainly with their property and their safety. In every *uezd* (district) there should be a *zemskii sud* (land court) to resolve landlords' disputes and commissars to resolve disputes among the peasantry. The way it was, he explained, nobles had to address petitions to urban agencies for the resolution of boundary disputes, and the cost of the legal proceedings was high. Land courts could resolve problems locally with lower costs and less expenditure of time.

Vorontsov aspired to create a class whose members could demonstrate their social superiority to those who toiled and not one that threatened the imperial power. His caution and tact were paramount. In his "About the Nobility" he included what he called a "Petition from the Nobility," where he alluded to corporate concerns, the heart of the work of this commission:

> The work we have now undertaken in compiling new laws is concerned with people
> of all strata; but the essential use of these [laws] and their necessary direction, as all
> can see, is to create our well being by [ensuring] the peaceful condition of estates
> and the preservation of the rights of the nobility.[57]

Vorontsov put forward his ideas with a constituency in mind—"as all can see"—
and a program statement with property rights and prevention of serf disturbances
the clearly defined motives and representation in government a less vital background interest. The nobility Vorontsov claimed to represent was fearful and uneasy, concerned with protecting its property but not eager to shoulder burdens.
Vorontsov concluded his "Petition from the Nobility" with a special attestation of
loyalty to the tsar: "In comparing the history of Russia with that of all European
states one finds no end to examples where the Russian nobility has shown as much
loyalty to the Russian monarch as have the nobles of other states to their rulers."[58]
Vorontsov's limited concept of the need of the nobility for political representation
is open to interpretation. Whether he did not envision a strong nobility or whether
he was delaying that agenda cannot be known. His strategy, in any case, was non-
confrontational. He presented the autocracy with words to elicit privileges other
"enlightened" rulers granted in other states of Europe and to persuade rulers of the
benefit of improving agriculture and eliminating "coarseness."

As mentioned above, land and agricultural development forms an essential part
of the background of this proposal. The falling land/labor ratio made land relatively
more valuable than labor. New buyers were coming into the land market, raising the
prices and threatening what was perceived as a scarce resource.[59] By the 1760s
something still remained of the two different types of landholding, the *pomest'e*, or
land held in lifelong tenure, and *votchina*, or land owned in perpetuity. Although
the forms had merged under Peter I, some of the most highly prized pomest'e land
near Moscow was still reserved for temporary distribution in reward for services.
Numerous circumstances, including a fall from favor, evasion of service, or other
disgrace, could put that property at risk of confiscation, so that the state always
maintained a reserve of assets to distribute.[60] Competition for new land grants for
service was intense, especially after the removal of internal tariffs in 1753 encouraged grain growing.[61] Elite nobles, such as the Vorontsovs, must have feared that
every clerk with pretensions to nobility would purchase land, leaving less for the
nobility. "In purchasing estates and land," the Vorontsov version read, "nobles are
obstructed by such people" (article 18).[62]

The point in history when property rights become an acute issue is a gauge of
consciousness as well as demographic expansion. A. Alchian and H. Demsets remarked about the relationship between pressure on the land and legal restraint:

> twelfth-century England experienced a relative rise in the value of land which led to
> efforts to convert the existing right structure into one that allowed for exclusive own-
> ership and transferability. During the thirteenth century, England experienced the
> development of an extensive body of land law, the initiations of enclosure, and, fi-
> nally, the right to alienate land, and there were similar experiences on the
> Continent.[63]

The demand for exclusive rights in the private ownership of land and villages, a demand which was a foundation of chapter 22 (the Vorontsov version), has special significance in the decade when the General Land Survey was initiated.

The Land Survey, fully launched only in the 1780s, was an effort whose results defined legal boundaries, closed off the common forest from general access by neighboring peasants, and more closely regulated competing access to vital resources. Rise of interest in law in Russia at mid-century cannot be separated from nobles' concern over their rights to land in a changing world.[64]

The same fear of encroachment on nobles' privileges by an upwardly mobile servitor class inspired Vorontsov's other project of 1761–1762. He sought to prohibit non-nobles from owning other kinds of rural property and to keep merchants from purchasing serfs and land for factories. All proposals to come from the Codification Commission recommended giving nobles monopoly rights in various branches of manufacturing, leaving only commerce for the merchants. Catherine II found the same attitude among noble representatives to her Codification Commission of 1767. Like those nobles, Vorontsov identified the improvement of agriculture with the "peaceful" life in the countryside and secure rights. Some of Peter's advisors, including Volkov and Glebov, were openly physiocratic in their economic orientation. This project bears clear marks of physiocracy, hinting at their role, but it was even more a political act, having to do with rights and privileges. Emancipation was the basis of a larger plan for the expansion of nobles' prerogatives; it was a declaration of independence and freedom from an especially constraining obligation to the state. A principle of personal rights was introduced, not replacing the service obligation but substituting moral suasion for force. This amelioration of political conditions had a significant impact on ushering in a new era of greater freedom, at least for the nobility. The guarantee of the right to choose a career and a life became a powerful incentive in the economic as well as political realm. Without granting all of the economic privileges that Vorontsov tried to win, it did encourage the emerging dominance of nobles in provincial manufacturing.

The Role of Volkov and Glebov

When the draft law code was discovered seventy years ago, it was thought that the manifesto must have preceded it. When the two documents—the manifesto and the draft law—were placed side by side, the latter seemed to be an expansion of the former.[65] Then the two documents were properly dated and the chronological order reversed, causing confusion. By tradition, in granting nobles their freedom from obligatory service, Peter III, passive or incompetent, had granted his noble advisors whatever they wanted in return for their support for his accession to the throne. Proper dating now made it necessary to find a new explanation, one that accounted for the discrepancy between what nobles must have requested and what they received. If Peter acquiesced to any of the nobles' demands, then why did he not grant the full charter of rights that they sought?

To explain the government's reticence, it has been customary not to attribute any decision-making to Peter III. Instead, Peter's advisors, Vorontsov, Volkov, and

Glebov, have each been credited with this enactment. M. M. Shcherbatov provided an anecdotal account of Dmitrii Volkov's role. Shcherbatov's credibility was such that for a long time this attribution was accepted. Yet Volkov came from a family of lesser nobles who possessed no title and few lands, and this project explicitly sought to diminish the stature of such nobles relative to the more distinguished stratum of higher officials.[66] A more plausible attribution was made in an article published in 1867 by M. I. Semevskii. Based on testimony by Jakob von Staehlin, Peter III's tutor, he credited Glebov, a noble of more distinguished birth, with the idea.[67] In 1874, Volkov's granddaughter replied to Semevskii in *Russkaia starina* that she had actually seen a draft of the manifesto among Volkov's papers with comments in his handwriting. This shifted historians' attention once again to Volkov. But the manuscript disappeared, and the testimony was subsequently discredited.[68] The historian G. V. Vernadskii, summing up the evidence in an article of 1915, concluded, in line with logic as well as instinct, that it must have been Glebov, who was at that time the general procurator of the Senate.[69]

Rubinshtein provided an entirely new analytic framework. He saw in the draft project of Vorontsov a single embracing vision, diminished and frustrated by critics within the ruling group of Peter III, both Volkov and Glebov and possibly others. To Rubinshtein, the manifesto was the result of a conflict over the nobles' desire for economic privilege and Volkov's and Glebov's desire to steer policy on a more neutral course in satisfying the interests of both nobles and merchants. His interpretation, as mentioned above, has been criticized and dismissed for excessive emphasis on "class conflict over economic issues."[70] Yet its critics have not expressed any better the thinking that went into emancipation. Raeff wrote that on February 18 Vorontsov's aristocratic interests were not represented:

> The act of February 18 remained silent on those rights and functions that would have offered the nobility an alternative to the service obligation that had been their very raison d'être. Seen in this light, the manifesto can hardly be considered to have expressed the point of view of the Vorontsov group, who wanted to give noblemen a greater stake in private and local concerns.[71]

He continued:

> D. V. Volkov, Peter's private secretary and mainspring in the administration, who probably drafted the manifesto, may have expressed the thinking of P. Shuvalov, whose protege he had been. Shuvalov believed that a small, closed oligarchy should control Russia's economic life by means of monopolies and regalias with rank-and-file nobles continuing to provide most of the military and bureaucratic career personnel.[72]

One fact that stands in the way of understanding emancipation is that the physiocrat Volkov was not Shuvalov's protege. His loyalty to any political position was uncertain, as his desertion of his patron Bestuzhev-Riumin shows. His ideas were his own.

Another reservation about the attribution to Shuvalov's heirs is more complex. In contrast to Raeff's summation—"After the death of Elizabeth, Rubinshtein argues, the idea of freedom from service was separated for tactical reasons from the Shuvalovs' proposed general statute on the rights and privileges of the nobility"[73]—Rubinshtein did not argue that the Shuvalov/Glebov group proposed emancipation. His dating demonstrated otherwise. Rubinshtein in fact had argued "that the aristocratic program of the Vorontsovs came up against sharp opposition of the 'Shuvalov party.' "[74]

Shuvalov's position on emancipation or estate rights is by no means clarified by these hypotheses. On the whole, there is excessive emphasis in the writing about the Codification Commission on the rivalry of groups and divergent positions. It is imperative, indeed, to see Shuvalov's position in an entirely different light. Peter Shuvalov was the single most influential figure in state policy in the 1750s—in part because he was the husband of one of Empress Elizabeth's closest friends and in part because of his enormous wealth, derived in large part from monopolistic entrepreneurial operations, for example, fishing and salt mining, operations protected by a lucrative exclusive contract for their sale (*otkup*). He was friendly toward merchants and waged a successful struggle in the Senate against efforts to eliminate all merchant-owned manufacturing. Shuvalov was, as Rubinshtein insisted, the advocate of privileges for merchants because of their vital role in the expansion of foreign trade (see chapter 1). Shuvalov was largely responsible for the shift of government policy in the mid-1750s in this direction, which Kahan summarized as follows:

> In one respect the establishment of the Bank for Commerce in St. Petersburg Port in 1754 was a break with age-old traditions of Russian domestic policy. That was probably the first time that the government acknowledged not only the need of Russian merchants for credits, but also admitted that the need was legitimate by its own merits, not only because of reasons of state. This was a new tone, markedly different from the attitude that the merchant class was a state servitor that could be drafted into state service, forcibly resettled, and heavily taxed, the old Muscovite attitude that totally ignored the welfare of the individual merchant and considered his accumulated capital a legitimate prey when government revenue had to be increased.[75]

But Peter Shuvalov was thoroughly Petrine in his outlook, and he was no opponent of monopolies or of the Vorontsovs' aristocratic programs.[76] On the contrary, he sought to protect nobles' monopolies in industry, where his own fortunes were at stake. Among other means chosen to protect his own monopolies, he eliminated the saltworks in Novgorod to the enormous disadvantage of the local peasantry so that they would not compete with his own further north.[77] When he died, because of the idiosyncrasy of his position no Shuvalov party in the sense either Raeff or Rubinshtein meant survived him. What historians miss by giving Shuvalov too great a role in the late 1750s and 1760s is the intellectual shift of enormous importance in economic thinking and the unique political convergence of Vorontsov and Volkov, both, in very different ways, physiocrats. Rubinshtein's position makes Shuvalov out to be much more consistent than he was; to call Shuvalov entirely pro-merchant is to affix a false label, to put both Volkov and Glebov in the Shuvalov camp is to miscast at least Volkov. Raeff, equally wide of the mark, referred to the same two statesmen and to Shuvalov as opposing Vorontsov who has been exclusively identified with the aristocratic proposal to exclude lesser families from landownership.

The position of Shuvalov, Volkov, and Glebov on this issue is by no means clear; nor is there any possibility of clarifying it.

One must remove the original texts from layers of interpretation based on Rubinshtein's notion of nobles' aspirations in the 1750s. There was no disagreement between the Shuvalov/Glebov commission and the Vorontsov commission on the exclusion of merchants from broad areas of manufacturing—the extent of the exclusion was a matter of degree. The Shuvalov/Glebov version did not intend to separate nobles into lesser servitors and hereditary nobles; neither version would have prevented emancipation from affecting all the nobility.

Both versions were offensive to merchants. Invited to St. Petersburg in 1762 to comment on the proposed code of laws, a group of merchants vigorously protested: "In place of anticipated advantages, merchants find to their regret that provisions of the newly created Code impose great and unbearable burdens on the poor Russian merchants, as if they were entirely unimportant in the state."[78]

Indeed, this was not a time in Russia when merchant ownership of enterprise was considered essential to growth. The limited way in which economic growth was perceived meant that improvements in manufacturing were balanced against the loss of labor in agriculture. Over merchants' protests, their role in manufacturing was constantly being challenged. This pattern of law favoring noble enterprises was so widespread that it is surprising, in view of the concurrence of both Shuvalov and Vorontsov on this issue, that neither the Shuvalov/Glebov group nor the Vorontsov group got their way. The provisions entirely barring merchants from some manufacturing sectors were omitted from the manifesto promulgated by Peter III.

Glebov, as author of the Shuvalov/Glebov version, would not have omitted these provisions. He left no direct testimony about his political position on nobles' rights.[79] However, he had produced one version of the law code that offended the merchants. Moreover, he demonstrated by his management of the Senate during Peter III's reign that compromise and avoidance of conflict constituted the very fabric of his style. On February 1, for example, the day Vorontsov proposed his measure to prohibit merchants' purchase of settled estates for their factories, regardless of the branch of manufacturing, a sweeping law to which Glebov—were he "Shuvalovian"—would have objected at least in part, and a discussion that as general procurator Glebov should have conducted, he was absent. A month later, on February 28, he let the measure pass in revised form.[80] It is clear from his absence on February 1 and lack of comment on February 28 that he chose not to oppose Vorontsov on estate rights. Therefore he cannot be considered the author of the emancipation project as it emerged in Peter III's reign. As general procurator Glebov may have drafted a final version.[81] However, the excision must already have been made by the time the draft came to him.

Volkov, Peter's key advisor, was surely the source of the problem as historians have conceived it: opposition to the extended rights desired by Vorontsov. Volkov was an articulate member of his class, but a different kind of physiocrat than Vorontsov. In 1760, when he first confronted Shuvalov about the role of the nobility in the economy, he wrote a friend, Ivan Chernyshev, chair of the Commerce

Commission, "With my whole heart, I wish the nobility well, but we should not take over the function of merchants."[82] In his capacity as Conference secretary under Elizabeth, he must have seen numerous drafts of emancipation. He must also have approved the one that went to the Senate, since it issued from the imperial chancery where he worked. The enumeration and restraints on privileges that comprise the peculiar substance of this decree logically can be traced to Volkov's physiocracy, which was shaping other reforms of Peter's reign.

As discussed above, physiocrats like Volkov believed in the relaxation of restrictions on the "natural" economic activity of elites as well as peasants among the rural populace. They sought the removal of obstacles to the flow of capital into agriculture. They wanted to eliminate arbitrary and irregular taxes, and, to cite a familiar passage from Mirabeau's *Tableau Economique* (1758), "On the price side, the main means must be the removal of all physical and legal restraint on internal and external trade in corn and the stimulation of the internal demand for corn by such measures as the abolition of the 'exclusive privileges.'. . . . "[83] Emancipation was timed to coincide with the liberation of the grain trade and should be viewed, at least in Volkov's conception, as a complementary act. The withholding of monopolistic privileges from nobles is entirely consistent with the views of Volkov and, from what is known, Peter III himself.

It is vital to distinguish, in sum, between Volkov and Shuvalov. In some respects, Volkov's views were in agreement with those of Shuvalov and Glebov—about the importance of banking, the expansion of commerce, and provincial development. Yet on key issues he opposed Shuvalov: the financing of the war by raising the salt tax and customs rates; the selling of tax farms and commercial monopolies to wealthy nobles. He agreed with Shuvalov's monetary policy, in other words, but he opposed noncompetitive commerce that excluded merchants from the grain trade and from industry. Key restrictions in the Shuvalov/Glebov draft law code as well as the Vorontsov version would have offended the physiocrat Volkov.[84] There is no doubt that Volkov did not stand alone, as is argued in chapter 4.[85] Whoever else his supporters may have been, the critical figure was Peter III, who conducted affairs in accord with these new views that were sweeping Europe.

As leader of the coalition that included the Vorontsovs, Volkov had no reason to obstruct emancipation itself. Indeed, he and Peter III conceived of emancipation as essential within the context of financial as well as social reform, since nobles' indebtedness was a critical problem which they repeatedly confronted in law.[86] Volkov certainly did not draft the original project, which emerged from the law code drafted by Vorontsov, Mel'gunov, and others. In his confessional letter to Orlov, Volkov declined a role in reform. His achievements, he wrote, were secularization of the ecclesiastical estates (1757); the creation of a bank (1762); and the decree on commerce (1760). Moreover, he was appointed privy secretary only at the end of January, after the initiation of discussions at the Senate.[87] His thinking nevertheless was in the spectrum of interests represented by emancipation, and since he was Peter's closest advisor, his thinking must be considered paramount in Peter III's reform. The complexity of the manifesto is one of the clearest indicators of coalition politics, the new broad Shuvalov/Vorontsov/Volkov consensus that channeled diverse interests into policy in 1762.

The Emancipation Manifesto

On January 17 Peter III announced to the Senate his intention to grant nobles freedom from obligatory service. In a brief statement, borrowing from the Vorontsov draft, he declared, "nobles may continue to serve as long as and wherever they wish, on a voluntary basis. In time of war, however, they must appear [for duty] as do the nobles in Lifland."[88] The key words are "may continue." The senators may have believed that compulsion itself as a form of rule would no longer govern their career choice or their lives. This was not exactly the outcome.

In contrast to other measures from Peter's reign, this proclamation was not accompanied in the Senate record by analysis and commentary on provisions. Unlike other proposals from the draft law code, this one was not sent back to the Codification Commission. It was an imperial decree. Coincidentally, roughly in mid-February, about the time of the promulgation of emancipation, Volkov's name began to appear more and more frequently in the Senate record (he is first mentioned on February 19). Clearly, reform was prepared in the imperial cabinet.

Peter III has nearly always been left out of the history of this reform.[89] Raeff wrote:

> obviously, Peter III did not personally make the major policy decisions, nor did he even define the pattern or determine the ultimate direction of the legislation issued in his name. . . . For convenience as well as brevity, I shall use the name of the monarch as synonymous with his government, with the clear understanding that I by no means believe that Peter played a paramount role.[90]

Yet there is both direct and indirect evidence that he did play a critical role. Diplomats credited Peter III with decisive influence over the outcome of this reform. The French ambassador Breteuil wrote, "The emperor . . . has rejected two separate drafts of the project as 'too expensive,' thus showing his intentions as more restrained than he initially indicated in using the nobles of Livonia for his model."[91] In the same vein, the Austrian ambassador Mercy d'Argenteau commented, "His Majesty has turned down two drafts of the project, each granting fewer rights than the Lifland nobility holds; all the same, both were rejected by the tsar for just that reason, that the freedom granted in them was too great."[92]

These comments are basically the same, showing a single source. In contrast to foreign policy, domestic policy information provided by diplomats was usually untainted by point of view. Diplomats drafted their comments with precise wording and quotations from manifestos and decrees. Mercy characteristically derived information from Glebov, who had no reason to dissemble on a matter of no consequence to the Austrian ambassador. That Peter found nobles' requests to be excessive is precisely what one would expect in view of the failure of previous projects on this theme since the 1730s and from the extreme obsequiousness that characterized Vorontsov's proposal in the draft law code and the "Petition from the Nobility." The excision of "too great" demands also intuitively follows if the decree is seen as somewhat narrowly contrived to rectify a mistaken policy rather than broadly conciliate a social class. The preface begins by stating that the manifesto was basically a response to specific complaints:

> it is true that in the beginning the institution [of obligatory service] seemed intolerable to the nobility, disturbing its peace and separating nobles from their homes. Nobles performed military and civilian service and enlisted their children against their will, and some evaded it, suffering punishments in fines and by confiscation of their property.[93]

The compulsion had been offensive to the nobles but useful:

> Although . . . it was linked at first with force, it was very useful, and was therefore continued under Peter the Great's successors . . . and this principle has produced infinite benefits in destroying coarseness for the universal good, changing ignorance into wisdom; it improved the military by increasing the numbers of knowledgeable, diligent, skillful and brave generals; it augmented in the civil service competent officials who are well suited to political positions.

The preface concluded, "We do not find it necessary to enforce service which up to this time was considered necessary."[94]

The use of force was not itself rejected, as historians have underscored. The limitations of this reform have been raised repeatedly in the literature. However, by restricting the areas of policy subject to compulsion, a new important line was drawn. The authority of the law to punish those who did not educate their children was still in place, as dictated by enlightenment principles, but administrative law chose a more responsible distance on the issue of service.

The preface about the use of force ("although [service] was linked at first with force") was taken from a passage in the Vorontsov draft dealing with education. Where the word "service" appeared in the manifesto, "education" had earlier been drafted by Vorontsov or some other author. "Education"—which destroyed coarseness, transformed ignorance into wisdom, and so forth, rationalized the end of compulsion in service.[95] The editing of the manifesto shows the combined efforts of perhaps A. P. Mel'gunov, the codification commission's editor for education and a member of Peter's inner council, and Ivan Shuvalov, the new head of educational institutions in Russia, to make it appeal to Peter III, whose interest in education was well established.

Compulsory education had been in effect since the reign of Peter I. Anna Ivanovna established the Cadet Corps in 1731 to enable young nobles to rise rapidly in the ranks, since graduates automatically were promoted to full officer rank. Teenage graduates entered service at the fourteenth rank, i.e., officer level, after "passing through the ranks" while in the school as youths. Placement in the Cadet Corps, however, was difficult to arrange. Hence it was common to find early enrollment, since the same result was obtained by registering little boys in regiments at very young ages. Thus the importance of the manifesto was not that it reiterated the principle that education was compulsory but that more than words were involved. The decree was accompanied by enormously increased funding for educational institutions, Peter's pet project, and an expansion of the Cadet Corps, and this automatically meant that more elite nobles could guarantee career advancement for their sons.[96] Implicitly the government acknowledged the insufficiency of educational institutions since the expansion of the Cadet Corps was to be coordinated with new institutions which were only being designed at the time of Peter's fall from power.[97]

Thus the Cadet Corps was not an inessential part of the emancipation project, and it suggested Peter III's personal role in this reform. According to the manifesto, nobles were required to enroll their children in the Cadet Corps at the age of twelve. Wealthy nobles, with more than a thousand serfs, were exempt and could hire tutors, although if they did not, the decree stipulated that "those who spend their lives in idleness and those who do not educate their children . . . We order to be despised and degraded . . . and excluded from Our Court."[98] The fact of nobility was less important than the handling of it; the strong warning revealed a point of view typical of both Petrine (referring to Peter I) and enlightenment didactic statutes.

The linkage of the manifesto to Peter III by stressing the importance to him of education and of enlightenment principles in general (apart from what the nobles sought) is made more explicit in his own later remark about what he thought he had accomplished by this reform. In April, in an address to the Senate, he observed that in his February 18 enactment he "had shown His desire" for the state to assume greater responsibility for education.[99]

Provisions

Despite its narrow focus on the Table of Ranks and on education, the decree was actually constructed as an elementary charter of rights. It contained an absolute lifting of restrictions on retirement and travel abroad, on the right to form local assemblies, and on mobility after retirement from service. Nobles could leave service at any time other than during a campaign or three months before. "No noble will be obliged to serve against his will in any of our administrative institutions," the manifesto read. The terms provided a two-tiered service. Nobles requested leave in accordance with their service rank. At the top, in the upper eight ranks, servitors had to request retirement directly from the emperor, and lower-ranking servitors from the bureau chief (article 1). The incentive to retire was enormous. Noble servitors would be rewarded with elevation by one rank, providing they had served at the previous rank for at least a year. This promotion made retirement particularly appealing to civilian servitors at certain ranks: the barrier between lifetime and hereditary nobility could be leaped by means of retirement; higher ranking servitors could attain great salary advances by retiring and reentering service because salary scales were weighted at the upper end.

In addition to the main freedom that nobles sought, Peter granted a fundamental law. Freedom to serve or not to serve would be permanently observed under his successors, he wrote. This was the first instance in which an estate (*soslovie*) became legitimized by such a guarantee.[100] The growing power of the central government had been essentially alien to the emergence of new jurisdictional authority and to independent status for the nobility. Centralization had undermined the legal foundations of the nobility's real power, as the reforms of the reign of Peter I made clear. The fundamental principles in emancipation halted but did not in the very long term reverse that development. Peter's establishment of fundamental rights served as a precedent for later legislation and affected legal thought in eighteenth-century Russia, although perhaps not legal consciousness.[101] The interests of the cameralist state in an abstract sense were not personified by the ruler but by the state itself, which preceded the interests of any class or institution within the state.[102] In line with newer theory, the state should divest itself of some prerogatives on behalf of the national economy and the well-being of the people. Emancipation could be rationalized in this way. However, the manifesto failed to grant nobles any sort of prerogatives that could be a springboard to challenge the state's power.

The ideas in the enactment had powerful echoes elsewhere among Peter's proclamations, where the concept of estate rights took preeminence over other legal traditions. For example, Peter responded favorably to a petition by the Protestant nobility of Courland demanding the deposition of a Catholic prince appointed by Elizabeth. Peter sided with the nobles, who claimed a right to choose a Protestant ruler, even though political theory dating to the Treaty of Westphalia of 1648 gave the ruler the right to determine the religion of his or her subjects.

His concept of estate was not of an exclusive elite but of a large and powerful instrument of autocratic rule. He allowed his advisors no carte blanche over the law. He refused, for example, to allow the senators to hold back the careers of non-nobles in the bureaucracy. Reversing his aunt's policy, he opposed the Senate and granted non-nobles the right to attain hereditary nobility when they rose to the appropriate rank. In an important decree of April 20, Peter ruled that non-nobles could be promoted to the position of "secretary" (sekretari) in the colleges and chancelleries, a rank conferring nobility, and the best servitors from the "towns" should be recruited for service in the capital and be promoted to this rank. "For otherwise," he concluded, "many will be deprived of the reward which they deserve by their qualifications."[103] Peter's policy in general demonstrated the continuing interests of the state in autocratic, not class, control over the staffing of the central agencies of government.

The rejection of some elements of the sweeping Vorontsov version reinforces an impression of the central importance to the government of administrative efficiency. Though the principle of merit had to some extent officially governed the service since the reforms of Peter I, the obligatory nature of service and the principle of seniority and time in service had made this principle difficult for the state to sustain in practice. By eliminating the obligation and maintaining the requirement of promotion through "capacity," Peter facilitated the realization of the administrative goals of the Table of Ranks, by which non-nobles were to be promoted, and he would not allow this point to be reversed by exclusionary demands of the nobility. To summarize, this in some respects showed a departure from trends of the

1750s, when estates belonging to nobles with questionable claims or to non-nobles were confiscated. Both Vorontsov and Shuvalov had wanted to create a closed caste of powerful landowners; Peter III, relying presumably on Volkov, was more concerned about the quality of service.

The Revised Concept of Service

Despite its endorsement of nobles' rights, the decree allowed service to remain the avenue of advancement and path to nobility. The decree clearly emanated from a confirmation of the Table of Ranks and did not entirely clash with its central principles. The emphasis in the manifesto was on competency, "capacity and skill," a vague but essential requirement for position, given an existing vacancy. The bureaucracy was not to take on inessential personnel: those who had served at a rank lower than the eighth without promotion for twelve years were ineligible for reentry; just as those who had served twelve years without promotion had to accept involuntary retirement.[104] Peter's emphasis on professionalization of the service corps—repetition of such phrases as "if he is found capable" and "if there is a vacancy"—recalls, once again, emphasis sustained by all the autocrats in the eighteenth century on merit over birth in the review of promotions.[105] The manifesto firmly reflects both tradition and innovation; faithful to the aims of Peter I, it showed commitment as well to the administrative efficiency of the contemporary models of the Prussian and Austrian bureaucracies.

The planners of the manifesto endorsed the essential principle of the Table of Ranks in using rank as an incentive system. They needed such incentives for a variety of purposes. For example, they sought to use the ranking system as an incentive for colonizing the south. On April 19, Peter approved a proposal offering hereditary nobility and land grants to servitors who would move south to the border areas.[106] We find the pull of colonization reinforcing what was paramount in the manifesto, Peter's refusal to limit access to the nobility and make the class more exclusive. In another example, the planners made the ranking system an inducement to the expansion of provincial government. With explicit provisions and encouragement of reentry into service, emancipation accompanied the simultaneous establishment of a provincial police force and the opening up of management positions on former ecclesiastical estates. These positions were filled even before the Senate had approved all of the secularization acts. The manifesto eased the transfer from military to civilian service, thus helping demobilization procedures, and increased the salary of retired servitors upon reentry into service. It envisioned a flexible civilian service, which would allow and encourage landowners to participate in governance if they wished.

A final provision showed more fully the intellectual dispositions implied in the proposal. Although the desired economic monopoly in property rights was cut from the manifesto, the procedures Vorontsov had designed for the election of permanent representatives to the Senate and its branch for proportional representation by regions were preserved. The principle of right of assembly, repeatedly rejected by Peter III's predecessors, entered law under Peter III. During Catherine's reign, this right was translated into the notion of regularly convened provincial assemblies.

In summary, the goals of Peter III, Dmitrii Volkov, Aleksei Mel'gunov, and Ivan Shuvalov, among the possible authors of the last draft, and of Roman Vorontsov, the certain author of the original draft, can be inferred from the text of the manifesto. The planners sought to facilitate the rationalization of service and to enable the nobility to achieve the autonomy essential to its further development as an estate. The first goal was traditional, established by the reform of Peter I, yet it showed the particular perspective of Peter III through its reiterated emphasis on education and training of nobles on the one hand and administrative efficiency on the other. The second goal, corporate status for the nobility, represents at least a qualified endorsement of the essential aim of Vorontsov, and arguably something stronger, given Peter's and the physiocrat Volkov's capacity to envision both immediate and long-range effects of the measure. The manifesto reveals, then, the shaping influence of the interests of autocracy at mid-century: a vision of provincial development, a landholding nobility, an expanded bureaucracy, a educated elite, and efficiency in recruiting officers for campaigns.

Consciously grounded in the Vorontsov draft, the text of Peter's version nevertheless departed from it in significant ways, omitting sections pertaining to immunity from the arbitrary will and authority of state power. Insofar as there was theory in this omission, it was that the autocracy would still not relinquish punitive authority over the first estate. Peter III continued to confiscate nobles' estates, including the domains and palaces of Bestuzhev-Riumin, still under house arrest. This, rather than the lack of regalias and monopolistic privileges, may have been the source of the reference in the two diplomatic comments quoted above to aspirations that "went too far." Yet Vorontsov could view the manifesto as a qualified success. He did gain emancipation: the principle of voluntary service which changed the definition of nobility from a function in the state to a privileged estate with rights and exclusionary privileges. In its effects emancipation was the essential first step in the development of a landholding gentry.

Too often, following Rubinshtein, the manifesto has been seen as the victory of the Shuvalovian party.[107] To the extent that it represented success for any faction, that success should be granted to Vorontsov (especially since soon afterwards, on March 29, 1762, his power in the Senate was boosted further by the passage of another proposal prohibiting merchants from petitioning for the further purchase of land and peasants[108]). Peter was clearly engaged in balancing rival interests at court; what he removed from the manifesto was restored in part on March 29, when he put merchants at a competitive disadvantage in obtaining labor for manufacturing without, however, granting Vorontsov's addition that merchants be deprived altogether of their manufacturing enterprises.

Implementation

In bringing the enactment to fruition, Peter allowed nobles to retire even before demobilization from the Seven Years' War began. Each week he granted retirement "on the basis of the manifesto of February 18" to nobles listed in the *St. Petersburg*

Gazette, some individually, some in groups of fifty and sixty; some with promotion, some without; some from civil service, many more from the military. In all, given that his government was less than three months from a campaign, his grant of close to five hundred petitions for retirement seems substantial evidence of the intent to follow through. From the listings in the *St. Petersburg Gazette,* it is impossible to tell how many more nobles retired less conspicuously at lower ranks.[109]

One representative instance of the willingness of nobles to take advantage of their new freedom occurred in connection with the dissolution of the imperial body guard. The body guard was comprised of a special group of soldiers and nobles (company of grenadiers of the Preobrazhenskii guards regiment) who had been rewarded by appointment to this regiment for placing Empress Elizabeth on the throne in 1741. Its members consisted largely of nobles from the eighth rank and above, "the flower of the nobility," as one contemporary observer put it.[110] Peter's motives—whether he was offended at the lack of discipline of these regiments (the nobles dissipated their youth at the barracks and, when called up for a real military service, refused or performed poorly) or whether at the expense they represented— led to their disbanding on March 21 with a choice of retire or transfer to another corps or to the army. Over three-fourths of the 332 men in the company, or 252 of them, chose to return to private life.[111] The overwhelming desire of these nobles to leave service entirely rather than join some other regiment or transfer to the civil service illustrates that nobles did take advantage of the opportunity to retire when it was offered. The significance of this observation grows in the breakdown of the group represented by the sampling, a mixture of old families and newly ennobled ones but a group predominantly young. Those who chose to return to the provinces rather than to join another guards regiment or the officer corps of the army or transfer to the civil service, were, with two exceptions, men who had served only five to ten years.[112] Given an average age at entry into service of fourteen or fifteen, these were men of twenty to thirty years of age. Without the customary motives of ill health or advancing age to prompt them, the members of this young, exclusive company chose for the most part home over service.[113]

The case of the imperial body guard is not an isolated instance of nobles' warm response to emancipation. There is ample evidence of how the manifesto was received. The Senate suggested that a gold statue to Peter III be erected. General reactions at court were immediately favorable;[114] and on March 18, 1763, when the commission that Catherine had established to study the issue of nobles' emancipation gave its report, an almost unanimously favorable recommendation was made (the dissenting member being Grigorii Teplov, Catherine II's representative on the commission). On that commission were Senator Nikita Panin, Field Marshall Aleksei Bestuzhev-Riumin, Chancellor Mikhail Vorontsov, Senator Iakov Shakhovskoi, Generals Zakhar Chernyshev and Mikhail Volkonskii, Count Grigorii Orlov, and Hetman of the Ukraine Kyril Razumovskii, a group which included military commanders as well as the most eminent civilian officials. Their response to Peter's enactment, echoing not the language of the manifesto but its motivations, was to advise Catherine "to allow young nobles to serve or not serve at will; for those who retire will work on their private lands and will enrich themselves with factories, mills and mines. They will thereby enrich their fatherland as well, and support the people who work for them. . . . ''[115] S. M. Solov'ev had portrayed the manifesto as bereft of what nobles most wanted, immunity from corporal punishment and from confiscation of their estates.[116] The consensus of this commission in 1763, accepting the principle of voluntary service and not demanding the additional privileges and immunities, attests by contrast to the acceptable provisions of the manifesto.[117]

This point was well supported in the literature of the time and was accepted by historians until Korf. Arguing that Catherine II was not an enthusiastic supporter of emancipation, Korf placed weight on her lack of response—nonconfirmation—to the commission report discussed above. The commission was disbanded and its records sent to the archives. Unwilling to repeal the manifesto of emancipation and incur the anger of the nobles, Catherine chose other means, according to Korf, to defeat its purposes. Legal restraints were exercised, he wrote, so that over a long period a service mentality remained tenacious, and that, in itself, was the real reason nobles did not choose to retire to their estates.[118]

Catherine's confirmation or nonconfirmation of emancipation is of obvious relevance to the question of implementation. She did not rescind or confirm emancipation upon ascending the throne, as she did with other reforms enacted by Peter III. In any case, it would have been impossible to rescind and unnecessary to re-promulgate a measure granted in perpetuity by her predecessor. Peter had written, no future sovereign of Russia shall revoke this right given to the Russian nobility.[119] Her decree convening a commission to study the enactment shows her awareness of her difficult position. Without revoking the decree, she declared that it was "incomplete" and needed further work. Thus she reopened the subject for debate and allowed the possibility of an expansion of nobles' rights, not curtailment. Something of the excitement of this moment at court is captured in a letter by Mikhail Vorontsov, who was serving on the commission, to Nicholas Korff, the senator. "We are working very hard now in the commission on the granting of freedom [vol'nost'] to our nobility," he wrote. "I beg you to inform me openly of your views . . . useful for the discussion of rights and privileges on the example of nobles of other nations and appropriate to our own circumstances."[120] The discussion of the commissioners ranged over a variety of questions, from the usefulness of entail to voluntary service. Its results serve as a link between the work of the two commissions of 1754–1762 and 1767–1768. During this time, the nobles' opinions on the whole changed very little; it was the state that was slow in responding to the nobles' consistent demands.

The Legacy in Legislation

Catherine's Charter of Nobility of 1785 was, over twenty years later, her confirmation. In articles 17, 18, and 19, she confirmed the freedom of nobles to serve or not to serve.[121] The introduction conferred corporate status, and remaining articles granted the immunities. This was the sense in which she found the manifesto incomplete, the rectification seems to be in line with what her commission had sought. The twenty-five years that passed before Catherine formally endorsed emancipation in no way constituted a lapse in the right of nobles to make use of their freedom. The archives of the Senate, published in part for Catherine's reign, provide a written record of the many nobles she allowed to return to their estates on the basis of the manifesto. Gradually this favorable reaction to emancipation was reflected in the residency of nobles on their country estates.

Catherine took power on June 28, 1762. Immediately nobles began to submit their requests for retirement from service, as they had done under Peter III. She duly granted their requests, using the exact words of the manifesto, as she confirmed each application: "On the basis of the established law of February 18, 1762, by which the Russian nobles are granted liberty and freedom to continue in service as long as they desire and to request freedom from service. . . ."[122] Documented in the published journals of the Senate for the 1760s is her confirmation, repeated many times over, of the nobility's emancipation. The petitions of assessors, state chancellors, army officers, of men from twelve to sixty in age: all were received and granted.[123]

The petitions requesting retirement from service caused considerable comment during the early years of Catherine's reign. A secretary at the French legation observed in 1767 that "many nobles now request retirement from service, for they say that they can no longer stand it."[124] The state had obviously even received petitions for retirement from non-noble servitors, since Catherine was forced to issue a law in 1766 excluding non-nobles from the privilege of requesting freedom from service on the basis of the manifesto.[125] The opportunity for advancement in rank by withdrawing from service, attaining nobility in that way, must have increased the number of claims to nobility by lower-ranking clerical and military personnel. By the mid-nineteenth century, the noble estate was so inclusive that a statistician such as Petr Koeppen could no longer determine precisely what that category represented.[126]

Impact on Society

Catherine wrote in 1775 that "the majority of nobles live on their estates."[127] In recent years, historians have been reluctant to confirm this conclusion. For most historians, the manifesto had the effect of a routine and temporary demobilization. One reason, as Raeff has shown, was that the service retained many wealthy nobles—Bolotov is seen as an exception[128]—and many poor nobles (for example, those near Moscow who had difficulty living exclusively on the returns from a backward agriculture). Raeff wrote, "even after the abolition of its compulsory character, state service remained the most popular way of life for the nobility . . . and . . . the prime factor in defining the status of members of the upper class in the Russian empire."[129] The point is not that nobles abandoned the service entirely or ceased to derive their status from once having served, but that more and more of them lived on their estates after a brief period in service.

The Russian nobility cannot be compared, even after emancipation in 1762 or the founding of provincial government in 1774, to the English or Prussian nobility, since it was subject to no customary obligation nor to any compulsory regulation binding it to contribute to local government. All narrative evidence indicates that the Russian nobility was more similar to the Austrian aristocracy. The life of the noble was bound up within the estate, and that the exercise of authority and taking of responsibility was limited to that smaller community. Indeed, even within the small economic community over which nobles potentially exercised considerable control, most of them did not demonstrate responsible management techniques— for example, record-keeping, the creation of incentives, and the policing of bound- aries—until well into the late eighteenth century. I. Dubasov from Tambov described the first attempts at building community spirit in the late eighteenth century:

> The first attempts at self-government by the Tambov nobility were very unsuccess-
> ful. We had rights and powers, but almost no one worthy of exercising those rights
> and powers. Noble deputies were elected, but rarely were they willingly drawn into
> service. They refused for a variety of reasons . . . pretending illness, one . . . went
> with his hunting dog to the outlying fields, islands and along the Oka river,
> fishing.[130]

Prince A. M. Golitzyn's memoir on nobles' rights, which he wrote for presentation to Catherine's Codification Commission, is an example of the resistance of nobles to the imposition of major responsibilities. To him, responsibilities should consist of the administration of justice within an estate and the education of one's children, rights of participating in imperial court functions, traveling abroad, and residing in the countryside.[131]

Nobles such as Golitzyn were proud of their service record but chose to live on their estates. One memoirist commented, "Men of service coming into the land market have tripled the price of estates."[132] In the latter part of the eighteenth cen- tury, the new provincial nobility was so visible that it became the object of satire by Russian writers, for example, Denis Fonvisin.

Even with such strong narrative evidence, historians deny that this was so. It is therefore important to present data about the relative numbers of urban and pro- vincial nobles in the late eighteenth century. For this purpose, topographical records of the late eighteenth century are adequate. Topographical surveys, ar- ranged by guberniia, list the numbers of nobles actually in residence at their pro- vincial homes. In order to explore the significance of these numbers, it will be necessary first to estimate the size of the service and non-service nobility before determining the extent of their residence in rural Russia and their retirement from service life.

Examining the revizii for the eighteenth century, Kabuzan attempted to derive a rough figure for the nobility as a whole at the time of their emancipation (the third revizii, 1762). In sum, on the territory excluding the left-bank Ukraine, the Baltic, and Polish lands incorporated into the empire after the partitions, male nobles in- creased from 37,326 in 1744 (before females were included in the revizii) to roughly .59 percent of the populace in the 1760s, or 62,500 males. Attempting to define how many of these were service nobles, Troitskii used a bureaucratic census, lists of servitors compiled in 1754–1756, which he checked against heraldry lists of active and retired servitors compiled up to 1762.[133] The census is limited to service nobles. Like the "Adres-kalendar'," first issued in 1766 and regularly compiled thereafter, it did not include retired or under-age nobles.[134]

The difficulty in making judgment from these data can be seen in the following breakdown: in 1755, Troitskii found that civilian servitors in central and local office numbered 5,379. Of these, hereditary nobles comprised 21.5 percent, or 1,160, but 38.16 percent, or 2,053, were listed as owning settled land. Troitskii acknowledged that the number of noble landowners must be much larger, since the youthfulness of servitors made it likely that not they but their parents were the landowners. Consequently, the civil service lists cannot be used with confidence as a basis for estimating the total number of nobles in general or nobles eligible to own land and reside in the countryside.

The military service presents an equally great difficulty for estimates of nobles in service. Commissioned officers, according to Walter Pintner, numbered about eight or nine thousand.[135] In addition, an undetermined number of nobles served in the lower ranks.[136] It is perhaps easier to derive a figure for the early eighteenth century (1699–1701), for which period Ia. Vodarskii counted 15,492 nobles in twelve dragoon and other infantry and cavalry regiments.[137] Assuming no decrease after obligatory service was imposed and being confident of an increase, 15,000 nobles would by no means be the base figure. As time went on, nobles served not only in the officer corps. The Cadet Corps was available only to a very few, and throughout the eighteenth century poor nobles were largely illiterate. As a consequence, a large part of the guards units in the capital (from five to six regiments of up to ten thousand men) consisted of nobles fulfilling their obligation as ordinary soldiers because they did not qualify for rank.[138] In summary, the figure for male nobles in service at mid-century can with confidence be estimated as up to 60 percent of all male nobles, which would comprise most of the cohort at risk.

The task is to determine residence. The critical problem in deriving that information is the inaccuracy of survey data. Of the civil service nobility, the *verkhushka*, or highest-ranking servitors, 110 members (6.4%) owned 53.3 percent of all the serfs, which meant their estates were spread out over various provinces.[139] Even middling landowners, however, owned estates in different provinces, which confounded all eighteenth- and nineteenth-century estimates of where they resided.[140]

The reason for determining the residence of nobles is to gain an understanding of the impact of emancipation; the above inaccuracies are the main obstacle to that understanding. Equally daunting is lack of government efforts to record the residency of nobles before the 1760s. Reports by pre-emancipation provincial governors have been presented above. They comprise impressionistic evidence that nobles were not available in the provinces to do even routine tasks—collect the poll tax, supply surveyists with documentation, participate in local government. It seems a fair assumption, in view of the enforcement of the service requirement, that a large part of the nobility before 1762 either did not live on their estates or did so at peril, which had the same bleak significance in an era when the nobility dominated the distribution of services as well as government office.

Wha happened after 1762? In the second decade after emancipation, Aleksandr Vorontsov claimed that there was a visible transformation of rural life. "Among nobles [in Iaroslav province] are many who are relatively well off and educated. There are already numerous nobles who have never served, who, due to imperial kindness, now have the opportunity not to leave home yet serve their country."[141] Topographical surveys confirm his impression.

In Kostroma by the 1780s there were 1,771 male nobles in residence; in Iaroslav there were 2,046 in residence; in Nizhnyi Novgorod 1,425; in Kursk, 2,190.[142] Guessing that 2,000 was an average for the central provinces, since these four provinces would have been relatively unsettled compared with the more agricultural and densely settled central and western gubernii, and estimating on the basis of the figures for the remaining gubernii and oblast regions (52), one can easily arrive at a figure that represents the large part of the nobility. On all the territory of Russia at the time of the fifth revizii (1794–1795), the ratio of nobles in residence on their estates (104,000) to the total number of male nobles in the populace (193,132) is considerably over half, when age cohort at risk for service (60%) is used as the denominator instead of the total male population.[143] Provincial capitals boomed in the 1780s; nobles lived there as well as on their estates. In the city in Riazan, for example, there were 576 male nobles; in Zaraisk, 194; in Pereslav-Zalesk, 28; in Borovsk, 158; in Rostov, 473; in Maloiaroslavets, 224; in Tula, 237, and so forth.[144]

Evidence from Kursk province provides a more detailed look at the residence pattern of the Russian nobility. The survey for Kursk offers a comparison of local nobles in residence and local nobles living elsewhere for this guberniia. In Kursk province, three out of four local nobles were in residence on their estates; one out of four lived on some other estate in another province. Kursk province bears out the evidence of the larger sampling.[145]

Ruza district of Moscow province offers a select example of long-term developments. When the topographical survey was published in 1787, there were 41 nobles living in their homes in the district and 5 in the capital. In 1812 a count was taken of effects of the Napoleonic invasion. The information incidentally provided showed that out of a total of 130 landowners, 61 were in residence. These, wealthy nobles who possessed estates near Moscow, had on the average 120 serfs on their Ruza estates (for 84, only one estate in a larger portfolio of holdings). Of the total of 130 owners, 31 lived in an urban environment, whether in the capital city, Ruza, or elsewhere (16 lived in Moscow, 6 in St. Petersburg). Of the 84 most wealthy, 65 chose to live in rural Russia. A high percentage (41%) of the total were female (widows, wives, daughters); however, looking only at males, the share in residence and away are much the same as for the general totals. Of the 75 male owners, 40 lived in Ruza district (not Ruza city).[146] To summarize, noble landowners in this illustration preferred to live on their estates by a margin of roughly 3 to 1.

These surveys do not confirm the hypothesis that emancipation reflected Peter's "efforts at separating the nobility," enforcing service for lower career officials and allowing those who had greater wealth to retire as a leisured group of economically active serfowners.[147] Evidence shows both poor and wealthy landlords in residence.

Figures for Nizhnii Novgorod province—again, a small but representative illustration—show that a majority of the 1,425 landowners in residence were petty proprietors, who had two to three serfs. Ten families in the region owned 60 percent of the serfs; thirty-nine owned one thousand serfs or more.[148] For Iaroslav province (a report by the governor general on the number of nobles living in their villages), 806 of 1,200, a number which includes nobles of all ranks, 72 percent, were at the rank of second major or below.

It was certainly true, as many historians have written, that service rank remained one determinant of status. Judging by the proliferation of civilian and military ranks on lists of landowners, few nobles wished to be categorized simply as landlords (*pomeshchiki*). Widows and wives were listed by their husbands' rank; only daughters, merchants, and impoverished landlords were listed without reference to rank as, respectively, *doch'*, *kupets* or *meshchanin*, and *pomeshchik*. For Iaroslav province in the late eighteenth century, 33 nobles, only 4 percent, declared themselves as non-serving. Among the branches of service, a small fraction, 3 percent, of nobles in residence on their estates in Iaroslav belonged to the civil service; the overwhelming majority of noble landowners had served in the military.[149] Military servitors were wealthier on the average and better positioned in service to acquire the better located estates as their reward for service.[150] Titles to land do not reveal a numerical preponderance of military landownership (by contrast with residency),[151] but they do reveal a qualitative superiority of military holdings.

To summarize, the small sample introduced above does not lead to the conclusion that retirement to the provinces was only characteristic of higher or lower ranking nobles, although if status is measured by all possible means, the fact that military servitors tended to retire and civil servitors did not is an indication that retirement both implied and produced a relatively high status. This conclusion goes against the thinking that retirement from service was either legally or informally restricted, since so many nobles retired. It also demands a closer analysis of the proposition that service remained the only definition of status. It is more likely that access to the best located estates, high status in service, and the financial means to do without service are linked. Unfortunately, limitations of the evidence do not permit much speculation about stratification among the elite. One point can be made. The broadening of the estate in the first half of the century and enhancement of opportunities in the second greatly affected both the aspirations and status determinants among the Russian nobility.

The rough evidence for the residence of nobles at their estates helps explain the success of one of the most significant enactments of late eighteenth-century Russia, Catherine's statute on provincial self-government of 1775.[152] The consequences of this act radically changed the character of nobles' life in the countryside. Yet it could not have been promulgated without the presence of nobles in the provinces. The act of 1775 helped define a new role for those who had been relocated out of the capitals. The definition of provincial administration assisted the gradual transformation of rural Russia and the rise of a larger urban network.

The statute on provincial government had little in common with plans for reform in Elizabeth's reign. Discussion of provincial government began in Catherine's reign as early as the summer of 1762. On July 23 and August 9 Catherine established a new commission to examine relevant statutes.[153] She appointed Iakov Shakhovskoi, returned to court life after the coup, to head the commission. Shakhovskoi's research resulted in the conclusion that the failure of local government was due to two principle causes: too few nobles resided in the provinces, and provincial officials were appointed rather than elected; that is, he drew the familiar conclusion. Shakhovskoi argued that the state should loosen central controls and increase local salaries to match those in Moscow and St. Petersburg. Like Vorontsov, he suggested that nobles meet regularly in order to elect provincial officials and representatives to the Senate. Like Vorontsov, he also saw local self-government by nobles as a means to improve provincial life.[154] His project was rejected, and discussion was postponed.

The Pugachev peasant revolt induced Catherine to act.[155] The timely promulgation of her enactment of 1775 suggests a relationship between the functions of local government and police protection in the provinces, as M. Pavlova-Sil'vanskaia has pointed out.[156] However, the statute went well beyond policing measures. It provided an elaborate structure for town and district administration, for schools, chancelleries, police, courts of law, land magistracies and economic advisors. It also provided for regular meetings and representation in the central government. The law on provincial government both elaborated and greatly expanded the existing local bureaucracy.[157] In this way, it virtually depended on the presence of nobles at their estates in sufficient numbers to justify the elaboration of local government and to fill the posts it specified. The law on provincial government is a topic well researched in history; what is of concern here is the numbers.

Historians argue that the act of provincial self-government of 1775 existed on paper only, that the bureaucratic positions and administrative services specified by the act were never realized.[158] This follows of course from the related but misleading assumption dealt with earlier that nobles did not reside in sufficient numbers of the provinces for effective implementation of the act. The evidence about provincial government suggests otherwise: the posts were filled, and filled largely by local nobles residing in the provinces. A detailed example is provided by the case of Kostroma, a northern guberniia where textile mills and agriculture were the mainstay of the local economy. Provincial government was established in Kostroma in 1779. By 1785, the governor of the province could report that all but three of the new positions created by Catherine's reform were filled by local men, most of them nobles.[159] The posts included administrative assistants to the governor, judges, economic advisors, lawyers, secretaries, scribes, and clerks. For Kostroma that meant a total of 58 new positions. Moreover, an assembly of nobles came into existence in 1785. Participating in this assembly were 82 nobles, elected by district by the 1,771 nobles living in the region. The enactment of 1775 brought to Kostroma a school, a system of judicial review, courts, a police agency, and many other tangible and intangible amenities of life.[160]

The story of provincial political development in Kostroma is also a study in social change. Aleksandr Vorontsov continued, in his report on his trip to the northern gubernii in 1778, that he was astonished at the growth and efficiency of new services. "It does not seem the same land nor the same towns," he wrote, "that I saw six years ago."[161] The nobles who returned to their home provinces in ever-increasing numbers found in the enactment of local government not only the instrument of political authority and local development, but also the means to the growth of awareness for individuals and for communities. The act brought jobs, buildings, services to the provinces; it affected, less tangibly but just as significantly, the minds of the provincial nobility. Both kinds of changes are essential elements in the transformation of the countryside in late eighteenth-century Russia.

The social and psychological implications of the act of 1775 were emphasized in a work on provincial society in the second half of the eighteenth century by N. D. Chechulin. His argument had been ably summarized by the historian who sought to challenge it, S. A. Korf: "We can speak about the introduction of new world views and understanding, brought back by nobles who returned from the frontiers and . . . by officers who served in Europe during the Seven Years' War."[162] Chechulin isolated for analysis aspects of culture which were introduced by these retired servitors, many of whom had spent years in Europe during the eighteenth-century wars. The development of doctors' services and pharmacies, post offices, libraries, schools, and even literary circles marked a change in the horizons of provincial nobles, who before 1762, Chechulin wrote, "did not look further than their farthest grove and last field." After the 1760s and 1770s, Chechulin continued, writers of memoirs described their neighbors as men fluent in several languages, men of learning and leisure.[163] In the nineteenth century, some of these formed the basis of a rural squirearchy.[164] This segment of the nobility rarely resided in the capitals and led a life not patterned around service.[165]

Chechulin concluded by stressing particularly the significance of the manifesto for the process of change he examined:

> the manifesto is a most important act in the development of rights and privileges of the nobility; especially, it transformed the nobility into a privileged estate, granted nobles special rights. . . . The period between 1762 and the 1770s was a preparation for a new life which began in the 1770s with the introduction of guberniia governments.[166]

By a new life, Chechulin meant a change in circumstances as well as a change in outlook. Both kinds of change are documented in records of the provincial life of late eighteenth-century Russia. Each is necessary for understanding the other. The fusion of the two, the growth of practical opportunities and the growth of cultural awareness, was a consequence of the shifts in policy emerging from a rejection by both Peter III and Catherine II of the rigidity of the Petrine administrative regime.

In its impact on society, the manifesto was one of the major acts of legislation in the hundred years preceding the abolition of serfdom. By detaching service from land tenure, this enactment was decisive in the development of estates' rights. Confirmed by the Charter of Nobility in 1785, security of land tenure and various immunities and rights increased the importance of the private in comparison with the public interest. The manifesto had far-reaching social consequences. By 1775, because of the number of nobles in residence, it was possible to establish local self-government and create hundreds of district centers with schools and courts, a reform that could not have been envisioned in the years prior to Peter III's reign. Most historians believe, as Iurii Got'e wrote, that "a new epoch in the internal history begins with the reign of Catherine II." In regard to provincial Russia, the change began earlier.

One source of the confusion surrounding this issue is Catherine's apparent unwillingness to confirm the manifesto explicitly, even after its unanimous approval by a commission she established to study it. Catherine's delay did not reflect a lukewarm acceptance of the enactment of emancipation; as an absolute monarch, Catherine, jealously guarding her powers in a changing world, did hesitate to codify the rights of nobles. But she did not, nevertheless, suspend or halt the practical effects of the manifesto of 1762.

The manifesto came as a practical measure. In the years preceding emancipation, years of the Seven Years' War, nobles complained that they were not receiving their pay and that the obligation of service brought expenses that most of them could ill afford. Their accumulated debts came under the scrutiny of the Emperor, who repeatedly called in overdue loans. The complaint that they were not able to tend to their estates acquired significance in that they could not collect either the poll tax or the serfs' dues in order to meet their obligations.[167] Service to the state limited nobles' personal and professional opportunities; the employment of all nobles impaired the efficiency of the civilian and military service.[168] To eliminate these limitations, Peter III dissolved the obligatory bond between the nobility and the state and replaced it with a voluntary union with mutual benefits for both.

Emancipation also represented a political accomplishment for a relatively large and powerful configuration of nobles at court. Nobles were able to win freedom from one form of political compulsion. From evidence provided by the proposed law code of the 1750s, the terms of emancipation were not all that some aristocratic nobles sought. However, they were well satisfied in 1762 by the state's renunciation of a course of policy that their resistance and petitions had previously been powerless to stop.

III

SECULARIZATION OF THE ECCLESIASTICAL ESTATES

In the eighteenth century, anticlericalism was a protean force, capable of embracing divergent political and intellectual movements. In Russia, the spread of the attack on ecclesiastical authority affected most powerfully the practical considerations of the absolute monarchs. In the first year of the Great Northern War, Peter I confiscated some of the lands of the Church and from 1711 to 1724 grouped a portion of these confiscated lands under a special domain upon which he levied a tax. On March 21, 1762, three months before the onset of a military campaign in northern Germany, his grandson, Peter III, announced a more sweeping secularization of all ecclesiastical estates.[1] By the time this reform was completed by Catherine II in 1764, it added nearly one million former ecclesiastical peasants, now called "economic" peasants, to the state tax rolls and an untold, uncounted remainder to the landed estates of nobles.[2]

The reform's main legal accomplishment was to deny the Church's long-held claim to land and villages. In a dramatic recasting of the law, Peter III's enactment went beyond the previous confiscations of land and prohibitions of land grants to the Church. In the past, the Church had always retained a legal basis for its claim to land, and its sacrifices were in essence a subsidy to the state in periods of war. The law of mortmain, preventing the Church from further acquisition of land, had been in effect since the sixteenth century, but even under Peter I the hierarchy retained full control even over the synodal domain. Peter I's successors kept up his effort to survey ecclesiastical property and inspect collections to squeeze more payments out of the Church. Until 1744, the Petrine supervisory agency, the College of Economy, continued to exist, conduct surveys of property, and look after government revenues. The College of Economy, however, was not empowered to use force. The hierarchy, therefore, only intermittently complied with the request for property assessments and payment of taxes to the state. Under Elizabeth, the effort to collect inventories was abandoned and the College was closed, although her advisors repeatedly urged her to reconsider. In view of the failure of Peter I's immediate successors to complete his partial secularization of Church lands, it is difficult to agree with Pavel Miliukov that after the reign of Peter I "it was only a matter of time before secularization of Church property was completed, and when it was accomplished in 1764, it meant only a slight administrative change."[3]

Imperial policy in the intervening years between Peter I and Peter III reflected the lack of will to remove the Church entirely from the political sphere of government.

The first proposal for partial secularization was advanced in the late 1750s during the Seven Years' War. It gained approval by Elizabeth's Conference at the Imperial Court, but neither the Senate nor the Empress was willing to implement it. By 1762, there was no attractive alternative. Peter had ended Russian participation in the Seven Years' War, which promised a savings for the treasury. However, he was planning a new campaign to realize a dynastic claim to Holstein land occupied by Denmark, and his search for additional taxation revenues from other sources was stymied. Government officials considered the salt tax too high already; potential peasant unrest made the government wary of raising the poll tax. The offers of subsidies by which the Church had palliated rulers in the past were insufficient to meet the needs of even one season's campaign.

Financial need does not explain the ferocity of reform. Peter III elected to use force rather than conciliation and to overturn the imperial law without so much as consulting the Synod. As much as secularization met practical needs, pressure for reform had also gathered popular support in the eighteenth century. During the Enlightenment, ecclesiastical landholding became the focus of one of the sharpest and most sustained attacks on clerical "abuses" since the Reformation. Voltaire's dictum, *écrasez l'infame,* was a passionate commitment of the enlightened monarchs, especially Joseph II, who interfered with the affairs of the Church, canceling some Papal bulls, reorganizing episcopal sees, suppressing the Jesuit order, and instigating a large scale dissolution of monasteries and confiscation of their property. Peter III combined his attack on ecclesiastical landholding with an attack on parish schools,[4] private chapels,[5] and the proliferations of icons.[6] On January 29 he issued an edict of tolerance for Old Believers, who had been persecuted by the black clergy and fled to Poland.[7] Peter interfered in the ecclesiastical courts, claiming on March 27 that "the Synod watches out for the eminent clergy, when its proper mission is to be arbiter of justice and to defend the innocent and the poor."[8]

Among the threads of anticlericalism in the eighteenth century, the judicial writings of the cameralists had a particularly powerful influence in Russia. One of two proposals for secularization in the 1750s emerged from work on a new code of laws being drafted by a Senate commission which had cameralist principles as its main frame of reference. In Prussian cameralist tradition the law looked upon members of the Church as officials of state.[9] The Prussian cameralist model of law undermined concepts such as dual power, referring to continued authority of ecclesiastical law on a par with secular authority.[10] Under Peter I dual power was challenged; under Peter III and Catherine II it was finally suppressed.

Instances of secularization, according to chronicles, occurred in the fourteenth century when crowds of people led by government officials seized lands belonging to the Church.[11] In the fifteenth and sixteenth centuries, the idea of secularization took root in political theory.[12] Members of the clergy began to question the worldliness of life in the monastery, and they proposed that the lands of the Church revert to the state. Their challenge touched off a prolonged and intense debate. Proponents of secularization were on one side and clerical supporters of monastic wealth, led by Joseph of Volokolamsk, were on another. Volokolamsk strategically upheld the absolute authority of the monarch against those who wanted a larger share of power for the ecclesiastical hierarchy, and the debate ended in his decisive victory. His opponents were executed, and the Church won confirmation of its Mongolian *tarkhani,* or tax-free grants of land and villages.[13]

In the sixteenth century, the Church's ownership of land persisted, although rulers introduced the law of mortmain, an important step in the reduction of ecclesiastical landholding.[14] Ivan III, his son Vasilii, and especially Ivan IV attempted to curtail unauthorized grants of land in order to prevent the Church domain from expanding. "No land shall be taken out of service," Ivan IV wrote. However, he also personally approved the considerable donation and sale of land to the Church.[15]

In the first half of the seventeenth century, Church landholding continued to be governed in theory by the law of mortmain, although the state in practice was indifferent to the expansion of ecclesiastical landholding. The Church supplied grain to the peasants during famines, for example, during the reign of Boris Godunov.[16] It entered a period of relative economic prosperity, when losses from earlier centuries were regained.[17] In the second half of the century the Church witnessed a considerable erosion of its power. In his *Ulozhenie* [law code] of 1648, Aleksei Mikhailovich eliminated the tax-free status of the land, the tarkhani, thereby reducing the Church's revenues from land and mills. He also strictly upheld mortmain.[18] In a separate reform he established the Monastery Bureau to supervise collection of dues for the monks.[19] His weak successor, Feodor, allowed the Church a temporary victory by abolishing the much-hated Monastery Bureau; but Peter I reinitiated reform. Beginning with the abolition of the patriarchate and the reestablishment of the Monastery Bureau in 1701, he subjected the Church to an incremental loss of its power.

Peter I's excuse was that he intended to rectify the "great disorder" in the financial affairs of the Church. His revenue-finder, Aleksei Kurbatov, drew his attention to the potential gain from an administrative reform. Peter used the Monastery Bureau to "collect and preserve revenues, which decline under the capricious [management] of the owners."[20] The new managers, the boyar Ivan Musin-Pushkin, who headed the Monastery Bureau, Kurbatov, and a dozen other servitors, received lavish grants from the Church's holdings in reward for their assistance.[21] Peter I posted advertisements on the Kremlin gates offering for sale empty plots and other lands of the Church to anyone who wanted to buy them.[22] No estimate of the Church's loss after 1701 has ever been attempted, although historians assume that nobles acquired much land, especially rivers, forests, and mills.[23]

Without denying the importance of that transfer, it should not be exaggerated. This reform was not used for the same purposes as secularization was used by rulers in Reformation England and in Germany. Elsewhere, rulers broadened their support and enriched their subjects by making more land available to a commercially minded elite. In Russia, confiscation of land and supervision of the synodal domain was intended to supply revenues for Peter I's practically uninterrupted military campaigns.[24] When the wars were over in 1721, Peter I gave the lands back to the Church.[25] Indeed, some of the land already given out to servitors was also returned.[26]

Peter I's Church reform fell into two periods, 1701–1721 and 1721–1725, dividing years of war and peace. In the first period, revenue was confiscated. Some portion covered the salaries of the clergy and other personnel; most went to the state. In the second period, confiscations were stopped, but a more elaborate scheme was devised. Some monasteries, classified as *opredelennye* (designated), were to be taxed. Those in outlying regions of the empire were classified *zaopredelennye* (beyond secular supervision). "Designated" monasteries included at least seventy of the largest and most centrally located monasteries and eleven bishoprics, mostly in Moscow and St. Petersburg.[27] At designated monasteries, sometimes a part of the land was set aside for the state's needs and the rest was used by the Church. Sometimes there was no precise division of land but only a fixed rent. The unevenness of this system was its main feature, encouraging conflict between ecclesiastical and secular authorities. The advantage in the conflict belonged to the local ecclesiastical authorities because of the state's powerlessness to spare personnel to enforce central decisions. In 1724, for example, Peter made a decision to billet retired officers and invalids at monasteries. He established a ratio of one monk to two or three invalids and a salary scale for the black clergy (monks) equivalent that of the invalids they cared for; he prohibited further induction of monks and began an inventory of designated monasteries, a process completed by 1725.[28] None of these decisions could be enforced.

Peter's Church reform, in summary, reflected the practical concerns of the state. After the war, as is clear from what follows, he intended to use the hold he had gained over some Church revenues to resolve administrative and financial problems linked with demobilization. His death in 1725 prevented the realization of those aims.

The Church had so vigorously defended its prerogatives under Peter I that after his death only a small part of the confiscations remained in effect. Even among designated ecclesiastical institutions there were some, including the Synod, which were not subject to secular supervision. The Synod's lands were managed by the so-called synodal command, which lasted into Catherine's reign. Separate from the designated domain, the considerable property of "undesignated" monasteries was by definition not supervised by the state. Together with the synodal property, the undesignated untaxed property embraced 217,050 peasants (24% of the total)[29] and a great portion of all Church institutions, including eight bishoprics and 537 monasteries, among them Troitskaia Sergievskaia lavra with its 100,000 peasants.[30] Finally, in the designated sector, only a part of the peasantry was subject to tax, 151,000 in 1762. Thus 16 percent of a total of 910,866 ecclesiastical peasants in the early 1760s were categorized as under secular jurisdiction.[31]

Because such vast amounts of Church land were excluded from Petrine reform, for the the next decades the Synod made the case that Petrine law actually protected the ancient rights and traditional privileges of the Church landholding. This argument appears in the records of debates which broke out during 1742–1744 when members of the Synod, pressing their advantage with the deeply religious Elizabeth, requested that she remove secular collection agents from their lands, allowing ecclesiastical authorities to collect state payments. "The Synod accepts the existence of the College of Economy, Platon Krutitskii argued, "as long as it does not exceed in its ordinary expenses the budget allowed by the blessed tsar of eternal memory, Peter the Great."[32] In coming years, Petrine precedents would be used tactically both by government officials and by the Synod to politicize their practical concerns.

From the beginning, the Church adopted a defensive posture. It resisted state officials on both designated and undesignated monasteries. The matter of inventories (*opisi*) was the main arena for the much larger contest between Church and state over the practical reality of a shortfall of transfer payments agreed upon between Church and state. Secular officials sought in vain to update Petrine cadastral surveys and inventories of monasteries and to incorporate data from undesignated as well as designated institutions.[33] In the early 1740s, reformers exceeded their responsibilities in pursuing their inventories. One procurator of the College of Economy, Platon Musin-Pushkin, secularized property in the course of routine collection and management. The Church hierarchy complained:

> those officials of the College of Economy who were sent to "designated " estates took the dues that had been paid along with edibles and grain reserves which had been sent to bishoprics and monasteries for the consumption needs of the clergy, and they seized cattle and other goods from the villages. The peasants on those estates no longer work for the bishoprics and monasteries. For this reason, the Church is slipping into poverty.[34]

Between 1737 and 1742, Musin-Pushkin and Ivan Chaplygin, procurator of the Synod's Economic Chancellery, collected over twice the usual revenues; even undesignated monasteries in Novgorod began to pay something into the treasury, and the synodal command, supposedly free of secular jurisdiction, was also taxed.[35]

The efforts of these two reformers reveals the vitality in this period of Peter I's larger vision. This was the first open attack on Church property after his death. In a report to the Empress dated November 30, 1742, Chaplygin moved from a justification of the current state of affairs to an argument based on finances for more sweeping reform:

> The resources of the College of Economy and other institutions established by Peter I . . . are for extremely necessary present military needs, for salaries, for maintaining retired servitors, and other expenses. . . . [To guarantee these resources] the ecclesiastical peasants should be liberated from excessive and burdensome dues above what the state requires, from abuse and responsibilities imposed [by the Church], so that they will not fall into arrears in their payments to the treasury.[36]

The 1740s witnessed the rise of anticlericalism in government circles. Chaplygin's successor, Afanasii L'vov, wrote in his report of 1744: "Monks lead a life of celebration. They pay nothing to the treasury, and they do not perform any services."[37]

It was common in the early eighteenth century to attack local authorities for mismanagement of revenues, thievery, and resistance to the state.[38] Peter I had created a bureaucracy with reform-minded officials. The reason reforms of all kinds were stalled in later years is that Peter's successors on the throne varied in their commitment. In 1744, without any decree, the College of Economy ceased to exist. Synodal economic affairs were quietly transferred to its chancellery.[39] Elizabeth continued to allow taxation of designated institutions. She relied, however, mostly on extraordinary revenues, emergency subsidies from the Synod. During the war years of the 1740s she resorted to metallic inflation and transfers directly from the Synod to the treasury, an irregular kind of income which sometimes left the army undersupplied but did not bring her into conflict with the Church.

This situation lasted through the Seven Years' War, which placed a greater burden on the treasury than it was able to bear on the basis of ordinary revenues supplemented by extraordinary taxes. Still, the revival of the idea of supervising the allocation of Church revenues came not from Elizabeth but from her Conference at the Imperial Court, which had responsibility for financing the war. Among its first recommendations was reform of ecclesiastical landholding.

Preparation for Reform

The reform, announced on September 30 and circulated as a decree on October 6, 1757, was referred to as *pereobroka,* transfer of ecclesiastical peasants from labor services and payments in kind to a single payment of monetary dues.[40] Peasants would belong to *pomeshchichii oklad* (a tax category consisting of the bundle of obligations, chiefly *obrok*, due from peasants on private and state-owned land). This reform fell far short of a full resolution of either the legal claims by the Church or the practical need of the state for additional revenues. The terms of the reform revealed that Chaplygin's argument about the necessity of state intervention for the sake of helping peasants pay their dues to the state was the guiding inspiration to reform. Chaplygin had complained that peasants' arrears were caused by the excessive obligations imposed upon them by the monks; this reform intended to monetize and oversee the collection of dues. Secular overseers would be the retired officers and servitors of lower ranks already resident on ecclesiastical estates. These supervisors would not only collect dues but also manage expenditures. Net revenues over expenditures on necessities, such as salaries, would be spent on hospitals, repairs, and construction.[41] Supervisors would confiscate for the state only an amount equal to arrears already owed by the monasteries and a fine if the monks refused to care for invalids. This transfer was to be held in reserve in a bank for management expenses.[42]

The rationale for this reform was expressed in several ways. The authors, who are unknown, prefaced the text of the proposal with a striking statement of anti-clerical attitudes. They sought to remove the servants of God from their worldly concerns. They turned to the unifying political principle of the Petrine reforms, that the state dictated the amount and purpose of all expenditures by institutions controlled by the government. They cited Petrine law and the Prussian cameralist principle that "monasteries do not have the authority [*vlast'*] to use their revenues for any purpose that is not officially prescribed.'' The authors stopped short of revoking the traditional right of the Church to keep the land it had been given in donations by nobles and by the tsar.[43]

Since no significant transfer of funds was to occur from the Church to the state, no central enforcement agency was set up. Abolished after the death of Peter I, revived in the 1730s, and again abolished in the mid–1740s, the College of Economy was not mentioned. The main function of the reform, apart from reducing peasant arrears, must therefore have been to provide support for retired officers by billeting them to monastic estates. The pressing circumstance was the mounting number of casualties from the war, invalids with no other means of support. Peter I had attempted to billet retired and wounded officers at monasteries; Elizabeth first decided on the construction of a special residence and hospital, for which there turned out to be no funds. Then she determined to use the monasteries, but once again, the Synod would not cooperate.[44]

Although promulgated by the Conference as a law, the 1757 proposal did not go into effect. Its failure to be implemented has been attributed to Elizabeth, who received substantial personal gifts from the Synod to cover emergency expenses.[45] Presniakov wrote that her personal religious sentiments were what limited the possibility of reform in the 1750s.[46]

The repositories of laws and institutional records of the 1750s, filled with complaints against synodal and monastic authorities, reveal that her advisors were differently inclined. In the 1750s a strong bureaucratic initiative against Church landholding was launched. After the recommendation of the 1757 proposal, approved by the Conference at the Imperial Court, a council consisting of key government officials, numerous other efforts were made that attest to the readiness of the Russian government for reform in 1762.

After the 1757 proposal had been set aside, bureaucratic initiative surfaced in another institution. In 1758, General Procurator of the Senate Nikita Trubetskoi tried to persuade Elizabeth to appoint a special procurator to the Synod's Economic Chancellery, with the idea that a secular official might gain some control over the disputed revenues and the stalled process of reform. The Empress rejected his proposal,[47] but he succeeded in promoting his protege, Aleksei Kozlovskii, as procurator in the main office of the Synod. Kozlovskii, who later dominated the reform process, submitted a report on August 9, 1759, urging the Empress ''to make an example of just one eparchy,'' since ''there are 12 bishoprics and 400 monasteries'' that ''pay nothing into the treasury.'' ''I have examined your decrees about cadastral surveys and about the pereobroka of estates,'' he continued, ''and it would be a simple administrative matter'' to complete this reform. Kozlovskii continued that he needed her support against the members of the Synod, ''who ignore my suggestions,'' and members of the Economic Chancellery, ''who refused my requests, saying that they are not subject to secular supervision.'' His report was marked ''not approved.''[48]

In a simultaneous attack on Church landholding from a different direction, Trubetskoi and the other senators created a commission in 1758 to investigate the causes of rebellions at monastic estates (the Novospasskii Monastery Commission of 1758). In their reports, the commissioners drew attention to peasant petitions.[49] Peasant protest in the 1750s manifested itself in empty unploughed fields and such petitions as well as in revolts. In one instance, peasants at the Dalmatovsk monasteries refused to do labor services for an entire year.[50] In the periphery, as at Viatka, more distant from secular authority, revolts broke out frequently.[51] Complaints from designated estates centered on the continuing demand for labor services against the regulations. If peasants refused to work, they complained, the monks denied them passports so that they could not carry their grain to market.[52] Culling through these complaints gave the senators further ammunition.

In the early 1760s the subject of secularization was raised again. The Senate's Codification Commission proposed a law on ecclesiastical landholding.[53] This Senate proposal, which cannot be dated exactly, began with the concept of pereobroka but its substance dealt with the more serious principle of the Church's rights as landholder.[54] This is the first instance in the eighteenth century when the Church's claim to settled land was explicitly denied. The timing of the attack on the Church's legal claim is best explained not only by anticlericalism but also by the Senate's concern with property rights. The proposed law on ecclesiastical landholding emerged as a provision in the general law code being drafted by this commission, "On the Status of Subjects," in which the key question was the landholding rights of state institutions and social groups. The right to own settled land was to be the exclusive prerogative of the nobility and the state.

Faced with opposition by the Holy Synod, the Senate did not maintain a firm resolve. Iakov Shakhovskoi, general procurator, proposed allowing the Synod jointly to determine with the Senate the issue of ecclesiastical landholding. Shakovskoi apparently anticipated that the Synod would be willing to open its account books to the Senate and that the hierarchy would agree to be placed on the state payrolls. Discussions produced no such resolution. In a meeting jointly convened by the Senate and the Synod on July 24, 1760, Archbishop Dmitrii Sechenov declared that in return for complete freedom from secular supervision, the Church would make an annual payment to the state of 300,000 rubles. The Senate rejected the proposal, and the idea of joint determination was abandoned.[55]

Shakhovskoi blamed the lack of action on the political process and the reluctance of the Senate and the Empress to overcome the objections of the clergy.[56] The reality was more complex. Although the Seven Years' War made secularization increasingly attractive,[57] the war also created a special constraint on the ability of state officials to carry out such a measure. The officer corps was not available to enforce the law in the countryside. This was the central dilemma faced by Peter III.

Reform under Peter III

In the first week of the new regime, Kozlovskii summarized for the Emperor the state of the discussion and advocated sweeping measures. He wrote that the Church's wealth was being squandered and that the ambiguities and double collections resulting from previous reform efforts and ecclesiastical resistance had left the peasantry unable to pay and in disobedience.[58] Kozlovskii argued that the 1757 project be implemented so that "the authorities and monks would be satisfied with their salaries. The peasants would be certain of what was expected of them. All the present multitude of commissions and injustices would come to an end, and peace would be restored."[59] Kozlovskii's phrasing matched the tone of the Conference and Senate projects. His report showed how deeply the bureaucracy was influenced by concerns of state and, at least for the purposes of persuading the imperial power, in the destabilizing effects of peasant revolt.

Peter presented this reform proposal to the Senate on January 17. Initially he seemed open to conciliation. He announced that he would bring Elizabeth's project to completion, but he would begin with a joint meeting between Senate and Synod.[60] The new general procurator of the Senate, replacing Shakhovskoi, was Aleksandr Glebov, to whom the reform has with excessive confidence been attributed.[61] In the long history of this reform, no single government figure stands out. Dmitrii Volkov, secretary of the Conference at the Imperial Court; Nikita Trubetskoi and Iakov Shakhovskoi, the former general procurators; Kozlovskii, continuing as procurator of the Synod—all were equally likely to have framed the draft version of secularization.

Indeed, the Senate under Glebov's leadership began cautiously. It met with the Synod in January, agreeing to the pereobroka in a compromise where the Church and state should jointly determine the use of revenues. One-half of each ruble should go to the state and one-half to monasteries.[62] Peter III was dissatisfied with this agreement. On February 16 he dictated new terms to the Senate. "Out of all the fruitless confrontations and sessions between the Senate and the Synod," he said, there was nothing more to be gained by dialogue. The Conference project would be put into effect. "Our Aunt Empress Elizabeth," he began, "combining good will with purpose and wisely differentiating between abuses and prejudices of dogmatists, on one hand, and the pure foundations of Our Eastern Orthodox Church, on the other, chose to relieve the monks, who have vowed to live apart from this earthly life, from all worldly cares."[63] In the future, he concluded, there would be no further induction of monks.[64]

The rationale of the 1757 project was to remove from the clergy the burden of worldly concerns; similarly, the February 16 declaration emphasized that neither the enjoyment of revenues nor the burden of worldly concerns was consistent with monastic vows. Peter's wording was even more anticlerical than the earlier document. He called ecclesiastical landholding an "abuse and prejudice of dogmatists of the faith." The Senate scribes referred to this reform as "the enactment about the abuse and prejudice of the dogmatists."[65]

Peter ordered the implementation of the decree "as quickly as possible" according to the "exact guidelines" and "without any omissions" from the Conference project of 1757. The Senate complied. It strengthened the terms of reform, clarified the peasants' status, and elaborated an administrative apparatus to guide implementation of reform. All the substantive changes were accepted. The final decree of

March 21 was as the Senate created it. Volkov later made reference to editorial changes in the final version. He complained that the senators omitted his introduction tracing the origin of reform in Elizabeth's reign.[66] The materials no longer exist to follow these editorial changes.

The Senate formulation of February 19 imposed a firmly secular design. The land would be managed by retired officers rather than monastic servitors. (Peter's final enactment of March 21 strengthened this provision: "Among the administrators there shall be no monks, clergy or monastic servitors, and just as they shall not be appointed, those who already occupy those positions shall be removed.")[67] Once in residence at monasteries, managers were to compile cadastral surveys and inventories which the government had requested but which the Synod had refused to supply.[68] In order to accomplish these goals, the College of Economy was re-established. Provisions for the peasantry were strikingly new. The land would belong to the peasants, the Senate enactment went on, and a tithe of 10 percent on net profits would be placed on excess land rented out to them.[69] The expression, "the land will be given to the peasants" ("otdat' zemlia krest'ianam,")[70] framed in a legal document, was an experiment unique in the eighteenth century. The apparently inflammatory formula was removed from later enactments.[71]

The intent of the Senate to pacify the peasantry was evident in a passage declaring amnesty for some peasants who had participated in rebellions of the 1750s. The Senate halted the investigation of revolts and disturbances from the 1750s, except where murder had been committed and where the peasants had been unjustly treated:

> As for all the complaints that we have examined about the burdensome, excessive taxes on the peasantry, about their exhaustion, about their protests and disobedience in various places, about the commissions and investigations that have been conducted, and about the petitions that have been submitted, except in the case of murder, would not your Imperial Highness consider dropping all of this and destroying the records; for there never was any regulation governing revenues collected at monasteries. Now the levy has been established. The College will be opened and the officers assigned. Peasant payments found by the officers to have been seized by monastic servitors in excess of the required amount will be returned immediately to the peasants.[72]

This Senate resolution expressed the appearance and even prominence of concern with the position of the peasants in this reform as conceived in the late 1750s and early 1760s. The framers of this enactment demonstrated a physiocratic concern with the ability of the peasant household to pay, and they showed the intent to rectify the diminishing marginal value of labor by taxing output rather than input.

Peter signed the Senate's recommendations on March 6 and promulgated the decree on March 21. He appointed the Moscow senator Prince Vasilii Obolensky as head of the College of Economy and located it in Moscow, near the majority of ecclesiastical estates. The College was to generate instructions for the officers, who were to regulate the activities of the peasants as well as the disposal of revenues.[73] The officers—one staff officer per province and a regular officer for towns where there were at least 1,000 peasants—had to be capable, "and not old men living at monasteries."[74] Officers should be hired "according to their capabilities" and provided with salaries and rations to "avoid any burden on the peasantry." These officers were to be trained as managers of a new fiscal regime.

The 1757 plan had been without stipulations or clear guidelines for implementation. The Senate's decree removed that imprecision by reestablishing the College of Economy. The clear control by the College over revenues removed the previous ambiguity about the peasants' status. The College was given all responsibilities: it initiated the administrative process, defined categories of taxes, started inventories of Church property including livestock not used in farming, grain reserves, and other items, and transferred the Church officials to state payroll schedules. The scale it used was from 1724. So was the existing inventory. Bishops received separate salaries; monasteries were divided into three classes and received stipends depending upon the number of resident monks; for reclusive monks who had no land, no provision was made. With this manifest inadequacy, the adoption of outdated pay scales, the Senate's decree was a trial subject to modification. The intention was to revise the provisions as officers gathered information and updated cadastral surveys.[75]

The Synod's Economic Chancellery did not actually relinquish control over ecclesiastical revenues until late spring.[76] On April 27 the Senate demanded that the 1,358 officers who were located at monasteries begin to implement the reform, and that others be chosen to assist them.[77] In May and June the Senate sent officers, twenty at a time, to various provinces[78] to start the reform: peasants were given mills, salt mines, factories, industrial shops, fisheries, grain, wood, and land.[79] Horses were immediately requisitioned for the army.[80] On May 24, the College delivered its questionnaires to the monasteries, where inventories began. The questionnaires covered both the peasant population (dues, quality of land, and state of buildings) and military residents (number, literacy, salaries, and dependents).[81] By mid-June the College was established. Six officials met daily for six hours, studying petitions and responses to the questionnaires. Before Peter's overthrow, cadastral surveys had been received from Tver, Belgorod, Kursk, Iaroslav, and parts of Moscow.[82] The main difficulty in implementation, according to the records of the College, was resistance by the clergy. Some bishoprics and monasteries concealed their assets.[83] Without sufficient personnel to suppress it, clerical opposition spread.[84] Monasteries prevented the gathering of information and sometimes continued to collect dues from the peasantry, demanding labor services. One decree cited illegal collections in two eparchies, St. Petersburg and Pskov. "Taxes have been unfairly collected," declared Nikita Trubetskoi to the Senate on April 4, "and they will be returned to the peasants."[85] On June 1, the Senate stopped all collections from the peasants until the end of the year.[86] Until the demobilization of the army, there could be no speedy implementation of this reform.

On June 25 the Senate issued a confirmation of the peasants' right to forests and groves previously belonging to the monasteries; again the clergy resisted.[87] By the end of Peter's reign, dual power and excess taxation resulted in some peasant unrest. However, rebellions which marked this brief reign were, on the whole, not led by monastic peasants.[88] Unrest can largely be attributed to the new disparity between the position of economic peasants and serfs. On May 30, there was a revolt of 2,840 peasants from the districts of Tver and Klin, belonging to four different pomeshchiki, who had petitioned to be transferred to the crown, "where their payments of rent would be less than they are now."[89] By June 3 another thousand had joined in. They were suppressed "with guns and cannons" on June 13.[90] The clergy also protested. They sent a petition to the Emperor, complaining that he wanted to "encloister the servants of God in their monasteries."[91] In a more significant form of protest, several members of the clergy took part in the coup that overthrew Peter III.

Resistance and lack of personnel prevented the realization of secularization in Peter's reign. The most important barrier to reform, not new to this reign, was the shortage of manpower created by the Seven Years' War. Peter's government was forced to postpone collection of obrok until the end of the year, and it was unable to stifle protests of the clergy and serfs. Counterbalancing the relative weakness of the reform in these two respects, a weakness caused by poor timing, was its strength: immediate settlement of demobilized and wounded officers from the Seven Years' War and resolution of long-standing complaints of the monastic peasants.

In the absence of more direct indications, the provisions of the reform and pronouncements in the course of its implementation can be used to gain insight into the motives for the reform. Peter and his advisors sought to resolve the grievances and encourage the peasant economy in the state sector by removing the ecclesiastical authorities, renting the land to the peasants, and granting amnesty to rebels. Although the reform had its origins long before new economic thinking appeared in Russia, the new thinking helps explain why there were so many new features of benefit to the peasantry in this enactment. Violent breaches of order in the manorial sector, some of the consequences of agrarian reform, in turn surely account for the retraction of "liberal" elements of reform in Catherine's reign.

The essential aspect of secularization was the transfer of land as well as of peasants. From 1700 to 1764 the state sector continued to expand. In proportion, the manorial sector declined until Catherine's capture of new lands made possible the distribution of land to favorites and many others. It is surprising that in that era of enhanced noble privilege in the 1750s this kind of reform with so little in the enactment for the nobility should have been so widely sponsored, especially since there is a record of nobles attempting to gain the land for themselves throughout the eighteenth century. The answer must be that the nobles in charge of finding revenues for a state with an overextended budget sought to secure their own rights against confiscation and deflect the weapon of confiscation against a vulnerable institution, the Church.

Fiscal policy dictated some solution to the shortfall of tax revenues, and the amount the Church was willing to cede was apparently deemed insufficient. Nevertheless, the Church could surely have been commanded to provide a larger subsidy and allowed to retain the lands. Because of the numerous alternatives and more moderate steps that could have been taken, this decree seems the product of complex and interconnected fiscal, political, and economic purposes. It was the first instance in the eighteenth century of real interest in agrarian reform.

Reform under Catherine II

Catherine did not immediately rescind secularization after her ascent to the throne. Despite the claims of her manifestoes about the immediacy of danger to the Church from Peter's policies, she delayed doing anything about the decree for over a month. Thus it would seem that rescission was not necessary for the consolidation of her power. It was also clear that her sensibilities were the same as those of the reformers. A diplomat had found in her in the 1750s the same sort of anticlericalism that was characteristic of her husband: "The Muscovite clergy detest the Grand Duke and the Grand Duchess for it is known that they are much less attached to the Greek religion than to the Lutheran."[92] Catherine's failure to take the side of the Church is apparent in her first decrees, going ahead with collections.[93] On July 24, at a joint meeting of Senate and Synod, she listened to arguments of the Church for the restoration of its land.[94] In August she still vacillated, as can be seen from her letter of August 8 to Aleksei Petrovich Bestuzhev-Riumin. "Little father," she wrote, "give me your advice! Should I set up a commission now, not giving the lands back; or should I give the lands back with the provision that a commission be established later?"[95]

It is plain that Catherine's maneuver, whatever path she chose, would be temporary and tactical. On August 12 she announced her decision to close the College of Economy and return the estates. At the same time she revealed her contrary long-range intentions. She would create a commission, she announced, consisting of secular and clerical members who would "bring the entire matter of assessments to completion."[96]

There was some administrative confusion and peasant disobedience. On the next day, she issued the decree again and commanded it to be sent to all eparchies and monasteries.[97] On September 19 the Synod reported that it had not yet been received at many monasteries.[98] On October 4 the bishop of Pskov complained that the provincial chancellery refused even to acknowledge that there had been such a decree, and the eparchal administration had not received it.[99] On October 10 she was forced to confirm her decree for the third time.[100]

Catherine's apparent vacillation fueled the peasant uprising. Although she spoke of returning land to the Church, she nevertheless continued to collect obrok from peasants on designated monastic estates. At a loss for available manpower, she ordered the peasants to begin their fall labor at the monasteries, to collect receipts from the monks after the labor was done, and to turn them in at the provincial chancellery. Complaints would be submitted in the future to the Synod rather than the Senate.[101] What this meant was a return to the system of dual authority of the 1740s, the era of Chaplygin and Musin-Pushkin, when secular officials and ecclesiastical authorities both imposed their exactions.[102]

Catherine described in a later ukaz the violent resistance of the peasants to the reversal of the reform:

> On almost all bishopric and monastic estates they have taken the sown wheat given to the monastery by the treasury and distributed it among themselves . . . they have refused to sow next year's wheat . . . as if by special permission, these simple and irrational people, as peasants are, with evil thoughts have cut down the forests . . . stolen the fisheries.[103]

Revolt spread to bishoprics and monasteries in Tver, Tambov, Moscow, and the Don, building in September, October, and November to conflict with authorities.[104] Peasant revolts broke out at the iron and copper factories in Kazan and Orenburg.[105]

On November 29, Catherine established a commission to draft a new law. It included among others the Archbishop Dmitrii Sechenov, Aleksei Kozlovskii, Grigorii Teplov, and Aleksei Kurakin, later president of the College of Economy. Kozlovskii's inclusion may point to his critical role even at this stage in the process of reform. The commission was ordered to reestablish the College of Economy, compose instructions for the officers, send out questionnaires, and draft a budget for the College.[106] These orders contained all the provisions essential to reform, decided by the "secular command."[107] Teplov urged her to go further, to clarify what was demanded of the peasantry. Publish a decree, he advised, "stating how much and no more that monastic authorities can demand from the peasants"; "transfer all immovable property of the Church" to secular supervision.[108] No further instructions were issued, however, until the inventories were complete in 1764. As a result, the year 1763 stands out as one of the most violent episodes in eighteenth-century history before the Pugachev uprising. The peasant revolt, later called the Dubinshchina, after the peasant's club, was finally suppressed in the fall of 1763.[109]

By including Sechenov on the commission, Catherine restored a role to the Synod in her reform. She removed control over the substance and progress of reform from the Senate, turning down its request to manage the College of Economy.[110] In November, she appointed a single senator to her Commission, Ivan Vorontsov from the Senate kontor in Moscow.[111]

The College was reestablished on May 12 with orders to continue implementing previous laws: only designated estates were taxed; others were under observation to prevent "excessive" burdens on the peasantry.[112] 160,428 peasants paid obrok in 1763, roughly the number of those on designated estates.[113] Arrears for the year were 7,591 rubles.[114] The reform thus far was without promise.

A more sweeping measure was enacted on February 16, 1764, when Catherine adopted the provisions of Peter III's enactment. The distinguishing feature of this enactment was that the privileges and salaries of the most eminent clergy had been increased.[115] Average salaries were raised; monasteries were given a stipulated amount of land; the hierarchy was reassured of its position. For this reason, there was little protest over secularization. The lone protesting voice, that of Arsenii Matseevich, a gifted and fanatical archbishop, was stifled by trial and exile.[116] On the whole, Catherine commanded the loyalty of the hierarchy.

Monasteries and other ecclesiastical institutions retained enough land, in theory, to cover consumption. Those which, even so, could not meet expenses because of a large staff turned away their clergy; some monasteries were closed.[117] As a result, mendicancy rose. Within the first year of reform, 2,887 monks and nuns were counted in St. Petersburg without lodging.[118] By 1770 in Moscow guberniia, there were as many as 17,000 monks, all of whom were drafted into the army.[119]

The impact of this measure on the white clergy, or village priests, by contrast, was insignificant. They retained their position and their land. At first Catherine abolished fees for confession and other services, but in 1765 she reinstated them in fixed amounts and allowed charges for all sacraments.[120] Retired officers were also well provided for. They were now to be cared for in special hospitals and homes. Persons insane, criminal, or ill were no longer sent to monasteries but to special homes provided by the College.[121]

The peasant question was resolved as Peter III's government had intended except that the wording of the decree differed. Instead of the words "give the fields that formerly were ploughed for bishops, monasteries, cathedrals, Churches, and hermitages to the peasants," the commission substituted that the College of Economy would "take as its own" all votchiny and immovables of the secularized institutions, along with the legal matters and investigations connected with governance.[122] "Economic" peasants were initially distinct from state peasants, because of the intent that they be supervised by the College of Economy. Catherine doubled the supervisory personnel at monasteries (to 6,000) and issued instructions about the management of economic estates, but the experiment was abandoned in 1784 when the College was closed.[123]

The treasury took its share by raising obrok by 50 percent. This brought an annual revenue of 1,366,000 rubles, and, subtracting 460,000 for salaries and other expenses, a net gain of 903,430.[124] The increase in obrok was in some places a hardship, especially where the prevalence of labor services had inhibited the market. On July 15, 1765, 4,542 peasants previously belonging to the Trinity St. Sergius lavra (Moscow votchina, Bezhetsk district) petitioned for an increase in allotment land; "the one and a half ruble obrok has caused many to fall into extreme poverty." The petition went on to say that "there never had been any trade, and as a result, peasants have fled to places where obrok is not required."[125] Similarly, an anonymous report to the commissions described the spread of infanticide among impoverished households, where ecclesiastical authorities had been less demanding.[126]

The peasants' position did not decline as a result of increased obrok. Land allotments had improved. Before secularization the average allotment was between 0.6 and 2 desiatiny (one desiatina = 2.7 acres).[127] After secularization, according to data from the land survey, peasants on economic lands held anywhere from 5 (in Tula) to 34 desiatiny (near Novgorod) as an average allotment; a discrepancy due to variation in forest land. The range compared favorably with average allotments of serfs, who previously had been better off. Only in Moscow and St. Petersburg was the average share less than 3 desiatiny (2.6 and 2.7 respectively); in eleven provinces of the central region it fell between 2 and 4 desiatiny; and in Smolensk, Novgorod and Tambov, economic peasants held between 4 and 5 desiatiny of land.[128]

Secularization did constrain mobility, although, even so, economic peasants were better off than serfs in this respect as well. Under ecclesiastical supervision, to flee had been easy; fugitive monastic peasants formed a large part of the urban poor. Between 1726 and 1730 almost one-third of the guild merchants in Moscow were former (fugitive) monastic peasants.[129] During Peter's reign monastic peasants took advantage of the new order to leave in large numbers. From a single monastery (Volokolamsk) in 1762 over a thousand left.[130] From 1762 to 1764 the confusion of command encouraged further flight; new registrants in the merchantry from this stratum reached 75 in Moscow, 70 in Rostov, and 76 in St. Petersburg. After 1764, the law in theory was restrictive; greater supervision may have slowed down illegal departure.[131] Peasants complained of more interference in every respect, although mainly about collection of obrok in excess of the established amount.[132]

Ideas of reform, once called into being as a political force, have a life of their own. Secularization was largely a bureaucratic reform, given life by both the anticlericalism and unusual financial need of Peter III and Catherine II. The final enactment passed through three revisions, correspondingly the work of the Conference and Senate under Elizabeth, the Senate and synodal Chancellery under Peter, and the Commission on Ecclesiastical Estates under Catherine. The first proposal reflected the impetus to reform in the bureaucracy, where physiocratic ideas were discussed in connection with numerous projects for fiscal reform. The second stage, under Peter, led to specific reform measures, the Senate's resolution of February 16, confirmed by edict on March 21, 1762. The third stage began with Catherine's rescission of the decree of March 21 and ended with her own secularization decree of February 16, 1764.

In view of Catherine's avoidance of any reference to Peter III—her ukaz announcing secularization cited as historical justification her predecessors in reform, Aleksei Mikhailovich, Peter I, Anne, and Elizabeth—it bears emphasis that by denying to Peter's regime even the status of predecessor, Catherine was concealing a substantial debt. After June 28, 1762, because of peasant resistance to repeal and because of the broad consensus at court, the reform could not really be halted. It was carried along also by sheer bureaucratic momentum despite synodal opposition. The dimensions and the framework of reform were fixed by the time it came under discussion in her reign, and there was no real difference between her decree and his except in distribution of funds.

The enactment in 1762 was a landmark in Russian political history. Although as early as the fifteenth century Russian rulers began to consider establishing greater secular control over ecclesiastical lands, and Aleksei Mikhailovich's Monastic Bureau and Peter's tax of "designated" monasteries served as important precedents, realization of reform was out of reach in the intellectual climate of the seventeenth and early eighteenth century. Peter I's legacy was a tax; under Peter and Catherine secularization had broader significance. It meant a change in property rights and signaled a restructuring of social wealth. In view of the intense interest in property rights in Elizabeth's Codification Commission, and the survey of property in the 1750s, this particular reform has a parallel history in the aspiration of nobles to secure their land against confiscation.

Secularization benefited the nobility considerably less than it benefited the state. There is no comparison here with the hearty advantage to commercially minded English gentry that secularization brought in England in the sixteenth century. Peter chose not to auction off the land and peasants, and he did not transfer these peasants directly to the state, to be doled off to court nobles. Catherine, on the whole, respected the difference between economic and state peasants and also did not allow significant numbers to be alienated as private property.[133] Thus, however many parcels they may have added unobtrusively to their estates, nobles gained no substantial advantage from secularization under Peter or Catherine. And the managers of the estates, retired officers above the eighth rank, encouraged to rent factories, mills, and fisheries on former ecclesiastical estates, did not acquire either the prestige or authority of manorial lords.

The fiscal purpose of the reformers ruled out the private exploitation of the economic peasantry. However, there is a sense in which this reform satisfied the nobility. High-ranking nobles, eager to restrict their own exclusive privileges, at least prevented lesser nobles from acquiring settled land at lower prices. Therefore the transfer of monastic land to the state was not an act by reformers indifferent to the interest of the highest stratum of the noble estate.

Why, then, if nobles supported secularization and bureaucrats repeatedly proposed it, was it so long in coming? "Absolutist theory," J. H. Hexter wrote, "wrenched the idea of hierarchy from its context in the nature of things and made it a matter of the prince's will."[134] Until this test of power, absolutism in Russia was not fully developed. Elizabeth failed to provide the forceful leadership essential to this reform. The slow pace of reform also showed to what extent a state, relying on the military to implement reform, could not both wage war and tend to domestic affairs.[135] Finally, one of the greatest barriers to stronger government was between capital and countryside. In the eighteenth century local ecclesiastical authority was exceptionally strong. Among its accomplishments, secularization opened the way to the expansion of local civil government by reaffirming the central authority over local tradition.

IV

NATIONAL REVENUES

A forceful foreign policy demands a forceful economy. During the Seven Years' War, enormous debts had accumulated.[1] Peter III was greeted at his accession by a stunning accomplishment of Russian forces in Europe and no means to follow it up.[2] He tightened control over the budget and spent the next six months cutting expenses. He withdrew his army from central Europe. He slashed inessential military and civilian personnel by eliminating a corps of the imperial Russian guards and retiring hundreds of noble servitors. He permitted landlords to collect the poll tax on their estates, further reducing the need for military personnel.[3] He resorted to a savage confiscation of the wealth of the Church for the sake of new recruits and revenues, and he debased the currency. He stopped the funding for the construction of buildings and of a canal from the Volga to the Volkov River.[4] He used all of the methods of asset-pawning that were the usual means of borrowing by kings under emergency situations. He renewed tax-farms and monopoly concessions to merchants. He repossessed state land rented to nobles who did not pay their debts.[5] Then on May 23, when the Senate submitted a budget estimate, and the deficit still proved to be substantial (see Table I),[6] he took measures of final resort. Only five months into his reign but two months away from his intended campaign, unable to squeeze out any more revenue or remint coins fast enough,[7] he called in overdue loans and created a new state bank to issue paper money, in effect, a partial repudiation of debts.[8]

Peter's unusual effort to overcome the financial crisis demonstrated that in times of pressing need the Russian mercantile economy was driven back on inelastic revenues. The fundamental predicament of the government was that it was not creditworthy. Peter requested loans from Dutch merchants to cover the costs of the campaign,[9] but he had no means of promising repayment. "The ordinary emergencies," wrote John Hicks, "such as harvest failures or attacks by the 'usual' enemies, would not require new decisions; ways of dealing with them could be incorporated within the traditional rules."[10] Four million rubles needed to launch a campaign in the summer and four million more for the coming year suddenly required a new set of rules.

The export expansion policy of 1761–1762 can be seen mainly in this light. Liberalism took hold in a tight credit environment where aggressive mercantilism and constant warfare had led to deficit financing. Peter announced that restrictions would be removed on the export of grain and other raw materials; customs would

TABLE I

Budget Report by Senate (June 5, 1762)*

Income	Rubles	Percent
Poll tax	5,212,685	34
Spirits monopoly (1750)	986,950	6
Salt tax (1749)	1,302,867	9
New spirits and salt tax (1756)	1,440,905	9
Customs collected by Shemiakin	1,405,711	9
Reminting silver, Shemiakin's monopoly	597,383	4
State and other peasants	455,514	3
Siberian customs	591,495	4
Misc. other collections	2,400,545	16
Extraordinary collections	956,579	6
Total	15,350,634	
Total revenue from salt and spirits	3,730,722	24
Total revenue from customs	1,997,206	13
Expenses		
War (commissariat, artillery, provisions, irregular troops)	10,418,747	63
Imperial cabinet	1,150,000	7
Court	603,333	4
Hetman of the Ukraine	98,147	1
Salaries and other payments	4,232,432	26
Total	16,502,659	
Deficit	1,152,025	

*"O podnesenii Emu Imperatorskomu Velichestvu o vsekh godudarstvennykh dokhodakh i roskhodakh perechen' vedomstvu," *TsGADA, f.* 248 *pr. Senata, kn.* 3383, *l.* 430.

be reduced and equalized at all ports. All items previously prohibited, including iron, cloth, and hemp, would be permitted to be traded through ports and other trading points in the Caspian area. Merchant trading concessions and state trade would be abolished. The tallow industry in Arkhangel, where the Dutch were dominant in trade, would be freed of export restrictions, and the port would be given more favorable status. Finally, no factories would be allowed to import raw materials or instruments free of tariff duties.[11] This measure was designed to serve as a powerful stimulus to agriculture and to the merchantry, as a means of dismantling the vast network of trading monopolies established in the 1750s by the now deceased Peter Shuvalov, as a tool of expansionism and foreign policy, and, not least among its purposes, as potential security on a loan from merchants of the United Provinces.

Even though the new policy was perceived at the time as a sharp turn away from established policy,[12] it had deep roots in a long political tradition of protest against mercantilist restraints on trade.[13] Freedom of trade was a popular notion in late seventeenth-century Russia,[14] just as grain-centered liberalism in France was in the anti-mercantilist, Christian-agrarian, and utilitarian currents of the second half of the seventeenth century.[15] In the first half of the eighteenth century, although policy was governed on the whole by protectionism and restraints on trade, occasionally there were periods of liberalism. From 1713 to 1718, for example, export restrictions were liberalized. For a brief period after the death of Peter I, A. I. Osterman, A. A. Menshikov, and others relaxed restrictions.[16] Again, in the mid–1750s, liberalism became prominent in the writings of the philosopher M. V. Lomonosov,[17] the secretary of the Senate, F. I. Sukin, the merchant N. Korzhavin, Senator I. I. Nepliuev, and Conference secretary D. V. Volkov.[18] Fueled by resentment of the way private fortunes of some courtiers had accumulated, to the detriment, they believed, of the treasury and the populace, they criticized the manipulation of tariffs, monopolies, and taxes to the personal advantage of individuals.[19] They pointed to corruption and mismanagement, excessive reliance on direct and indirect taxes which led to peasant flight, missed opportunities in the exotic eastern trade, and contraband that flourished under the regime of monopolies.[20] An indictment of the corruption of the system of tax-farming by G. N. Teplov during Catherine's first year on the throne, for example, led to one of the most liberal measures of the 1760s, the elimination of that method of collecting customs duties.[21]

The liberals did not maintain themselves solely by the appeal to end a corrupt regime. In a caustic criticism of mercantilism, the author(s) of Peter III's enactment claimed that the theory itself was wrong and was leading to the depletion of silver and gold.[22] They condemned a tradition they believed to be backward. Their method of open attack as well as their advancement of a full program of economic policies show the adaptation of the more traditional liberalism to a new current of physiocracy, itself a few years old in France.[23] Physiocracy grew to be an even greater part of liberalism during Catherine's reign in a multitude of laws granting freedom to all to enter into manufacturing and to set up a workbench or industrial enterprise and to nobles to freely exploit the subsoil and growth on their own lands; imperial declarations were to deplore state interference in the production and distribution of goods and to advise a minimum of regulation in the interests of the national economy.[24]

Nineteenth-century liberalism—which stood for the labor market, the gold standard, and freedom of trade—barely existed in embryo in the eighteenth century. Mercantilists were still a powerful force, preventing the implementation of law in Peter's reign and opposing the work of Teplov in Catherine's reign.[25] Rumor spread that Peter III would not be able to eliminate trading monopolies after all, and he was not entirely able to.[26] Those who opposed the policy wrote a lengthy retort to the enactment, filled with references to "the sanctity of contracts" and the correct reasoning of Peter's predecessors.[27]

Even when it triumphed in reforms, liberalism in the eighteenth century was not an organizing principle so much as a tendency. Karl Polanyi justly cautions against misspecifying its significance. The conditioning level of economic development as a backdrop for new understanding, according to Polanyi's theory of economic transformation, appeared only in the nineteenth century, when "trade had become linked with peace," and finance acted as a powerful moderator in the councils and policies of sovereign states. In Russia, even basic features of an advanced economy were missing: banks and credit, joint stock companies, and a labor market. Polanyi wrote,

> To antedate the policy of laissez-faire, as is often done, to the time when this catch-word was first used in France in the middle of the eighteenth century would be entirely unhistorical; it can be safely said that not until two generations later was economic liberalism more than a spasmodic tendency. . . . All that the Physiocrats demanded in a mercantilistic world was the free export of grain in order to ensure a better income to farmers, tenants, and landlords.[28]

This interpretation is correct, providing the focus of discussion is modernity. If the object is to know why these important changes in the nineteenth century happened at all, it is necessary to start with thinkers who discovered the weakness in their existing institutional order and anticipated how to adapt policies in trade and finance to the long-term interests of the state and the economy. Before understanding the concepts of production, distribution, and banking, the government had to examine the principles of a self-regulating system of markets, or an economy directed by market prices, about which the "economists" the eighteenth century were unusually clear.

The critical insight of 1762, about the beneficial effect on merchants and peasants of increasing the volume of exported raw materials and about the responsiveness of output to higher prices, had to compete against a very powerful fear of famine and its effect, peasant flight from the insufficiency of grain. Against such a response, the liberals could only fall back on their theories,[29] but these theories were persuasive to Peter. Catherine confirmed and expanded the new commercial policy on July 31.[30] Her confirmation was a direct acknowledgment that a firm course of policy had been set by her predecessor. She fully embraced the idea of making Russia's markets considerably more open to foreigners than they had been in the past, confirming that Russia's role in the world market was that of a seller of raw materials. This support for agriculture-centered liberalism marked a move in the direction of contact and competition with the West that was not reversed in ensuing years when the bureaucracy in practice continued to prohibit the export of specific grains.

The Mercantile Tradition

By removing restrictions on the export of raw materials, Peter III claimed to be "following in the footsteps of Peter the Great." This was true only in a literal sense of Russia's exports expanding along the route of southern territorial conquests. Peter III's commercial policy was not Petrine: by a single enactment, he removed control over commercial policy from the Petrine Senate and changed the premises of export policy. An account of the history of policy is important to an understanding of what was new about the ideas his advisors advanced in the early 1760s which he put into law in 1762.

Peter I was one of the most determined practitioners of bullion-oriented policy identified with mercantilism. Beginning in 1715–1717, after his travels abroad and his acquaintance with German cameralism, Peter I turned his back on free-trade advocates in his government and launched a new program to raise custom revenues while protecting industry.[31] He reversed the relatively liberal tariffs of the seventeenth century. In his tariff of 1724 he raised duties on exports and placed a stiff ad valorem duty of up to 70 percent on imports in order to provide protection for industry by import substitution and to encourage the flow of specie into the country.

This strategy had little economic abundance to draw on. Russia had a poorly developed commodity and money market, low yielding agriculture, no merchant marine, and an unskilled and unreliable supply of labor for new industry. Because of its insecure foundation and lack of promise, extreme protectionism was abandoned after Peter I's death. His former advisors retreated to a milder form of protectionism. Not turning their backs on agriculture as he had, they introduced the export of hemp, grain, and flax.[32] In 1728 they lifted restrictions on ravenduck cloth, grain, and tobacco and eliminated some state monopolies, including the salt monopoly.[33] Duties on rye and wheat were reduced.[34] In 1731 they produced a moderately protectionist tariff that brought down ad valorem import duties to a maximum of 20 percent from 70 percent.

For the next few decades, policy vacillated. Export restrictions were re-imposed in the mid–1730s, then in 1741 again removed to allow export of 100,000 chetverti of rye and 15,000 chetverti of wheat from St. Petersburg. From 1739 to 1742, because of protests by the Dutch, limited exports were also permitted from Arkhangel. Between 1746 and 1756 restrictions were reimposed, and in 1756, lifted for a limited amount of 255,000 chetverti of grain (15% wheat) from the two ports together, a limit which is probably a general guide to the level of exports, except during years of prohibition.[35] Meanwhile government interference by direct state trading monopolies and direct subsidies to import-substitution industries grew. Monopoly privileges, which throttled economic growth, were accompanied by the constant resort to the debasement of coinage and confiscation of land, which brought one-time gains. During the Seven Years' War, the Russian government averaged about 240,000 rubles a year from the trading monopoly of grain, thus saving the costs of customs collections and providing steady revenues for war.[36] Nearly constant warfare explains the persistent pattern of fiscal priorities of early modern monarchies. Survival was at stake, as Douglass North and Robert Thomas wrote: "a monarch could seldom, if ever, afford the luxury of contemplating the consequences of reform and revenues several years hence."[37]

Alternating restrictions and relaxation were in large part a consequence of fear that exports would cause a rise in prices. The Senate claimed to be using customs revenues in part for the construction of off-estate storage facilities, so that the volume of exports would not affect supply in a given year. In an economy where primitive agricultural technology prevailed, both law and public sentiment were powerfully affected by the extreme circumstances that could occur. The low yield of rye in the north, where wheat would not grow, guaranteed frequent food shortages, which were used to justify the attempt to control food production rather than risk experimentation with exports. "Fear of want," wrote Joan Appleby about seventeenth-century England, "secured the poor's support for laws that controlled the rich, and the rioting that often accompanied grain movements during times of scarcity made the laws acceptable to the gentry and nobility who had the responsibility for maintaining order in the countryside."[38] In eighteenth-century Russia, where the main implement was the simple wooden plow (*sokha*), and the labor force was enserfed, the uncertainties of the weather and the inadequacies of the transportation network combined to produce a timid approach to exportation. Exports were blamed for price hikes and famine during periods of harvest failure.[39]

Liberals of the 1750s found their point of entry in this unproven association between exports and higher prices, the rationale upon which the entire edifice of barriers to trade rested. The volume of exports was a very small portion of the volume of the yearly grain crop. Exports to the army during the war had not in fact affected prices.[40] Even mercantilists, who were fearful of the rise in prices, sometimes puzzled over the value of holding back the export of grain and other raw materials.[41] The most convinced mercantilist and self-proclaimed upholder of Petrine principles, Peter Ivanovich Shuvalov, was the most enthusiastic exponent of export expansion. He recommended in 1758 that a Commission be created in the Senate to expand commerce, create new credit facilities, open commercial consulates, encourage new starts in manufacturing, and examine the effect of state trading monopolies to determine if products such as grain should be exported freely, at least through Arkhangel.[42] He was responsible for the most important single enactment of commercial policy before the 1760s, the abolition in 1753 of all internal tariffs, including local "bridge" taxes paid by the peasants, and transport and other taxes paid by urban dwellers, as well as tariffs which inhibited transport of goods and internal trade.[43]

Yet Shuvalov occasionally opposed what the liberals sought. He compensated for the 13 kopecks per ruble loss from repeal of internal tariffs, to increase revenues by 13 percent. These rates were confirmed in a stiff protectionist tariff issued in 1757, designed to help finance the campaigns of the Seven Years' War.[44] He raised the salt tax. His many projects in the 1740s and 1750s, including the creation of the first two Russian banks, the Nobles' Bank and the Bank for the Improvement of the Trade of St. Petersburg, known as the Commercial Bank,[45] mainly subsidized wealthy merchants and nobles and their enterprises, although they also improved conditions of commerce, and, most important, put money into circulation. His great achievement was the debasement of copper coins in 1756. From nearly 11 million rubles minted between 1757 and 1761 came a profit of 6 million rubles for the treasury. Head of the project, he avoided paying the market price for copper, since, as artillery master, he was able to melt down cannons and procure copper from treasury factories.[46] In other words, much of his effort was designed to relieve the treasury from some of its dependence on direct taxes.[47]

The criticism Shuvalov encountered was for the corruption he had fostered.[48] Critics pointed out that all of his policies were in some measure designed to assist the accumulation of his own fortune.[49] He used state monopolies over fisheries and tobacco sales to perpetuate a life of extreme luxury and an income of more than 200,000 rubles.[50] His critics observed that the bank for commercial credit he created in 1754 loaned out almost its entire reserve to a few leading merchants, and that it was a failure as an experiment because of corruption and mismanagement.[51] Shuvalov was the driving force behind economic development in the 1750s, but he

TABLE II

Revenues in Russia in the Eighteenth Century* (in millions of rubles and percent)									
Sources	1724		1749		1758		1769		1795	
	R	%	R	%	R	%	R	%	R	%
Direct	4.7	55	5.4	55	5.4	36	10.5	43	26.0	36
Indirect	2.8	33	3.3	33	7.6	51	10.3	43	35.1	49
Other	1.0	12	1.2	12	2.0	13	3.3	14	10.7	15
Total	8.5	100	9.9	100	15	100	24.1	100	71.8	100

*I. G. Spasskii, A. I. Iukht, "Finansy, Denezhnoe Obrashchenie," *Ocherki russkoi kul'tury XVIII veka* (Moscow, 1987), p. 110.

differed little from his mercantilist predecessors and fellow members of the ruling Senate who believed in subsidizing and farming out the management of state trade to the wealthy court nobles and merchants, considered to be the most "productive" individuals.[52] This kind of regime had efficiencies in the collection of customs duties and security for the state against the risk of uncertain revenues, but corruption and contraband were its pernicious effects.[53] As J. H. Hexter wrote, "The eighteenth century was no doubt the twilight of the old regime, but only a bold prophet could have been certain that it was the moment before the dawn of the new."[54]

Russian Exports

The formation of an opposition, its penetration by physiocracy—the maturation of a new point of view about prices and markets—and its persuasion of the monarch to use his or her vast powers over law to direct the course of economic growth: these intellectual developments were responsible for some of the most significant and formative changes in policy in the eighteenth century. The vying for influence over economic policy reflected a political transition that can scarcely be understood without considering the growth that the government was witnessing. In a steady climb, exports rose from roughly 5 million rubles in the early 1740s to 53 million in current rubles in 1793–1797, or by 1,058 percent.[55]

Much of this rise took place as a consequence of activity at ports. The government became aware that Russia was potentially a sea power. "Can we think of a country better positioned for commerce than Russia," wrote Sukin in 1760, "with its command over five seas!"[56] By contrast, as the senator N. E. Murav'ev wrote to Catherine in 1763, overland foreign trade was considered "of very little importance."[57] Even virtually without a merchant marine, statesmen believed Russia was capable of considerably expanding its overseas foreign trade.[58] Russian merchants failed to reap the profits that countries dominating shipping could acquire. In the 1770s, two-thirds of all the ships carrying Russian goods belonged to England and Holland (the Dutch had more in number, the English more in tonnage.)[59]

TABLE III

**Trade Turnover
and State Revenue from Customs Collections***
(in thousands of rubles)

Year	Imports	Exports	Balance	Revenue
1742	3,568	4,567	8,135	950
1743	4,501	4,240	8,741	1,060
1744	3,703	5,916	9,619	1,001
1745	3,899	5,249	9,148	1,031
1746	4,193	5,268	9,461	1,055
1747	3,499	5,402	8,901	950
1748	4,304	4,624	8,928	886
1749	4,508	5,337	9,845	1,052
1750	6,013	7,153	13,166	1,227
1751	5,957	6,596	12,553	1,230
1752	7,003	5,932	12,935	1,427
1753	5,915	7,458	13,373	1,460
1754	5,160	7,240	12,400	2,134
1755	6,642	8,183	14,825	2,412
1756	6,601	8,005	14,606	2,320
1757	6,084	8,195	14,279	2,516
1758	6,353	8,663	15,016	2,559
1759	8,003	9,602	17,605	2,654
1760	7,358	9,875	17,233	2,625
1761	7,181	9,724	16,905	2,669
1762	8,162	12,762	20,924	2,881

*S. M. Troitskii, *Finansovaia politika russkogo absoliutizma v XVIII v.* (Moscow, 1966), pp. 185–186.

The consequences of the lack of a merchant marine were outweighed to Russian statesmen by the enormous potential that ports provided in a sea-faring age. Government officials looked for models for expansion to the sea powers of Europe. The Dutch in particular represented a kind of "anti-fairy tale," having earned their riches by prudence and manipulation of markets. Amsterdam was the great commercial and banking center of Europe; the Dutch were indispensable neutral carriers, and the regulator of rates of exchange.[60] "Envy and wonder," as Joyce Appleby wrote in reference to England, "stimulated a great deal of economic thinking."[61] Murav'ev called the Dutch "the new Phoenicians."[62] Peter III, wrote a member of his court, "preferred the Dutch to all other nations."[63] He made plans to send members of the Evreinov family, relatives of the president of the Commerce College, to open a consulate at The Hague,[64] and at the time of his death he was about to sign a treaty of commerce with the Dutch.[65] His plan for a new commercial policy favored both the British and the Dutch in their seafaring capacity: in separate enactments he lightened tariffs and eased restrictions in the Baltic ports they dominated. By a special decree on January 30, 1762, for example, before his general commercial enactment, he allowed unlimited export of linseed from Revel (present-day Tallin), a trade dominated by Dutch merchants.[66] He hoped to rebuild the navy and establish a merchant fleet, and he planned to send twenty to thirty apprentices to work in the British navy.[67] One of the technical schools that he planned to carve out of the former Cadet Corps was for the training of shipbuilders and seamen.[68] His grand aspiration to create a new era is captured in the preface to his enactment of March 28: "We have superior ports. We can reach Asia . . . and through Orenburg, we can travel to India . . . and to the shores of America. The road to . . . Egypt and Africa by the Black Sea is there if unexplored."[69] This was a vision of empire based upon the expansion of trade.[70]

To Peter, the needs of trade compelled Russia to take a different approach, to depart from the system of preferential tariffs by which Peter I had given the port of St. Petersburg dominance over trade. St. Petersburg—and the British who were the main traders there beginning in the 1730s and 1740s—commanded the country's export of hemp, flax (used for cordage and sailcloth), timber, masts, tar, and pitch, strategic materials used in shipbuilding. Demand was steady. Russian hemp and flax were "much wanted by all nations in a state of warfare."[71] The British were also vital in the sale of Russian iron, upon which British industry depended until the end of the century when its own iron became more competitive. Because of their primacy in trade, beginning in the trade treaties of 1734 and 1766, the British had special privileges in Russian ports, including after 1766 the right to pay customs duties in Russian currency.

Peter aspired not so much to reverse this outcome of Petrine tariff policy as to restore closer connections with the Dutch, by attending to conditions of trade at Riga, Revel, and Arkhangel where the Dutch trade remained vital. Goods sold through Riga, Revel and Narva (hemp and flax seed, grain, and hides), largely from the Baltic and the Ukraine, were of a high quality. They were used in Dutch whalelines and fisheries—particularly hemp, which was of a strong harle and better than the hemp sold in St. Petersburg.[72] The emphasis that Peter III's policy would bring to Russian trade through these Baltic ports showed both that Russia intended to be more competitive on the market for higher quality goods and that in the world of finances, the Dutch still commanded some influence over the Russian government. The rate of exchange on the ruble for almost the whole century continued to be estimated by the exchange at Amsterdam.[73]

Competition for Markets

The central arena for Russia's commercial expansion was the Baltic. Russia's trade relations with Sweden, Prussia, and Poland, the other suppliers of raw materials to western Europe, were constrained. At mid-century, Russian iron exports did not yet surpass those of Sweden. Much of the grain exported from Narva and Revel was grown in the Baltic and Poland. Early in the century, the best hemp and flax came from the Baltic. The necessity of confronting evidence that exports of grain from the Baltic were producing abundance in that region while dearth persisted in Russia produced—with help from physiocracy—the belief that the government could and should create better conditions for agriculture. Physiocracy gave the government in the 1750s new guidelines by which it would actively interfere to create mechanisms for improving production, rerouting trade to save costs, and controlling quality in order to become more competitive.

Competition in the Baltic with the Swedes and Prussians in the export of iron and grain made all the more attractive the development of new trade outlets in the south and east, where Swedish and Prussian competition would not stand in the way. The lucrative trade with Iran through Astrakhan, the only port to be dominated by Russian ships, had particularly lustrous potential. Trade relations had formed in the 1580s, when formal diplomatic ties were established. The state trade consisted of raw silk, carpets, and jewels from Iran traded for Russian furs, metals, and foreign textiles. Private traders imported silk wares, leather goods, and cotton used in Russia's rising domestic cottage production and exported Russian and transshipped foreign goods. The steady profits, amounting to about 24,000 rubles a year in the 1750s,[74] and local hazards of trade led the government to believe it might control the risk more effectively by creating a trading company on the model of the Dutch and English companies. The state farmed out monopoly trading concessions to Russian merchants in Astrakhan.[75]

The Lessons of Failure

The disastrous effect of state interference was a strong rebuff in the 1750s to the principles that had generated it. Experiments aroused the protest of local merchants and claims of damage done to trade. The Russian trading company went bankrupt in less than two years, whether through incompetence and/or underinvestment of capital, and the price-fixing and other advantages given to the monopolists in fishing suppressed local trade.[76] Before, with sufficient investment, a merchant was able to sustain a loss of several hundred thousand rubles in a single year; afterwards, in one year the total value of goods exported from Astrakhan to Iran did not amount to more than 29,367 rubles.[77] Silk ceased to be delivered to Russian factories; state revenues fell to one-tenth of what they had been.[78] There was a reduction of silk shipped abroad. This sudden loss was perceived as a lesson in policy formation.

Russia's experience with the China trade was another lesson. The Treaty of Kiakhta of 1727, which governed Russo-Chinese trade, set up a government monopoly, which restricted sales. In 1737, cabinet ministers questioned the benefits of the state monopoly. They drew on the counter-example of "Holland and the East India company, which permitted a public auction every three months."[79] In 1739, the government attempted to disband the state trade, but since no other traders expressed interest in taking it over, reimposed it in 1753. Government-organized caravans crossed the country in principle every three years. Yet the trade was continually disrupted by border disputes, and due to fears of losing the cargo the government sent no other caravans after 1755. The goods were sold on public auction.[80] Between 1728 and 1760, the China trade was broken off entirely six times.[81] The items traded were potentially of value. Imports through Kiakhta consisted of silks, cotton goods, rhubarb, and tea and exports of furs and textiles.[82]

Rhubarb was one of the main staples of the "distant, exotic, and chancey" commerce overland from China to Europe, where it was considered a remedy for gastric disorders and was much in demand.[83] It was singled out as a reason for abandoning the state monopoly. Because of fixed prices, excess supply rotted in the bins at St. Petersburg.[84]

Complaints about the state of trade and ambitions to achieve economic goals through manipulation of trade converged into a common program during the Seven Years' War. Inevitable interruptions of trade during the war were worrisome: foreign sources of silver and reserves were depleted. Meanwhile, the demand for Russian grain in the Baltic rose, in part due to wartime supply needs and in part due to incidental harvest failure in Finland in 1760 and 1761.[85] Affected by the popular movement in Europe for freeing the grain trade from restrictions, which had reached a pitched battle cry in France,[86] Russian policy makers moved to follow their direction.

The Opposition

Institutions and the Conduct of Trade

The attraction of new markets and complaints about state trade prompted the rise of an opposition at the highest levels of government during the intensely competitive years of the Seven Years' War. The reason why criticism was not immediately followed by a shift in policy was that a single institution, the ruling Senate, maintained command over commercial affairs with rights to conduct the state trade and to distribute monopolies and concessions to its own members. It had a stake in maintaining its protectionist policies and a responsibility for meeting the fiscal demands of the ruler. To challenge commercial policy was to challenge the very agenda of government.

Customarily, the Senate managed exports by delicate maneuvers and rescindable partial measures. Typical of its approach was the effort to improve quality of output of hemp, Russia's main export, by exhortation. As it had been doing since the early years of the eighteenth century, the Senate issued decrees and launched investigations of the discipline of brackers of hemp, officials charged with enforcing and certifying uniform standards.[87] One decree complained that "because brackers do not fulfill their responsibility, half-cleaned Polish hemp transported through Prussia is considered better than fully cleaned Russian hemp. It is extremely important that we restore the 'credit' of our hemp."[88] Equally typical was a tendency to allow liberalizing laws to stay in force only briefly. It was difficult for the senators to anticipate the consequences of laws affecting trade, such as lifting restrictions in general or at a single port. Overland exports of Russian hemp, flax and their seeds, iuft (a low-quality tanned leather), rope, and other goods, for example, were permitted on November 18, 1754, for the sake of expansion of commerce, but prohibited again on December 11 because of fear of the effect on trade through St. Petersburg.[89] The virtue of such an approach lay in its flexibility, since the volume of grain exports could respond quickly to foreign demand in time of famine and also be mindful of problems of local supply.[90] Its flaw lay in its unpredictability for foreign customers and local peasants.

The Senate returned proposals for a drastic change in policy, including one by its own general procurator, Nikita Trubetskoi, who in 1758 advocated freeing the grain trade from restraint.[91] The consequence of its resistance during a period when revenue needed to be expanded was that a more dynamic leadership began to gain control. During the Seven Years' War, foreign commerce was moved to the agenda of several institutions. In 1760 and 1761, the Senate's newly created commerce commission reviewed numerous projects for the improvement of foreign trade submitted by merchants, factory owners, and statesmen.[92] The Senate's codification commission also assumed it had the right to make laws regarding foreign trade. All the proposals tended in the same direction. The bluntest exposition of the liberal position of the Russian court in the 1750s and early 1760s is from a passage in a version completed sometime before 1760 of Part III of the new proposed law code:[93]

> Nothing is so harmful to the merchantry or so damaging to the public as monopolies . . . because prices are fixed. . . . We will not have laws granting privileges or establishing monopolies in the export, shipping, and exchange of any good . . . and we will abolish those that exist, firmly granting merchants freedom in commerce and manufacturing.[94]

This passage illustrates the scope of the attack launched against the Senate's control over trade by one of its own commissions.

The most important of the Senate's rivals in commercial policy was the Conference at the Imperial Court, which had responsibility for coordinating the war effort and financial means of supporting it. Without consulting the Senate, the Conference allowed the Anglo-Russian commercial treaty to remain in force after it had expired.[95] In 1756 without requesting permission the Conference took on the task of "improving trade at Riga in order to attract Polish goods now sold through Prussia, and to increase Russian trade thereby diminishing Prussian trade."[96] It sought to use the grain trade as a tool of foreign policy. Diplomats were ordered to gather detailed information about prices for Russian and foreign goods in order to estimate the capacity for increasing Russian exports and improving the rate of exchange.[97] In 1760 and 1761, new proposals were made for further liberalization.

In the difficult campaigns of late 1760 and early 1761, the Conference took advantage of a low point in the war to assume broad regulatory authority over the Senate's activities in general and foreign trade in particular. On January 5, 1761, the Conference sent a message to the Senate that there would be a new order of command for the sake of administrative efficiency. Colleges would prepare reports; the Senate would examine them and send comments to the Conference; the Conference would make the decision; and the monarch would either confirm or seek further consultation on disagreements that arose between the Senate and the Conference.[98] The idea, as historian of the Senate A. P. Presniakov put it, was that "Russia should have an institution . . . with generally broad authority over the whole political system and control over internal politics."[99]

Having attempted in this way to challenge the Senate's prerogatives, the declaration of January 5, which was written by the Conference secretary, Dmitrii Volkov, went on to dictate an entirely new commercial policy.[100] The Senate was not prepared for this. Shuvalov in particular struggled to keep certain questions off the agenda of the Conference.[101] Volkov later described the outcome.

> The ideas . . . which I submitted in writing to the previous Conference, remained unrealized because no one had the courage to confront Peter Ivanovich [Shuvalov.] This matter was by no means conceived incautiously. I had taken the advice of Ivan Ivanovich Kostiurin,[102] Adam Vasil'evich Olsuf'ev,[103] and Iakov Matveevich Evreinov,[104] who declared orally and Olsuf'ev even in writing, that they could view nothing better or more useful . . . [105]

On February 8, Shuvalov had it sent back to the commerce commission with the observation that the proposal was "not useful to the state."[106] The disagreements between Shuvalov and his opponents are on record.[107] The political liability of high grain prices and the immediate loss from the lucrative monopolies that many of the senators enjoyed led the government into a serious political conflict.

The Volkov Proposal

The substance of Volkov's proposal is important, since it is the foundation of all future enactments on commerce in the early 1760s. His position can be seen in two documents prepared while he was developing this proposal. In a letter to his friend and colleague, the chair of the commerce commission, Ivan Chernyshev, on December 19, 1760, Volkov showed a clear sense of the need to reformulate commercial policy. State trading monopolies were among "artificial mechanisms" which interfered with trade to its disadvantage. "We should begin freely to export agricultural products, including those which have been prohibited from time to time. We should remove all duties from items or subject them to light duties that cannot be felt." Lumber and wood products should be allowed to be exported from Narva. "From such a fertile country as Russia," grain should be able to be purchased at all ports. Iron, he acknowledged, was "not competitive with Swedish iron." Nevertheless, it could be exported in much greater quantities to the English, who would purchase the cheaper product. Citing the example of the decline of the silk trade with Persia as a consequence of mismanagement by the Russian trading company in Astrakhan: "We have been clearly shown that trade dominated by the state tends to decline."[108] Where trade and profits cease to expand, the state should cease interference. The most important reason for the new policy was to stop the outward flow of gold and silver, "the exhaustion of the reserves of the treasury and of the country itself."[109] The urgency that he and others felt, not knowing when the war would end, is captured by his comment that "We could sit quietly until peace brings the monetary crisis to an end, or, since peace may not come for years, we can watch the silver ruble disappear."[110]

The second document was the Conference proposal advanced by Volkov and Chernyshev less than a month later at the January 5, 1761, meeting of the

Conference.[111] Here Volkov attacked non-"economic" thinking with some stridency. He accused those who had made policy in the past, i.e., the senators, of "error larger than the limits of one's astonishment."[112] He complained of the futility of attempting to affect the balance of payments by curtailing the import of luxuries. Our trading partners, he wrote, "are clever people experienced in commerce" who will respond by not purchasing Russian goods. Our own subjects will be thrown out of work and will be good for the state "only in the sense that they eat bread."

Decisions taken in the past had an enormous and negative impact on markets and profits, he wrote. For example, yarn and cloth, which were in demand in the 1740s but prohibited from export in the 1750s, lost their markets. In Europe substitutes were found. By allowing such products to once again be freely exported, the treasury might lose a hundred or two hundred thousand rubles in customs—a sum lost in any case when exports were prohibited. As trade expanded, millions of silver rubles would flow in the country and peasants would find work.

Limits on the export or iron and lumber were unwarranted, he continued. "The only guiding principle has been the conservation of forests." Forests did need to be preserved; replanting compensated society in the future. But exports were the least source of deforestation, by contrast with the use of wood for houses, fuel, manufacturing, and particularly distilling. True, prices had risen so that barges cost more than the load the bore. The problem was not fixed resources but the way the resource was managed.

To have permited monopolies was a mistake. "The more workers in a craft, the less we need a monopoly." Gains in trade were temporary and small by comparison with uncompensated long-term loss. For example, in the case of Iran, "in 1732 and 1735 we ceded territory to Persia," he wrote, "but won important trading rights." Merchants became rich. What had led to ruin was the imposition of monopolies. If trade were freed from restraint, foreigners might settle in Astrakhan again with guarantees of freedom of worship, freedom from local taxes, and the right to build factories that were not taxed.

Grain was the last point on his list. Citing the example of the province of Lithuania, "exports [from Riga] greatly encouraged agriculture" and did not result in scarcity "as everyone had believed." In the fall, grain could be withheld from the market, and a portion of the harvest saved in storage. Eventually, as the supply of grain became more abundant, the amount to be stored could be reduced. Town governments could take over storage arrangements. Prices would rise. But if, by contrast, they remained low, no one would be better off but owners of distilleries.[113]

In summary, Volkov's proposal rested on an "economic" approach to trade and a cameralist approach to politics. Under his leadership, the opposition achieved both political force and a new program. Volkov challenged the Senate. In Elizabeth's reign, he was unsuccessful. In Peter's reign, the atmosphere was more amenable to a new trade policy. What was different was a new set of imperatives—the Emperor's plans for another war—that made the expansion of revenues and the overcoming of opposition in the Senate an urgent priority.

The Fiscal System and Commercial Policy: 1762

The extravagance of Elizabeth's court and her expenditures on the army abroad, which amounted to over 43.4 million rubles in the first four years of war[114]—almost three times the annual revenues of the empire—made every item of revenues a target of concern. One of the key sources of revenue in the 1750s was the state monopoly of the trade of salt and spirits.[115] These taxes on salt and spirits, which had been one of the bases of Shuvalov's policies, now reached some 24 percent of all revenues (see Table I) and this was the maximum considered collectible. The rigidity of these revenues is the main reason that the search for new resources was launched and along with it the careers of the Russian physiocrats. A description of budgetary resources under Peter III helps explain his acceptance of a full program of policy reversals.

The largest part of revenues, 34 percent of the total, derived as in all early modern states from direct taxation. In Russia, the poll tax was levied on adult male peasants and serfs, and paid directly to the government by the serfs and by the ecclesiastical peasants, until the completion of secularization in 1764. The remaining peasants and taxable population also paid an obrok (or money due per male soul) raised in 1760 from 40 kopecks for peasants and free householders and 50 for townspeople to 1 ruble for all, and raised again for former ecclesiastical peasants to 1 ruble 50 kopecks. The fact that despite the rise in obrok, the poll tax itself remained at 70 kopecks for almost the entire eighteenth century and that it was sometimes lowered during years of famine, shows that this was not an area in which a new ruler would seek an increase.[116]

During periods of war, there was a tendency for indirect taxes to grow relative to direct taxes, in part to relieve the nobles from burdens other than recruitment. In the category of indirect taxes, however, were only the already high salt and spirit taxes, along with the many "chancery" taxes on miscellaneous items such as stamped paper, bridges, and leases of government-owned or -controlled enterprises such as fisheries, flour mills, and so forth, which amounted to 6 percent of the annual budget.[117] To turn to indirect taxes was not a solution that would be effective in a financial crisis.

A more vital source of revenue expansion during periods of unusual need was the reminting operations and the debasement of the currency. During the reign of Peter I, the silver content in coins was continually reduced, an operation producing a steady revenue of about 200,000 rubles a year; beginning in 1723, the government also minted copper coins and considered issuing paper notes.[118] In this way, financial needs were met. Concern in subsequent years about contraband led in 1731 to retreat from debasement; silver coins were reminted with a higher silver content, while copper was maintained at a fixed value. That situation lasted until the Seven Years' War, which produced further manipulation of the money supply. In 1756, copper pieces were reissued at 16 rather than 8 rubles per pud. The copper money was placed in circulation by loans (at 6% interest compared to rates of up to 20% on the private market) from two new banks created for that purpose, the Bank

Comptoir for the Circulation of Copper Money within Russia and the Bank of the Artillery and Engineering Corps.[119] From 1757 to 1761 10,977,349 rubles were created, two and one-half times more than the entire amount of copper money issued for the past sixteen years.[120] Pressure on finances continued to mount. In 1760 Shuvalov offered an even more ambitious proposal for the further debasement of copper and silver. He suggested increasing the supply of copper money to 16 million rubles in all and issuing new coins minted at 32 rubles a pud, rather than 16. Together with the reminting of silver, he promised a gain of over 20 million rubles over the next 16 years. This was the idea to which Peter would immediately turn.[121]

Recovery

At his accession, Peter had to deal not only with the deficit but also with additional debts that came due immediately: his own debts as Grand Duke, a million rubles to those who helped his elevation to the throne, 700,000 of his aunt's debts, 50,000 run up by his mistress, and 200,000 already incurred for the defense of his duchy.[122] Military and civilian staff had not been paid for the second half of 1761, and the treasury was short by an unknown amount.[123]

To pay personal debts, he used a stash of gold coins and silver found in Elizabeth's wardrobe at her death. The silver he reminted over the next six months.[124] Then he began to scour existing accounts for unused funds. He demanded a financial statement from the Senate.[125] He stalled projects that required personnel, including the Land Survey, claiming an insufficiency of staff and funds.[126] On January 17, 1762, a few weeks after taking power, he accepted the Senate's recommendation to revive Shuvalov's proposal for reminting coins. He recalled sixteen million copper rubles for reminting at twice the value and announced a similar measure for silver.[127] In part a defensive measure, since Prussia and Sweden had devaluated currency in 1761, increasing the necessity for Russia to do the same,[128] reminting was also a way to subsidize the indebted nobility. He increased the capital available for loans from the copper bank from two to six million rubles, using funds from the debasement of copper and silver.[129] He claimed to have wanted to subsidize industry and commerce by small loans.[130] The result of the expansion of capital, however, was the same pattern of lending as in the past. Mikhail Vorontsov, for one, borrowed 180,000 rubles at once and within months requested another 300,000, this time obtaining it without interest.[131] On May 25 Peter III announced yet another experiment, the establishment of an assignat bank (which never came into existence)[132] backed by three million rubles both in silver and copper, a sum he intended to increase over a period of three years.[133] By the end of six months, there was a two and one-half million ruble increase in the volume of money in circulation[134] and the promise of more, which encouraged the Senate to help finance his campaign.[135]

This operation showed that the government could gain money for war by enlarging domestic resources.[136] The consequences of debasement, however, were costly both in domestic disturbance and foreign financial markets. There was discouraging news on the negotiation of a loan from two Dutch bankers. Under no circumstances could they give the preferred rate of 4 percent, and even at the higher rate of 6 or 7 percent the bankers declined to lend.[137] The market for lending in the eighteenth century was narrow, since only those with something to pawn could borrow. The only way to widen the market was to offer different kinds of security and to promise an increase in revenues apart from the reminting operation. Beginning in 1762, with Peter III's unsuccessful request, and ending in 1768,[138] with a successfully negotiated loan, the government used commercial expansion as a means to gain confidence of bankers of the United Provinces who could take customs revenues in the Baltic as security on a loan.

The Enactment of March 28

The provisions of the commercial enactment of March 28, 1762, therefore turned first to the issue of grains, which were likely to increase Dutch trade in Russia. The first provision opened up all ports, including St. Petersburg, Arkhangel, and ports on the Caspian and Black Seas, to the export of grain, with one-half of the customary charge at Baltic ports, Revel, Riga, and Pernov (present-day Piarnu). This provision reversed the preferential structure of Petrine tariffs by which St. Petersburg maintained its advantage. In the second provision, attention was paid to Ukraine, where reform in the 1750s had already opened up free trade in grain.[139] This provision allowed salted meat and livestock to be exported overseas. Ukrainian bulls were traditionally herded through Poland, with a loss in profits due to costs of transportation. The object of this provision, which allowed export and reduced tariffs at ports to half the rate collected at overland crossings, was to redirect the herding of cattle to Baltic ports to make cattle and cattle products cheaper for Russia's maritime trade partners and more profitable for the treasury.

The third provision was focused on Arkhangel, where the tallow industry had been protected by export prohibitions and import tariffs since the beginning of the century.[140] It removed this protection, letting cattle, seals, and other sources of tallow, along with tallow itself, be traded freely to bring advantages to shipping which had been stymied by export prohibitions and protected by import tariffs at St. Petersburg. Another provision improved general conditions of trade at Arkhangel by the removal of a 2 percent surcharge on imports and of all prohibitions. Arkhangel was a valuable port in that the sea lanes leading into the harbor could not easily be blocked in times of war, and, as a consequence, there was always a steady flow of customs revenues. Beginning in Peter's reign, there were increased exports of forest products (pitch and tar), tallow, linseed, and grains, for which demand by northern German cities and the Netherlands was constant. Dutch ships were large, producing the benefit of economies of scale, and Russian grain markets in Kazan and Siberia were accessible by the northern Dvina and Volga Rivers.[141] Hopes of expanding trade at this port can be seen by the intent to establish a commercial office in Arkhangel for the roughly 250 foreign merchants to give them "all the privileges, advantages and freedom that they enjoy at other ports."

The seventh provision released the more costly products, rhubarb, cloth and yarn, pitch, tar, and potash, from prohibitions and monopolies, and protected cloth and sugar factories from duty free import of technology and chemicals. The ninth eliminated merchant companies and state monopolies in the Persian trade and through the Black Sea to Constantinople to encourage local traders, Italians, and Greeks to find easier access to Russian cities and ports. Further study was recommended of the consequences of exporting lumber and wood products,[142] and no comment was made in reference to the export of iron, but the decree ended by remarking, "All trade should be without restraint."[143] The rationale as advanced in the enactment was physiocratic, the encouragement of "producers and traders."

> Our grain could feed the world, as witnessed by the large quantity of grain used up by distilling spirits, and . . . prices still so low that peasants only harvest enough grain to pay their dues. The richest grain areas have vast unsown fields. . . . We began to think that We could conduct extensive trade in grain while encouraging output.[144]

There was also concern about the fall in the rate of exchange of the ruble, which would not improve with further debasement. There was embarrassment at the damage that government interference in trade had done: "The English use trading companies in India to make profits, build fortresses, and enhance the grandeur of the nation while surmounting the hazards of private trade." The Russian companies were, by contrast, "a refuge for bankrupt merchants." For all these reasons, because of the mistakes of the past and the necessity of an overhall of policy, it was not enough, the decree stated, to cut expenses and reduce consumption of luxuries. "Economic principles" taught that "crafts and industry must be made more profitable." "Each and every able person should participate in trade . . . earn a little more than his needs. . . . Only commerce can produce this result."[145]

In its sweep of all ports and nearly all exported products, the decree would bring monumental change with foreign policy implications. Peter for the first time allowed Persia to import iron and hemp, used for military supplies, as well as grain. In order to create new opportunities for trade and rebuild a relationship that had faltered, he ordered a commercial consulate to be founded there.[146] By allowing unlimited quantities of raw materials, new finished products such as linen cloth, and a general large-scale reduction of tariffs, for example on grain of 80 to 20 kopecks per chetvert', he sought to enhance conditions of trade for British and Dutch merchants, but particularly the Dutch who had more trade at previously disadvantaged ports, such as Arkhangel. Another direct beneficiary, Sweden, which by custom included permission to buy grain in its treaties with Russia, was gratified in its current petition during Peter's reign to renew this deal, broken off during the war. Since trade at Kiakhta was opened up to all merchants, Peter could now hope to resolve the border difficulties with China. He sent an envoy to Peking "to confirm a treaty of peace between our two great states and to solidify relations."[147]

The Senate's Response

The boldness of the idea was in contrast to the tentativeness of the wording. At once inexperienced and ambitious, Peter struck out a half-century of prohibitions. Meanwhile, reaffirming his hesitance in his first announcement of January 17, where he noted that if there were reservations, existing regulations "would not be lifted entirely,"[148] in the concluding words of the enactment, he added: "We recommend freeing trade from restrictions, but this recommendation should not be taken as compulsory. . . . Specific implementation needs a great deal of further planning. . . . The Senate should present a plan about precautionary measures." In Peter's enactment, there was a deliberate softening of the language and clear effort to compromise with those who disagreed. A careful distinction was made between merchant (kupecheskie) companies, which would be abolished, and state trading monopolies, which would be subject to further review.

His hesitance points to the political difficulties of encouraging acceptance of change among a powerful elite which had for almost a half century dominated commercial policy in its own way. The link between the political and economic spheres under absolutism had by now been strengthened by thirty years of government-sponsored monopolies. Throughout the 1750s, merchant and noble monopolies multiplied.[149] New trading concessions were confirmed during Peter's reign, as was the vast fortune the merchant Shemiakin had built upon the farming of customs revenues, an empire within an empire allowed to exist "because there have not been any specific complaints,"[150] which was not the case.[151] Even under Catherine, despite prohibitions, monopolies continued to exist, and state assets were given in large amounts to the elite of the nobility. The long-established link was not likely to be attacked in Russia as decisively as it had been attacked by an autocrat such as Joseph II. Neither Peter for financial reasons nor Catherine for political reasons could entirely dismantle privileges of the elite at court.

Peter's predicament was that the Senate, the chief legislative body since the Conference at the Imperial Court had been abolished, was determined to resist this new challenge to its authority. There is no sign that the senators had any intention of abiding by the new legislation. On January 30, the procurator general and the vice chancellor granted themselves an eight-year renewal of their monopoly of the export of Ukrainian wheat from Riga and Revel and Russian wheat from Arkhangel.[152] By March, the Senate was ready for confrontation. Peter III and Volkov were proposing commercial regulations that contained the same provisions that the Senate had rejected the previous year. General procurator of the Senate Aleksandr Glebov gave Volkov an "oral report about Commerce."[153] "Not receiving an answer to his report," Volkov wrote, Glebov "waited, assuming it would be accepted, due to some mistake or misunderstanding."[154] A sense of heated discussion is felt in Volkov's attack on "false theories" advanced by the senators.[155] Later, apparently still in anger, Volkov remarked to Chernyshev that "a very small number of greedy people profit while society suffers."[156]

The senators used in their response a summary of the essence of the decree as they saw it, "The Destruction of Monopolies and the Establishment of complete Freedom of Trade."[157] On April 18, April 22, and May 20, they urged its repeal.[158] Although they concurred that trade with China should be open to all merchants, they restored the rhubarb monopoly, among the most lucrative of the state's regalias to be abolished, at least until the present supply was sold. "The treasury must not suffer such a loss."[159] Lumber and wood products could be freely exported at only one port, Narva.[160] Tar could be exported freely, they wrote, but not potash and pitch because of the threat to the supply of lumber. Customs on narrow cloth and rough yarn, needed by the army, should be retained. Customs at Riga and Arkhangel should not be reduced because of the loss to the treasury. Monopolies formerly belonging to Shuvalov (seals and fisheries at Arkhangel, and the export of tobacco abroad) and those for the sale of glue and fish in Astrakhan could be dismantled, but trading concessions in general were governed by contracts which should be held "sacred and inviable"[161] The senators criticized Shemiakin's abuse of his tax-farming operation, but they confirmed the contract.

Coming to the most important provision, the senators urged that "with God's help, much more wisdom and concern might be shown for grain storage and shortages, as weighed against the expansion of trade."[162] This was especially necessary, they wrote, at Arkhangel; grain should only be exported when there was an abundance. They wrote that for 1762, there were already signs of coming danger:

> Governor General Braun of Lifland [present-day Latvia] has submitted a report about the effects of grain export, shortages and higher prices. He has therefore petitioned us to prohibit grain exports. . . . We agree with the Governor General's recommendation, although we know that we are powerless to command that grain be exempted from export after an imperial ukas has [decreed otherwise].[163]

Not all senators shared this objection. Roman Vorontsov's response is interesting, since too often he has been misidentified as an opponent of the issues important to the Shuvalovs and Volkov and Glebov.[164] Roman allied himself on this issue with the physiocrats and wrote a statement that vindicated himself with the Emperor:

> It can be anticipated that the response of the ruling Senate will have harmful effects on the economy of the country and the monarchy, and I could never concur; in the first place, a rise in grain prices would benefit Russian grain producers and thus create incentives for the improvement of agriculture; in the second place, allowing exports from Riga, which attracts grain from Russian provinces as well as from Poland and Kurland, will benefit merchants involved in the export trade; third, if grain is not permitted to be exported, grain will not be brought to Riga and shortages and high prices will result.[165]

The Vorontsovs shared a concern with Volkov about market development, as in a report to Mikhail Vorontsov in 1762 that "if the grain trade is halted, then foreigners will find other markets . . . and peasants will stop bringing their rye to Riga."[166]

Heartened perhaps by Vorontsov's support, over the Senate's objection, on June 1 Peter repromulgated his decree.[167] The same day he issued his well-known admonishment that the senators had no power to make or confirm laws independently.[168] He did not, however, alter any of the Senate's revisions pertaining to monopolies and trade, and so he left the issue of the Senate's prerogatives and the freedom of trade itself as matter for future resolution.

To summarize, the commercial enactment of 1762 went into effect despite opposition. It was motivated in part by physiocratic thought and sponsored by a now politically powerful group at court. On balance, political weight in commercial policy had already shifted in a liberal direction by the time Peter III ascended the throne. The resistance that he encountered in his brief reign was due to institutional conflict: what institution would decide commercial policy? Senators had fixed views about how to deal with scarcity, and they had vested interests in monopolies. They temporarily succeeded in thwarting the implementation of parts of the enactment they were powerless to repeal as a whole. In none of his other enactments did Peter so pit himself against the power and privilege of some of the noble senators. The extent to which he brooked confrontation on this issue is a measure of the importance of this enactment to his financial position and to his foreign policy. He sought to resolve conflict with China and complaints about the Iran trade; he sought advantages with Great Britain, Sweden, the northern German cities, and the United Provinces. The curious twist of the enactment was emphasis on trade through Arkhangel, a city that had long endured a drastic decline. This provision shows on one level Peter's interest in restoring balance and opportunity in all parts of the empire and in emerging from extreme dependency on the British by selecting for special privilege a city frequented by Dutch ships. On another level, he seemed to have been trying to use a rich asset, the vast monopolies of the deceased Shuvalov, as a bargaining chip in the difficult bid for foreign credit. This manipulation of commercial regulations, resented by the senators, was continued with great success by Catherine, who gained for her war against Turkey loans from several countries, including the United Provinces.

Catherine II and the Grain Trade

Peter's housekeeping measures were adopted by Catherine II. His debasement of coins was endorsed. Although Catherine halted the printing of paper money, in a few years she revived the idea in an assignat bank, which lasted through the early nineteenth century.[169] Her main means of emergency financing was much the same as Peter III's had been. The difference was a few years of peace, which gave Catherine time to create a more credible budget and accumulate savings. Her budget was entirely different from Peter's by the late 1760s, when salaries started to be paid for lower-level officials and assignation of revenues to cover costs went through a central clearing office. These operations were so significant that they introduced a new era in Russian financial history.

On July 31 Catherine issued almost the same new commercial regulation as the one of March 28. She announced the abolition of almost all state trading monopolies, excluding, for example, rhubarb.[170] She would no longer renew private monopolies when they expired, and she abolished some immediately. Private trade with China was permitted, and uniform customs would be collected at all ports and border crossings. The export of grain was permitted. This was a beginning of fairly consistent liberalization, leading toward moderate tariffs of 1766 and 1782. However, high export duties continued to be maintained on sheet iron, pitch, and tar in the 1760s.[171] Her policy in commercial affairs did not greatly depart from the policy which was initiated in the 1750s.[172]

Liberalization established a principle in policy. By the end of the century there was a significant increase in the export of all grains, particularly wheat, and considerable improvement in the trade of cattle and timber. Cattle produced nearly half the profits of the principal grains, and timber exports multiplied in value seven times.[173] In 1797 prohibitively high duties were levied on timber exports— increases of two, three, and often five and six times the former rates for various sorts of wood—and in the following year timber export was forbidden entirely. The initial effect of the prohibition, coupled with the impact of the Napoleonic wars, caused a permanent loss to Russia of part of its western European timber market, which had turned to the United States for timber supplies.[174]

Grain in fact was not exported for the better part of the 1760s.[175] The government regularly interfered to prevent it. In France, "Exportation loomed as a mammoth, tentacular pump which voraciously drained the grain from the lifestream of the kingdom."[176] Not so in Russia. Military conflict in the south in the 1760s initially disrupted the implementation of commercial policy. Nevertheless, afterwards, grain exports became significant. In the long term, the general dynamic shows the 1760s and 1770s to have been a turning point: grain was exported only sporadically in the sixteenth and seventeenth centuries; from 1701 to 1761, the average yearly volume was .225 million puds, reaching 2.6 million puds by 1801 and 521 million puds by 1910.[177] The impact of exports on production was felt in areas that serviced the Baltic and White Sea trade. For the second half of the eighteenth and first half of the nineteenth century, the maximum harvests in central and northern Russia were obtained in Baltic and near Arkhangel.[178] Prices in Viatka, Kazan, and the Baltic reflected the fluctuations of the world market.[179] As B. N. Mironov remarked, "Concern for improving the efficiency of grain production was a new phenomenon in the economic life of Russia. Here one must consider the influence of the export of Russian grain. Although the importance of grain exports for agriculture in the 1760s is rarely mentioned in the sources, all the same, it was significant."[180] Although for the country as a whole the percent of output consumed by exports remained small, it increased over the century. In 1700, the export market amounted to an estimated 2.9 percent of output;[181] by 1810, it claimed 25 percent of commercially grown grain.[182] The general effect of exports on productivity cannot have been large. The almost sixfold increase in grain prices in the eighteenth century, particularly after 1761, was due to a large number of factors, only one of which was demand.[183] The number of contributing factors to poor agricultural productivity is large, and so it would be difficult to say that exports on the whole could have had any broad effect on productivity. The state of agriculture was much the same in 1790 as it had been in 1760.[184]

The main material effect of the shift in policy may well have been in its combination with other powerful forces pulling population and agriculture south. The land in the south was better; there was more of it. In the 1770s the entire Caspian and Black Sea trade was opened up and a permanent and important avenue for the export of Russian wheat maintained the pull to settle the rich lands of the south. The population grew rapidly. Between the first tax census (*reviziia*) in 1719 and the tenth in 1857, the annual population growth in the Lower Volga region was 2.43

percent, compared with .38 percent for the central non-agricultural and .77 percent for the central agricultural regions during the same period.[185] The real effect was on wheat production in the south, where, because of its quality and price, it came to dominate the export of all grains in the country as a whole.

The two enactments of 1762 also had the effect of attracting foreign and domestic merchants to the south and east. Imports of tea, cotton goods, and silks into Russia and exports of furs and textiles rose. Trade with Persia and China doubled in volumes of sales in the decade of the 1760s.[186] These were results of the general attention to exotic trade.

A final note should be made that the drop in export duties had even broader historic significance for Russia's role in the world market than emphasis on grain exports alone would reveal. The purchasers of Russia's raw materials, the shipbuilders of Western navies and merchant marines, the producers of ironwares, soap and candles, linen and ropes, and American slaveowners, who bought coarse linen to clothe their workers,[187] made Russia, like other suppliers from central and eastern Europe, a major contributor to the Industrial Revolution by support for a process of capital accumulation without loss to living standards.

The Monarch and the Economy in Mid-Eighteenth-Century Russia

An effect of physiocracy was that Russian rulers acquired at least a partial vision of the macroeconomic structure of growth and, equally important, a rationale binding them to intervene so that growth could be stimulated. Freeing the networks of internal trade from restraints and improving foreign markets became for the first time the specific responsibility as well as a goal of the monarch, who could override any institution to do so.

The monarch's purpose was to enrich the economy while enhancing revenues and this justified a new social as well as economic policy. For example, the urban population, however small relative to the countryside, posed severe problems of supply which could only be resolved by drawing peasants off the land.[188] Mobilizing the factors of production to get grain to the urban markets, in turn, brought governments into confrontation with the landholding elite and demanded a revision of the most fundamental of social laws affecting departures from the land. Landlords struggled to maintain the system of production based on forced labor; their object was to introduce more controls and improve monitoring to ensure a docile labor force during the process of commercialization of agriculture. Monarchs by contrast sought to reduce monitoring in part to save expenditures and personnel and in part to mobilize the production of grain. In the eighteenth century, the conflict between economic policy and the resentful landholding elite was not resolved, although, beginning in the 1750s, the benefit of encouraging the labor market was more and more often heard in government circles and more and more clearly elaborated.

As Heckscher has pointed out, the central purpose of mercantilism was to place the economic life of the people in the service of the power politics of the state.[189]

Peter III's thinking both derived from that tradition and departed from it. His specific goal was described in laws as the enrichment of the country and the populace rather than the state. Mobilization of factors of production, labor in particular, was the repeated goal of different kinds of laws. His reign is an example of how monarchs began to try through law to encourage mobility, even as they were forced to compromise and compensate an elite whose labor force was newly threatened by military recruitment and flight.

Mobilization of labor was a key issue in the 1750s and 1760s as the background for the debate over peasant trade.[190] The expansion of peasant trade was a recurring theme of discussion in commissions on commerce and codification. Although peasant trade in principle supported nobles' consumption interests by supplying supplementary income that could be taxed, nobles were generally concerned about their serfs' flight. Because of the geography of Russia, serfs could easily be caught, but they could also easily escape. Miliukov estimated that in the early eighteenth century, flight comprised 37.2 percent of all departures (death by illness, recruitment, exile, transfer to another estate or class).[191] Between 1765 and 1767, Mironov cited 1,129 instances of flight from one district in western Pskov gubernia, or roughly 5 percent of the populace.[192] During the entire period of the 1740s and 1750s, nobles made the curtailment of flight and return of fugitive populations a main emphasis of policy, an aspiration which helped introduce a measure of tolerance for Old Believers the government wished to bring back from Poland.

With this background, one may look at Peter's laws encouraging peasant mobility as a challenge to the landholding nobility as well as evidence of his and his advisors' liberal convictions. One of Peter's most important measures, which has been overlooked in the literature, was a law prohibiting the police from checking passports of peasant traders coming to Moscow.[193] Since these *bilety* or permissions to travel off the estate were virtually the only means by which departures were policed, the state was abdicating its role in Moscow of distinguishing between fugitives and traders with proper papers. In the eighteenth century, the tide was in favor of serfs' production and sale of industrial and agricultural crops, largely produced on allotment land. In part, the state's abdication was a way of recognizing that its personnel were insufficient to restrain trade and other forms of non-agricultural activity to those who were permitted off the estate.[194] In the tide of liberalization, nobles lost their ability to prevent one of its main effects, the change in peasants' opportunities as well as their own.

At the same time, the government was not in favor of inter-estate mobility, and the ruler of eighteenth-century Russia was one who attempted to defend rigid boundaries between social groups, even as they were being broken down. For example, on January 31 there was another law prohibiting crown, ecclesiastical, and privately owned peasants from entering the merchantry without special permit.[195] In other words, peasants who regularly enjoyed the right to trade and frequently joined merchant guilds were now denied that access.[196]

Peter's most controversial labor law, prohibiting merchants from purchasing serfs for factories, exemplifies a similar duality, a commitment to the new liberalism and a simultaneous deep-rooted sense of social distinction. The measure both clarified the division in law between nobles and merchants, one permitted to own serfs and the other not, and managed strongly to support the use of hired rather than serf labor in manufacturing. That the policy had ambiguity from the beginning is clear from its history. The decree overturned a permissive statute—allowing merchants and nobles equivalent privileges in industry—which had been in effect, except for a brief prohibition of purchases in the 1730s and early 1740s, since the reign of Peter I. In the 1740s and 1750s, merchant rights were opposed by nobles who argued that merchants might be led to speculate in trade and buy land and serfs for non-industrial purposes.[197] In 1752 the senators sought to repeal the law of Peter I and instructed the College of Manufactures to watch out for merchant "abuses."[198] The issue was raised again in the codification commission of the early 1760s by Roman Vorontsov, author of a chapter entitled "Rights of Factory Owners," barring to "non-nobles, either from the merchantry or from the middle class, the right to operate factories or mills until the completion of the new law code."[199] Vorontsov wanted to eliminate the merchants' role in society entirely except for trade[200] and recommended to the Senate on February 1, 1762, "That the right of non-nobles to own factories be abolished, along with the right of merchants to purchase land and villages." The Senate agreed that non-nobles should not possess the right to own serfs for any purpose,[201] but that according to the laws of 1719 and 1723, people of all ranks could own factories and buy land for them, and that providing that the labor they used was hired, they could not be barred from their right to be factory owners. On February 28 the Senate responded to a petition that the merchant Foma Mal'tsov be exempt as before from prohibitions to buy forests and villages for his crystal and glass factory. He was turned down. The new law was ready for promulgation.[202]

The law is properly perceived in the context of the ongoing discussion of the necessity of substituting hired for serf labor in manufacturing. The political context of the law and its use by senators has been described above. However, the fact that this law was promulgated in Peter III's reign draws attention to its physiocratic purposes as well. Documents dating to the mid–1760s show Volkov, now president of the Manufactures College, and Sukin, the vice-president, preoccupied with means of implementing a transition to hired labor. Volkov and Sukin argued later in the 1760s that European experience demonstrated that forced labor in factories was costly and inefficient: workers could not be trained without considerable expense, and this was wasted if serfs were recruited; the provisioning of whole families was a further waste of scarce capital.[203] In cannot be proved that Volkov was the dominant force behind this decree, but it seems likely that this was a compromise decree that suited both his economic interests and the nobility's aspiration for exclusive privileges.

The law thus came into being as a proposal by the aristocratic nobility, who sought to exclude merchants from a privilege they possessed. In a society where around 50 percent of the working populace was enserfed,those who were denied the purchase of labor were certainly disadvantaged. They would have to put up with discontinuities in the labor force when serfs failed to return after the harvest and a

competitive disadvantage in costs. Since nobles had the advantage of choosing between free and unfree labor, and merchants did not, this law discriminated in favor
of the nobility.[204]

The bias of the law makes it a mistake to argue, as historians have, that at this
time factory owners in general lost the right to purchase serfs. Such a misreading
fails to explain the persistence of serf labor in factories.[205] This measure contained
one of the provisions essential to a free hiring market system, which would have
entailed relocating factories off the estate and in towns, setting limits and constraints on noble serf-ownership, and making residence in a town the only criterion
necessary for an escape from serfdom. As confirmed by Catherine on August 8 and
kept in force throughout the eighteenth and early nineteenth century, except for a
period of rescission from 1798 to 1816,[206] this measure explicitly allowed serf and
hired labor to coexist. It defined a political compromise that suited the mix of economic opinions in the eighteenth century.

Did compromise limit the ability of merchant manufacturers to compete with nobles in industry? Merchants vociferously complained that it did. "Without enough
workers to live at the factory," one merchant complained, "there is no way for the
merchant owner to improve or maintain any of his factories."[207] Then merchants
began to escape the constraint by ennoblement. Peter ennobled several particularly
eminent non-nobles, like Brigadier de Bressan, director of the famous Gobelin por-
celain factory and director of the College of Manufactures, and the merchant Peter
Evreinov.[208] Later in the century, it was common for second-generation factory
owners to be ennobled.[209] Those who were unable to escape the constraint in this
way found that in reality they were at no disadvantage. In spite of merchant fears
that the new conditions would limit their operations, this decree encouraged profits
from the use of hired labor, as can be inferred from the relative inefficiency and
decline of forced labor in some industries.[210] By the end of the century, the pos-
sessional factory was on its way out, and hired labor predominated in manufacturing in sheer numbers of laborers in the central region of Russia.[211]

The results of the enactment of March 29, the ennoblement of many merchants
and the steady increase in the use of hired labor, render the law of some importance. It should be noted, however, that hired labor—meaning only that serfs or
peasants were offered a wage—was already widespread at mid-century (as much as
40% of some industries), and since ennoblement proceeded at a very fast rate in any
case, any linkage of the decree and its effect is exceedingly difficult. In textiles,
where both hired labor and non-noble ownership of factories predominated over
serf-operated factories belonging to the nobility, a percentage increase for the eighteenth century as a whole is striking. In the linen industry, hired labor moved from
52.1 percent in the 1760s to 65.1 percent of all workers in the 1790s; the same was
true for silk production, from 40 to 65 percent hired labor.[212] By the time of emancipation, a great deal of industrial labor was paid, although figures as high as 82
percent, while widely quoted, are utterly misleading, since they exclude those
branches of industry, such as distilling and mining, where servile labor was almost
universal.[213] In any case, the sharp rise of merchant purchases of enterprises in the

1760s seems to prove that the obligation to use hired labor did not really discourage the merchantry from becoming factory owners, however much they complained.[214]

Peter III's social and commercial policy reveals the stability of his monarchy and his new directions in policy. He showed himself to be a good housekeeper, who improved on the administration of his aunt by his demand for accuracy in accounting, reduction in expenses, and expansion of revenues. He aimed to start the process of recovery from the war and succeeded. He encouraged agriculture and sought to bring more traders into markets.[215] The relaxation of restrictions on the export of grain and other raw materials and the eventual curtailment of state and private monopolies responded to and promoted vigorous economic expansion. A half-century later, foreign trade had more than doubled its ruble value, adjusted by the rate of inflation, and within another century grain occupied a central place in foreign trade.[216]

Peter's policies were designed to help him regain an advantage in foreign policy that Russia lost just before his accession due to the financial crisis caused by wartime expenditures. At the outset of his reign, he had no resources to plan the campaign that he considered vital to his interests. As a consequence of his savings and the debasement of currency, his problem was solved. But even as he exercised more power through control over the budget, he had less room to maneuver. His ambitious foreign campaign, for which he had made a place in the budget, was overshadowed in its importance to his reign by the mounting force of sentiment against it.

V

FOREIGN POLICY

Between the Peace of Westphalia of 1648 and the Napoleonic era it was commonly recognized that the security of Europe depended on the balance of power. This political understanding did not prevent the dismemberment of small countries, such as the partition of Poland and the separation of Ingria, Livonia, and Estonia from Sweden. Indeed, the balance of power presupposed meaningless international agreements and contempt for national boundaries in its premise that expansion could be checked only by conflicting ambitions. The interests advanced by this concept were those of the great powers, Austria, France, and England, and the emerging states of Russia and Prussia. Savage but serviceable, the principle that no one state should become too strong and that all members of the system should be maintained led to nearly constant warfare without serious territorial readjustment.

The outcome of the continental conflict in the Seven Years' War (1756–1763) may be seen in this light as a victory of the principle of partition where the interests of Europe were held to be more important than the interests of individual states. The conflict began as one for the survival of Prussia. Supported only by a subsidy from England, Prussia fought France, Austria, Russia, Sweden, and some of the smaller states of Germany. This bloodiest of eighteenth-century wars, costing 850,000 lives, not including deaths from disease and other indirect causes, nevertheless did not bring about Prussia's defeat. Prussia was rescued, to become a world power, a rival to Austria for leadership in the Germanies. Russia became more securely a part of Europe. England defeated Prussia's enemy, France, and became the dominant colonial power in the world. Among the losers, France was forced to evacuate its German conquests—Hanover, Hesse, and Brunswick—much of North America, and all of India. Austria ceded Silesia to Prussia.

Austria and France were defeated in part because their overwhelmingly agricultural resources did not suffice for a decisive victory in protracted warfare. Inadequate resources prevented them from devising a means to compensate for the anticipated reversal of their interests when Elizabeth of Russia died. Even before that event, the anti-Prussian coalition in Russia was not secure. An ingrained orientation favoring the preservation rather than the destruction of established boundaries of great states could be seen in the remarks of a powerful Russian statesman under Elizabeth near the end of her reign. This key official, Mikhail Vorontsov, the vice-chancellor for foreign affairs, declared at court in November 1760 that the Russian government should pull back its forces and help bring an end to the war.[1]

Once Elizabeth died, Austria, the main belligerent, could neither prevent nor prepare for a policy reversal, although such a reversal might have been foreseen.

After Elizabeth's death Vorontsov became the sole imperial counsel in foreign affairs. Peter changed sides, becoming Frederick's ally. He explained his policy position to the College of Foreign Affairs on April 6, 1762: "Europe became engulfed in this unbearable war because of circumstantial events and because of too great an aspiration for change in the European system." Hostility to Prussia was not in Russia's long term interest, he wrote, or in the tradition of Russian foreign policy.[2]

Background

The Prussian king retained support at the Russian court during the Seven Years' War. The future ruler and his wife, Peter and Catherine, were both of German origin. Equally important, Russia's foreign policy tradition was based on ties with Prussia; Russian rulers perceived alignment with Prussia as useful for becoming a Baltic power. Russia's presence in the Baltic threatened all the neighboring powers except Prussia. Denmark, Sweden, England, and France resisted Russia's advancement in the north, while Prussia and the other German states did not. After conquering several Swedish provinces, Peter I used his German ties to gain a further foothold by marrying his daughter into the house of Holstein. In this way, a member of his dynasty acquired a claim to the Swedish throne and to valuable German land. The territorial claim was pursued diplomatically by Peter I and by his grandson, who was the product of the dynastic alliance.

Peter III's aim was "to restore Schleswig," as he put it, to the ducal house of Holstein. These words and this ducal ambition with Russian support had figured in the treaty between Russia and Sweden after the northern war, when Schleswig was recognized by England and France as a Danish conquest.[3] To restore Schleswig, actually to lay claim to the Schleswig part of the occupied ducal domain, was a consistent purpose of Russian policy and the rationale for Peter III's solicitation of Frederick's support and threatened military action.

The contested territory—the domain in Schleswig and Holstein claimed by the duke of Holstein, as contrasted with the Danish parts of Schleswig and Holstein—had been formed by a territorial endowment in the mid-sixteenth century by Frederick III of Denmark, who divided up his kingdom among his sons (1581). He gave part to the house of Holstein-Gottorp, a branch of the Danish royal family. The succession of the ducal domain was guaranteed in 1658 by England, France, and Holland, a guarantee renewed in 1689 after an interlude of Danish occupation. The duke's fortunes fell in the early part of the next century when his lands were again occupied by the Danes. Duke Karl Friedrich was forced to cede the possession of his territory, although not the claim.[4] A treaty in 1720 and general agreement in 1721 confirmed the territorial transfer.[5]

The settlement promised to bring peace to long troubled lands. France, England, Sweden, and Russia were guarantors of what they called "the repose of the north," by which was meant the Danish possession of Schleswig and ducal Holstein, leaving Kiel and the surrounding countryside in the possession of the duke.

Russia was an early defector from this agreement. Peter I decided that Karl Friedrich, who was son of the oldest sister of Charles XII and heir to the Swedish throne, should marry his daughter, Anna. In 1723, Peter I made a declaration to the Danish Court that the resolution of the territorial question was unsatisfactory. A treaty with Holstein in 1724 and the marriage agreement of November 24, 1724, included secret articles by which the Russian government agreed to work for Karl Friedrich's inheritance of the Swedish throne and for his repossession of Schleswig and ducal Holstein.[6] Negotiations began. Once duke Peter, now heir to the Russian throne, began to conduct his own negotiations, Denmark sought and achieved new guarantees for its possession of the land—by Sweden in 1745, the year Peter attained his majority as Duke of Holstein, and by Austria, England, and France in 1746 (renewed in 1758). The Russian court persisted in its support of the duke. In 1746 Elizabeth released Peter from Russia's agreement to the settlement of 1721 and permitted him to conclude his own convention with Denmark.

When the Seven Years' War began, Peter had been negotiating with the King of Denmark for over ten years. The king proposed an exchange of territory. In place of Schleswig and ducal Holstein, Peter was to accept two counties, Oldenburg and Delmenhorst, along with compensation for the loss of revenues in the past and for the average difference in revenues between the two territories.[7] Peter rejected this offer. Oldenburg and Delmenhorst were located in a position difficult to defend, to the southwest of Schleswig.[8] Peter agreed to reconsider if Denmark were to guarantee Holstein's possession of Lübeck, the gateway to the Baltic, and secure an elevation of Oldenburg and Delmenhorst to the status of duchies. The two critical points for him were the strategic and commercial advantage of Schleswig and ducal Holstein and the power and prestige he commanded with the ducal lands.[9] The Danish foreign minister, Johan H. E. Bernstorff, acknowledged that as long as the Danes held Lübeck as well as all access routes to the Baltic, Russia would essentially be cut off from its counties, a situation to the advantage of northern Germany's independence.[10] Pressed by France and Austria to bring the affair to a resolution, rather than granting the duke the conditions he sought, Bernstorff hinted that Danish neutrality in the war could be abandoned in favor of support for Prussia, and such a move might depend on a settlement with the Grand Duke.[11]

This communication ended hopes of reconciliation. Vorontsov replied that such a menace was inconsistent with assurances of friendship, that "all of Europe would blame the king of Denmark as the aggressor if in order to obtain his goal, Holstein, he seized it from a friend."[12] "We gave the Danish king no reason for complaint," Elizabeth formally responded. "We do not see how the king calls the grand duke his enemy, only because his highness was opposed to giving up land belonging to him in all his rights." There will be no exchange "until the grand duke himself is so inclined. It does not follow that he must lose what he had when he acquires new lands."[13] In September 1761, acknowledging the deadlock, Bernstorff took the Grand Duke's response as "a refusal, terminating negotiations for the King."[14]

Peter's practical position was weak, since his domain had been occupied for half a century, but his claim was in principle respected. He had his aunt's indulgence and the enormous increase of Russian power during the Seven Years' War to encourage him.[15] Indeed, Elizabeth's refusal to force him to negotiate with Denmark[16] made it seem that the claim was in sight of realization. In June 1761 the existing Russo-Danish treaty expired, and no new one was proposed.

Deploring the bloodshed and domestic sacrifices necessitated by the continental war, Peter nevertheless made policy decisions that posed a new threat of war to Europe. In the most controversial act of his reign, he gave up Russian conquests in Prussia and offered 12,000 of his troops to convince Russia's former enemy, Frederick, to join him in a new alliance. As the two rulers exchanged proposals, their ambitions grew. Frederick came to guarantee all of the lands that Peter wanted and could win, including Danish Holstein, in return for a reciprocal open guarantee of whatever Frederick could obtain before the coming of peace with Austria. The last days of Peter's reign immersed the entire Russian and Prussian courts in the Holstein question, but this proved to be a fragment of the larger issues that the partnership called into being.

The consequences of raising the larger issues by the conclusion of a sweeping new military alliance form an essential part of the history of Russian foreign policy through the 1760s and 1770s. Peter III's removal from power on June 28, 1762, did not save Europe from the threat of Russian and Prussian cooperation and aggrandizement. The northern German question faded for a time in importance. The Danish government won a settlement from Catherine, completing the exchange in 1765. However, the Russo-Prussian partnership survived. Catherine found the alliance with Frederick to be her best strategy in international affairs.[17] Initially, she used it to reduce the independence of the Polish government and, later, with Austria's help, to partition Polish lands. Catherine's advance into north central Europe showed in what direction the dramatic victories during the Seven Years' War could immediately lead. It simultaneously and necessarily also showed that Peter III's policy had much the same significance.

Far from a victim of fortune, Peter should more accurately be seen as among the most aggressive and cynical of the eighteenth-century monarchs. Acting decisively, he virtually imposed the terms by which peace was later concluded, status quo ante bellum, and forced open a breach between Prussia and England which had lasting significance in European affairs.

The Seven Years' War

The war began in 1756 with Frederick's invasion of Saxony and attack on Austria at Lobositz, a strategic offensive designed to confront his opponents before they were entirely ready for war. The aims of war emerged from the previous War for the Austrian Succession and the Treaty of Aix-la-Chapelle of 1748, to whose terms— the loss of Silesia—Maria Theresa had never acquiesced. In 1753, she had appointed as ambassador to Paris Prince von Kaunitz, chancellor and foreign minister, who reopened the issue. Kaunitz sought an alliance with France, Austria's enemy of many centuries, since he believed France was the only power in Europe capable of defeating Prussia. Seeking security against such an alignment, Frederick turned to England, agreeing to defend Hanover for George II if the French attacked it, and negotiating a subsidy agreement, the Convention of Westminster (January 1756), for his own defense. This was all Kaunitz needed. With assurances from Elizabeth of Russia that she would attack Frederick and help Austria recover Silesia, Kaunitz achieved his "Diplomatic Revolution," a defensive alliance and treaty of friendship between the two enemies, France and Austria (Treaty of Versailles of May 1, 1756).

After the invasion of Saxony, a second Treaty of Versailles (May 1, 1757) involved France more deeply by commitment to the partition of Prussia, an annual subsidy, and the maintaince of an army on the continent. In return, France would gain a portion of the Netherlands. Acquiring a principality in the Netherlands and containing Prussia were notions of such force that Louis XV failed to see that French strength was needed for the war against England in America and India. Additionally, he did not see that to pursue the war bound him to relinquish the "secret diplomacy" in clientele states of Poland and Sweden where he sought to undermine Russian influence. The multiple French aims—to defeat Prussia, persuade Russia to break off with England, undermine Russia in Sweden and Poland, and stave off defeat in the colonies—were incapable of realization. In 1758 a new minister of foreign affairs, Count Étienne de Choiseul, now Duc de Choiseul, redirected French foreign policy back to the maritime conflict. "Austria had no interest in our war," Choiseul later wrote; "our subsidies amounted to 52 million *livres* and were impossible to pay."[18] By new treaties in 1758 and early 1759, the third Treaty of Versailles, he reduced the subsidy and the French commitment to Austria. But it was not enough. In 1759 and 1760 the French were defeated in Quebec and India, and they were expelled from Hesse. The French and Austrian alliance had not been based on a firm foundation.

The allies' weakness was displayed in Frederick's brilliant victories at Rossbach and Leuthen in 1757. Because of these victories, he increased his subsidy from England. His enormous levies in Saxony and the quality of his army allowed him to survive in a position of strength.[19] He retreated through Silesia after the failed seige of Olmütz in 1758 but meanwhile defended Brandenburg from a Russian invasion; he lost considerable numbers at Zorndorf on August 25 and Hochkirchen on October 14, but his opponents failed to follow up their victories. The Russians retired into Poland, the Austrians under Daun into Bohemia. The Russians achieved a great victory at Kunersdorf in August 1759, but again failed to follow it up. The Austrians continued to rely on the cautious general Daun, restraining the more capable Laudon from designing Frederick's defeat. As a consequence, in 1760 the Russians crossed back over the Oder, and the Austrians in Silesia were checked. Frederick was still in possession of Saxony, and Frederick of Brunswick defended Westphalia and Hanover from the French advance.

The year 1761 ended critically for Frederick. In the fall the Austrians under Loudon captured Schweidnitz. Silesia and Glatz were occupied by Austrian and Russian troops. On December 1, the fortress of Kolberg fell in Pomerania, and Russian forces occupied most of Pomerania except for the fortress of Stettin. In a last effort to save the position of the French, Choiseul succeeded in concluding a Family Pact uniting the Bourbons of Spain with the rulers of France and Austria, a union Choiseul hoped would be strong enough to prevent France's defeat. Frederick II's correspondence in 1761 indicates his discouragement.

Nevertheless, these battles did not introduce a clear difference in Frederick's position. He had the advantage of fresh supplies and ready access to them. In February 1761 the French envoy at St. Petersburg, Baron Breteuil, wrote, "One can say without fear of being wrong, that the present weakening of the forces of the King of Prussia is only temporary, and that if one does not profit from it, he will promptly reestablish himself, stronger than before."[20] On September 1, the British envoy in Prussia reported that Frederick's position, "critical as it is, seems less dangerous than it was last year before the Battle of Leignitz."[21] At the end of 1761, British agents estimated his troop strength at 100,000.[22] "The army in Silesia has suffered little," wrote a British observer in November 1761, "and it is in perfectly good condition."[23]

The Russian Court in 1761

Because no one had yet really won, peace proposals at the Russian court met with resistance. Although France sought consistently to stop the continental war, Austria and Russia had little to gain from peace apart from financial relief. To be sure, circumstances were affecting governments' considerations. War finances had inflated prices, increased taxes, enlarged the public debt, and caused considerable internal dissension in Austria and Sweden.[24]

The vice-chancellor for foreign affairs, Mikhail Vorontsov, believed policy should be responsive to this dissension and to the desire in France for peace. Vorontsov attempted to shape Russia's posture toward Europe with moderation and traditional balance of power politics. In November 1760 he spoke to the Conference at the Imperial Court, over which he presided, about the necessity of peace. Difficulties of supply combined with military expenditures of nearly forty million rubles and a deficit of eight and one-half million rubles were the reason "peace is necessary, the sooner the better."[25] He did not gain the day, but the *St. Petersburg Gazette* picked up his refrain in a new year's wish for 1761 for "the conclusion of a worldwide peace."[26] The ruling Senate was occupied with effects of prolonged warfare—massive desertion from the army, discontent among the peasants because of taxation, and arson committed by returned deserters, who destroyed in one instance two million rubles' worth of hemp and tallow.[27] The incidence of arson reached three and four fires a day.[28] The Senate's ledgers were piled with debts. In December 1761, the Senate could not find funds to pay the army a million and a half rubles due in back pay.[29] At one moment it seemed to Gregors von Haxthausen, the Danish special envoy at St. Petersburg, that Elizabeth's inclination and "the will of the nation" was to make peace this winter.[30]

Even so, at another moment it seemed to the same ambassador that the court wanted to wage war until it was won, putting Russia in possession of eastern Prussia. Haxthausen wrote on September 14, "All are discontent. They reproach the

French for failing to do battle, the Swedish for their weakness and inertia, and the Austrians for their bad faith in wanting the Russians to bear the essential burdens of war."[31] On the whole, there was a desire to hold off making the peace. Robert Keith, the British envoy, had the impression that the taking of Schweidnitz on October 1 stimulated the desire for one more campaign; "the good dispositions of this court for peace are now quite vanished."[32]

The difficulty of defeating Frederick and internal exhaustion therefore did not add up to an end to the war. The questions that prolonged the war were the territorial issues for which it had been fought and ones raised by conquests. "The taking of Schweidnitz and successes in Pomerania," Keith continued, "have elevated them so much that they talk again of keeping Prussia, which idea they had seemed to have put aside."[33] To be sure, Russia had no prior claim to eastern Prussia. Vorontsov argued against keeping it. "Russia will acquire no advantage in acquisitions in Europe," he said, "since acquisitions by conquest will attract only the jealousy of other countries."[34] "It will be difficult to harmonize so many divergent interests [among the warring powers]," he wrote; "each will have to yield in its demands and be satisfied with however little it receives."[35]

European powers had guaranteed Russia's possession of eastern Prussia, at least until there was a congress of peace, but the point was still contended. The British had an informal agreement by late 1761 that the territory of eastern Prussia would be returned to Frederick in return for an English subsidy of 16 million rubles at one million annually.[36] As the war was coming to a conclusion, it was obvious that new questions of power and position had been raised. The Austrians and Russians were gaining in the east, but the French were losing in the west. At the end of 1761, statesmen sought a way back to a situation where power was evenly balanced. To produce such a situation, the British, as the victors, would necessarily intervene. The French could not maintain a continuing hold on the client states, Sweden, Denmark, and Poland, against the influence of either England or Russia. The secret diplomacy by which this hold had been maintained was not working because of the same chain of events, administrative mismanagement and relative military weakness that were leading to a general French defeat.[37]

The Holstein Cause and European Response

To keep the peace between Denmark, Sweden, and Russia and to prevent any further Russian advance in the north was the greatest aim of French diplomacy in northern Europe. The main obstacle was the dynastic connection that gave Russia, through the ducal house of Holstein, a claim to the Swedish throne. Resisting dependence upon Russia at the end of the northern war, Sweden exacted a promise from the Russian Emperor in 1721 not to interfere in Swedish domestic affairs, disturb the order of succession, or permit the subversion of the Constitution of 1720. In return, by a treaty of February 22, 1724, Sweden agreed by secret article that Peter's son-in-law to be, the Duke of Holstein, would be in line for the Swedish throne, provided he renounced his succession to the Russian throne, and they agreed that Russia and Sweden would attempt to get Schleswig and ducal

Holstein returned to the Duke.[38] Swedish diplomacy, successful in constructing plans, failed in entirely negating Russia's demands. During the thirty-year period after the death of Peter I, Sweden faced threats from Russia in 1726–1727, 1743, and 1747–1750.

For small powers such as Sweden and Denmark, it was imperative to design some system of guarantees. The Danish government was concerned about the combined threat of Sweden, Russia, and Holstein. In the 1740s Elizabeth of Russia imposed a member of the Holstein family, Adolf Frederick, the Protestant bishop of the secularized sees of Lübeck and Eutin, on the Swedish throne. Adolf Frederick renounced his contingent claim to Holstein and accepted the notion of an exchange of counties for duchies, but his renunciation did not produce confidence from either side, Swedish or Danish, in an alliance. For reconciliation, Denmark and Sweden needed the mediation of a third power, France.

The first French alliance and subsidy agreement with Sweden was signed but not ratified by France in 1735. Following a period of political maneuvering, a clearer pro-French policy was achieved and the subsidy was granted. Those who struggled for a pro-French policy formed a government guided by a new political party called the "Hats." They acquired power through election to the Riksdag, appointments to commissions, and in the bureaucracy, then got Sweden into a disastrous war with Russia. In 1745, Russia bound Sweden to declare for the Holstein cause. Meanwhile another party appeared, the "Caps," that looked to England for support against French influence. A rupture in relations with England lasting from 1748 until 1764 forced the Caps to accept Russian aid. The necessity of falling back on Russia was not to their benefit. This dependency, along with a failed coup attempt, helped make the Hats unassailable in the 1750s. With the Hats in power in Sweden, during the leadership of the pro-French J. H. E. Bernstorff as foreign minister in Denmark, the "French system" fell into place: both Sweden and Denmark were put on peace- and wartime subsidy. The period of the Seven Years' War was the height of French influence in the north, where Denmark remained a "passive" neutral power and Sweden an "active" one that was expected to produce troops for engagement with France against its enemies and not to sign any treaties without French consent.

Grand Duke Peter's pretensions to lands in Schleswig and ducal Holstein threatened to disturb the reconciliation by forcing the Hats to take sides. The aim was to prevent an invasion. Bernstorff turned to Prussia and England for guarantees and subsidies and sent his nephew Andreas to discover what France and other former guarantors would be able to provide.[39] Andreas Bernstorff found that "circumstances" rendered his mission impossible.[40] Choiseul was powerless to respond to Denmark with assurances: critical financial shortages incurred by France during the war introduced a new element of insecurity into the system, "the secret of our exhaustion," as Choiseul called it, France's default on its subsidies.[41] To Choiseul, it was desperately important to keep Elizabeth alive as long as possible to prevent "the catastrophe" that would befall French policy in the north when Peter asserted his claims.

The Armistice

Peter III ascended the throne on December 25, 1761. Unable to see any rationale for destroying Prussia, he immediately stopped Russia's participation in the war. He notified his generals in Pomerania and Silesia to halt all movement of troops. General Zakhar Chernyshev, commander of troops in the south, was ordered on December 25 to return to Russia via Poznan.[42] Prince Mikhail Volkonskii, newly designated commander-in-chief, was to prepare for an armistice; he was to accept a proposal for cessation of hostilities if one were offered by Prussian officers.[43] On Vorontsov's suggestion, Peter also sent Frederick a special emissary, Andrei Gudowitz, who carried a message "to renew, extend, and confirm in a durable and good friendship that understanding which has always existed under our predecessors."[44]

These first steps removed any doubt that Peter intended to break loose from diplomatic engagements of the war years. He instructed his ambassadors to convey a hope that all of Europe would "end the senseless waste of human blood, which in Russia was the ruin of the treasury and the destitution of the people of Our empire."[45] "This war," he said, "has already cost thirty million rubles and it has so destroyed the army that Russia will need ten years to repair the damage."[46] At dinner, Peter spoke of his desire to place himself at the center of European diplomacy, "and have the glory of giving peace to Europe, finishing this abominable war at any price."

He moved quickly toward a separate peace. On March 5, Prince Volkonskii and August Wilhelm, the duke of Braunschweig-Bevern, signed the armistice, lifting restrictions on trade and separating Russian troops from the Austrians. By the armistice, Frederick agreed to provision General Zakhar Chernyshev's corps as it returned to Russia.[47] The armistice did not reveal what kind of peace would follow.

Peter camouflaged the details of his peace efforts to avoid antagonizing Austria and France. He called for a review of all treaties and received reports of Vorontsov's views of all questions relating to foreign affairs.[48] For the month of January, Vorontsov claimed to be seriously ill, and Peter failed to convene the imperial advisory conference, Elizabeth's Conference at the Imperial Court, maintaining that he wished to include Vorontsov at its first meeting.[49] Its abolition on January 28 bought him still more time.[50] He urged Volkov and Vorontsov to discretion.[51] One diplomat accused him of acting behind a "veil of secrecy."[52] Vorontsov explained to Mercy d'Argenteau that he had to educate the emperor who was "in complete ignorance" of affairs. Mercy came to realize that the Emperor was "better acquainted with affairs than Vorontsov wanted to tell me."[53] At last Peter came forward with Vorontsov still as his chancellor, possibly because Vorontsov supported his ducal claims.[54] Peter's first statement to the ambassadors of Austria and France conveyed an impression of neutrality. He told Olsuf'ev, who told Breteuil, that he "did not at all wish to break his ties with the allies in thinking of peace, for he had no direct alliance with France, and as for the house of Austria, he would be on the same good terms as had existed before the war."[55] He allowed his advisors to conduct affairs as if his arrangements with the former allies continued to subsist. For example, work on the French commercial agreement proceeded, although relations with Breteuil fell apart.[56]

The precautions concealed the exact nature of his plans, but Peter was clearly not the man of peace he claimed to be in circulars to the European courts. As Breteuil wrote on 7/18 January,

> The political system that he has proclaimed, loudly enough for the greater and lesser lords to know it, is that Russia should draw subsidies from all the powers and maintain a large army at her frontier so that he will have money for domestic affairs and the means to determine the outcome of the general dispute according to his own will.[57]

As his reign progressed, he showed a desire to force the conclusion of peace and drive the Austrians out of Prussian territory. He devised new alliances and, by bold unexpected moves, revealed broad ambitions not related solely to Holstein. Peace was the first phase of his strategy. He made the peace for the sake of financial recovery, but he discovered in the course of negotiations that peace could be used to derive new commitments from foreign powers. In the second phase, he gained the promise of an alliance with Prussia. In the final phase of his policy, he attempted to create a number of other alliances as a diplomatic base for imminent mobilization of troops against Denmark.

His experience in the Danish negotiations made him believe that war might be necessary to assert his claim to ducal Holstein and Schleswig. Since no European power was in a position to defend Denmark,[58] haste had strategic advantages. From late December to mid-March, Peter was occupied in the first phase, acting moderately in the interests of strengthening bonds of friendship and commerce with all powers, regardless of potential alliances. From mid-March to late May, he pursued alliances with northern powers, England, Sweden, and Prussia, more vigorously, relinquishing the cautious diplomacy of the first phase for more blunt and confrontational methods. More and more intent on satisfying his Holstein claims before fall and winter rendered battles more difficult and Denmark's defense more formidable, he formulated, fast and frequently, requests for aid and offensive alliances. Important markers of a turnabout in England and neutrality on the part of Sweden occurred toward the third phase: the promise of an alliance came first; promises were also made by the king of England and the Swedish government that despite their guarantees to Denmark they would not interfere in the Holstein affair if war broke out.

Meanwhile, the king of Denmark stopped neutral ships and sent troops to Mecklenburg and Hamburg in part to show how difficult the problem of supply would be for Peter anywhere in the vicinity.[59] Not having a problem of supply nor one of exhaustion of troops,[60] Denmark risked moving to an offensive position. Peter was informed by Frederick and others that Denmark was "on the warpath."[61] He perceived the threat in the advance on Mecklenburg and Hamburg, and grew unsure. "Denmark," he wrote Volkov, "has begun an immense expansion of its armaments at the very time when we are not far from negotiations."[62] In May, Peter agreed to cede Schleswig in return for some districts of Holstein and absolute separation of his ducal domains from Denmark. Vorontsov was of the opinion that Denmark "will make no sacrifice and, with her superiority in the Baltic, will use the first opportunity to impose a settlement."[63] In this third phase, Peter backed away from an outbreak of war, and he continued work on an alliance with Frederick that reflected his broader goals—hegemony in Poland and Courland, the incorporation of White Russia into the empire, and troop support for mutual interests. While drafting an alliance, Peter established a commission to investigate methods of repairing the fleet.[64] Twenty-four Russian warships—one-fourth without a crew—were ready to set sail in June.[65] But he kept open the option of negotiations.

The three phases of Peter's policy reveal consistent and sustained objectives, but his methods of achieving the new alignments that he thought might yield him Holstein did change.[66] His efforts to achieve a general peace and new alliances were effective, in part because of the circumstances and in part because of his handling of his peacemaker role. To gain advantage with Frederick he exploited the sudden shift in British policy toward the subsidy; to use that advantage, he pressed England and Sweden for stronger commitments and freed himself from entanglement with former alliances. The evaluation of Peter III's foreign policy is complicated by the distorting lens of hindsight and the brevity of his reign. His schemes for alliances were scarcely developed in six months. From hindsight, particularly in the light of Catherine's accusations, one might see in the brevity of the reign remote ambitions and few real accomplishments. Yet the goals and effectiveness of his policies show their major limitation to have been neither their idiosyncrasy nor their immoderate scope but rather their failure to achieve the confidence and support of key members of his court, some because of their continuing loyalty to the Austrian alliance and others because the outcome was insecure.[67] It has been said that Peter III's foreign policy was an embarrassment to Russia. As S. V. Bakhrushin put it,

> At the time of Catherine's accession, the prime task confronting Russian diplomacy was restoration of Russia's international prestige, which had suffered badly during Peter III's reign in consequence of his withdrawal from the Seven Years' War and the sudden shift of alliance from Austria to Prussia.[68]

This assessment ignores the milieu in which his foreign policy emerged, one in which financial strains had opened the way for breaches in treaties.

The Conclusion of Peace

In 1762, Peter III succeeded in imposing his doctrine that peace was an overwhelming priority. With the excuse of extreme financial circumstances, he challenged the idea that alliances bound him to continue the war for any other power's sake. In all of Europe 1761 and 1762 were years of resolute steps toward peace. In 1761, Choiseul requested a congress to negotiate an end to the war.[69] Also in 1761, William Pitt resigned as director of the war effort in England. Support for the war was waning, and Pitt, the statesman who had brought England to a position of first ranking importance in Europe and firmly established its colonial empire, was replaced by the king's favorite, the relatively inexperienced James Stuart, Earl of Bute. Bute dropped the Prussian subsidy, tried to abandon all continental connections, and sought peace at any price. Also, late in 1761, because of financial and political considerations, the Swedish government initiated discussions in preparation for concluding peace. The Secret Committee of the Diet decided on December 11, 1761, that Sweden must try with its allies to reach a peace settlement or reach a separate peace with Prussia. This secret decision was communicated to the Council of the Realm, and on December 22, three days before Elizabeth died, Chancery-President Claes Ekeblad sent the Swedish ambassador at Paris secret instructions along these lines.[70] In 1762, the Russian peace and Sweden's separate peace at Hamburg, leading to the cessation of hostilities along the entire northern line, brought an end to the war. By fall Frederick drove the French out of Germany and the Austrians out of Silesia, forcing the French and the Austrian governments to accept the fact of their defeat.[71]

That Peter should not be bound by alliances with whose fundamental premises he disagreed was a problematic corollary to the doctrine of peace at any price. Peter sent a rescript to European courts on April 9 in which he declared that the war aims of the allies were contradictory and impracticable.

> To wait for a general peace, such as the peace of Westphalia, means to wage endless war and even so not be confident that the ensuing peace would be satisfactory. At Westphalia, each was confirmed in the territory, rights and freedoms that once were held; now, it is a matter of satisfying pretensions and desires arising out of the war, and these are so diverse that there is no possibility of coming to an agreement.[72]

Vorontsov attempted to conceal the implications of the treaty of peace and maintained that it was inoffensive, or "innocent."[73] Choiseul understood the document to be more offensive, "heinous to our interests."[74] The first provisions of the peace, which was published on April 24, confirmed the armistice and the exchange of prisoners of war, which had taken place in February. The remaining provisions touched off fears. Out of "deep friendship" with the Prussian monarch, Peter surrendered territory captured during the war. A deal of some kind was clearly being struck. Peter's promise of assistance to bring all of Europe to peace and "to end all previous engagements that were not . . . pacific in nature" broke several engagements that Russia had made with Austria. The cordiality of tone inviting Sweden to join Prussia and Russia and embracing the idea of harmonious relations with Prussia hinted at what was actually put in a secret article, the intention of extending the treaty of peace into an alliance.[75]

Peter's image of himself as peacemaker in this document no doubt harmonized with his ambitions to influence European affairs. He gave an impression of frankness and openness in contrast to his wife, who had a reputation for cunning and secrecy.[76] His explosive temper and frequent arguments contributed to the impression that he was forthright, direct, undissembling.[77] "He is open to reason," wrote Robert Keith.[78] Historians have believed that he was easily manipulated and that Frederick's envoy to Russia, Baron Goltz, virtually dictated the terms of peace.[79]

But he had a mind of his own. Joseph Yorke reported to his court on the basis of communications from his informants,

> No one knew the King of Prussia while he was a boy and the same is true of Peter III. People are certainly mistaken in their opinion of him. He will appear to be a Frank and Open Prince, but with Ideas peculiar to himself, which he certainly has; The frankness of his Character was the reason that so much indulgence was showed him in the last reign.[80]

Peter's self-defined role as peacemaker did not coincide with his aims in concluding an alliance with Frederick. The frankness with which he conducted diplomacy suggested only the kind of image he wished to portray. Personal correspondence shows that he was acting under restraint.[81] The cause of peace was not really one he intended to support, unless it served his interests.

European observers were correct in identifying an emerging pro-Prussian policy couched in terms of peace. Peter wrote in his memorandum of April 6 that the treaty of peace had "satisfied issues arising out of the war itself, but not our permanent interests, which will take more time."[82] Having gained a promise of a future alliance from Frederick, he had to devise a way of making that alliance what he wanted it to be. Frederick firmly believed and wrote him to the effect that the intended campaign against Denmark was ill-advised, against Russian and Prussian interests.[83] Peter sought a way to change that opinion.

Russian Ascendancy in Europe in the Early Postwar Period

Peter's policy toward Prussia, Austria, and England developed as a series of political expedients as he moved toward war against Denmark. While separating from Austria he moved closer to Prussia, England, and Sweden, which was necessary both for a military alliance and for neutralizing Denmark's potential allies. He did not have it all his own way. Among his accomplishments, however, were the crystallizing elements of a more permanent structure for foreign policy, one which would draw its strength for over a decade from impressive military performance and the alliance with Prussia.[84]

Peter's withdrawal of his forces from the war compelled the Austrians to follow suit. After the fact, Frederick would encourage Peter through his envoy at St. Petersburg, Baron Goltz, to believe in the "knavishness of the Austrians and the Saxons." Inspire the Russians, he wrote, "even to the point of jealousy." Tell them, he wrote on February 7, that while the Austrians watched, the Russians ran all the dangers in the war; explain that the Austrians have guaranteed to both the king of Denmark and to Peter his ducal domains in Holstein.[85] By January 19, Peter III had already made the decision to break free of the Austrian alliance.[86] He requested proof of Austria's intentions to guarantee to him the ducal domain, but when Mercy offered a subsidy to keep him in the continental war, he refused it.[87] He entangled his relations with the ambassadors of Austria, France, and Spain in formalities. He demanded that all foreign ambassadors present themselves to his uncle Prince

George Ludwig of Holstein before being presented at an imperial reception.[88] Anticipating a refusal by the monarchs of Austria and France to be treated like minor rulers of Europe, he thus bought time.[89] In March, the ambassadors still had not been received—France still resisted the visit to Prince George on the grounds of protocol.[90] Peter meanwhile demanded that Austria withdraw from the war, or he would remobilize Russian troops,[91] since Austria had increased its forces by twenty thousand troops to compensate for the Russian withdrawal.[92] On April 10, the Austrian ambassador conceded.[93] "Far from being against peace-making," Mercy said, "we will offer a Truce as proof of it. . . . "[94] Instead of responding to the offer, Peter preferred a break with these diplomats who were part of the old alliance system. He urged Breteuil to leave, "the sooner the better," and encouraged the departure of Mercy.[95] At the time of his overthrow, Peter was organizing a Protestant party to challenge the Hapsburgs in the Diet of the Holy Roman Empire.[96]

The Separate Peace with Sweden

As Peter distanced himself from Austria, he attempted to expand Russia's influence in Sweden. In that country, French policy was in a shambles, with the secret diplomacy losing force as the subsidy went unpaid.[97] This was the opportune moment to do so, as one historian wrote with exaggeration—"over the corpse of French power."[98] Choiseul wrote to his king, "It was Your Majesty who lost this Power [Sweden], in great part, by engaging her in a war against Russia in 1740 and in the one which was just concluded against Prussia. These two wars did more harm to the Swedish state than the misfortunes and follies of Charles XII."[99]

There was still little room for Russian influence in Sweden. The party opposed to Russian influence, the Hats, was in the ascendance for over a quarter of a century after 1738 by means of its elected representatives in the Riksdag, the lawmaking body which met every three years. The Hats were in full control during the Riksdag meetings of 1751–1752 and 1755–1756, and a disastrous attempt to undermine that control and place the king more fully in power—a coup attempt in which the Russians had played a role—only confirmed Hat dominance. Russian statesmen were forced to stop all efforts to meddle in Swedish domestic politics. England was virtually without a diplomatic representative in Stockholm.[100]

The Seven Years' War altered this situation somewhat. Against the general will of the Riksdag, the Hats had led Sweden into war against Prussia largely as a consequence of the exigencies of the French alliance. The legitimate grievances of Sweden against Prussia, arising from Frederick's interference in Swedish commerce and from Swedish fears that Prussia would seize the last of its possessions in Pomerania, would probably not, alone, have induced Sweden to join forces against Prussia. Franco-Swedish cooperation, moreover, never worked as planned. The Naval Union of 1757 with Denmark was too much of a risk to Denmark's profitable neutrality, collaboration with French and Russian troops failed, and the Hats' inflationary policies and maladministration led to the unpopularity of the war.[101] The French declared that there could be no increase of subsidies,[102] and the Hats were unable to stop the slide of a parliamentary majority toward peace.[103]

At his accession, Peter hoped to use the political instability and relative weakness of France to reestablish Russian interests in Sweden, that is, to gain a supportive policy for peace and for his claims in Schleswig and Holstein. The dance of diplomacy shows Peter to have taken advantage of every opportunity to enhance his personal influence there. In the beginning, there were nothing but false steps and mistakes. He started with an incorrect assumption that he might deal with the royal house rather than with the parties of the Riksdag, the Hats and the Caps. He ordered the Russian ambassador at Stockholm, Baron Osterman, to declare support for the royal couple and for the Caps at the Riksdag and crossed out the cautionary words, added by Vorontsov, "do not work for a change in the form of government."[104] He invited the queen to send an envoy to St. Petersburg and sent Peter Buturlin, the general's son, to Stockholm to investigate possible cooperation on a peace treaty and campaign against Denmark.[105] The queen's emissary, Joachim von Düben, a representative of the Caps, came to St. Petersburg. It is unclear precisely what his mission was, apart for a request that the Russian government send financial support and Nikita Panin to replace Osterman.[106] Among his other missions, however, he told Peter,

> However good and sincere are the intentions of the King, . . . his Majesty sees regretfully that the usurpation made from time to time on the rights accorded him by the constitution of the kingdom allows him to do salutary services neither for the kingdom which God gave him nor for his allies and friends. . . . He wishes to preserve Russia's grandeur in Holstein, but He can do this only if he is in full powers in Sweden.[107]

The Caps "pushed through peace" in the Riksdag.[108] But the conclusion of a separate peace did not bring full power to the monarchy. Indeed, when the Caps came to power at the Riksdag in early 1765, they were firmly supportive of the constitutional order.

Peter's attempted negotiation of support for his intended war against Denmark was therefore bound to fail. There was little chance that Sweden would take any part in the Holstein affair. A small Danish party began to form at Stockholm, but fear of one would not drive Sweden into alliance with the other.[109] However, Peter opened up a vexing question. Would Sweden come to Denmark's defense? This question was resolved in the third phase of Peter's policy, by which time Peter had already become a realist—he was now dealing with the Hats, the party in power.

Relations with England

Although ties between England and Russia had never been broken during the Seven Years' War, there was a discontinuity of considerable importance in that the fall of Pitt led to the formation of a new government with little experience and new ideas about British interests. The new government, led by Bute, believed England to be in a position to impose a European peace.[110] King George III disliked the war; popular antiwar pamphleteering had risen to a feverish pitch.[111] Financial considerations were not least among the considerations that made Bute pursue a policy of peace.[112] In regard to Russia, Bute believed that no special care need be taken to prepare the court for peace. The assumption was that Russia would be a passive partner to the larger European arrangements. Bute had the impression that Russia was governable in this fashion because he and the other members of the government allowed themselves to be convinced by an agent who had formerly served in St. Petersburg, Thomas Wroughton, that the former Grand Duchess Catherine was really "the ruling genius."[113] Through Wroughton she had engaged in a correspondence with the King of England, and among other things requested that Wroughton be made resident.[114] Bute could be certain of Catherine's and Peter's pro-English and pro-Prussian sympathies, openly expressed during the Seven Years' War, rendering Russian military performance at times totally unreliable.[115] Catherine's liaison with Sir Charles Hanbury-Williams in 1756 and 1757, and her dealings with Bestuzhev-Riumin, who came to trial in 1758 for countermanding Elizabeth's military orders, were two events that must have encouraged her credibility with the British government. Bute initially assumed that if he were to send Wroughton to Russia as resident, he would have special access to the court through Catherine.[116] "In this Critical Juncture," he instructed Robert Keith, "as he [Wroughton] is acquainted with His Majesty's Intentions you will communicate your Instructions to Him, and act with him in everything, in the most perfect Harmony and Concert."[117]

The first blow to his confidence was Keith's information that Bute would not be able to control the court through Catherine: "Your opinion that the Empress is not like to have any great credit in the present Reign was very unexpected here. That circumstance may make your conduct more delicate in some Respects and adds difficulty to the Part which you will both have to act."[118] The second was the announcement of Peter's intent to sacrifice conquests in concluding a separate peace. "What has happened . . . far exceeds political credibility, and will require much prudence and adress [sic] to bring it to perfection," wrote Bute to the Duke of Newcastle.[119]

On January 6, Bute held a conversation with Prince Golitzyn that showed that his command of the Russian situation was by no means complete. He was attempting to find a course to peace. Golitzyn reported back to the Emperor, in a famous letter reviewing that conversation, that Bute had told him "he could not continue the war forever to please the King of Prussia," and as a result, Prussia should consider yielding to the Austrians. As for Russia, Peter should prevent Frederick from further prolonging the conflict, which he could do by keeping his troops in Europe. Recent research has clarified details of this conversation. Golitzyn greatly misrepresented the opinions of Bute, who had spoken of the urgency of peace without specific prescriptions. Bute was unquestionably interested in driving a wedge between Austria and France, but not in dictating terms that would prolong the war.[120]

Even though Bute, acting out of lack of knowledge of the Russian court, had seriously miscalculated, he was not entirely responsible for what happened. In the Golitzyn dispatch Peter had information he needed to further cement his ties with Prussia. He sent an extracted copy of the dispatch to Frederick which further misrepresented the conversation so that Frederick could no longer have any faith in

British support for Prussian territorial claims.[121] The Golitzyn letter, as communicated, persuaded Frederick that Bute was treacherously shifting sides to support a peace satisfactory to Austria. The consequence was that Frederick demanded the subsidy from England, without regard for British terms, and Britain declined it. Bute used Peter's policy as an excuse. "After receiving the important declaration of the Emperor of February 23 where he openly exhorts the King of Prussia's enemies to put an end to the war, and declared his intention to restore all conquered territory, We can no longer be expected to give the subsidy."[122] The subsequent rift in relations between England and Prussia and deep hatred on the part of Frederick toward the British government would work years later to the disadvantage of England, isolating it in Europe.[123]

The combined effect of the Golitzyn dispatch and the denial of the subsidy caused a coldness to develop in Anglo-Russian relations. Peter had begun his reign by developing close relations with the British. Keith was one of the first to know on December 27 about the command to Volkonskii to agree to an armistice.[124] Early in February, Peter had already requested British support against Denmark.[125] After March negotiations on a commercial treaty were postponed,[126] and relations declined to the point that Keith requested his recall.[127] Wroughton was asked to leave Russia because of his "secret maneuvers and intrigues,"[128] and Keith volunteered to leave because his government's purposes were no longer those he had helped shape.[129]

Relations with England were soon restored. Bute vacillated in his communications, as if evaluating the likelihood of Peter's success.[130] Peter's boldness in demands from England was uncompromising: he asserted the legality of his claims and refused to negotiate from any other basis. "What could he expect from England," he asked Keith again on April 5, "in case of a Rupture with Denmark?" Keith answered that he had never received any orders on that subject.[131] Peter went on, "we had no Reason to be uneasy about War, for if we would enter into a League offensive and defensive with him and the King of Prussia he would send such a Body of Troops to our Assistance . . . as would leave us at liberty to employ our own where we pleased."[132] The difficulty of this case was presented to Peter III by Vorontsov, who was responding to Peter's request for naval assistance from England: "About my orders to speak to the English minister Keith about sending us naval assistance this summer, . . . you do not have a treaty with Great Britain, and given that she is now engaged in a two-sided war, . . . what advantage does she have in sending a number of ships?"[133] Hardwicke commented to Newcastle, summing up the very different fears not touched upon by Vorontsov:

> the Grand Duke's desire for a guarantee touched not the Dutchy of Holstein or the Ducal Possessions but the Ducal Dominions, including Schleswig. If Schleswig is to be attacked and the king of Prussia to cooperate in it, what is to become of England's guarantee of that Dutchy to the king of Denmark? And what will become of the counter-guarantees given to the Elector of Hanover for Bremen and Verden? This may be a very hampering business.[134]

On April 9, a response was drafted at Whitehall:

Upon the whole, the King cannot but hope, and believe, that his Imperial Majesty
will receive, with pleasure and approbation, the assurances you are to give him of
his Majesty's taking no part in those unhappy differences, if they should, contrary
to his earnest desires, produce an open rupture.[135]

The Earl of Hardwicke, writing to the Duke of Newcastle, emphasized the friend-
liness of this assurance. As he wrote on April 10, "the King's answer to the Czar,
that he will remain neutral [is] full strong enough."[136]

This arrangement could not be the keystone of his northern policy, yet it was a
concession that Peter would have taken as encouragement. After the offensive dispatch, he had removed Golitzyn, and in his appointment letter to Golitzyn's successor he described the new mission as one to "destroy entirely" the agreement
between Denmark and England over the Holstein issue. More important, "by any
means," Peter wrote, "draw England into the alliance with the king of Prussia,
stressing on the one hand the good it would do for commerce and on the other the
harm to commerce that might otherwise occur."[137]

In this last phase of his foreign policy he also attempted to draw the Hats into an
alliance. He told Mauritz Posse, the Swedish envoy, that Denmark was striving to
rival Sweden's supremacy in the Baltic; he repeatedly mentioned "lands to the
west," i.e., Norway, which Sweden might want in return for support against
Denmark.[138] In May, he frankly inquired if the Hats were interested in a quadruple
alliance of Russia, Prussia, England, and Sweden.[139] He had a substantial need for
naval assistance from Sweden: Denmark's reputed 48,000 troops, twenty-four ships
of the line and twelve frigates, all ready to move immediately, "were more than he
had reckoned with," wrote Posse in code to the Chancery President, "and he seems
to be thinking things over carefully. The Russian navy is in bad shape."[140] Yet, at
the same time, Peter placed more confidence in Prussia's help than in Sweden's,[141]
and his real goal, more modestly expressed in a dispatch to Baron Korf at Copenhagen, was, "if Sweden is not in any condition to assist us against the Danes, nor
will she hinder us, for she has many reasons for wishing us success in our
venture."[142] In June, the Hat government offered neutrality, and, without promising actual naval assistance, extended the offer to include provisioning of Russian
ships at the port of Stralsund, provided ships entered the harbor one by one and not
as a fleet.[143]

At the last minute, England and Sweden were making military concessions. This
suggested that Peter was laying a solid basis for a new structure. The cornerstone
of this policy was also coming into its proper position.

The Prussian Alliance

Peter won an alliance with Frederick essentially because he was winning a war.
Yet one of the reasons the alliance endured was that it was based on tradition as
well as circumstances. Russia and Prussia had been allies for much of the early
eighteenth century. Peter "had never heard of any former quarrel between the
House of Brandenburg and the Emperor of Russia,"[144] wrote Keith. All Russo-
Prussian treaties set forth terms of mutual interest, the succession of a mutually

acceptable monarch in Poland, for example. In the treaty of 1762, whose terms were never realized, the two monarchs agreed to cooperate in placing Henry, the King's brother, on the throne, after which Henry would give the Prussian part of Poland to Frederick. Lithuania would be ceded to Courland, which would become a part of Russia. [145] England would receive the Duchy of Osnabrück to be attached to Hanover. Denmark would receive Oldenburg and Delmenhorst. [146]

In his memorandum of April 6 Peter wrote, "If our interests demand it, then following the treaty of peace we will conclude an alliance." [147] Despite Peter's advantage over Frederick, the treaty of alliance took time. In 1760 Frederick had written, "the true interests of my state demand that I always support ducal Holstein in the hands of Denmark, rather than incorporated, so to speak, into the Russian empire." [148] In March 1762, Frederick had "not yet decided on the essentials you ask," Peter was informed by George Ludwig. [149] By May 11, however, a draft of the alliance was complete. Mikhail Vorontsov presented it to the Prussian plenipotentiary, Baron Goltz, who submitted another draft on May 18. Two days later a final draft was reviewed by Vorontsov, Goltz, and Prince George. [150] Goltz hesitated. [151] The signing was delayed until June 8, when Frederick ratified it.

The first twenty articles of the treaty set forth the terms of friendship which were to last twenty years and to include reciprocal privileges, most favored nation status in commerce, and mutual guarantees of troops in case either country was attacked (except if Prussia was attacked by England or France, or Russia by Persia or the Tatars, under which circumstances both powers would assist with money rather than troops. These arrangements were aimed in Frederick's case against Austria and in Peter's against Denmark. The first secret clause made this clear. It guaranteed to Frederick Silesia and Glatz, and to Peter the duchy of Schleswig and the ducal portion of Holstein along with other territory he might conquer in a war against Denmark. [152]

Other articles concerned Europe. In a second, separate article, Prussia and Russia agreed to protect the rights of Polish dissidents. Peter and Frederick resolved in the third secret article jointly to determine the Polish succession. Peter preferred that there should be a guarantee of constitutional forms, Frederick did not, and this guarantee was left out. No mention was made of boundaries, which had been a matter of discussion. [153] Peter favored guarantees of territorial integrity of the smaller states, and he made a diplomatic effort to get England to intervene with Austria so that Polish and Saxon territory would not be divided by Austria. [154]

Among Russian concerns was the protectorate of Courland, and this most Protestant agreement guaranteed that a Protestant prince should rule in the northern duchy. Prince Charles of Saxony, the Catholic son of Augustus III, had become duke of Protestant Courland in 1758 following the lapse of the claims of the previous duke, Johann Ernst von Biron. [155] When Peter ascended the throne, he replaced Charles at first with Biron, whom he recalled from exile. Then he demanded that Biron renounce his claim in favor of George Ludwig. [156] The advantage was that while the appointment of a Protestant would please the nobility of Courland, who had sent a delegation to Peter III in protest of Charles's persecution of Protestants, a cause with which Peter was sympathetic, Russia would also gain

Courland.[157] The third secret article of the treaty of alliance between Russia and Prussia thus dealt primarily with the deposition of Charles. Continuation of the purposes of this treaty in Catherine's reign led to the even closer attachment of Courland to the Russian empire.

The Russo-Prussian alliance gave expression, precision, and weight to Peter's foreign policy objectives. It also encouraged Peter's plans for war. The Holsteiners at Peter's court, although they tried, could not calm the escalating tensions. Saldern, selected by Peter to head negotiations for a last effort at reconciliation with Denmark, attempted to mediate between Peter and the king of Denmark. Although he served in Peter's court, Saldern was simultaneously in the Danish service.[158] He worked secretly with the Danish envoy Haxthausen, informing him of critical memoranda from Peter's councils. When a breech seemed likely, he sought to prevent it. Saldern tried to ease the impact of Peter's ultimatum of March 12. Peter had asked, "Does the King want to restitute Schleswig or not?"[159] Saldern sent the following message to the King of Denmark through Haxthausen:

> Korff's proposed declaration is not at all conceived in the desired terms . . . at heart, it [the declaration] is good, if too strong; and it mentions actually only Schleswig; we beg you not to react formally to the style; we can respond in generous terms; the proposal to arrive promptly at a goal so salutary should be agreeable to his Majesty.[160]

George Ludwig, Peter's uncle and military advisor, also urged caution. He advised Peter III on February 24,

> Although this seems the moment to establish the luster of the House of Holstein and to reacquire ancestral rights, I am persuaded that your Majesty would not want to alter the Repose of the North, the happiness of its present population, and the true well-being of its future population. To the contrary, I suppose that your Majesty will in the future work in accord with your future allies, England and Prussia, in the firm persuasion that these two kings will do all possible to terminate the differences in a friendly manner. . . .
>
> Although it appears convenient for you to invade Denmark through Pomerania and Prussia, you are not thereby stopped from tentatively negotiating with the assistance of your good allies. Your Russia languishes only after peace. Where is the Prince who would not choose the means of an amicable resolution before beginning a war?[161]

Ludwig's remarks point to a considerable antiwar sentiment at court. The writings of Lomonosov and Sumarokov similarly attest the common denunciation of war.[162] On May 31, Peter's council of war, the two Holstein princes (Georg Ludwig and the Prince of Holstein-Bek), Ernst von Münnich, Nikita Trubetskoi, Mikhail Vorontsov, Mikhail Volkonskii, Alexander Villebois, Aleksei Mel'gunov, and Privy Secretary Dmitrii Volkov, unanimously recommended "on behalf of the nation" that he not begin the campaign or leave the country. Vorontsov wrote a separate letter to that effect. "Even the favorites," wrote Keith, are "throwing pitchforks into the fire to stop the Emperor from going, after urging him on."[163]

Peter vacillated. He was confident in his armed forces and his strategy. He proposed negotiations, first in Hamburg, then Berlin. A congress was set for July 1, with Frederick II or his minister, Finckenstein, to serve as mediator. Keith pondered that "his Council has persuaded him to negotiate."[164] Peter was discouraged.[165] "Having passed so much time with the Danes, I have to go to negotiations now to see the little they will add to their present propositions."[166] Meanwhile, Danish forces advanced on Lubeck and Hamburg. Peter viewed these incidents as acts of war, happening "at a bad time, after the King of Prussia had consented to be mediator."[167] Haxthausen feared that such a provocation would be sufficient to produce war. The emperor was restrained from attacking: "All examples in this war," Haxthausen commented, "prove the truth that when they [the Russians] must act offensively they can do nothing." Peter would not want "to seem the aggressor." This provocation, however, according to Haxthausen would seem to "give his cause an air of justice."[168] On the last day of his reign, indeed, war broke out. Mitchell in Berlin reported on June 27, "Rumiantsev has already begun his march from Pomerania on the news of the Danes marching into Hamburg."[169]

Alliance with Prussia was the last of Peter's political expedients designed to strengthen the empire for this conflict. However, as the army abroad was strengthened, his regime at home was weakened. Some elements of his foreign policy had remarkable promise, but stability eluded him. Foreigners' reports of the last days at court heightened the sense of instability because they were focused exclusively on the campaign and the conspiracy, in which the diplomats had some stake. The conspirators accepted gifts and financial support from the courts of Austria and France.[170] Rumors of Peter's impending overthrow filled every dispatch. "Panin had contacted Schumacher [Danish commercial consul]," wrote Haxthausen on June 10, "to tell us the Empress' position. We are to assure our courts that he is also discontent . . . his liaison with the Empress gives you rich matter for thought about what will happen when Peter departs."[171]

The striking achievements in foreign policy, which all stemmed from the keystone of his alliance with Prussia, had a jarring effect on diplomats. The changed situation within just a few months fueled European fears that this was just a beginning. "One cannot dissimulate," Choiseul wrote, "that these developments could cause a revolution in the affairs of Europe and dislodge part of our system."[172] "England must fear even more than we do the aggrandizement of Russia on the Baltic."[173] The primary aim of French and Austrian policy in the north was to prevent the outbreak of war. Peter's failure to restore stability and peace, despite enormous concessions to Frederick, gave moral force to successive oppositions, first within his council and then on the part of the conspiracy. In the end, Peter fell victim to his own doctrine of peace at any price.

VI

WHY THE COUP?

Observers of the coup d'état of June 28, 1762, adduced highly biased evidence to demonstrate that Peter's fall from power was caused by his betrayal of tradition and offense to the nation. Diplomats cited, sometimes appended, Catherine's first manifesto, in which she explained the coup as a national revolt. The danger, she wrote, was "a threat to Our Greek Orthodox dogma," presumably referring to secularization. The withdrawal of troops from the Seven Years' War meant that "Russian glory, brought to its height by the victory of arms and by much bloodshed, has now fallen in complete enslavement to the enemy [Prussia] by the conclusion of peace."[1] Robert Keith, among others, subsequently attributed Peter III's fall from power to his "taking away the Church lands . . . joined to his neglect of the clergy; . . . and this after the Emperor had just sacrificed the conquests made by the Russian arms."[2] "Greatly discontent with the government of Peter III, the Russian nation deposed him on the 9th of this month."[3] The French chargé, Laurent Bérenger, elaborated, "Not content with abjuring the religion of his throne in the face of his subjects, [Peter] forced his courtiers to take part in ceremonies of this foreign cult [the consecration of a Lutheran chapel at Oranienbaum]."[4]

Catherine's manifesto endowed the coup d'état with a rationale drawn from political theory, where regicide was occasionally permissible but justifications had to be offered and sustained. From a Christian point of view, Thomas Aquinas had suggested leaving tyrants to the punishment of God, since God was the source of royal authority. In a practical vein, John of Salisbury had recommended assassination. The sixteenth-century Dutch pamphlet *Vindicae contra tyrannos* advocated popular resistance. However, because neither revolt nor conspiracy was tolerable as a general rule, it was left for the actors to find solutions and seek justification. Revolt could only be sanctioned, in any case, by contractual theory where kings could be convincingly accused of having abused power, breached the rights of the estates of the realm, and overturned traditions.

After the coup, Catherine's maintenance of Peter III's discredited foreign policy and most of his domestic enactments clearly necessitated a special reworking of the evidence. In an elaborate manifesto (July 6), designed to replace the initial proclamations by a more sophisticated justification, Catherine shifted ground to the war Peter was planning against Denmark, and, more fully than before, to his personal contempt for native traditions, an easier charge to prove than one based on his legislative enactments.[5] Robert Keith was fully aware of the artifice in her rationalization: "Several other little circumstances greatly exaggerated, artfully represented and improved contributed to the fall of this unhappy Prince, who had many excellent qualities."[6] One observer rejected Catherine's accusations altogether. "It is absurd," wrote Charles T. de Laveaux, the French commercial envoy, "to look for the causes of the overthrow of Peter III in the pretexts which Catherine II published in order to attempt to justify her crime."[7] Louis XV of France was moved by Rhuliere's *Revolution 1762* to a narrow view: "*the fault of Peter III* consists in having given his spouse too much independence and in having been insufficiently watchful of the party of ambitious men around her."[8] Louis XV sensed that the final blow could have been avoided. Keith also had noted a false sense of "security that proved fatal to [Peter]." He had a mistaken notion that "he had . . . secured the affections of the nation by the great favors he had so nobly bestowed upon them."[9]

To St. Petersburg

The road to the capital led from the palace of Peterhof, where Catherine was spending the night of June 27, to the suburbs named Izmailovsk, after the guards whose unit was stationed nearby. Catherine's route had been chosen in advance. Awakened at 6:00 A.M. by Aleksei Orlov (1737–1807), officer of the Preobrazhenskii regiment and one of four brothers who organized the conspiracy, she was informed about the arrest of one of the conspirators. Catherine made her move. She and Orlov and two other officers arrived in the early morning at the barracks, where they were met by twelve members of the Izmailovskii regiment, a drummer, and a priest.[10] She explained to the crowd that her life had been threatened, and that the position of her son as heir to the throne was also in jeopardy. The story of her impending arrest, wrote one diplomat, was "spread around to excite the people."[11] There were also rumors that the Emperor was dead, which, when proven false, were to evoke a sense of guilt among the guards, who, a week later, claiming to have been deceived, revolted again.[12]

Following the route toward the capital, she made the same appeal at the other barracks, the Semenovskii, where she had the help of its captain, Fedor Orlov (1741–1796), and the Preobrazhenskii and cavalry guard barracks, where thirty-six and forty-three officers respectively, later given awards for special services, joined her forces.[13] The streets filled with men in uniform. Catherine later made an effort to count them:

> We had full confidence in a great number of captains in the guards regiments. The ins and outs of the secret were in the hands of the three Orlov brothers . . . The plotters were divided into four separate sections and only the leaders met for the execution of the plan. . . . Toward the end from 30 to 40 officers and about 10,000 of the lower ranks had been included in the secret.[14]

Lists of rewards provide evidence of the extent of the conspiracy, which was considerable. The leaders came mainly from the Izmailovskii, the unit mobilized for the planned Holstein campaign, the cavalry guard, and some from the Preobrazhenskii and Semenovskii regiments.[15] The freely flowing spirits at the *kabaki* (pubs) added to the celebratory atmosphere on June 28.[16] One eyewitness reported soldiers dancing in the streets, hatless, waving their sabers and shouting.[17]

They celebrated their success and their release from mobilization orders. Their commanders were moved to assist them in this spreading wave of military disaffection, and some of their commanders were already on Catherine's side. The guards that started the rebellion, the Izmailovskii, were under the command of one of the leading conspirators, Kiril Razumovskii, the Hetman of Ukraine (1728–1803).[18] Razumovskii was Catherine's most valuable military commander, apart from Grigorii Orlov, her lover. General Aleksandr Villebois, commander of the infantry artillery corps, a position he obtained through the help of Orlov, came over to Catherine's side after the revolt began.[19] General-in-chief and commander of the cavalry guard Mikhail Volkonskii (1713–1788) was one of the highest-ranking officers in the conspiracy.[20]

The high command was "not merely an association of military leaders," wrote John LeDonne, but also "the political core of the ruling class."[21] Catherine later conceived of the government as welcoming her to power. It was not a government in the sense tradition implied; it was a shadow government of men without any political views except the advancement of their special interests. The memoirist Bolotov has left a powerful description of the charismatic Orlov, master of the artillery and treasurer of the guards. During the war at the Russian camp in Königsburg, he was immensely popular, gay, charming, and irresistible. He was imaginative and honest. He had "so many fine and attractive qualities that it was impossible not to love him."[22] At Königsburg, he made friends with Nikolai Korf, Vasilii Bibikov, and Grigorii Potemkin, co-conspirators who helped him mobilize the guards.[23] Catherine, writing to Poniatowski, described by Orlov's role:

> My advent to the throne had been planned for the last six months. . . . I kept my ears open to the offers made to me since the Empress's death. Orlov . . . used to follow me everywhere and committed innumerable follies. His passion for me was openly acknowledged and that is why he undertook what he did. . . . The guards were all prepared. . . . It was agreed that in case of treason we would not wait for his return but assemble the guards and proclaim me Empress. [After Passek's arrest] the whole regiment was astir. A report of what had happened reached Oranienbaum during the night and caused alarm among our confederates. They decided to send the second of the Orlov brothers to fetch me back to town while the other two spread the news that I was arriving. The Hetman, Volkonskii, and Panin were in the secret.[24]

Catherine's civilian support was drawn from long-standing opponents of Peter III. She was blessed at the cathedral by the archbishop of Novgorod, who had been won over. Nikita Panin, tutor of her son, Paul, was by her side. At the cathedral she was supported by two high-ranking nobles, Mikhail Skavronskii and Peter Sheremetev, former senators excluded from Peter's government. These political figures led the oath of allegiance from the soldiers and officers.[25]

From the cathedral, Catherine led the troops to the center of government. "I then went to the Winter Palace where the Synod and Senate were assembled. A manifesto and the text of the oath were hastily composed. From there I walked to the troops."[26] The manifesto had been composed the day before and was ready for distribution; many of the senators were absent; six new senators were placed in office. One eyewitness reported that the debates that day about the takeover "ran very high."[27] Two senators (Trubetskoi and Aleksandr Shuvalov), arriving late, took the oath with reluctance; Glebov remained at home; Mikhail Vorontsov submitted his resignation.[28] The palace was besieged by troops and guards. The Senate gave its approval, something of a formality, and Catherine departed for Peterhof leaving the military in command.[29] Skavronskii, Sheremetev, Senator Ivan Nepliuev,[30] director of the police Nikolai Korf, and lieutenant colonel of the guards Feodor Ushakov were elevated to head the Senate and the country in her absence.[31]

Renunciation

At Oranienbaum Peter III was in ignorance of events. Before the coup, preparing to leave the country, he had attempted to protect himself; there had been arrests and police measures.[32] But on the day of the coup, he lost the support of the director of the police; his spies were arrested, and access to him was cut off by barricades around the capital. Only at 10:00 A.M., when he went to Peterhof for Catherine, was he informed about the coup by a note sent from the capital.[33] He acknowledged to a friend that his wife had been more of a threat than he had been willing to admit.[34] He remarked, "I knew she was capable of [this]."[35]

He had nothing comparable with which to fight. The content of the note, which itself no longer survives, may have given him little hope. There was no outrage, only confusion at the sudden appearance of unfathomable and unbeatable opposition. As Keith put it, Peter had "no recourse either in his Friends or his own Resolution."[36] He was urged by Ernst Münnich to turn to his Holstein guards in his defense.[37] But he thought of escape. He released his courtiers, Alexander Shuvalov, Nikita Trubetskoi, and Mikhail Vorontsov; only Volkov and Münnich remained at the palace. He then headed by boat for Kronstadt, after dispatching an officer in advance to secure the fortress for him. Arriving at Kronstadt, however, he discovered that his officer was under arrest and that the new commander of the island, Admiral Lukian Talyzin,[38] refused passage and permission to land. This consumed twenty-four hours.[39]

Meanwhile, after a day of celebration, Catherine left St. Petersburg at night at the head of a force of 14,000, four guards and four infantry regiments. Changing the guards uniforms back to what they had been before Peter III, she herself dressed in the style of Peter I in a uniform of the Preobrazhenskii regiment. She arrived at Peterhof the next day. Peter, taken captive at Orianienbaum, after his failed attempt to flee, was brought to Peterhof. He had surrendered without struggle and had signed a renunciation of the throne.[40] The following document, existing only in copy, is generally attributed to Teplov:

> During my brief reign in Russia, experience itself made me aware that my abilities were not equal to the task; that I was not fit to govern the Russian state either as

autocrat or in any other capacity. And so even I became aware that there were changes of my own doing that would have led to the utter ruin of the state and to its eternal disgrace.[41]

His abject apology had the effect of reinforcing the impression, as Frederick II saw it, that "he allowed himself to be put aside as like a child trundled off to bed."[42]

On the day after publishing his renunciation, which she appended to her revised manifesto on her reasons for taking power, Catherine was informed that he had died at Ropsha, his place of imprisonment. She now had to account for what was clearly an assassination. On July 7, Catherine issued a new manifesto, claiming Peter had died of hemorrhoidal colic.[43] One diplomat commented that those who had not accepted his renunciation and had never been content with the transfer of power would now "have to be courted."[44] For others, the death of Peter III was a revelation. Béranger now wrote, "She has opened a vast field for discontent and factions. . . . In one case, the grandson of Peter I is deposed and put to death; in another, the grandson of Tsar Ivan languishes behind bars. A Princess of Anhalt-Zerbst usurps the crown beginning her reign as a Regicide."[45] Catherine was now less secure on the throne and threatened by new revolts by some of the guards, who wore the uniforms Peter had given them as a sign of rebellion.[46] According to several sources, the number of "discontents" was considerable.[47] The threat of conspiracy continued through the autumn, after her coronation.[48]

Motives

The difficulties that Catherine had throughout the fall in dealing with disaffection cast significant doubt on the substance of her claim to represent the popular will. To ascribe motives to her supporters on June 28 is arbitrary, especially in view of later regrets. Some must have participated in hopes of reward, some because they were caught up in the events, and some because they were persuaded by their peers or officers. The later regrets demonstrate that some could not fully justify to themselves what they had done. At the end, Peter may have wielded greater power than he believed.

The court did not entirely defect on June 28. Catherine's circle moved against him. Members of his own group either remained loyal or were silent. His brilliant and determined rival organized a conspiracy, but it is difficult to identify her supporters as a political opposition with a community of shared interests. Catherine's support came from personal networks; her military power drew force from the personal charisma of the leader of the guards, Grigorii Orlov, with whom she had an intimate liaison and a child in 1762.

Catherine generally denied that she had any role in planning the coup: "We never had the intention or the desire to ascend the throne in this manner," she publicly announced.[49] But she confessed to Poniatowski, "Everything was done, I will not conceal from you, under my own direction. . . . [T]hings had been more than mature for a fortnight."[50] Few concrete details were offered in diplomatic dispatches. Foreign diplomats themselves were implicated. Ministers of France, England, and Austria were troubled by Peter III's threat to the balance of power in the north, to British possessions in Hanover, and to French hegemony in Denmark and Sweden: the conspiracy was a source of encouragement and hope. They described Catherine's relations with various courtiers and they enclosed notes from her to their respective courts on her policy positions.[51] Beginning in March, they recorded money paid to "secret channels"[52] and described her moods, upon which their hopes rested.[53] Catherine's ties with Mercy, Breteuil, Sievers, Panin, Shakhovskoi, Razumovskii, and Teplov were charted with precision.[54] Informal discussion of Peter's plans to depart for the campaign were linked with a prognosis of his fall from power.[55]

Catherine made no secret of her determination to rule in her own right. In her memoirs, she wrote that the crown of Russia always attracted her more than her husband.[56] She described the obstacles, staked out her opponents, and estimated her chances. During the illness of Empress Elizabeth, Catherine referred to her fear and hatred of Peter Shuvalov—"that second Godunov"—who, she wrote, wished to establish a regency council for himself and send her back to Germany.[57] She frequently referred to her son as the source of inspiring loyalty to herself. She wrote in 1756 to the English envoy, Sir Charles Hanbury-Williams: "This is my dream. After being informed of her death, and being certain that there is no mistake, I will go straight to my son's room. If I meet, or can quickly get ahold of the Grand Master of the Hunt Aleksei Razumovskii, I shall leave with him and ten men under his control."[58] "I shall either perish," she concluded, "or reign."[59] "There is no doubt," wrote Haxthausen in 1762, "that this Princess has coveted for a very long time a great and ambitious design."[60]

In the fall of 1757 and 1758, rivalry over the succession began in earnest. The Bestuzhev-Riumin arrest and trial was at first threatening, then reassuring. Catherine was accused of conducting a personal and political correspondence with General Apraksin, who was accused of intentions of moving his troops back to Russia to help out in the succession at the moment of the Empress's death.[61] Catherine proved immune to attack presumably because of her great ability to persuade. Rumors persisted that she had not given up plans to seize power at the moment of the Empress's death.[62] "As much as the present Czar is open, the Czarina his wife is cunning, secret and dissembling."[63]

The Orlov conspiracy was probably initiated in early 1762.[64] Catherine's pregnancy, which she tried to conceal in mourning clothes, prevented her from making her claims as an aggrieved spouse until April, after she gave birth.[65] Peter provided the pretext in May by announcing his intended departure for the front by early summer. This may have been Catherine's achievement. "I am badly mistaken," wrote Haxthausen, "if the Empress did not put it into Peter's head to leave at the head of his army."[66] Peter then left for Oranienbaum to celebrate the start of the campaign.[67] Catherine remained at Peterhof. Between June 26 and June 28 she was busy composing decrees and planning her first acts as Empress.[68]

The accession manifesto was composed by Grigorii Teplov. Kyril Razumovskii, president of the Academy of Sciences, reproduced it on the Academy's printing press.[69] Nikita Panin, tutor of the Grand Duke, went to the summer palace to secure the safety of his ward.[70] These preparations would help immediately after the revolt to reestablish the operating principles and legal assumptions of autocracy, which would be badly shaken by intervention in the normal political process. Their work was critical to their success on June 28.

Teplov, Shakhovskoi, Sheremetev, Skavronskii, and Panin were civilian officials of enormous distinction but without portfolio. Their authority was a sign of the power that eminent nobles, without any base of authority, could hold over the bureaucracy, regardless of established and legitimate procedures of rule. Their independent power by virtue of their names may indeed have been one reason that Catherine later was to keep the nobility in check. The coup d'état must have seriously weakened the case for nobles' rights in Russia. S. O. Shmidt wrote, "these court storms had little to do with the bureaucracy."[71] But it was over the entire bureaucracy, which showed some reluctance, that this small group triumphed. If the possibility of governing was closed to them because of Peter III's appointments, then their exclusion had vital political meaning for the instability of the succession.

As for motives, the conspiracy was constructed upon well-established patterns of loyalty. Bestuzhev-Riumin was clearly a key figure in the beginning of the polarization of the court and a key figure in the opposition throughout the period, even from exile.[72] Bestuzhev's enemies (Volkov, Vorontsov, Mel'gunov, Shuvalov) became Peter's allies and defenders on June 28. Bestuzhev's relatives and friends were Peter's opponents.[73] Rubinshtein's polarization of the court into two parties, Shuvalov and Vorontsov, does not make much sense as a description of the nature of antagonisms at court. The two groups were divided differently. The first included the Shuvalovs and Vorontsovs, the Trubetskois, Volkov, Glebov, Naryshkin, Chernyshev, and Mel'gunov. The second consisted of Bestuzhev-Riumin, Shakhovskoi, Panin, Nepliuev, Razumovskii, Teplov, Skavronski, Sheremetev, and Sievers.

Peter's confiscation of Bestuzhev's estate in 1762 was an important act of antagonism,[74] and it was accompanied by other signals to the opposition.[75] Catherine's friend Teplov was arrested;[76] Panin was threatened with a diplomatic post in Sweden;[77] Prince Ivan, a possible substitute for Paul, was given improved accommodations in the fortress, an implied threat to Catherine.[78] Iakov Shakhovskoi, former general procurator of the Senate, and Iakov Sievers, a courtier, were retired from the court and possibly threatened with exile.[79] Nepliuev, a senator, feared his own demotion as a consequence of that of Shakhovskoi and submitted his resignation, which was not accepted. His son also experienced demotion under Peter III.

In this divisive situation, family connections were clearly not insignificant. They seem less important than the imponderables of long-time association and power, however. For example, although Mikhail Vorontsov was married to the sister of a leading conspirator (Skavronskii), he remained loyal to Peter III. General Rumiantsev, commander of the northern army, was also connected to the conspirators by family line, but refused to shift his loyalties and was retired when he returned to Russia.

The core of Peter's supporters had been united by years of political work and friendship. As they acquired power through a shared sense of political compatibility and the achievement of their goals, they adhered to each other and to

Peter. In the eighteenth century the appearance of proto-parties, especially in France, was one of the most important results of the broader discussion at court of ideas about tax reform and public policy. Similarly, the formation of political loyalties in eighteenth-century Russia, a phenomenon of extraordinary complexity, cannot be explained exclusively by patronage networks and/or by family connections, although, to be sure, group identity was not entirely separate from those networks and connections. David Ransel has written about Peter's rule as a period when a ruler attempted to govern without traditional familial and personal patronage networks that dominated the court and upper administration. To Ransel, the lesson was that "Rulers could not govern without them and rely solely on the bureaucracy. Those who tried, like Peter III and Paul I, enjoyed but brief and stormy careers cut short by assassination."[80] However, this misrepresents Peter's base of support and mistakes the nature of the coup d'état. Peter did not lack powerful political support; he lacked temporarily the ability or the will to mobilize that support.

In Catherine's coup, officers and commanders of the guard were critical to her success. In Peter's reign, loyalty to commanders had been intentionally enhanced by new laws changing the name of the unit to that of its commander.[81] This only fueled Catherine's advantage, gained by access through Orlov to the treasury of the artillery corps to money for bribing the guards.[82] The two loyal regiments, for example, the Ingermanland and Astrakhan regiments, were led by Mel'gunov, Peter's ally.[83] The disloyal regiments were almost all under the command of conspirators. The cavalry guard was no exception. "The Regiment of the Horse-Guards were among the first to appear and showed greatest Animosity against the late Regime and against Prince George, their Colonel." Volkonskii, however, one of the conspirators, was appointed late in Peter's reign general-in-chief and commander of the cavalry.[84] With Volkonskii and forty other officers part of the secret, it would have been surprising had the cavalry gone the other way. Opposition in the military was clearly focused on the campaign, even though here too personal considerations in some cases were decisive. Mikhail Volkonskii, for example, had been relieved of his general command of the army under Peter III for negligence in supplying his troops.[85] His appointment to Peter's council on military affairs, it would seem, did not erase his resentment, which was possibly increased by Peter's obstinence on Holstein.[86] Volkonskii joined the opposition at roughly the time of Peter's announcement of his coming departure.[87] Razumovskii, although given land and serfs by Peter, was a long-time admirer of Catherine[88] and a friend of Teplov, who was threatened by Peter with arrest.[89] Aleksandr Villebois, "Grand Master" of the artillery and head of the corps that came to Catherine's assistance on June 28, was presumably won over by Grigorii Orlov, whom he appointed treasurer of the artillery corps.[90]

Sources of Opposition

An understanding of the motives of the coup d'état and sources of opposition helps provide a clearer conception of the role of the autocrat at the eighteenth-century court. In an uncritical acceptance of eighteenth-century memoirs, Solov'ev made Peter III extremely unpopular and argued, for that reason, that his rule was without support.[91] Solov'ev, one of the authors of Peter's hopeless reputation, portrayed Peter as a ludicrous figure.[92] The implication is that there were implicit codes of behavior appropriate to autocrats, and that the court resented willful and arbitrary authority when it was combined with idiosyncratic behavior. The question of whether idiosyncratic behavior makes an autocrat vulnerable to attack is not worth serious consideration; the question of whether ludicrous behavior contributed to Peter III's unpopularity remains unanswerable. There is not enough reliable evidence, and too much contradiction, to confirm the anecdotes upon which Peter's reputation rests.

One charge that merits consideration is that an autocrat might encounter serious opposition for irreligious behavior. Catherine emphasized in her first manifesto Peter's lack of respect for Orthodoxy. She could hint but not argue openly that secularization was a betrayal of Russian imperial tradition, since Peter's enactment represented the culmination of repeated efforts.[93] Nor would she want a reputation as an enemy of Enlightenment reform. So, instead, she charged Peter with heterodoxy, since Russian law excluded rulers who were not Orthodox.[94] She turned his irreverent behavior in Church into an attack on icons; she exaggerated his consecration of a Lutheran chapel at Oranienbaum into an attempt to force an alien religion upon his country.[95] Was his tolerance of other religions a source of opposition, or did Catherine find this charge useful and convenient? Peter was not devout, and he did offend the clergy. However, it was an anticlerical age. It cannot be demonstrated that Peter's lack of faith made much difference. Catherine did not find it necessary to halt secularization altogether, and she also repromulgated Peter's other allegedly offensive laws.[96]

Another charge is that Peter's pro-Prussian sympathies lost him support at court. His tolerance of Lutherans and prohibition of private chapels were counted as deplorable departures from Russian custom.[97] It did cause note among diplomats that Peter sometimes wore the Order of the Black Eagle, which Frederick of Prussia sent him as a sign of friendship. However, in November 1762, Catherine was also wearing the Black Eagle, with which she was "very pleased."[98]

It is thought that the sacrifice of conquests ending Russia's participation in the Seven Years' War was done out of fanatical pro-Russian sympathies and, as such, was unpopular at court. With the aid of Catherine's distorting lens, the return of territorial gains in the treaty of peace has seemed a product of ambitions infinitely remote to the Russian national interest. Looking at this treaty differently, the Russo-Prussian peace, which did entail a sacrifice of conquests, was more than an end to an episode of war; it ended the likelihood that either England or France would be as powerful a force in central and eastern European affairs as Russia had become. Equally important, as discussed above, by late 1761, when Peter came to power, war had become a financial and social issue; up to 4,000 soldiers had deserted.[99] Colberg had not yet fallen, the Swedish government had determined to withdraw from the war, and Russian forces seemed weak. When Catherine came to power, despite the condemnation of the peace in her manifesto, she confirmed it and used it to secure her own alliance with Frederick and her independence from Austria and France.[100]

Peter unwisely gave priority to the territorial claims of his German duchy instead of to the restoration of his empire after the war. Catherine may have convincingly claimed that by planning a war against Denmark to reconquer lands once belonging to his native duchy of Holstein Peter had advocated a war "both untimely and extremely useless to the Russian state." Yet his dynastic orientation was not unusual in the eighteenth century—one may compare the preoccupation of the British monarchs with Hanover and of the Hapsburgs with Silesia. The opposition he encountered was not over the insignificance of Holstein to Russia but over financing a new campaign.[101] This opposition was not necessarily in favor of Catherine: his advisors sought to keep him on the throne.[102] Saldern wrote Frederick II, "I foresee that as soon as the war against Denmark will take place, a revolt is inevitable. Would you work for the preservation of this prince?"[103] On the whole, despite his reputation, Peter's reign was well received. Haxthausen, who had no reason to make Peter's reputation better than it was, wrote that he was "very popular."[104]

Conclusion

Some of the implications of Catherine's accusations have relevance to the broader culture she seemed to be describing in alluding to opposition to Peter III. Was there a fear of foreign influence in Russian government in 1762? Catherine's cynicism in using this accusation is clear in her letter of August 2 to the Polish prince Poniatowski, her former lover. "You should know that everything was done on the principle of hatred of foreigners; Peter III himself passed for one."[105] Hatred of the foreigner was a charge taken from Elizabeth's manifesto of 1741, and from earlier usages going back to the early seventeenth century. Xenophobia could be stirred up in Russia, but it can hardly have been a cause of revolt, especially among regiments of mixed origin. One regiment that took a particularly active part in the coup, for example, the cavalry, was "composed mostly of Livonians."[106] In Catherine's own immediate retinue were numerous foreigners, including the commander of the infantry, Aleksandr Villebois; two officers of the horse guard, Iakov Berger and Iurii Liven; Nikolai Korf, promoted by Catherine from director of the police to senator on the second day of the coup, and Jean Odar, her Piedmontese secretary, who helped plan the coup. On the day of the coup there was one recorded instance of violence against a foreigner.[107]

The implication that Russians were pushed aside by foreigners in government, one of the key features of Peter's modern reputation, is not spelled out in Catherine's manifestoes.[108] Nor in the memoirs of the senator Ivan Nepliuev, one of the few neutral Russian observers of the coup d'état, was there any suggestion that Peter's partiality to Prussia or the presence of Peter's German relatives at court had anything to do with his fall from power.[109] This is in part because under Peter III, Russians clearly dominated domestic affairs. "The Emperor," wrote Breteuil, "decides his affairs with each of his ministers, that is, for foreign affairs, Vorontsov,

for war, Trubetskoi, the marine, Admiral Golitzyn, the interior, Glebov, and with the Secretary of his Commands, Wolkonsky,"[110] In April, Peter began to rely on a council of state, which did include his Holstein relatives and Ernst von Münnich, but it also included the powerful Russian figures Dmitrii Volkov, Aleksei Mel'gunov, Mikhail Volkonskii, Mikhail Vorontsov, and Nikita Trubetskoi.[111]

More broadly, the appointment of Peter's Holstein relatives to government positions did not have the same significance it would have had in the nineteenth century. Nobles of Lifland, Kurland, and Holstein comprised a northern European nobility which mingled with the Russian nobility and Ukrainian nobility in school, at court, and in the countryside in the community of landowners. Only an incautious reading of select documents makes "hatred of foreigners" widespread in the 1750s and 1760s. Intellectual custom in Europe, in Voltaire's words, was judicious imitation or in Russia imitation of the West. Foreign literature was popular; foreigners held key positions in institutions of higher learning.[112] French was widely spoken by the francophile nobility, and German was also popular. Peter I favored Germans; Anne had delegated considerable power to foreigners, Elizabeth's heir designate was a Holstein prince with a German wife.[113] To peasants and townspeople, the family line of the tsar or tsaritsa was a matter of indifference. The Cossack rebel Pugachev acquired an enormous peasant following as Emperor Peter III.[114]

Catherine may have raised the issue of foreign influence because of her following among the guards, whose new uniforms had provided a pretext for revolt. Peter's discipline and Prussian-style drills were used symbolically by Catherine, who claimed that to restore Petrine uniforms was to restore tradition itself.[115] "He tried more and more to give offense by perverting all that had been established by the Great . . . sainted . . . Peter."[116] In an effort to improve discipline, Peter had indeed introduced new regulations and drills and prohibited the knout and gauntlet, which, in retrospect, may have appeared too lenient rather than too harsh. He apparently spoke openly of disbanding the guards, which, along with mobilization orders, would have tipped the balance against him.[117] Still, not all the guards regiments participated in the coup on Catherine's side.[118] After 1762, there were petitions to restore Peter III's innovations, and in 1763, aides-de-camp were allowed to wear the epaulettes Peter had given them, raising a question about what they really wanted.[119] The guards were easy to provoke and hard to pacify.[120]

Peter III lost popularity due to his fanatical pursuit of war against Denmark, which his advisors believed Russia could not afford. By his plans for war, Peter alienated the guards and their officers who were threatened with mobilization, just as Catherine independently was gaining their support through her association with the Orlovs. Peter maintained the support of his immediate entourage, but he failed to suppress a conspiracy among a group of courtiers who had long been opposed to him. He was oddly and inexplicably oblivious to the possibility that, once in power, he could still be challenged. He also apparently believed that his reforms gave him the command he needed over the bureaucracy. Peter was not wrong, but the weight of the military, whose favor he had not curried, proved to be more decisive. It is clear that his German background, with his assumption that discipline and loyalty were the same thing, misled him in this context. As a result, Peter was easily brought down by a rival who was better able to command at the right moment. Although Catherine was superior in the contest for power, his achievements stand untouched by her accusations. His failing was his inability to confront the conspiracy. His excessive self-confidence and false assumptions can be seen in his last letter to Frederick, "What do the Russians think of me?" He thought he knew.[121]

VII

CONCLUSION
RUSSIAN AUTOCRACY AT MID-CENTURY

A paradox persists in interpretations of the reign of Peter III. On the one hand, his regime is generally characterized as a failure—ephemeral reforms, offense to the clergy and the noble guards officers, and mismanagement of the administrative side of affairs. Sergei Solov'ev, in his history of Peter's reign, speaks of the growing antagonism to his reign, beginning with "The dissatisfaction of individuals . . . accompanied by dissatisfaction of the powerful estates, the clergy and the military." Deep discontent, he wrote, "spread through St. Petersburg, and even in distant localities it could not help but be observed that the government machine was breaking down."[1] On the other hand, it is common to find references to the long-standing power of certain ideas of reform, for example Peter's emancipation of nobles and secularization of Church lands, and to the efficiency of the reform process and wide popularity of some reform measures in Peter's reign. How can important and enduring reforms and the efficient promulgation of laws that the previous ruler had put to one side be identified so completely with failure and defeat for the autocracy in this brief period?

There is some truth in both positions. Peter initiated demobilization from the Seven Years' War, but his planned campaign for Holstein promised to stall the process. Officers were not brought back from the front, secularization was used to seize horses and grain from monasteries, the Senate was asked for funds it did not have. The prolongation of war was an issue that could easily have evoked some opposition, especially among the military.[2] But the argument by extension that there was massive discontent and that his reforms in general were not well considered or enduring is no more than accommodation to the self-justifying rationales advanced by Catherine II at her accession to the throne. By the end of his reign, astute financial measures brought him the funds he needed for the campaign. His other reforms were in progress; the change in rulers did not reverse their course. Nearly all of them were brought to fruition in his successor's reforms. The critically important enactments, the emancipation of nobles from obligatory state service, the secularization of ecclesiastical property, and the liberalization of commercial regulations underwent no essential alteration in substance. In other words, the state

[handwritten margin notes at top: M/C had political judgment + Peter's understanding of new process of reform so & got best of both worlds]

made great gains from the brief but active and strong leadership of Peter III, who was unquestionably a pivotal figure in the eighteenth century, despite his failure to make much of a personal impression on his contemporaries.

The European Enlightenment had the adherence of a series of remarkable rulers who exercised a large measure of control over image, advanced theoretical positions, and had a sophisticated sense of political mobilization. In the opinion of contemporaries, Catherine was one of the greatest of these. Her biographers confirmed, if they did not create, the partitioning of Enlightenment rule from the premodern past. Catherine's reputation and writings were used to distinguish her rule from what allegedly came before, rule-by-favorites despotism. For example, V. O. Kliuchevskii wrote that her coup d'état of June 28, 1762, was "an important turning point in Russian life."[3] Sidney Hook and Viktor Leontovich perceived Catherine as the first Russian ruler to move in the direction of liberalism, in particular, her grant of rights and advantages to the nobility.

To rehabilitate Peter III by measuring his success in comparable personal terms has its limitations. The numerous accounts written after the coup were contemptuous of his lack of literary interest and theoretical insight, his personal idiosyncrasies, and his poor leadership at the end. These narratives, which contain kernels of truth along with bias and exaggeration, stand in the way of a convincing portrait of a ruler of enormous erudition and ability. Yet Peter had a decisive impact on the laws of his country; the results of these laws encouraged economic growth and social change; he and his advisors were aware of the risks and anticipated the consequences of their acts. In sum, Peter III used his power to define the expectations of the politically effective elite. By his sweeping rejection of an earlier and more conservative generation's political position, he fit in practice if not in image what was expected of the Enlightenment ruler.

The misleading judgment that can come from excessive concern for the monarch's theoretical pronouncements suggests the weakness of the general model of political mobilization drawn from nineteenth-century discourse about Enlightenment monarchs. For example, Catherine was praised as an "enlightened despot" for having used persuasion rather than force to gain court opinion, sometimes called public opinion, to her side in 1762. The context in which the political options of courtiers was worked out, however, suggests the complexity of the conditions of her victory. A large and strategic section of the court was politically and financially dependent upon imperial patronage. The amassing of soldiers—that is, her choice of a military alternative on June 28—limited the options for those who still wished to govern. The intellectual leverage exerted by the court at this time has never been sufficiently recognized. Court opinion must have been exceptionally firm in its support of the reform program of Peter III to have it so quickly be restored despite Catherine's condemnation in her manifestoes. *[handwritten margin note: W! she didn't condemn reform there]*

In other words, the model should be revised to determine the shared assumptions and informal structures by which autocrats derived the limited necessary consensus.[4] Reform was the expression of an entire political culture which emerged gradually in the eighteenth century. The writings of Feofan Prokopovich had established the basis of autocracy of Peter I's reign as the monarch's will, an understanding conspicuously drawn from practice as well as theory. After the death of Peter I, absolutism was so deeply a part of political culture that it survived the five palace coups and other political upheavals that weakened the monarchy. To be sure, after 1725 a modification was made to the theory. A principle was introduced by the Supreme Soviet that law, not the monarch, was the source of authority.[5] The autocrat was thus bound to Petrine notions of the "national welfare" (vsenarodnaia pol'za) and to legal precedent, although monarchical authority remained the only mechanism that ensured compliance. In the years after 1741, an era of relative stability and rapid Europeanization of the court, Elizabeth showed scrupulous concern for legal precedent and some interest in proposals for reform. In 1753, she formed a commission to codify Petrine law and address new issues of welfare by a single statute on "the status of all subjects."[6] Along with routine codification, these commissioners devised new applications of the welfare concept.[7] Probably the most important new concept introduced into law, implying a shift of some responsibility for welfare from the monarch to his or her subjects, was that the Church was held to be responsible for welfare of the peasants on its lands. This was at least part of the rationale for the planning of secularization in the 1750s. Economic prosperity and social welfare were becoming an end in themselves, not just a means to more effective warfare,[8] and thus without incurring opposition the government could now rationalize its reform on the basis of efficiency and productivity, or welfare goals alone. The Enlightenment critique of clerical abuses is one example of an issue emerging as a problem of public welfare, one demanding action by the state.[9]

The general model of Enlightenment reform thus focuses primarily on the sources of political and social coherence under autocracy. In all three reigns, the main source of social coherence was the elite of the service nobility, which controlled the codification process.[10] Under Peter III, a broad coalition of these service nobles who had worked on the law—men who were steeped in the work of creating new statutes—came to dominate the highest posts in government. The first act of Peter III was to expedite their work by ridding his government of the complex and overlapping command structure that Elizabeth had used to prevent any single institution from becoming too strong. Peter based his power on the foundations Elizabeth had laid. However, he intervened more effectively than she had, and he invested his cabinet with considerable authority. Two acts in particular are worth noting, his *Machtspruch* (the weighting of verbal commands with the power of law) and his enhancement of the office of privy secretary, which Volkov used to revise Senate laws. The first of these acts repeated a previous instruction by Elizabeth to clarify the flow of command.[11] By the second, in an act unique to Peter's reign, a coalition acquired power to carry through legislative proposals.

Peter thus relied on a network of elite service nobles that was large and powerful but informal and without any single institutional base. His coalition included some of the most prominent statesmen and thinkers from Elizabeth's court: Dmitrii Volkov (secretary of her Conference at the Imperial Court), Aleksandr Glebov (her Commissar of War), Roman Vorontsov (senator and head of her Codification Commission), Mikhail Vorontsov, (Vice Chancellor for foreign affairs), Ivan Shuvalov (her favorite), Aleksei Mel'gunov (a scholar of German literature and friend of Shuvalov), Mikhail Lomonosov (a scientist), Lev Naryshkin and Andrei Chernyshev (courtiers), and others mentioned above. Their institutional affiliations are an intellectual mapping of the spread of the Enlightenment in Russia: the Academy of Sciences, the Cadet Corps, the Codification Commission of the Senate, and Elizabeth's Conference at the Imperial Court. Peter's Moscow supporters were distinguished intellectuals and writers. The confidence Peter derived from support by this group, the deference they could command, and their shared commitment to Enlightenment reform and bureaucratic efficiency must explain to a very considerable extent the more active style of government. Both Senate and imperial decrees found a common discourse in rationale for reform: to relieve the peasants of burdens, to protect the innocent, and to improve administrative efficiency. Most of the reforms also bore the weight of precedent, showing the origin of some projects going back to administrative work of the reign of Peter I. Yet too much should not be made of precedents. Peter III's design of secularization, for example—a project lifted down from the shelf virtually intact—also showed a firmly secular cast of thinking in a few administrative elements that marked an enormous change from the past. Volkov's liberalization of commercial regulations was also clearly representative of the intellectual breakthrough. It was an enactment containing a bold and entirely unprecedented attack on mercantilism and mercantilist understanding of prices not in the spirit of Petrine regulations; Peter III's edict of tolerance of Old Believers and repeal of an outmoded criminal code were other signposts of a transformation at court. Far from being the final display of rule-by-favorites despotism, this brief monarchy was the first confident step in the direction of Enlightenment reform, toward the perception of politics, like science, as a form of social reason.[12]

The Enlightenment model of centralized government must not overlook the monarch, as work on the reigns of Elizabeth and Peter III has tended to do. In contrast to his image, Peter steadily strengthened autocratic authority over law. He used his informal councils against the traditional powers of institutions such as the Senate. Throughout the eighteenth century, the autocracy remained bound by post-Petrine legal convention, which included the Senate's primacy in the legislative process, but rule by informal networks brought a subtle accrual of autocratic authority along with some demotion of the Senate's initiating role in the enactment of law. Catherine II unswervingly continued to strengthen the autocratic command. The Senate never regained its stature, and Catherine never relinquished the authority which Peter had acquired over legislation. "The Senate," she wrote to her general procurator, A. A. Viazemskii, "cannot make laws."[13] Catherine created advisory councils and commissions whose advice she sometimes heeded. More often, she dictated to the state institutions. By the end of the century, there was neither a supreme council nor a powerful Senate.

The sum of these developments, apart from the fragmentation of the power of institutions, was the enhancement of the social and economic status of autocracy's principle beneficiaries.[14] Nobles acquired greater personal freedom and security of land tenure, merchants gained control over the grain trade with the elimination of noble commercial monopolies and the reduction of internal and export customs barriers, and the state gained new sources of revenue, such as the tax imposed on former ecclesiastical, now economic estates.

Among the reforms, secularization was crucial to the success of the others. Church reform, conceived by bureaucrats possibly as early as the mid-1720s, was shunted from office to office in successive decades. It was finally carried out under Peter and Catherine by the military officers who returned from the front. The increase in the size of the nobility in the eighteenth century had put pressure on the entitlement to land, a battle which the Church lost and its former peasants and nobles won, the latter victory represented by emancipation from obligatory state service rather than gains from secularized land. The value of their land was finally assessed during the completion of the land survey, which provided a measure of judicial protection of property boundaries.

Trends favoring the expansion of noble landholding and merchant privilege were accompanied by—indeed, dependent upon—the strengthening of Russia's market position and its new foreign alliances. By ending Russian participation in the Seven Years' War, Peter III left Russia in a position of competitive advantage in Europe while he attempted to revive Baltic trade which had declined in the last years of war.[15] Peter thus gave Russia a credible alternative in Europe to weak alliances and also created a political climate advantageous to his domestic program.

Among the direct benefits of peace to domestic policy, the demobilization created an incentive for nobles' return to the land and allowed the state to dismiss staff. Further, the reallocation of officers to non-military tasks advanced long-stalled projects such as the land survey and secularization of ecclesiastical estates. Finally, the end of wartime expenditures brought orders for reallocating scarce funds to non-military purposes, education, commerce, and law enforcement, and to new military purposes, such as the training of officers and the building of a navy. The shift of budgetary priorities had already begun by the time of Peter's overthrow in June 1762.

Russia thus reaped domestic advantages from Peter's foreign policy, although territorial conquests were sacrificed along the way. Russia enjoyed postwar benefits of eased credit and a powerful new central European base of alliances. Meanwhile, delaying the peace, France suffered a staggering loss from the colonial war which was prominent among the factors that forced France into reform and revolution. Far from being incidental and insignificant, had Peter III's accomplishments been limited to withdrawal from the war, their history would have recorded a notable success. Given that he had not only executed a coup in foreign policy but also several in domestic affairs, which were targeted to bring in tax and customs revenues and to open up new opportunities for agriculture in the south—it is difficult to see any justice at all in the traditional dismissive treatment of his reign.

The legacy of Peter and Catherine, it can be emphasized, did not include major reforms accomplished by rulers elsewhere in central and western Europe at this time, for example, emancipation of the serfs, elimination of unfree labor in factories, or promotion of manufacturing in urban areas. Beginning in mid-eighteenth-century Europe, ideas of free trade, uninhibited commercial expansion, independence of agricultural producers, and development of manufacturing were everywhere. But Russian political leaders, with the exception of statesmen such as Peter III's advisor, Dmitrii Volkov, and Catherine's secretary, Grigorii Teplov, did not take these ideas much to heart.[16]

The central conception of reform brings the larger problem of historical transformation into focus, since the pace and extent of reform were carefully controlled by the autocracy. Apart from the lack of fundamental change in the social structure, the evolution of reforms after 1762 shows considerable hesitancy on the part of the autocracy, especially under Catherine II. Local government took twelve years of planning; many retired nobles returned to the cities after the Pugachev revolt in 1774–1775 since protection of their property and lives was insufficient. Trade made swift improvement, but guilds were not broken down and the mass of the merchantry only gradually obtained limited freedom within the economy and in urban government. The nobles waited two decades for a formal confirmation of rights and privileges. The pressure for these reforms, to be sure, was not very great.

Peter and Catherine enhanced the power of the state and cleared the way for reform by attacking some particularist interests. However, their autocratic methods created rigidity in the application of reform and stifled political dialogue. In social history wealth and social power were more broadly diffused by the end of the century than they had been under Peter I. The concentration of landed wealth greatly increased, but the number of small landowners also rose. The rapid growth of trade, the spread of domestic manufacturing which raised incomes, and vast new opportunities for "economic" peasants showed the expanding resources of the state which autocratic policy fully encouraged. In political history, however, far from creating a new epoch, the Enlightenment reformers further fragmented institutional authority and further enhanced imperial authority, giving informal access to power to the elite of the court nobility. With the rise of coalition politics, eminence at court remained as important and satisfying as it had been. The hierarchy of the central agencies of government and court posts remained relatively fixed, even as the scale and function of government grew. Peter III and Catherine II thus reinforced the political legacy of Peter I. They established broader but still rigid social boundaries, and they continued to grant land and privileges to a small political elite in return for service. In the nineteenth century, this form of rule was modified but not abandoned despite the pressure for reform coming from economic growth coupled with social stagnation, the rise of a legal profession, and a mounting force of public sentiment.

NOTES

Introduction

1. "It was clear to all true sons of the fatherland," she declared, "what danger there was to the whole Russian state, and above all, what threat to Our Greek Orthodox dogma." *Polnoe sobranie zakonov Rossiiskoi imperii, 1649–1913,* 234 vols. (St. Petersburg, 1830–1916), 15: 11,582 (June 28, 1762) (cited hereafter as *PSZ*).

2. *Osmnadtsatyi vek. Istoricheskii sbornik,* ed. P. Bartenev, 4 vols. (Moscow, 1868–1869), vol. 4, pp. 216–23.

3. As on her coronation medallion, "For Having Saved the Faith and the Fatherland."

4. Lynn Hunt's expression for the revolutionaries' break with the past during the French Revolution, "the instant of creation of the new community, the sacred moment of the new consensus." L. Hunt, *Politics, Culture, and Class in the French Revolution* (Berkeley, Calif., 1984), p. 27.

5. C. Leonard, "The Reputation of Peter III," *Russian Review,* vol. 47 (1988), pp. 263–92.

6. *PSZ* 15: 11,446 (*im.,* Feb. 21, 1762), pp. 918–19; 11,495 (*sen.,* Apr. 5, 1762), p. 969; 11,509 (*im. na doklad Senata,* Apr. 29, 1762), p. 981; 11,521 (*sen.,* Apr. 26, 1762), p. 994; "Protokoly," Mar. 4, 6, 1762, *TsGADA, f.* 248, *kn.* 3428, *ll.* 86, 185.

7. "To protect the innocent," he claimed as his purpose. He abolished the Secret Investigatory Chancery and ended the pronouncement of "slovo i delo gosudarevo" (the sovereign's word and deed), which carried a charge of rebellion or treason. Slovo i delo had been enhanced by Senate decree in 1714 and used as a means of suppressing the substantial opposition under Peter I. Peter III also pronounced against the use of torture, which may nevertheless have persisted. The archives and functions of the Secret Chancery were transferred to the Senate and thus recreated in a new Secret Expedition. J. Cracraft, "Opposition to Peter the Great," *Imperial Russia, 1700–1917, State, Society, Opposition: Essays in Honor of Marc Raeff,* ed. E. Mendelsohn and M. Shatz (DeKalb, Ill., 1988), p. 23; V. I. Veretennikov, *Iz istorii tainoi kantseliarii, 1731–1762, Ocherki* (Kharkov, 1911), pp. 117–20; *PSZ* 15: 11,445 (*man.,* Feb. 21, 1762), pp. 915–18.

8. *PSZ* 15: 11,420 (*im.* Jan. 29, 1762), pp. 894–95.

9. The continuity was noted by the Danish ambassador, Gregors v. Haxthausen. "As soon as she [Catherine] ascended the throne, she condemned all Peter did in her first sovereign acts, but scarcely a month later, she was already . . . beginning to march in his footsteps." Gregors v. Haxthausen (Danish ambassador to Russia) to Johan Hartvig Ernst Bernstorff (Danish foreign minister), November 5/16, 1762, *Rigsarkivet,* Copenhagen, *Tyske konsliets Udenrigske Afdeling* 80 (cited hereafter as *RAD TKUA*).

10. Wortman's interpretation of legal consciousness as the securing of legal justice is a somewhat separate matter. It was possible, for example, for Catherine to champion "a new expanded role of law and legal equality" and at the same time be "suspicious of the nefarious ways of judges." The antilegalist spirit of her autocratic disdain for the judicial function did not preclude the elaboration of estate rights presumably to be guaranteed by the courts. The manifestoes of Peter's reign similarly reflected the eighteenth-century legal literature, where the protection (or removal of protection) of privilege was guaranteed by institutions that were themselves vulnerable to incursions of the revenue-seeking state. R. Wortman, *The Development of a Russian Legal Consciousness* (Chicago, 1976), pp. 9–10.

11. Concepts of law were essentially the same in the 1750s and 1760s. See W. J. Gleason, *Moral Idealists, Bureaucracy, and Catherine the Great* (New Brunswick, N. J., 1981), p. 8.

12. See Wortman, *The Development*, pp. 9–33; M. Raeff, "The Enlightenment in Russia and Russian Thought in the Enlightenment," in J. G. Garrard, ed., *The Eighteenth Century in Russia* (Oxford, 1973), pp. 25–47, and other works listed in "Marc Raeff: A Bibliography (1946–1987)," in *Imperial Russia*, pp. 289–313.

13. V. A. Bil'basov, *Istoriia Ekateriny Vtoroi*, 2 vols. (Berlin, 1900), vol. 1, p. 458.

14. Revisionist historians have tried to reconcile the paradox of Peter's hopeless image and his activity as a reformer. Firsov argued that his behavior could be explained by alcohol, Bain by idosyncracies, and Fleischhacker, much the same, by mood swings. These revisionists' conclusion, in other words, admits the evidence from the tainted sources. N. N. Firsov, "Petr III i Ekaterina II—Pervye gody ee tsarstvovaniia," in his *Istoricheskie kharakteristiki i eskizy 1890–1922 gg.*, 2 vols. (Kazan', 1922), vol. 2, pp. 43–109; R. Nisbet Bain's *Peter III, Emperor of Russia* (Westminster, 1902), pp. 50–51, and H. Fleischhacker's "Porträt Peters III," *Jahrbücher für Geschichte Osteuropas*, vol. 5 (1957), pp. 127–89. M. Raeff accepts the traditional image (Raeff, "The Overthrow"). See more sweeping reinterpretations by M. Florinsky in *Russia: A History and an Interpretation*, 2 vols. (New York, 1970), vol. 1, pp. 496–513, and A. S. Myl'nikov in *Legenda o russkom printse* (Leningrad, 1987) and *Iskushenie chudom: "Russkii printz" i samozvantsy* (Leningrad, 1991), who reject, as I do, a large part of the substance of the reputation of Peter III.

15. These quotes from John Alexander's biography of Catherine and Bil'basov's biography, both based largely on her memoirs. See Bil'basov, "[Peter] was a terrible coward . . . he was cruel, and he took pleasure in torturing animals and playing for hours with tin soldiers" (Bil'basov, *Istoriia* vol. 1, p. 94); J. Alexander, *Catherine the Great: Life and Legend* (Oxford, 1989), p. 4; J. von Staehlin, "Zapiski Shtelina o Petre Tret'em Imperatore Vserossiiskom," *Chteniia v Obshchestve istorii i drevnostei rossiiskikh*, vol. 59 (1866), no. 4, pp. 67–118.

16. Staehlin, "Zapiski," p. 110.

17. See his "Kratkie vedomosti o puteshestvii Eia Imperatorskogo Velichestva v Kronstadt 1742 mesiatsa maia," *Istoricheskii vestnik*, vol. 31 (Jan.–Mar. 1888), pp. 251–52.

18. "I have always trusted in the protection of the good Lord." Peter to Frederick, May 15, 1762, *Politische Correspondenz Friedrich's des Grossen*, 46 vols. (Berlin, 1879–1939; hereafter cited as *PC*), vol. 21, p. 510. Münnich wrote, "No one knew what the personal religious persuasions of the emperor were," "Zapiski fel'dmarshala Minikha," *Russkaia starina*, vol. 9 (1874), p. 102; see also Staehlin, "Zapiski," p. 110. His pronouncements against the corruption of the Church hierarchy speak only of anticlericalism.

19. P. H. Reill, *The German Enlightenment and the Rise of Historicism* (Berkeley, Calif., 1975), p. 7.

20. Reill, *German*, pp. 7ff.

21. Staehlin, "Zapiski," p. 110.

22. Staehlin, "Zapiski," p. 111.

23. He was abducted and brought to Russia in part to prevent him from accepting an offer to be king of Sweden. Staehlin, "Zapiski," p. 105.

24. Lord Hyndford (British ambassador) to Earl of Harrington (Secretary for Northern Affairs), Apr. 12/24, 1746, *Sbornik imperatorskogo russkogo istoricheskogo obshchestva* (hereafter *SIRIO*), vol. 103 (1879), p. 39.

25. Hyndford to Harrington, p. 39; Staehlin, "Zapiski," pp. 74–84.

26. Simeon Todorskii, Bishop of Pskov (and Catherine's tutor), and Isaac Veselovskii. P. Shchebal'skii, *Politicheskaia sistema Petra III* (St. Petersburg, 1870), p. 20.

27. "Peter benahm sich dabey mit einem Anstände und einer Salbung. . . . Elizabeth, die Pathenstelle verträt, vergoss Freudenthranen, so geruhrt war sie." G. Helbig, *Biographie Peters des Dritte*, 2 vols. (Berlin, 1800), vol. 2, p. 38; Cyril Wich (British ambassador) to Lord Carteret (Secretary for Northern Affairs), Oct. 30, 1742, *SIRIO*, vol. 99 (1897), p. 120.

28. Staehlin, "Zapiski," pp. 112–13.

29. K. Staehlin, *Aus den Papieren Jacob von Stählins* (Berlin, 1926), pp. 102–15.

30. Memoirs purportedly by Caspar von Saldern, an advisor on Holstein affairs, note Peter's interest in arts and science. The Emperor was "greatly concerned to make the arts and sciences flourish . . . he frequented the meetings of the Academy of Sciences . . . [and] had a love of literature." C. von Saldern, *Histoire de la vie de Pierre III, Empereur de toutes les Russes, présentant sous un aspect impartial, les causes de la révolution arrivée en 1762* (Metz, 1802), p. 23.

31. A. T. Bolotov, *Zhizn' i prikliucheniia Andreia Bolotova opisannye samim im dlia svoikh potomkov* (Moscow-Leningrad, 1931) [reprinted 1973], vol. 2, p. 118.

32. Staehlin, "Zapiski," pp. 109–10.

33. Prince August, Stadthalter of Holstein, and his adjutant, Shil'd, Aleksandr Villebois, Ivan Chernyshev, and the Holsteiner von Drukker. Staehlin, "Zapiski," p. 78.

34. Staehlin, "Zapiski," pp. 89–90.

35. "Ce Prince était accoutumé à vivre depuis dix ou douze ans entouré 50 officiers allemands avec lesquels il passait familièrement sa journée." Louis Auguste, baron de Breteuil (French ambassador at St. Petersburg) to Etienne François, duc de Choiseul (Secretary of State for Foreign Affairs in France), Feb. 1/12, 1762, *AMAE CP Russie* 68.

36. He addressed friends and acquaintances with the familiar form and sometimes dressed in a uniform that was undecorated by stars or colors indicative of rank. "Zapiski grafa Briul'ia (iun') 1762," in Bil'basov, *Istoriia*, vol. 2, p. 658; Bolotov, *Zhizn'*, vol. 2, p. 118; "Bumagi Vorontsova," *LOII, f.* 36, *d.* 1071, *l.* 955.

37. T. Bakounine, *Répertoire biographique des francs-maçons russes (XVIIIe et XIXe siècles)* (Paris, 1967), p. xi; A. N. Pypin, *Russkoe masonstvo, XVIII i pervaia chetvert' XIX v.* (Petrograd, 1916), pp. 498–99.

38. "Peter lives such a life that he will certainly shorten his years," wrote the Swedish envoy, a hostile eyewitness. "He drinks every night. . . . Everyone around him smokes too much, and at a dinner a few days ago, the men smoked so much that the Empress and a number of other women felt ill and went home." "There are already stirrings against Peter . . . resentment of his drinking." M. Posse (Swedish ambassador to Russia) to Claes Ekeblad (Chancery President), Jan. 22/Feb. 2, Feb. 8/19, 1762 (Apostille), *RAS DM* 306; Bakounine, *Répertoire*, p. xi; *Grand Lodge* (Oxford, 1967), pp. 232–34; H. Carr, ed., *The Early French Exposures* (London, 1971), pp. 7–17, 142–43; *Zapiski Briul'ia*, pp. 655–58.

39. Bakounine, *Répertoire*, p. xi.

40. "As the Empress lies in state, the habitude of fear . . . is the only sentiment which bears mention," Breteuil to Choiseul, Jan. 11/22, 1762, *AMAE CP Russie* 68.

41. Anisimov places Ivan Shuvalov at the head of an opposition to Peter III's succession before Elizabeth's death, but his account is from Catherine, who acknowledged that Shuvalov's support for Peter at least after Elizabeth's death was secure. E. V. Anisimov, *Rossiia v seredine XVIII veka, Bor'ba za nasledie Petra* (Moscow, 1986), pp. 222–23.

42. Haxthausen to Bernstorff, Dec. 29/Jan. 9, 1762 (draft), *RAD TKUA Gregors Christian v. Haxthausens gesandtskabs Arkiv* 172.

43. For Peter's supporters, see M. I. Semevskii, "Shest' mesiatsev iz russkoi istorii XVIII veka, Ocherk tsarstvovaniia imperatora Petra III, 1761–1762, posviashchaetsia Efimiiu Borisovne Zubovoi," *Otechestvennye zapiski* (1867), no. 1, p. 80.

44. Breteuil to Choiseul, Jan. 11/22, 1762, *AMAE CP Russie* 68.

45. 120,000 rubles yearly. *PSZ* 15: 11,443 (*im.*, Feb. 18, 1762), pp. 911–12.

46. Elizaveta was described as kind but homely ("more than a little plump" and marked by smallpox), a companion rather than a lover, see Posse to Ekeblad, Feb. 12/23 (Apostille), Mar. 26/Apr. 6, 1762, *RAS DM* 306; Saldern, *Histoire*, p. 48; Brul', "Zapiska (June) 1762," pp. 663–64.

47. Posse to Ekeblad, Apr. 2/13, 1762 (Apostille), *RAS DM* 306.

48. Johan German Lestocq, Burkhard von Münnich, Biron (Ernst Johann Büren), and the Mengden family, *PSZ* 15: 11,445 (Feb. 21, 1762), p. 915; V. I. Veretennikov, *Iz istorii tainoi*

kantseliarii (Kharkov, 1911), pp. 116–18; Haxthausen to Bernstorff, Jan. 29/Feb. 9, 1762, *RAD TKUA* 78.

49. Nikita Panin (1718–1783), tutor to the Grand Duke, and Iakov Shakhovskoi (1705–1777), former general procurator of the Senate. Both statesmen later took part in the overthrow of Peter III.

50. Breteuil to Choiseul, Feb. 15/26, 1762, *AMAE CP Russie* 68.

51. "Peter is the only person in his country who does not see the Revolution," Haxthausen to Bernstorff, May 31/June 11, 1762, *RAD TKUA* 80.

52. "He dissimulates so little," Haxthausen to Bernstorff, Jan. 11/22, 1762, *RAD TKUA* 78; "the Emperor, while Great Duke, was rather imprudent in his conduct, by declaring too openly His Disapprobation of the Empress's measures," Andrew Mitchell (British ambassador to Prussia) to Earl of Bute (British Foreign Minister), Jan. 21, 1762, *PRO SP* 90/79. He openly disagreed with his aunt's anti-Prussian foreign policy, and in 1757 he refused to attend the meetings of the Conference at the Imperial Court, her council of war. Volkov, the Conference secretary, showed him the record of the conference meetings, but the absence of his signature on more than a handful of the conference records suggests that he did not regularly follow the protocols. H. Kaplan, *Russia and the Outbreak of the Seven Years' War* (Berkeley, Calif., 1968), p. 50; Staehlin, "Zapiski," p. 93.

53. Robert Keith (British envoy to Russia) to Bute, Feb. 12/23, 1762, *BMAddMSS* 35, 493.

54. Haxthausen to Bernstorff, Jan. 4/15, 1762, *RAD TKUA* 78.

55. Keith to Bute, Jan. 1/12, 1762, *BMAddMSS* 35,493.

56. Keith to Bute, Jan. 11/22, 1762, *BMAddMSS* 35,493.

57. Breteuil to Choiseul, Feb. 1/12, and Mar. 15/26, 1762, *AMAE CP Russie* 68.

58. Keith to Bute, Feb. 5/16, 1762, *BMAddMSS* 35,493.

59. Haxthausen to Bernstorff, Feb. 11/22, 1762, *RAD TKUA* 78.

60. Staehlin, "Zapiski," pp. 67–118.

61. Haxthausen to Bernstorff, Jan. 11/22, 1762, *RAD TKUA* 78.

62. "I have pardoned all my enemies, I have done nothing but good for the Russians," he said on the eve of his overthrow; "why would they wish me ill?" J. -Ch. T. de Laveaux, *Histoire de Pierre III, Empereur de Russie*, 2 vols. (Paris, 1798), vol. 2, pp. 160–61.

63. Breteuil to Choiseul, Mar. 15/26, 1762, *AMAE CP Russie* 68.

64. Frederick II to Peter III, May 1, 1762, *PC*, vol. 21, p. 412.

65. The imperial body guard was formed from a unit of the Preobrazhenskii regiment by Empress Elizabeth after she took power by a coup d'état in 1741. All the soldiers in this regiment were granted nobility; its officers were high-ranking nobles. Peter abolished the body guard, and Catherine reinstated it. G. Helbig, "Russkie izbranniki," *Russkaia starina* (April 1866), p. 151.

66. Catherine to Poniatowski, Aug. 2, 1762, *AKV*, vol. 25, p. 424.

67. V. O. Kliuchevskii, *Kurs russkoi istorii* (vols. 1–5 of his *Sochineniia*, 8 vols. [Moscow, 1955–59]), vol. 4, p. 353.

68. Compare Hunt, *Politics*, pp. 87–119.

69. The cultural frame of monarchical authority was founded in hierarchical ordering ascending to a sacred center. The king's charismatic body was at the center of political discourse. The new romantic identification added to the king's consecrated force. On medieval kingship, see E. H. Kantorowicz, *The King's Two Bodies: A Study in Mediaeval Political Theology* (Princeton, N. J., 1957).

70. C. Geertz, "Centers, Kings, and Charisma: Reflections on the Symbolics of Power," in J. Ben-David and T. N. Clark, eds., *Culture and Its Creators: Essays in Honor of Edward Shils* (Chicago, 1977), pp. 150–71.

71. The Byzantine emperor was traditionally acclaimed not just by the military, but also by the "Blues" and "Greens," the circus parties.

72. See S. E. Finer, *The Man on Horseback: The Role of the Military in Politics* (New York, 1962); D. L. Horowitz, *Coup Theories and Officers' Motives: Sri Lanka in Comparative Perspective* (Princeton, N. J., 1980); and others.

73. There is no holograph text in Peter's hand; see "Reskript," *TsGADA, f.* 3, *d.* 10, *l.* 6.

74. The number of pretenders to the throne rose noticeably in the second half of the century. From 1764 to 1796, 24 pretenders appeared in Russia, by contrast with 8 from 1730 to 1762. The first pretenders claiming to be Peter III were the Ukrainian Nikolai Kolchenko, the Armenian merchant Anton Aslanbekov, and the fugitive recruit Ivan Evdokimov. Support against the regime in the 1760s as in the 1770s was gathered among the Cossacks, soldiers, Old Believers, and lower clergy. S. M. Troitskii, "Samozvantsy v Rossii XVII–XVIII vekov," *Voprosy istorii* (1969), no. 3, pp. 134–46.

75. Laveaux, *Histoire*, vol. 1, p. 216.

76. For example, Dashkova wrote that Peter stuck out his tongue at the priests during the service, as an example of "meaningless behavior that could evoke no respect." Dashkova's attachment to Catherine dates to February 1759. V. V. Ozarkov, *E. R. Dashkova, ee zhizn' i obshchestvennaia deiatel'nost'* (St. Petersburg, 1893), pp. 22–23; E. R. Dashkova, *Zapiski* (St. Petersburg, 1907), pp. 21, 22, 24–41; Bolotov, *Zhizn'*, vol. 2, pp. 101–85.

77. Under Peter III, Shakhovskoi was replaced by Aleksandr Glebov as general procurator of the Senate. Ia. P. Shakhovskoi, *Zapiski kniazia Shakhovskogo, 1705–1777* (St. Petersburg, 1872); M. M. Shcherbatov, *O povrezhdenii nravov v Rossii* (St. Petersburg, 1906).

78. Nikita Panin's position as tutor to the Grand Duke naturally colored his view of Elizaveta Vorontsova, who posed a threat to Paul's succession and Catherine's position as Empress. Panin's recollections in A. F. von Asseburg, *Denkwürdigkeiten* (Berlin, 1842), pp. 315–42; quoted in D. Ransel, *The Politics of Catherinian Russia* (New Haven, Conn., 1975), p. 62.

79. Compare Coxe, "Peter was greatly beloved by those who had access to his person." W. Cox, *Travels into Poland, Russia, Sweden and Denmark*, 4 vols. (London, 1787), vol. 3, p. 43. See also J. Castera (trans. and rewritten, W. Tooke), "beloved of all who composed his more intimate circle," *The Life of Catherine, Empress of All the Russias*, 2 vols. (Philadelphia, 1802), vol. 1, p. 190.

80. Ransel, *Politics*, ch. 3.

81. As she remembered, he tortured animals or played excruciating music on the violin, while she read Plato and Voltaire. "His heart was timid and his mind simple." "One must have not contempt for him but pity," she wrote. "Zapiski, prodolzhennye v 1791 godu," *Zapiski Imperatritsy Ekateriny Vtoroi*, ed. A. S. Suvorin (St. Petersburg, 1907), pp. 104–105, 121–22, 151–69, and elsewhere.

82. Alexander Herzen, the first publisher of her memoirs, wrote, "In reading these pages, one *sees* her *arrive*, one sees her become what she was to be much later . . . she was already afflicted with the curse of the Winter Palace, the thirst for domination." *Zapiski*, ed. Suvorin, pp. iii–iv; *Mémoires de Catherine II*, ed. A. Herzen (London, 1859), p. v.

83. C. Rulhière, *Perevorot 1762*, ed. G. Balitskii (Moscow, 1909), pp. 6–7.

84. [C. F. Schwan] M. de la Marche, *Histoire et anecdotes de la vie, du regne, du détrônement et de la mort de Pierre III, dernier Empereur de toutes les Russes, écrites en forme de lettres* (London, 1766), p. 217.

85. See Schwan, *Histoire et anecdotes*, p. 217. That Peter threatened the archbishop with exile, a common allegation of pro-Catherinian accounts, is depicted as a false allegation; see also Laveaux, *Histoire*, vol. 1, p. 207.

86. The authorship of these memoirs has been questioned. Like Bil'basov, however, I find both the shortcomings and the strengths of this work a kind of signature. E. Hübner, "Fälschung oder korrekte Angabe? Zur Verfasserschaft der 'Biographie Peters des Dritten,' " *Jahrbücher für Geschichte Osteuropas*, vol. 33 (1985), pp. 231–38. Also, the theme is consistent with his earlier writings. See his Danish correspondence. For example, "Noch ist [sic] kein einziger Mensch unglücklich geworden, dahingegen tausende bereits glücklich sind. Man könte vorhin sehen, dass er eine grosse liebe bey den gemeinen Volcke und bey

den Soldaten haben wurde [sic]'' (Saldern to Fr. Vilh. Ottes, January 15/26, 1762, *RAD Rusland* 35, Korrespondance Akter, III, 1761–1766. fr Ottes arkiv); Saldern, *Histoire,* pp. 44, 261.

87. Laveaux, *Histoire,* vol. 1, p. 228.

88. Laveaux, *Histoire,* vol. 1, pp. 131, 180–81, 185–86, 212–14.

89. See K. Staehlin, *Papieren,* p. 232.

90. Helbig's informants, he wrote, were ''men of all ranks, and from towns and industrial firms and some were women,'' some who ''had been in the service of this prince,'' and some partisans of Catherine. Helbig, *Biographie,* vol. 1, p. v.

91. Helbig, *Biographie,* vol. 2, p. 6.

92. This clarification was provided by David Griffiths. See Castera, *The Life of Catherine II.*

93. J. Castera, *Histoire de Catherine II, Impératrice de Russie,* 3 vols. (Paris, 1800), vol. 1, p. iii.

94. In the 1740s, for example, Cyril Wich, the British ambassador, wrote, ''His Highness is possessed of many good qualities, which, being vested in a very agreeable Personage, make him everyway recommendable.'' Wich to Carteret, November 8/19, 1742, ''Doneseniia i drugie bumagi angliiskikh poslov, poslannikov i rezidentov pri russkom dvore s iiulia 1742-go goda,'' *SIRIO,* vol. 99 (1897), p. 134.

95. Mercy d'Argenteau (Austrian ambassador to Russia) to Count Kaunitz-Ritberg (chancellor), Jan. 10/22, 1762, ''Doneseniia grafa Mersi d'Arzhanto Imperatritse Marii Terezii gosudarstvennomu Kantsleru grafu Kaunitsu-Ritbergu,'' *SIRIO,* vol. 18 (1876), p. 30.

96. ''Elizabeth's short illness prevented what otherwise undoubtedly would have been a revolution in favor of a minority-regency for Paul Petrovich. The quickness of Elizabeth's death prevented such a coup.'' Posse to Ekeblad, Jan. 29/Feb. 9, 1762 (Apostille), *RAD DM* 306.

97. Leonard, ''Reputation,'' pp. 263–92.

98. A. R. Vorontsov, ''Pis'mo A. R. Vorontsova k Aleksandru Pavlovichu,'' *AKV,* vol. 29, p. 458.

99. For example, ''A chronology best of all reveals Catherine's awful position during these six months . . . it shows her move from dark thoughts to despair, destroying her health, and from despair to resolution. . . . '' S. M. Solov'ev, *Istoriia Rossii s drevneishikh vremen,* 15 vols. (Moscow, 1959–65), vol. 13, p. 79.

100. ''Romanticism encourages the idea that not only individuals but groups, and not only groups but institutions—states, churches, professional bodies, associations that have ostensibly been created for definite, often purely utilitarian purposes—come to be possessed by a 'spirit' of which they themselves might well be unaware—awareness of which is, indeed, the very process of enlightenment.'' Isaiah Berlin, ''Birth of the Russian Intelligentsia,'' in *Russian Thinkers* (New York, 1984), p. 119. Solov'ev, *Istoriia,* vol. 13, p. 25; Kliuchevskii, ''Kurs,'' vol. 4, p. 353.

101. N. L. Rubinshtein, ''Ulozhennaia komissiia 1754–1766 gg. i ee proekt novogo ulozheniia 'o sostoianii poddannykh voobshche' (k istorii sotsial'noi politiki 50-kh—nachala 60-kh godov XVIII v.),'' *Istoricheskie zapiski* (1951), pp. 208–51.

102. See chapter 2.

103. Solov'ev described Shakhovskoi's opposition to Shuvalov as largely a personal vendetta. According to Solov'ev, Shakhovskoi and Shuvalov each vied to appear the better friend of the people. Shakhovskoi lost the edge of advantage, as general procurator, by a ''childish shaming.'' ''You really think you are something!'' he attacked Shuvalov in public. Solov'ev, *Istoriia,* vol. 12, p. 587.

104. The ''Ebauche'' from which this quotation is drawn was written by Burkhard von Münnich (1683–1767) by order of Catherine II in 1763. As a consequence, the section that should have been lengthy on a ruler whom he knew well, consisted of a few paragraphs. B. v. Münnich, *''Ebauche'' du Gouvernement de l'Empire de Russie,* comments and notes by F. Ley (Geneva, 1989), 128.

1. Origins of Reform

1. The boldness of the opposition is in contrast to an earlier period, when vulnerability of the elite to exile and imprisonment may have been more decisive in their political behavior, for example, under Peter I. J. Cracraft, "Opposition to Peter the Great," *Imperial Russia, 1700–1917, State, Society, Opposition, Essays in Honor of Marc Raeff,* ed. E. Mendelsohn and M. Shatz (Dekalb, Ill., 1988), pp. 22–36.

2. On the rationale for emancipation, see M. Raeff, "The Domestic Policies of Peter III and His Overthrow," *American Historical Review,* vol. 85 (1970), pp. 1289–1310; P. Dukes, *Catherine the Great and the Russian Nobility* (Cambridge, 1967); R. E. Jones, *The Emancipation of the Russian Nobility, 1762–1785* (Princeton, N.J., 1973).

3. Another purpose of this measure was to encourage the use of hired labor. See chapter 4.

4. *Polnoe sobranie zakonov Rossiiskoi imperii,* 1649–1913, 234 vols. (St. Petersburg, 1830–1916) (hereafter *PSZ*), 15: 11,422 (*im.,* Jan. 29, 1762),p. 895; 11,437 (*im.,* Feb. 7, 1762), p. 909; 11,472 (*sen.,* Mar. 12, 1762), p. 941.

5. After their return to the countryside, as a result of the new supervision by landlords, there was a renaissance of barshchina. See M. Confino, *Systèmes agraires et progrès agricole: L'assolement triennal en Russie aux XVIII–XIX siècles* (Paris, 1963).

6. B. Meehan-Waters, "Social and Career Characteristics of the Administrative Elite, 1689–1761," in *Russian Officialdom: The Bureaucratization of Russian Society from the Seventeenth to the Twentieth Century,* eds. W. M. Pintner and D. K. Rowney (Chapel Hill, N.C., 1980), p. 104; M. Raeff, *The Origins of the Russian Intelligentsia: The Eighteenth-Century Nobility* (New York, 1966); J. LeDonne's *Ruling Russia, Politics and Administration in the Age of Absolutism, 1762–1796* (Princeton, N.J., 1984).

7. "Doklad," May 28, 1762, *TsGADA, f.* 203, *no.* 1 "Vnutrennye kollezhskie dela," *l.* 78; *PSZ* 15: 11,422 (*im.,* Jan. 29, 1762), p. 895; 11,437 (*im.,* Feb. 7, 1762), p. 909; 11,472 (*sen.,* Mar. 12, 1762), pp. 941–42.

8. The decree, transmitted through general procurator Glebov, for the sake of "the more speedy resolution of affairs," divided the Senate, the Justice and Votchina Colleges, and the Judicial Bureau into departments. *PSZ,* 15: 11,422 (*im.,* Jan. 29, 1762), p. 895; see also A. E. Presniakov, N. D. Chechulin, *Istoriia Senata za dvesti let, ch. II, v tsarstvovanie Elizavety Petrovny i Petra Fedorovicha* (St. Petersburg, 1911), pp. 75–77.

9. Decree of January 28, whose purpose was that "each College command its own affairs." *PSZ* 15: 11,418 (Jan. 28, 1762), pp. 893–94.

10. On January 29, Haxthausen reported, "Peter will establish a grand council called a Cabinet." Gregors v. Haxthausen (Danish ambassador in Russia) to Johan Ernst Hartwig Bernstorff (Danish foreign minister), Jan. 29/Feb. 9, 1762, *RAD TKUA* 78. This may have been in response to Vorontsov's advice, submitted in writing (undated), according to a rationale based ostensibly not on ministerial power and procedure but on autocratic efficiency and order, "if you were to attend the meetings, you would see gathered together in one place all the main affairs, there would be fewer complications, you would manage everything, and they [the council members] would loyally serve your interests." Mikhail Vorontsov to Peter III, undated, *LOII, f.* 36, *d.* 1073, *l.* 377.

11. This was the perception at the time, as well as the obvious implication in historical perspective. "The Council of State has not been used in a decision-making capacity. For the resolutions that the Tsar has passed—all is done 'à la Prussienne.' " Louis Charles Auguste le Tonnelier, baron de Breteuil (French ambassador to Russia) to Etienne François de Choiseul (foreign minister in France), Apr. 14/25, 1762, *AMAE CP Russie* 69.

12. Münnich claimed that it began as a council for military affairs and then turned into an intermediary institution between the Senate and the imperial power. He also wrote, however, that Peter relied more on Volkov than on any commission or council. B. von Münnich, *"Ebauche" du Gouvernement de l'Empire de Russie* (Geneva, 1989), pp. 129–30.

13. The council consisted of two civilian appointees, chancellor Mikhail Vorontsov and privy secretary Dmitrii Volkov, and military figures: president of the War College Nikita Iurievich Trubetskoi, chief of the artillery corps Aleksandr Villebois, commander-in-chief of the armed forces Mikhail Volkonskii, colonel of the Ingermanland guards Aleksei Petrovich Mel'gunov, marshall Burchard von Münnich, and the two Holstein princes, George Ludwig and Peter August of Holstein-Bek. The rationale for creating the council was "to issue decrees. . . . For the use and well being of true subjects," and "for the efficiency of processing affairs." *PSZ* 15: 11,538 (May 18, 1762), p. 1006.

14. Legal modernization introduced "an alien system," the legal profession, into a government that remained opposed to new standards of legality. R. Wortman, *The Development of a Russian Legal Consciousness* (Chicago, 1976), p. 288.

15. Although the given rationale in the decree was anticlerical: "so that it [residing in Russia] will not be prohibited to them on account of their customs," concern for resettlement may also have reflected interest in settling relatively unpopulated land in the eighteenth century. See Kiril Razumovskii's recommendation to Elizabeth, K. Razumovskii to Elizabeth, 1761, *LOII, f.* 36, *d.* 1134, *ll.* 7–8; Aug. 8, 1761, *TsGADA, f.* 248, *kn.* 3360, *l.* 120; *PSZ* 15: 11,420 (*im.*, Jan. 29, 1762), p. 984; 11,456 (*man.*, Feb. 28, 1762), p. 926.

16. Compare Dmitrii Volkov's proposal to eliminate restrictions on the personal freedom of merchants and other traders in the south of Russia. Volkov to Chernyshev, Dec. 19, 1760, *LOII, f.* 36, *d.* 550, *l.* 261; "Ekstrakt o torgovli," *f.* 36, *d.* 550, *op.* 1, *l.* 91.

17. *PSZ* 16: 11,725 (*sen.*, Dec. 14, 1762), pp. 129–30; S. P. Mel'gunov, *Religiozno-obshchestvennye dvizheniia XVII-XVIII vv. v Rossii* (Moscow, 1922), p. 123.

18. K. Staehlin, *Aus den Papieren Jacob von Stählins* (Berlin, 1926), pp. 102–15; *PSZ* 15: 11,515 (*im.*, Apr. 24, 1762), p. 985; "Ukaz senatu," Apr. 25, 1762, *TsGADA, f.* 248, *kn.* 3429, *ll.* 316–22. He doubled funds assigned to the Cadet Corps for elite education, Saldern, *Histoire*, p. 23; P. Viskovatov, *Pervyi kadetskii korpus* (St. Petersburg, 1832), pp. 73–88. His reform of higher and technical education united all branches into one corps under the direction of I. I. Shuvalov and created new specialized training for engineers. He planned to send "20 or 30" students to study in England. Robert Keith (British envoy) to Earl of Bute (Secretary of State), May 7/18, 1762, *BMAddMSS*, 35,493.

19. [C. F. Schwan] M. de la Marche, *Histoire et anecdotes de la vie, du regne, du détrônement et de la mort de Pierre III, dernier Empereur de toutes les Russes, écrites en forme de lettres* (London, 1766), p. 217.

20. *PSZ* 15: 11,444 (*man.*, Feb. 18, 1762), pp. 912–15; 11,441 (*im.*, Feb. 16, 1762), p. 910; 11,481 (*im.*, Mar. 21, 1762), pp. 948–53; 11,489 (*im.*, Mar. 28, 1762), pp. 959–60; 11,456 (*man.*, Feb. 28, 1762), p. 926; 11,446 (*man.*, Feb. 21, 1762), pp. 918–19; 11,515 (*im.* Apr. 24, 1762), p. 985; 11,477 (*im.*, Mar. 22, 1762), p. 744.

21. On May 28, he released the Justice College Vice-President Emme for six weeks from other responsibilities to complete the code. "Doklad," May 28, 1762, *TsGADA, f.* 248, *kn.* 3430, *l.* 473.

22. "Ekstrakt o kommertsi," Jan. 5, 1761, *LOII, f. 36, d. 550, l.* 97.

23. "Baron Korff arrived July 8 and declared that the Emperor accepts the proposed conferences but wants them to open July 12 in Berlin under the mediation of Frederick of Prussia," Haxthausen to Bernstorff, July 13, 1762, *RAD TKUA* 181; "Peter has finally replied . . . that he must resort to arms . . . but the council has persuaded him to negotiate," Keith to Bute, May 29/June 7, 1762, *PRO SP* 91/70; Peter III to Osterman, May 24, 1762, Schierensee 704; Walter Titley (British ambassador to Denmark) to Bute, July 13, 1762, *PRO SP* 75/113, *folio* 206.

24. On the abolition of the Secret Chancery (*PSZ* 16: 11,687 [*im.*, Oct. 19, 1762] pp. 82–83); on tolerance of Old Believers (*PSZ* 16: 11,738 [*im.*, Jan. 20, 1763], pp. 140–41, and *PSZ* 16: 11,725 [*sen.*, Dec. 14, 1762], pp. 129–30); on the prohibition of purchase of serfs for merchant factories (*PSZ* 16: 11,638 [*im.*, Aug. 8, 1762], p. 47); on the grain trade (*PSZ* 16: 11,630 [*im.*, July 31, 1762], p. 31); see also chapter 2.

25. *PSZ* 15: 11,630 (*im.*, July 31 1762), p. 31.

26. *PSZ* 18: 13,087 (*sen.* Mar. 24, 1785), p. 483.

27. N. L. Rubinshtein, "Ulozhennaia komissiia 1754–1766 gg. i ee proekt novogo ulozheniia 'o sostoianii poddannykh voobshche' (k istorii sotsial'noi politiki 50-kh—nachala 60-kh godov XVIII v)," *Istoricheskie zapiski,* vol. 36 (1951), pp. 208–51.

28. J. G. Gagliardo, *Enlightened Despotism* (London, 1968); L. Gershoy, *From Despotism to Revolution, 1763–1789* (New York, 1944); and others.

29. "I became a financier the moment the issues were simplified. . . . I regarded everything that had previously been done as though it was a creation of the Iroquois Indians." From a memorandum of 1765, Joseph II, quoted in D. Beales, *Joseph II, I. In the Shadow of Maria Theresa, 1741–1780* (Cambridge, 1987), p. 106.

30. A. Kulomzin, "Gosudarstvennye dokhody i raskhody v tsarstvovanie Ekateriny II, 1763–1773," *Sbornik imperatorskogo russkogo istoricheskogo obshchestvo* (hereafter *SIRIO*), vol. 27 (1880), pp. 224–27; LeDonne, *Ruling Russia,* ch. 3; S. M. Troitskii, "Iz istorii sostavleniia biudzheta v Rossii v seredine XVIII v.," *Istoricheskie Zapiski,* vol. 78 (1965), pp. 181–203.

31. "Odar [one of the conspirators—CSL] said (Wroughton overheard) that the Empress of Russia, when she accepted propositions from all sides, sent to Breteuil for money which he immediately furnished her with," Money to Bute, Aug. 21, 1762, *PRO SP* 88/86, *folio* 202; "D'ailleurs il pourait arriver tel évènement qui lui serait favorable. Il serait donc utile d'entretenir avec elle quelque correspondance secrete et de préparer des canaux pour la gagner et la mettre dans nos intérêts," Choiseul to Breteuil, Apr. 27, 1762; Choiseul to Breteuil, Jan. 24, 1762, *AMAE CP Russie* vol. 68. See chapter 5.

32. C. Wilson, "The Other Face of Mercantilism," reprinted in *Revisions in Mercantilism,* ed. D. C. Coleman (London, 1969), p. 120.

33. Quoted in L. Haney, *History of Economic Thought* (New York, 1949), p. 121.

34. On the cameralists, see A. W. Small, *The Cameralists* (Chicago, 1909).

35. E. Heckscher, "Mercantilism" [reprinted in *Revisions in Mercantilism,* ed. D. C. Coleman (London, 1969)], p. 33.

36. Solov'ev here evokes eighteenth-century poets such as A. P. Sumarokov and Gavril Derzhavin, S. M. Solov'ev, *Publichnye chteniia o Petre Velikom* (Moscow, 1984), p. 10 and n. 4, p. 206.

37. J. Justi, *Staatswirtschaft, oder systematische Abhandlung aller Oekonomischen und Cameral-Wissenschaften die zur Regierung eines Landes erfordert werden,* vol. 1 (1755), pp. 152–55, 173.

38. T. C. W. Blanning, *Joseph II and Enlightened Despotism* (London, 1970), p. 11.

39. Blanning, *Joseph II,* pp. 18–19.

40. S. M. Troitskii, *Finansovaia politika russkogo absoliutizma XVIII veka* (Moscow, 1966), p. 88.

41. On the physiocrats, see G. Weulersse, *Le Mouvement physiocratique en France de 1756 à 1770,* 2 vols. (Paris, 1910); H. Higgs, *The Physiocrats* (London, 1897); Norman J. Ware, "The Physiocrats: A Study in Economic Rationalization," *American Economic Review,* vol. 21, no. 4 (December 1931), pp. 607–19; O. H. Taylor, "Economics and the Idea of 'Jus Naturale,' " *Quarterly Journal of Economics,* vol. 44, no. 2 (Feb. 1930), pp. 205–41.

42. "Extract from 'Corn,' " in *The Economics of Physiocracy, Essays and Translations,* ed. Ronald L. Meek (London, 1962), p. 84.

43. M. Raeff, "The Enlightenment in Russia and Russian Thought in the Enlightenment," in *The Eighteenth Century in Russia,* ed. J. G. Garrard (Oxford, 1973), p. 25.

44. Blanning, *Joseph II,* p. 99.

45. "Catherine II (that 'Tartuffe in a skirt and crown,' as Pushkin put it) consciously exaggerated both the degree of backwardness on the eve of her ascent to the throne and the contribution to the Enlightenment in Russia of her reforms." S. O. Shmidt, "Vnutrenniaia politika Rossii serediny XVIII veka," *Voprosy istorii,* vol. 3 (Moscow, 1987), p. 58.

46. Among those who have argued most forcefully for this position, see A. Kahan, "Continuity in Economic Activity and Policy during the Post-Petrine Period in Russia," *Journal of Economic History*, vol. 25 (1965), pp. 61–85, and his "Observations on Russia's Foreign Trade," *Canadian-American Slavic Studies*, vol. 8 (1974), no. 2, p. 222.

47. I. I. Shishkin, "Artemii Petrovich Volynskii, Biograficheskii ocherk," *Otechestvennye zapiski* (St. Petersburg, 1860), vols. 128–30; M. T. Beliavskii, L. G. Kisliagina, "Obshchestvenno-politicheskaia mysl'," *Ocherki russkoi kul'tury XVIII veka, chast'* III (Moscow, 1988), P. 174.

48. P. Miliukov, *Ocherki po istorii russkoi kul'tury* (St. Petersburg, 1909), vol. 3, pp. 247–48.

49. On the history of education in the eighteenth century, see M. T. Beliavskii, "Shkola i obrazovanie," in *Ocherki russkoi kul'tury* (Moscow, 1987), vol. 2, pp. 258–93.

50. A. Viskovatov, *Pervyi kadetskii korpus* (St. Petersburg, 1832), pp. 83–88.

51. *PSZ* 15: 11,515 (*im.*, Apr. 24, 1762), p. 985.

52. Miliukov, *Ocherki*, vol. 3, pp. 247–48.

53. Beliavskii, "Shkola," p. 268.

54. A. P. Sumarokov, "Son—shchastlivoe obshchestvo," *Trudoliubivaia pchela* (St. Petersburg, May 1759), pp. 738–47.

55. P. N. Berkov, "Nachalo russkoi zhurnalistiki," in *Ocherki po istorii russkoi zhurnalistiki i kritiki*, ed. P. N. Berkov (Leningrad, 1950), pp. 32–44.

56. See S. M. Troitskii, *Finansovaia*, pp. 88–91; P. K. Alefirenko, *Krestianskoe dvizhenie i krestianskii vopros v Rossii v 30-kh-50-kh godakh XVIII veka* (Moscow, 1958), pp. 365–86.

57. "In the middle of the century, that is in the 1750s, already visible were the results of the Petrine reforms in Europeanizing Russia, . . . in two, as it were, very different spheres of life, in the military and in 'the philological sciences.' . . . literature, or more precisely, poetry, took upon itself the celebration of victories of Russian armies." I. Serman, "Rossiia i Zapad," in *Russia and the West in the Eighteenth Century*, ed. A. G. Cross (Newtonville, Mass, 1983), p. 57; G. Marker, *Publishing and the Origins of Intellectual Life in Russia, 1700–1800* (Princeton, N.J., 1985); P. N. Berkov, "Nachalo," pp. 11–44; cf. Gleason limits to western influence, in "The Image of the West in the Journals of Mid-Eighteenth-Century Russia," *Russia and the West*, pp. 109–15.

58. For the second half of the eighteenth century, see Iu. Ia. Kogan, *Ocherki po istorii russkoi ateisticheskoi mysli XVIII v.* (Moscow, 1962).

59. T. Bakounine, *Répertoire biographique des francs-maçon russes (XVIIIe et XIXe siècles)* (Paris, 1967), pp. 24–593.

60. Bakounine, *Répertoire;* M. F. Zubkov, "Istoriia masonstva v strankakh tsentral'nol i vostochnoi Evropy," *Voprosy istorii*, no. 12 (1988), 130–31.

61. D. V. Volkov, R. I. Vorontsov, A. P. Mel'gunov.

62. K. Craven, Review essay *Deism, Masonry, and the Enlightenment: Essays Honoring Alfred Owen Aldridge* [ed. J. A. Leo Lemay (Newark, Del., 1987)], *Comparative Literature Studies*, vol. 26 (1989), no. 2, p. 159.

63. Craven, pp. 159–60.

64. G. V. Vernadskii, *Russkoe masonstvo v tsarstvovanie Ekateriny II* (Petrograd, 1917), pp. 1–8.

65. Ivan Grigorievich Chernyshev to Ivan Ivanovich Shuvalov, Jan. 15/26, 1762, *Russkii arkhiv*, vol. 7 (1869), pp. 1805–1806.

66. Chernyshev to Shuvalov, January 15/26, 1762, *Russkii arkhiv*, vol. 7 (1869), pp. 1805–1806.

67. "Volkov seems to have his confidence in foreign policy, which he seems to understand perfectly." Extract of a letter from Robert Keith, in Goodricke to Bute, Feb. 20, 1762, *PRO SP* 75/113. After the coup d'état, he wrote a letter to Grigorii Orlov in which he explained that he had won the respect of the Empress and of all his "bosses" (*nachalniki*) for his work in foreign affairs. Volkov to Orlov, p. 485.

68. M. I. Semevskii, "Dmitrii Vasilievich Volkov," *Russkaia starina*, vol. 9 (1874), pp. 163–74.

69. Breteuil to Choiseul, Jan. 31/Feb. 11, 1761, *AMAE CP Russie* 66.

70. Mikhail Vorontsov was concerned about Volkov's exclusion from office after the abolition of the Conference. He wrote to the new monarch, Peter III, that he should promote Volkov to the College of Foreign Affairs and raise his salary. M. Vorontsov to Peter III, undated, *LOII, f.* 36, *d.* 1073, *l.* 376. See also "Dmitrii Volkov," in "Ukazy i postanovleniia imperatritsy Ekateriny II za fevral'–dekabr' 1764 g." *Senatskii arkhiv* (St. Petersburg, 1910), vol. 14, p. 259.

71. The following is a rare comment about Volkov, who in 1768 served on one of Catherine's commissions. The Earl of Buckinghamshire wrote, "there are amongst [the members of the commission] three or four very clever and industrious men, particularly Mr. Wolkoff." Earl of Buckinghamshire to Earl of Sandwich, July 29, 1768, *SIRIO*, vol. 12 (1873), p. 341.

72. Raeff viewed Elizabeth's reign differently. "A relatively well-working central administration that had waged a successful war in central Europe (the Seven Years' War) and that had achieved some stability on the basis of the controlling role of the Senate and the imperial council was overthrown overnight by the new ruler." M. Raeff, *The Well-Ordered Police State: Social and Institutional Change through Law in the Germanies and Russia, 1600–1800* (New Haven, Conn., 1983), pp. 221–22.

73. "Elizabeth turned out to be unprepared for the role of governing a large state. She was inappropriately educated, lazy, fond of amusements and soon tired of her responsibilities." N. B. Golikova, L. G. Kisliagina, "Sistema gosudarstvennogo upravleniia," *Ocherki russkoi kul'tury XVIII veka* (Moscow, 1987), vol. 2, p. 82; compare Shmidt, "She was, in fact, "Peter's daughter" (Lomonosov's words) and inclined to concern herself with reviving an active national internal and foreign policy, to encourage projects in the area of government structure and cultural beginnings." O. Shmidt, "Vnutrenniaia politika, p. 48; E. V. Anisimov, *Rossiia v seredine XVIII veka, Bor'ba za nasledie Petra* (Moscow, 1986), pp. 153–60.

74. V. N. Latkin, *Zakonodatel'niia kommissii v Rossii v XVIII st.*, vol. 1 (St. Petersburg, 1887), p. 90.

75. Rubinshtein, "Ulozhennaia," pp. 208–35.

76. W. H. Riker, *The Theory of Political Coalitions* (New Haven, Conn., 1962), pp. 11–12.

77. D. Ransel, *The Politics of Catherinian Russia* (New Haven, Conn., 1975), pp. 137–43.

78. Shmidt, "Vnutrenniaia," p. 49.

79. A. N. Filippov, *Pravitel'stvuiushchii Senat pri Petre Velikom i ego blizhaishikh preemnikakh (1711–1741)* (St. Petersburg, 1911), pp. 224–25; Troitskii, *Finansovaia*, p. 23.

80. Shmidt, "Vnutrenniaia," p. 49; J. F. Brennan, *Enlightened Despotism in Russia, The Reign of Elisabeth, 1741–1762* (New York, 1987), pp. 37–59.

81. Consisting of two field marshals, Iu. Iu. Trubetskoi and A. Messino, chancellor A. M. Cherkasskii, generals G. P. Chernyshev, A. I. Ushakov, and V. Ia. Levashov, admiral N. F. Golovin, A. B. Kurakin, privy secretary A. P. Bestuzhev-Riumin, the procurator general of the Senate, N. Iu. Trubetskoi, and privy secretary A. P. Naryshkin.

82. The Conference, which met twice a week, included Grand Duke Peter Fedorovich, chancellor A. P. Bestuzhev-Riumin, his brother, M. P. Bestuzhev-Riumin, vice chancellor M. L. Vorontsov, senator A. B. Buturlin, general S. Apraksin, senator P. I. Shuvalov, senator Prince M. M. Golitzyn, general procurator N. Iu. Trubetskoi, and the head of the Secret Investigatory Chancery, Count A. I. Shuvalov (10 members). The Senate included in addition A. D. Golitzyn, Prince I. A. Shcherbatov, V. I. Suvorov, and I. P. Chernyshev. It varied in size from 9 to 19. In 1760, after a provincial corruption scandal in which Peter Shuvalov and his friends were implicated, Elizabeth increased it to the largest it had been. To the Conference, to make a new total of 14, she added the son of her morganatic husband, A. K. Razumovskii, and the new favorite, I. I. Shuvalov, commissar of war, I. P. Shakhovskoi, and

Governor General of Orenburg I. I. Nepliuev. In the Senate, as general procurator Sha-khovskoi, first secretary I. G. Cherynshev; and new members, the vice-chancellor's brother, R. I. Vorontsov, A. P. Shuvalov, Nepliuev, Ivan Ivanovich Kostiurin, the general procura-tor's brother, M. P. Shakhovskoi, P. S. Suvorov, I. L. Khitrovo, I. I. Bekhmetev, I. A. Shcherbatov, I. V. Odoevskii, and A. G. Zherebtsov (total of 19 members). A. E. Presnia-kov, N. D. Chechulin, *Istoriia pr. Senata za dvesti let,* 2 vols. (St. Petersburg, 1911), vol. 2, p. 73; S. M. Solov'ev, *Istoriia Rossii s drevneishikh vremen,* 15 vols. (Moscow, 1959–65), vol. 12, p. 323; Keith to Bute, Sept. 16/27, 1760, *PRO SP* 91/68; "Spisok," Jan. 18, 1760, "Pis'ma Shuvalova," *Russkii arkhiv,* vol. 8 (1870), pp. 1399–1400.

83. V. P. Naumov, "Voprosy vnutrennei politiki v protokolakh Konferentsii pri vysoch-aishem dvore i Imperatorskogo soveta (1756–1762)," *Arkheograficheskii ezhegodnik za 1984 god* (Moscow, 1986).

84. Presniakov, *Istoriia,* pp. 23–25.

85. Small, *Cameralists;* G. Barchet, *Studien über die Entwicklung der Verwaltungslehre in Deutschland von der Zweiten Hälfte des 17. bis zum Ende des 18. Jahrhunderts* (Munich, 1885); W. Roscher, *Geschichte der National-Oekonomie in Deutschland* (Munich, 1874).

86. R. Vorontsov, "Ot konferentsii," *LOII, f.* 36, *d.* 1071, *l.* 87.

87. J. F. von Bielfeld, *Institutes Politiques* (n.p., 1762), pp. 92, 110, 223ff., 227.

88. N. Trubetskoi, M. Vorontsov, P. I., A. I., and I. I. Shuvalov, I. Nepliuev, and Ia. Shakhovskoi. "Ot konferentsii," *ll.* 87–88.

89. Latkin, *Zakonodatel'niia,* pp. 88–92.

90. Initiator of more than 20 legislative proposals, embracing the Land Survey, the ab-olition of internal customs, protectionist trade policy, merchant banks, the expansion of pro-vincial government, nobles' rights, and others, Peter Shuvalov wielded power at court in part because of his aristocratic lineage, in part because of his education and oratory, and in part because he had helped Elizabeth to the throne and married her close friend, Shepel-evaia. His enormous authority was further enhanced when his cousin Ivan Ivanovich became the Empress's favorite in the 1750s. S. O. Shmidt, "Proekt P. I. Shuvalova 1754 g. 'O raznykh gosudarstvennoi pol'zy sposobakh," *Istoricheskii arkhiv* (1962), no. 6, pp. 100–103; Troitskii, *Finansovaia,* pp. 62–79; M. P. Danilov, *Zapiski* (Kazan', 1913), p. 68.

91. Solov'ev, *Istoriia,* vol. 12, pp. 585–86.

92. Solov'ev, *Istoriia,* vol. 12, p. 582.

93. Breteuil to Choiseul, Mar. 11/21, 1761, *AMAE CP Russie* 66.

94. Breteuil to Choiseul, Mar. 11/21, 1761, *AMAE CP Russie* 66.

95. Ivan Ivanovich Nepliuev, governor of Orenburg, Ivan Ivanovich Kostiurin, comman-dant of St. Petersburg and governor of Kiev, Petr Grigorievich Chernyshev, governor of St. Petersburg, and his brother Aleksei Grigorievich Chernyshev.

96. Presniakov, *Istoriia,* vol. 2, pp. 75ff.

97. See *Zapiski Imperatritsy Ekateriny Vtoroi,* ed. A. Suvorin (St. Petersburg, 1907), pp. 383–430.

98. Presniakov, *Istoriia,* p. 24–25.

99. Anisimov, *Rossiia,* p. 100.

100. L. J. Oliva, *Misalliance: A Study of French Policy in Russia During the Seven Years' War* (New York, 1964).

101. Bestuzhev-Riumin had been a friend of Volkov's father and had assisted him in gain-ing access to proper schooling and excellent placement in the service. "Bumagi, otnosiash-chiiasia k pobegu C. V. Volkovu," *AKV* (Moscow, 1875), vol. 7, p. 497; G. Helbig, "Izbranniki, Dmitrii Volkov," *Russkaia starina* (July 1866), p. 2.

102. Solov'ev, *Istoriia,* vol. 12, pp. 444–53.

103. She leaves the reader to guess, as Trubetskoi must have, at her question to him: "What miracles have you found: more crimes than criminals or more criminals than crimes?" *Zapiski,* p. 432.

104. Other arrests included Ivan Elagin (Razumovskii's adjutant) and Vasilii Adadurov (Catherine's former Russian language instructor), *Zapiski,* pp. 430–32.

105. Chernyshev to Shuvalov, Jan. 15/26, 1762, pp. 1805–1806.

106. According to Haxthausen, Trubetskoi, Glevbov, and Mel'gunov formed "a secret committee," Shuvalov's inspiration. Haxthausen to Bernstorff, Dec. 30/Jan. 10, 1762, *RAD TKUA* 78; according to Breteuil, it was organized by Roman Vorontsov, "who wanted Peter to divorce Catherine, disinherit Paul, and marry Elizabeth," Breteuil to Choiseul, Jan. 1/13, 1762, *AMAE CP Russie* 68. Conflating the two dispatches and examining the rewards to both families produces the impression that this planning was the first act of the new Shuvalov/Vorontsov coalition.

107. Breteuil to Choiseul, Jan. 11/22, 1762, *AMAE CP Russie 68.*

108. Keith to Bute, Feb. 5/16, 1762, *BMAddMSS* 35,493; see promotions, mainly in the guards regiments (30–80 per "Pribavlenie") *Skt.-Peterburgskie vedomosti,* Jan. 1, Feb. 1, 1762, *Moskovskie vedomosti,* Jan. 22, 25, and 29, Mar. 11, and Apr. 10, 21, and 23, May 14 and 24, June 18, 21, and 28, 1762; "Ukaz po prikaznomu stolu," Jan. 22, 1762, *TsGADA, f.* 248, *kn. 3377, l.* 83; Haxthausen to Bernstorff, Dec. 30/Jan. 10, 1762, *RAD TKUA* 78.

109. Leonard, "Reputation," p. 290; see chapter 6.

110. It is significant that although Shakovskoi was among her supporters, Catherine did not turn to him as a replacement for Glebov after her ascent to the throne.

111. He remained general procurator until 1764. See "Bumagi iz dela o A. I. Glebove i sibirskom sledovatele Krylove," *SIRIO,* vol. 1 (1867), pp. 216–17.

112. "The result at the Conference is ordinarily based more on the opinion of this secretary than on those of the other members." Breteuil to Choiseul, Jan. 31/Feb. 11, Feb. 28/ Mar. 11, 1761, *AMAE CP Russie* 66. Buckinghamshire to the Earl of Sandwich, July 20/31, 1768, *SIRIO,* vol. 12 (1873), p. 341.

113. Peter Shuvalov's intimidation of his enemies made Nikita Panin later complain of the "power of individuals" over the "power of state institutions" in Elizabeth's reign. Presniakov, *Istoriia,* p. 30.

114. Extract of a letter from 29 January, included in John Goodricke to Bute, Feb. 20, 1762, *PRO SP 113/78.*

115. *PSZ,* 15: 11,411 (*im.* Jan. 11, 1762), p. 889; 16:11,592 (*im.,* July 3, 1762), pp. 9–10.

116. Keith to Bute, May 27/June 7, 1762, *BMAddMSS* 35,493.

117. I. de Madariaga, *Russia in the Age of Catherine the Great* (New Haven, Conn., 1981), p. 44.

118. Ransel, *Politics,* p. 118.

2. Emancipation of the Russian Nobility

1. "In contrast to [the experience of] Europe, private landownership in Russia did not have significance for local administration, nor was it a source of political rights and responsibilities, as elsewhere in the feudal era. . . . The holder of a *votchina* [hereditary estate] was never a part of local administration. He was considered an agent of the central government with dues to pay, like others." A. D. Gradovskii, *Istoriia mestnogo upravleniia v Rossii, II Uezd moskovskogo gosudarstva* (St. Petersburg, 1868), p. 23.

2. Evasion in the seventeenth and eighteenth century was extensive. Got'e wrote that 42% (231 out of 555) of the nobles did not appear when called up in 1625 (Iu. V. Got'e, "Zamoskovnyi krai v XVII veke, opyt issledovaniia po istorii ekonomicheskogo byta moskovskoi Rusi," *Uchenye zapiski imperatorskogo moskovskogo universiteta, otdel istoriko-filologicheskii* [Moscow, 1906], pp. 307–10); on evasion of service in the eighteenth century, see A. Romanovich-Slavatinskii, *Dvorianstvo v Rossii ot nachala XVIII veka do otmeny krepostnogo prava* (St. Petersburg, 1870), pp. 181–85.

3. The Bank for the Nobility was organized in 1754 with a capital of 750,000 rubles that was almost exhausted within the first year. The assessed value per male serf was set at 10 rubles; neither estate income nor holdings were used as security. For the first three years, the branch at St. Petersburg averaged 57,000 in loans per year. See A. Kahan, *The Plow, the Hammer, and the Knout: An Economic History of Eighteenth-Century Russia* (Chicago, 1985), pp. 313–14.

4. *Polnoe sobranie zakonov Rossiiskoi imperii,* 1649–1913, 234 vols. (St. Petersburg, 1830–1916) (hereafter *PSZ*), 15: 11,444 (*man.*, Feb. 18, 1762), pp. 912–15.

5. P. I. Iaguzhinskii, the general procurator of the Senate, recommended to Catherine I in 1725 or 1726 that nobles be freed of the obligation to perform lifetime service so that "peasants would be more closely supervised and state dues properly paid." P. I. Iaguzhinskii, "Zapiska o sostoianii Rossii," *Chteniia v obshchestve istorii i drevnostei rossiiskikh* (hereafter *COIDR*) (1860), vol. 4, Smes', p. 271.

6. With land in seven or eight districts, the landlord typically moved his/her peasants to a single estate, allowing the others to go untended, that is, at risk for someone or some agency (the state, monasteries) to seize; E. D. Stashevskii, *Zemlevladenie Moskovskogo dvorianstva v pervoi polovine XVII veka* (Moscow, 1911), pp. 21–32; Gradovskii, *Istoriia mestnogo,* pp. 67–71.

7. N. F. Demidova, "Biurokratizatsiia gosudarstvennogo apparata absoliutizma v XVII–XVIII vv.," in *Absoliutizm v Rossii,* ed. N. M. Druzhinin (Moscow, 1964), pp. 211ff.; N. I. Khlebnikov, *O vliianii obshchestva na organizatsiiu gosudarstva v tsarskoi period russkoi istorii* (St. Petersburg, 1869), pp. 10–11.

8. See R. E. Jones, *The Emancipation of the Russian Nobility, 1762–1785* (Princeton, N.J., 1973), pp. 3–18.

9. Miliukov discussed the "unintended" results of many of Peter's reforms, observing that the legislation was not thought through. Troitskii emphasized Peter I's involvement in the process of reform and far-sightedness. However, so much of the substance of the service requirement had to be modified to mitigate the unforeseen consequences, including nobles' diminished attention to their estates and to income, that there is justice in the position that Peter's reforms were driven by military necessity. P. Miliukov, *Gosudarstvennoe khoziaistvo Rossii v pervoi chetverti XVIII stoletiia i Reforma Petra Velikogo* (St. Petersburg, 1905), p. 545; S. M. Troitskii, *Russkii absoliutizm i dvorianstvo XVIII v.* (Moscow, 1974), pp. 47–118.

10. M. D. Rabinovich cited examples of noble officers who could no longer, after so many years away from the land, remember the size of their estates or the number of their serfs. M. D. Rabinovich, "Sotsial'noe proiskhozhdenie i imushchestvennoe polozhenie ofitserov regulariarnoi russkoi armii v kontse Severnoi voiny," in *Rossiia v period reform Petra I* (Moscow, 1973), p. 159.

11. The rigidity at the top ranks, however, as Troitskii pointed out, created a mestnichestvo of position and rank out of a mestnichestvo of rod (clan); Troitskii, *Russkii absoliutizm,* p. 130. See also A. I. Markevich, *Istoriia mestnichestva v moskovskom gosudarstve v XV-XVII vv.* (Odessa, 1888), p. 610; A. Z. Myshlaevskii, "Ofitserskii vopros v XVII v.," *Voennii sbornik,* no 6 (1899), p. 290.

12. For Peter's examination of the model of the French bureaucracy under Louis XIV, see Troitskii's *Russkii absoliutizm,* pp. 54ff.

13. N. L. Rubinshtein, "Ulozhennaia komissiia 1754–1766 gg. i ee proekt novogo ulozheniia 'o sostoianii poddannykh voobshche' (k istorii sotsial'noi politiki 50-kh—nachala 60-kh godov XVIII v.)," *Istoricheskie zapiski* (1951), pp. 208–51.

14. I. D. Nepomiluev, for example, used two of Peter III's decrees, one condemning persecution of Old Believers, many of whom were merchants, and another granting the nobility rights and privileges as examples of the state's mediation of class interests, see his "Kupechestvo v tsarstvovanie Ekateriny II" avtoreferat (Kandidatskaia dissertatsia, Moscow State University, 1974), pp. 2–3; V. V. Mavrodin, *Krestianskaia voina v Rossii v 1773–1775 godakh (Vosstanie Pugacheva)* (Leningrad, 1961), vol. 1, pp. 310–12; Troitskii, *Russkii absoliutizm,* pp. 140–51.

15. The dating is not entirely satisfactory; see chapter 4.

16. M. Raeff, "The Domestic Policies of Peter III and His Overthrow," *American Historical Review* (June 1970), pp. 1294–95; Troitskii, *Russkii absoliutizm,* p. 140.

17. Jones, *Emancipation,* p. 32.

18. Jones, *Emancipation,* p. 34.

19. Jones, *Emancipation*, p. 36.

20. "The non-serving nobleman remained the exception, . . . even until the 1840s" (M. Raeff, *Origins of the Russian Intelligentsia: The Eighteenth-Century Nobility* [New York, 1966], pp. 112–13); "Paradoxically, many members of the higher nobility celebrated the promulgation of the Manifesto, even though they had no intention of exercising the rights it had conferred upon them" (Jones, *Emancipation*, pp. 40, 44–46). See also P. Dukes, *Catherine the Great and the Russian Nobility: A Study Based on the Materials of the Legislative Commission of 1767* (Cambridge, 1967), p. 44.

21. S. A. Korf, *Dvorianstvo i ego soslovnoe upravlenie za stoletie 1762–1855 godov* (St. Petersburg, 1906), pp. 1–11.

22. See also M. Raeff, *The Well-Ordered Police State: Social and Institutional Change through Law in the Germanies and Russia, 1600–1800* (New Haven, Conn., 1983).

23. Raeff, "Overthrow," pp. 1292–93, 1309–10.

24. Romanovich-Slavatinskii weakened his case by inconsistency, for example, elsewhere: "our *shliakhetstva* was a *service* not a *landowning* elite." Romanovich-Slavatinskii, *Dvorianstvo*, pp. 118–19, 166.

25. Romanovich-Slavatinskii, *Dvorianstvo*, pp. 118–19.

26. M. Confino, "Histoire et Psychologie: Apropos de la noblesse russe au XVIIIè siècle," *Annales E.S.C.*, no. 6 (1967), pp. 1174, 1187.

27. J. LeDonne, *Ruling Russia, Politics and Administration in the Age of Absolutism, 1762–1796* (Princeton, N.J., 1984).

28. Between 1682 and 1711, 213 nobles acquired crown lands (to a total of 338,960 chetverti of land and 43,655 households). After 1714, servitors still received land grants, but only for the purpose of colonization. (They had to promise to settle the land within three years.) Romanovich-Slavatinskii, *Dvorianstvo*, pp. 152–53.

29. Miliukov, *Gosudarstvennoe*, pp. 526–31, 676–78.

30. *PSZ* 7: 4595 (*im.*, Nov. 13, 1724), p. 368.

31. *PSZ* 8: 7141 (*man.* Dec. 31, 1736); Romanovich-Slavatinskii, *Dvoriansto*, pp. 125–27.

32. Confino suggests somewhat earlier; see "Apropos," p. 1187.

33. Catherine's observation, when Grand Duchess; see "Bumagi Ekateriny Vtoroi," *Sbornik imperatorskogo russkogo istoricheskogo obshchestva* (hereafter *SIRIO*), vol. 7 (1871), p. 82.

34. M. Iablochkov, *Istoriia dvorianskogo sosloviia v Rossii*, 2 vols. (Paris, 1932–1933), vol. 2, p. 457.

35. S. M. Solov'ev, *Istoriia Rossii s drevneishikh vremen*, 15 vols. (Moscow, 1959–65), vol. 12, pp. 540–41.

36. "Spravka v Pr. Senate," Feb. 1, 1762, *TsGADA, f.* 248, *kn.* 3427, *ll.* 22–23.

37. "Sochineniia proekta novogo ulozheniia," *SIRIO*, vol. 4 (1866), p. 144.

38. W. M. Pintner, "The Evolution of Civil Officialdom, 1755–1855," *Russian Officialdom: The Bureaucratization of Russian Society from the Seventeenth to the Twentieth Century*, ed. W. Pintner and D. Rowney (Chapel Hill, N.C., 1980), pp. 203–204.

39. Report by G. P. Chernyshev, Moscow governor general, 1731–1732, cited in Iu. V. Got'e, *Istoriia oblastnogo upravleniia v Rossii ot Petra I do Ekateriny II* (Leningrad, 1941), vol. 2, p. 123.

40. The main substance of reports of this period was that "there were not enough institutions, not enough people, and not enough funds." Got'e, *Istoriia*, vol. 2, p. 124.

41. I. Nepliuev, *Zapiski Ivana Ivanovicha Nepliueva (1693–1773)* (St. Petersburg, 1893; republished Newtonville, Mass., 1974), pp. 137–43.

42. "Donoshenie komissii o monastyrskikh krest'ianakh," Nov. 21, 1761, Feb. 25, 1762, *TsGADA, f.* 248, *kn.* 3427, *ll.* 278–81.

43. "Doklad," N. Korff, Mar. 1761, *LOII, f. 36, d.* 1075, *ll.* 192–96.

44. Manpower shortage was critical, acting as a brake on the collection of data; on March 4, 1762, the Senate attempted to recall the officers who were collecting survey information;

and on June 12, a report by officers about the status of the survey read, ''Because of military priorities in both men and money, the survey has ceased everywhere except Moscow, where it goes on,'' ''Protokol,'' Mar. 4, 1762, *TsGADA, f.* 248, *kn.* 3429, *l.* 109; ''Doklad'' June 12, 1762, *TsGADA, f.* 1256, Kommissii o soch. ulozh., *d.* 91, *op.* 3, *l.* 234.

45. On the report of the Policemaster General's chancery, eighteen officers were needed to draw a map of St. Petersburg. The collection of geographic data, as one voevoda chancery reported, was a low priority. There were a few nobles to continue with the land survey, none were available to conduct geographic investigations. ''Protokoly,'' Mar. 4, 6, 1762, *TsGADA, f.* 248, *kn.* 3428, *ll.* 86, 185.

46. Solov'ev, *Istoriia,* vol. 12, p. 538.

47. ''Doklady,'' Mar. 4, 11, 15, May 15, Aug. 11, 1759, *TsGADA, f.* 342, *d.* 91, *ch.* IV, *ll.* 1–29; ''Protokol'' Jan. 10, 1762, *f.* 248, *kn.* 3426, *l.* 104.

48. Got'e, *Istoriia,* vol. 1, p. 269.

49. Got'e, *Istoriia,* vol. 1, pp. 120–46.

50. ''Bumagi Vorontsova,'' 1761, *LOII f.* 36, *d.* 1067, *ll.* 155–56.

51. Rubinshtein, ''Ulozhennaia,'' pp. 219, 225.

52. V. I. Latkin, *Proekt novogo ulozheniia sostavlenniyi zakonodatel'noi kommissiei 1754–1766 gg. (Chast' III 'o sostoianie poddanykh voobshche')* (St. Petersburg, 1893), pp. 174–88.

53. Two departments of the Senate were located in Moscow. See discussion of the central administration in LeDonne, *Ruling Russia,* pp. 30–37.

54. Got'e, *Istoriia,* vol. 1, p. 120.

55. Shuvalov proposed a network of commissars, elected locally and coordinated by a Department of State Economy. They were to have responsibility for overseeing prices and ensuring grain supplies during famines and for other tasks. The general coordinator of this Department was to be Shuvalov himself. See Got'e, *Istoriia,* vol. 1, pp. 135–44.

56. R. L. Vorontsov, ''Proekty,'' *LOII, f.* 36, *d.* 1068, *ll.* 68–73: *d.* 1067, *l.*11.

57. R. Vorontsov, ''Proekt o dvorianstve,'' *LOII, f.* 36, *d.* 1068, *ll.* 68–73.

58. ''Proekt o dvorianstve,'' *l.* 73.

59. Rubinshtein notes figures about the commercialization of the economy but provides no information about land values. Kahan also does not undertake an estimate. However, a glance at land sales from the *Sankt-Peterburgskie vedomosti* suggests a rise. See Augustine. Rubinshtein, ''Ulozhennaia,'' pp. 212–13; A. Kahan, *The Plow, the Hammer and the Knout, an Economic History of Eighteenth-Century Russia,* with the editorial assistance of R. Hellie (Chicago, Ill., 1985), ch. 2; W. R. Augustine, ''The Economic Attitudes and Opinions Expressed by the Russian Nobility in the Great Commission of 1767'' (Ph.D. diss., Columbia University, 1968), pp. 24, 51.

60. A decree in 1736, not found in *PSZ,* put an end to the informal distribution of *pomest'e* by the Votchina College. Since the death of Peter I, hundreds of desiatiny had been granted in return for service, and despite prohibition, the practice lingered. In return for service, Georgian nobles who had served in the guard were settled in the Ukraine; Serbians who served in Novorossiisk were rewarded with land and villages. Settled estates therefore continued to be a common reward for special service and personal proximity to the ruler. These lands that were subject to repossession by the state when nobles fell from favor. Romanovich-Slavatinskii, *Dvorianstvo,* pp. 152–62.

61. More than 800,000 serfs with land were granted to landlords in 1762 after the coup d'état. See Mavrodin, *Krestianskaia,* pp. 292–93.

62. See Vorontsov's project that nobles, non-nobles, clergy, and merchants be allowed to ''obtain by money, tender persuasion, and means other than force'' Tatars, Nogai, Kalmyki, Kirgiz, Bashkiri, and other Moslem peoples who are not enserfed for ''permanent servitude'' so that unsettled regions could be populated without removing peasants from the field, agriculture could be improved and conscripts could be drawn from estates other than those in the center. R. Vorontsov, ''Proekt ob umnozheniia naseleniia,'' 1761, *LOII, f.* 36, *d.* 1067, *l.* 11; ''O dvorianstve,'' 1761–1763, *d.* 1068, *ll.* 68–73.

63. A. Alchian and H. Demsetz, "The Property Rights Paradigm," *Journal of Economic History* (March 1973), p. 25.

64. See J. Blum, *The End of the Old Order in Rural Europe* (Princeton, N.J., 1978), pp. 11–28.

65. G. V. Vernadskii, "Manifest Petra III o vol'nosti dvorianskoi i zakonodatel'naia komissiia 1754–1766 gg.," *Istoricheskoe obozrenie*, vol. 20 (1915), pp. 51–59.

66. He wrote that on one evening when Peter wanted an excuse to be away from his mistress, having explained to her that he was engaged in important state business, he closeted Volkov with the command to produce something important. Prince M. M. Shcherbatov, *On The Corruption of Morals in Russia*, ed. and transl. A. Lentin (Cambridge, 1969), pp. 232, 233. The reason Volkov was not in the Senate, despite his prominence in government, was, Haxthausen understood, that Volkov was not "sufficiently titled" to hold a post of great distinction, such as senator or chancellor. Haxthausen to Bernstorff, Jan. 11/22, 1762, *RAD TKUA* 78.

67. M. I. Semevskii, "Shest' mesiatsev iz russkoi istorii XVIII veka. Ocherk tsarstvovaniia imperatora Petra III, 1761–1762 gg.," *Otechestvennie zapiski*, vol. 173 (1867), p. 770; see also J. von Staehlin, "Zapiski Shtelina o Petre Tret'em Imperatore Vserossiiskom," *Chteniia v Obshchestve istorii i drevnosti rossiiskikh*, vol. 59 (1866), no. 4, p. 97.

68. M.I. Semevskii, "Dmitrii Vasilievich Volkov, 1718–1785," *Russkaia starina*, vol. 9 (1874), p. 170.

69. Vernadskii, "Manifest," p. 53.

70. Jones, *The Emancipation*, p. 33.

71. Raeff, "Overthrow," p. 1292.

72. Ibid., p. 1292.

73. Ibid., pp. 1291–92.

74. Rubinshtein, "Ulozhennaia," p. 250.

75. Kahan, *The Plow,* p. 316.

76. E. P. Karnovich, *Zamechatel'nya bogatstva chastnykh lits v Rossii, Ekonomicheskoistoricheskoe izsledovanie* (St. Petersburg, 1874), pp. 255–280; about his achievements, see his own account in "Zapiski P. I. Shuvalova (okolo 1760)," *TsGADA Gosarkhiv razriad*, XI, no. 316.

77. See Got'e for a discussion of the series of limitations Shuvalov and others placed on merchants' rights to own land, serfs and factories beginning in 1754. Iu. V. Got'e, *Ocherk istorii zemlevladeniia v Rossii* (St. Petersburg, 1915), pp. 102–28.

78. Got'e, *Ocherk*, pp. 102–28.

79. "Bumagi iz dela o general-prokurore A. I. Glebove," *SIRIO*, vol. 1, (1867), p. 215.

80. "Donoshenie kommissii novosochiniaemogo ulozheniia," Feb. 1, 1762, *TsGADA f.* 248, *kn.* 3426 *l.* 1; Feb. 28, 1762, *kn.* 3396, *l.* 51.

81. "Bumagi Glebove," p. 216.

82. D. V. Volkov, "O kommertsi," Dec. 19, 1760, *LOII, f.* 36, *d.* 550, *l.* 264.

83. Translated in R. Meek, *Economics*, pp. 26–28.

84. Shuvalov would have granted to nobles the exclusive right to own land and trade in agricultural products. See Rubinshtein, "Ulozhennaia," p. 237.

85. Volkov to Orlov, July 10, 1762, p. 484.

86. Among Peter's last acts was one of several attempts to recall overdue loans to the state commercial bank. See chapter 4.

87. "Ukazy Petra III," Jan. 30, 1762, *TsGADA, f.* 9, *op.* 2, *d.* 43, *l.* 3; "Pis'mo," pp. 480–81.

88. Protocol, Jan. 17, 1762, *TsGADA, f.* 248, *kn.* 3426, *l.* 283.

89. See J. Castera, *Histoire de Catherine II*, 2 vols. (Paris, 1800), vol. 1, pp. 207–209; Solov'ev, *Istoriia*, vol. 13, pp. 13–14; Shcherbatov, *On the Corruption*, pp. 232–34; Raeff, "Overthrow," pp. 1291–93.

90. Raeff, "Overthrow," p. 1290.

91. Breteuil to Choiseul, Feb. 15/26, 1762, *AMAE CP Russie* 68.

92. Mercy to Kaunitz, Feb. 1/12, 1762, *SIRIO*, vol. 18 (1876), p. 116.

93. Compare Raeff, "There is no documentary evidence to show that it was a direct response to the demands of the nobility as a whole or even of an important segment of the 'ruling classes'." Raeff, "Overthrow," pp. 1292–93; *PSZ* 15: 11,444 (*man.*, Feb. 18, 1762), p. 912.

94. *PSZ* 15: 11,444 (*man.*, Feb. 18, 1762), pp. 912–13.

95. Latkin, *Proekt*, p. 267.

96. G. Helbig, *Russkie izbranniki* (Berlin, 1900), pp. 271–77; Troitskii, *Russkii absoliutizm*, pp. 271–82; I. I. Shuvalov to D. V. Volkov, 1762, *TsGADA, f.* 11, *d.* 318, *l.* 1; *PSZ* 15: 11,515 (*im.* Apr. 24, 1762), p. 985; Viskovatov, *Kratkaia istoriia pervogo korpusa* (St. Petersburg, n.d.), pp. 30–36.

97. Separate projects were to be created by Aleksandr Villebois, Ivan Shuvalov, and Aleksei Mel'gunov for instruction in history, geography, mechanics, and military tactics. In the expanded Cadet Corps there was to have been an engineering school for non-nobles with training for future naval officers and a special engineering school for nobles. Villebois submitted his plan after the coup, and it was approved October 25, 1762. Ivan Shuvalov also represented continuity after the coup, when he continued to be involved in education policy. *PSZ* 15: 11,515 (*im.* Apr. 24, 1762), p. 985; 16: 11,697 (*utv. doklada senata*, Oct. 25, 1762), pp. 94–96.

98. *PSZ* 15: 11,444 (*man.*, Feb. 18, 1762), p. 915.

99. "Protocol," Apr. 20, 1762, *TsGADA, f.* 248, *kn.* 3498, *l.* 178.

100. See G. Freeze, "The Soslovie (Estate) Paradigm and Russian Social History," *American Historical Review*, vol. 91, no. 1 (Feb. 1986), p. 25.

101. On legal consciousness in the eighteenth century, see chapter 1 of R. Wortman, *The Development of Russian Legal Consciousness* (Chicago, 1976), ch. 1.

102. On the substitution of the Church's moral authority by state authority, see Raeff, *Well-Ordered Police State*, pp. 188–89.

103. *PSZ* 15: 11,510 (*Vys. utv. doklada senata*, Apr. 20, 1762), p. 982; 11,540 (*sen.*, May 19, 1762), pp. 1010–11; 11,422 (*im.*, Jan. 29, 1762), p. 895; 11,548 (*im.*, May 23, 1762), p. 1021; 11,564 (June 5, 1762), pp. 1032–33.

104. This clause, Point 8, is important. Although the wording is complex, upon close examination the meaning is clear. It has been misinterpreted, and therefore demands a brief review. "Nobles who are now in the military service, who are soldiers and who are at a rank below officer, and who have not been promoted to officer, will not be retired. Except [razve] nobles who have continued in service for more than twelve years; these will receive freedom from service." Troitskii has taken this clause to mean that nobles who had served at the lower ranks up to twelve years without promotion were ineligible for retirement, which puts an entirely different cast upon the manifesto. See his *Russkii absoliutizm*, p. 143; "Doklady Senata," Feb. 18, 1762, *TsGADA, f.* 248, *kn.* 3427, *l.* 137.

105. "Doklad," Feb. 18, 1762, *TsGADA, f.* 248, *kn.* 3427, *l.* 137.

106. Particularly officers and rank-and-file soldiers, "who do not have their own means of subsistence," to be resettled on the borderland area between Tsaritsyn and Astrakhan, with lands in perpetuity, "Protokol," Mar. 8, May 8, 1762, *TsGADA, f.* 248, *kn.* 3430, *l.* 168.

107. As in N. B. Golikova and L. G. Kisliagina, "Sistema gosudarstvennogo upravleniia," *Ocherki russkoi kul'tury XVIII veka*, ch. 2 (Moscow, 1987), p. 83.

108. See chapter 4.

109. *Skt.-Peterburgskie vedomosti*, April 5, 14, 23, May 17, 1762; *Moskovskie vedomosti*, May 7, 28, 1762; Romanovich-Slavatinskii, p. 191; *TsGADA, f.* 248, *kn.* 3428, *ll.* 86, 109, 185, 211, 316.

110. F. Algarotti, *Brieven* (Harlingen, 1770), p. 98; I. Pushkarev, *Istoriia imperatorskoi rossiiskoi gvardii* (St. Petersburg, 1844), pp. 251–53; *Istoricheskoe obozrenie leib-gvardii, 1730–1850* (n.p., n.d.), pp. 1–79.

111. Schwan, *Histoire*, pp. 114–19; *PSZ* 15: 11,480 (*im.*, Mar. 21, 1762), pp. 945–48.

112. *PSZ* 15: 11,480 (*im.* Mar. 21, 1762), pp. 945–48.

113. Catherine II, however, reinstated the company. Helbig, "Griunshtein," *Russkaia starina* (April 1866), p. 151.

114. Romanovich-Slavatinskii, *Dvorianstvo*, p. 195.

115. These commissioners examined once again the issues Vorontsov covered in his proposal in 1762. They looked at various papers on "fidei kommiss" (the Austrian model of inheritance), and their final proposal to Catherine included, in addition to a recommendation on emancipation (which they held to be "incontrovertible"), a recommendation for a new inheritance law. "Doklady komissii," Feb. 21, Mar 18, 1763, *TsGADA, f.* 16, *razriad* 16, *d.* 235, *ch.* 1, *ll.* 35–175.

116. Although he also writes that after its promulgation, the senators came in a group to thank Peter for the manifesto, Solov'ev, *Istoriia,* vol. 13, p. 12.

117. A false impression of this commission's work would be obtained from Solov'ev. Solov'ev presented only the critical remarks by Bestuzhev-Riumin as if this were all that remained of the documentation. "Among the responses by members of the commission," he claimed, "we have only the report of the elderly Bestuzhev." Solov'ev, *Istoriia,* vol. 13, pp. 222–23.

118. Korf, *Dvorianstvo,* pp. 1–11.

119. *PSZ* 15: 11,444, p. 915.

120. M. L. Vorontsov to N. A. Korff, Feb. 21, 1763, *LOII, f.* 36, *d.* 1067, *ll.* 339–40.

121. *PSZ* 18: 13,087 *(sen.,* Mar. 24, 1785), p. 483.

122. For example, see *PSZ* 16: 11,951 *(sen.,* Oct. 16, 1763), p. 401.

123. *Senatskii arkhiv,* 15 vols. (St. Petersburg, 1888–1913), vol. 16 (1907), pp. 301–308, 479–83, 502–505, 552–53, 567, and others.

124. "Description politique de la Russie, servant à faire connâitre l'état actuel des forces du Souverain," 1767, *AMAE Mémoires et Documents Russie,* 11, no. 10.

125. *PSZ* 17: 12,665 *(im.,* May 29, 1766), pp. 797–99.

126. "Evidence about the numbers of nobles is inaccurate, since the category is too inclusive and since other categories of citizens have not been created." P. Keppen, *Deviataia reviziia, issledovanie o chisle zhitelei v Rossii v 1851 godu* (St. Petersburg), p. 7.

127. Quoted in Korf, *Dvorianskoe,* p. 5.

128. Confino, "Apropos," pp. 1174, 1187.

129. Raeff, *Origins,* p. 12.

130. I. Dubasov, "Iz Tambovskikh letopisei," *Istoricheskii vestnik,* 3 (1880), no. 11, p. 141.

131. A. M. Golitzyn, "Zapiski o pravakh russkogo dvorianstva dlia predstavleniia v komissiiu po sostavleniiu ulozheniia zakonov," n.d., *Biblioteka im. Saltykova-Shchedrina, f.* 871 (Ia. Ia. Shtelina), *d.* 67.

132. Augustine, "Economic Attitudes," pp. 24, 51.

133. Troitskii, *Russkii absoliutizm,* pp. 161–63.

134. Troitskii, *Russkii absoliutizm,* p. 163.

135. W. Pintner, "The Burden of Defense in Imperial Russia, 1725–1914," *Russian Review,* vol. 43 (1984), p. 255.

136. See Romanovich-Slavatinskii, *Dvorianstvo,* p. 129.

137. Ia. E. Vodarskii, "Sluzhiloe dvorianstvo v Rossii v kontse XVII–nachale XVII v.," *Voprosy voennoi istorii Rossii XVIII i pervaia polovina XIX vekov* (Moscow, 1969), p. 234.

138. P. Dirin, *Istoriia leib gvardii Semenovskogo polka* (St. Petersburg, 1883), vol. 1, p. 281.

139. Troitskii, *Russkii absoliutizm,* pp. 299–301.

140. V. M. Kabuzan, *Narodonaselenie Rossii v XVIII–pervoi polovine XIX v. (po materialam revizii)* (Moscow, 1963), pp. 66, 152–53, Tables 15, 18.

141. A. R. Vorontsov to A. A. Bezborodko, Mar. 15, 1778, *TsGADA, f.* 19, *d.* 286, *ch.* III, *l.* 457.

142. V. L. Iur'ev, *Sostoianie goroda Viatka v tsarstvovanie imperatritsy Ekateriny II* (Viatka, 1885), pp. 54–57; M. Shcherbatov, "Materialy po Iaroslavskoi gubernii 1785 g.," *Biblioteka imeni M. E. Saltykova-Shchedrina, f. Ermitazhnoe sobranie,* 116/2, *bk.* 2;

Opisanie kurskogo namestnichestva iz drevnikh i novykh raznykh o nem izvestii v kratse sobrannoe seriem (Moscow, 1886), pp. 36–37, 43–44, 56, and 68–69; *Materialy dlia istorii goroda XVII i XVIII stoletii, Riazan, Zaraisk, Pereslavl'-Zalesk, Borovsk, Rostov, Maloiaroslavets, Tula* (1883–1888); *Topograficheskoe opisanie kaluzhskogo namestnichestva* (St. Petersburg, 1785); *Topograficheskoe opisanie iaroslavskogo namestnichestva* (Iaroslavl', 1794); *Topograficheskie izvestiia vseia Rossii* (Moscow, 1771).

143. Kabuzan, *Narodonaselenie*, p. 154.

144. Figures are not available for all major towns. It should be noted that from these figures, it is not possible to determine how many of these were in service and how many were simply landowners.

145. The total for rural areas surrounding towns was 2,190 nobles in residence, 492 away. *Topograficheskoe opisanie kurskogo namestnichestva* (Kursk, 1786), pp. 68–79.

146. "Vedomost' po dannym po ruzskomu uezdnomu predvoditel'iu ruzskoi okrugi pomeshchichim i votchinnym ikh starostam svedeniiam o preterpennom ot nepriiatel'skogo nashestviia razorenii," Mar. 15, 1813, *TsGIA g. Moskvy, fond ruzskogo uezdnogo predvoditel'ia dvorianstva*, no. 394, *d*. 43, *op*. 1, *ll*. 5–131; *Topograficheskoe opisanie Moskvy*, pp. 262–80.

147. Raeff, "Overthrow," p. 1302.

148. L. F. Zakharova, "Pomeshchichie krest'iane Nizhegorodskoi gubernii i ikh klassovaia bor'ba vo vtoroi polovine XVIII veka" (Kandidatskaia dissertatsiia, Gorkii Pedagogical Institute, 1954), pp. 44–52.

149. "Kratkaia vedomost' skol'ko v Iaroslavskoi Gubernii kakogo zvaniia nakhoditsia dvorian zhivushchykh v svoikh derevniakh," Feb. 4, 1778, *TsGADA, f*. 16, *d*. 1012, *ch*. 1, *ll*. 56–57.

150. In one district in Iaroslav province, Maloga, estates along the Volga river, i.e., those with commercial potential, belonged overwhelmingly (82%) to military service families. The data are from the 1830s. "Atlas Iaroslavskoi Gubernii s ekonomicheskimi primechaniiami," 1837, *TsGVIA, f. Voenno-uchenoi arkhiv, d*. 19187, Maloga; hereafter *TsGVIA, f. VUA*.

151. From the same source. "Atlas," 1837, TsGVIA, f. VUA, d. 19187, Maloga. In the Ruza list, out of 130 owners, 34% were civilian and 37% military; the remaining 29% were listed as pomeshchiki rather than by service rank. "Vedomost' po dannym po ruzskomu uezdnomu," *ll*. 4–109.

152. *PSZ* 20: 14, 392 (*Uch.*, Nov. 7, 1775), pp. 229ff.

153. "Doklad," *TsGADA, f*. 370, *d*. 21, *l*. 36.

154. Got'e, *Istoriia*, vol. 2, pp. 161–63.

155. M. P. Pavlova-Sil'vanskaia, "Uchrezhdenie o guberniiakh, 1775 g. i ego klassovaia suchnost' " (Kandidatskaia dissertatsiia, Moscow State University, 1964), pp. 1–7.

156. Ibid.; M. T. Beliavskii, "Trebovaniia dvorian i perestroika organov upravleniia i suda na mestakh v 1775 g.," *Nauchnye doklady vysshei shkoly, Istoricheskii nauki*, no. 4 (1960), p. 125.

157. *PSZ*, 20: 14,392 (*Uchrezhdeniia*, Nov. 7, 1775), pp. 229ff.

158. Augustine, "Economic Attitudes," pp. 35ff.

159. "Materialy po Kostromskoi gubernii, 1785 g.," *BSS, f*. 116/8, *ll*. 55ff.

160. *Materialy dlia istorii goroda Kostromy* (Kostroma,1883), pp. 225–26.

161. A. R. Vorontsov to A. A. Bezborodko, Mar. 15, 1778, *TsGADA, f*. 19, *d*. 286, *ll*. 457–58.

162. N. D. Chechulin, *Russkoe provintsial'noe obshchestvo vo vtoroi polovine XVIII veka* (St. Petersburg, 1889), pp. 28, 34; and his "Cherty iz zhizhi russkikh dvorian v kontse XVIII veka," *Moskovskii nabliudatel'* (Moscow, 1836), pp. 133–45; Korf, *Dvorianstvo*, p. 6.

163. Chechulin, *Russkoe*, pp. 28, 34.

164. A comparison can be made with French development; see J. B. Wood, "Social Structure and Social Change among the Nobility of the Election of Bayeux, 1463–1666" (Ph.D. diss., Emory University, 1973), pp. 5–92.

165. W. Pintner, "The Social Characteristics of the Early Nineteenth-Century Russian Bureaucracy," *Slavic Review,* vol. 29, no. 3 (1970), p. 433.

166. Chechulin, *Russkoe,* pp. 54–62.

167. Solov'ev, *Istoriia,* vol. 12, pp. 235–36, 541, 643–44.

168. A. Kahan, "The Costs of Westernization in Russia: The Gentry and the Economy in the Eighteenth Century," *Slavic Review,* 25 (1966), no. 1, pp. 45, 61. See also Raeff: "Nor was it easy for a Russian nobleman in the eighteenth century to make a career in the so-called free professions. Obviously, the obligation of service acted as a barrier until 1762. . . . moreover the young nobleman was frequently forced to withdraw from school to enter service, leaving . . . other *raznochintsy* to pursue the full course of professional training." *Origins,* p. 117.

3. Secularization of the Ecclesiastical Estates

1. *Polnoe sobranie zakonov Rossiiskoi imperii,* 1649–1913, 234 vols. (St. Petersburg, 1830–1916) (hereafter *PSZ*), 15: 11,481 (*im.,* Mar. 21, 1762), pp. 948–53.

2. For example, in 1818 the Musin-Pushkin inventories listed 36 desiatiny of Church land in the family's votchina. "Reestr i obmere zemlei za rekoi Malogoi Rozhestvenskikh i peremutskikh vladenii," *TsGADA, f.* 1270, *op.* 1, *d.* 554, *ll.* 94–95.

3. P. Miliukov, *Ocherki po istorii russkoi kul'tury,* 3 vols. (fifth ed.; Petrograd, 1909, 1916), vol. 2, p. 162; I. A. Bulygin, *Monastyrskie krest'iane Rossii v pervoi chetverti XVIII veka* (Moscow, 1977); N. Rozanov, *Istoriia moskovskogo eparkhial'nogo upravleniia so vremeni uchrezhdeniia S. Sinoda s 1721–1821 gg.* (Moscow, 1870), 2: 328–37; V. Miliutin, *O nedvizhimykh imushchestvakh dukhovenstva v Rossii* (Moscow, 1862), pp. 505ff., who stresses strong continuity of laws from the seventeenth century; and others. Cf. G. Freeze, *The Russian Levites: Parish Clergy in the Eighteenth Century* (Cambridge, Mass., 1977), p. 16.

4. [C. F. Schwan] M. de la Marche, *Histoire et anecdotes de la vie, du regne, du détrônement et de la mort de Pierre III, dernier Empereur de toutes les Russes, écrites en forme de lettres* (London, 1766), p. 217.

5. Considered an abuse of church regulations. On April 12, 1722, Peter I forbade the construction of private chapels for any family other than the tsar's, and he gave existing ones to parish churches. Both Peter and Catherine prohibited private chapels. See *Istoriko-statisticheskiia svedeniia S.-Peterburgskoi eparkhii* (St. Petersburg, 1878), ser. 6, pp. 81–83, 115–16; *Rukovodstvennye dlia pravoslavnogo dukhovenstva ukazy Sv. Pravitel'stvuiushchego Sinoda, 1721–1878* (Moscow, 1879), no. 53, p. 52; *PSPR* (1910), p. 29.

6. See also his aunt's regulation of icon production, *PSZ* 15: 10,935 (*sin.,* Mar. 16, 1759), p. 334; 10,977 (*sen.* July 26, 1759), p. 363.

7. *PSZ* 15: 11,420 (*im.,* Jan. 29, 1762), pp. 894–95; Feb. 7, 1762, *PSPR* (1912), no. 5, p. 1749; *PSPR* (1912), no. 4, p. 1751.

8. "Ukaz nashemu Sinodu," Mar. 26, 1762, *TsGADA, f.* 18, *d.* 193, *l.* 1.

9. A. Stözel, *Carl Gottlieb Suarez* (Berlin, 1885), p. 185.

10. On the Synodal command, see Freeze, p. 18; P. Miliukov, *Gosudarstvennoe khoziaistvo Rossii pervoi chetverti XVIII veka i reforma Petra Velikogo* (St. Petersburg, 1905), p. 161; T. V. Barsov, *Sinodal'nyia uchrezhdeniia prezhnego vremeni* (St. Petersburg, 1897).

11. In the Russian provinces of Novgorod and Pskov, Miliutin, *O nedvizhimykh,* pp. 415–17.

12. Miliutin, *O nedvizhimykh,* pp. 417–19.

13. M. Gorchakov, *Monastyrskii prikaz (1649–1725)* (St. Petersburg, 1868), pp. 19–20; A. Zav'ialov, *Vopros o tserkovnykh imeniiakh pri imperatritse Ekaterine II* (St. Petersburg, 1900), pp. 138–41.

14. Zav'ialov, *Vopros,* pp. 36–7; Gorchakov, *Monastyrskii,* pp. 33–37; *PSZ* 14: 10,588 (July 24, 1756), p. 602.

15. Miliutin, *O nedvizhimykh,* pp. 443–53.

16. Ibid., pp. 465–71.

17. See the Synod's response to Musin-Pushkin's report of March 6, 1740, in Barsov, *Sinodal'nyia*, pp. 196–201.

18. I. A. Bylygin, *Monastyrskie krest'iane Rossii v pervoi chetverti XVIII veka* (Moscow, 1977), pp. 62–63.

19. On the sixteenth and seventeenth century, see A. Pavlov, *Istoricheskii ocherk sekuliar-izatsii tserkovnykh zemel' v Rossii, ch. I., popytki k obrashcheniiu v gosudarstvennuiu sob-stvennost' po zemel'nykh vladenii russkoi tserkvi v XVI v. (1503–1580)* (Odessa, 1871); and Zav'ialov, *Vopros*, pp. 51–52.

20. A. M. Borisov, "Krizis tserkovnogo i monastyrskogo zemlevladeniia khoziaistva v 40-kh-60-kh godakh XVIII v.," *Istoriia SSSR* (1968), p. 168.

21. See document no. 17, "Vedomosti tserkovnym votchinam, rozdannym iz Monastyr-skogo Prikaza v techenii 1701–1723 godov raznym litsam, s ukazaniem vremeni i uslovii razdachi i chisla dvorov sostavlennaia na osnovanii svedenii, nakhodiashchikhsia v delakh sinodskago arkhiva," in Gorchakov, *Monastyrskii*, pp. 70–72.

22. *PSZ* 4: 1897 (*im.*, Feb. 27, 1702), pp. 188–89.

23. See most recent treatment in chapter 5, Bulygin, *Monastyrskie*, pp. 180–201.

24. Cracraft argues, in the tradition of Miliukov and other nineteenth-century scholars, that Peter's reform was a temporary resolution of financial stringencies associated with fre-quent military campaigns (see J. Cracraft's *The Church Reform of Peter the Great* [Stanford, Calif., 1971], p. 87). Soviet scholars, including Bulygin, emphasize instead that Peter I's reform should be seen as movement toward secularization (see Borisov, Bulygin, and oth-ers). Peter's restraint in church reform, in any case, was evident. He allowed the synodal domain considerable freedom in the conduct of affairs and tax collection. On the other hand, his designation of certain estates for special taxation was not temporary. By the end of his reign, grain as well as money was levied from designated church institutions. This solution seems to have been satisfactory in the early years of the century. Peter's advisor, Musin-Pushkin, who wanted a more sweeping reform, failed to persuade Peter's successors that anything more was necessary; see P. Verkhovskii, *Naselennyia nedvizhimyia imeniia Sv. Sin-oda, arkhiereiskikh domov i monastyrei pri blizhaishikh preemnikov Petra Velikogo* (St. Pe-tersburg, 1909), pp. 10–11, 13.

25. *PSZ* 4: 1829 (*im.*, Jan. 24, 1701), pp. 97–8; 1886 (*im.*, Dec. 30, 1701), p. 181; 2415 (*sen.*, Aug. 13, 1711), p. 727; 8: 3659 (*im.*, Oct. 16, 1720), p. 248; 7: 3632 (*sen.*, Aug. 24, 1720), pp. 232–33.

26. See Musin-Pushkin's report of March 6, 1740, in Barsov, *Synodal'nyia*, p. 198.

27. Seventeen of the twenty-eight eparchies were located in central regions, comprising 60% of all monasteries. In numbers, ecclesiastical peasants were distributed as follows: among the central provinces, in Moscow there were 342,467, Voronezh 124,509, Kazan 80,538, Belgorod 38,161, Nizhegorod 38,090, altogether a total of 73% of all ecclesiastical peasants. In Novgorod there were 130,400, Archangel 43,657, Siberia 8,159, and in Oren-burg 4,476 ("Kratkaia vedomost': kolikoe chislo v vsekh guberniiakh, provintsiiakh, gor-odakh i uezdakh po nyneshnei revizii muzhskago pola dush, podlezhashchikh v podushnom oklade, iavilos', i v kakom zvanii i chto s nikh podushnykh deneg iavstvuet nizhe sego," *Zhurnal ministerstva vnutrennykh del* [1839] vol. 33, no. 8, pp. 252–53).

28. Miliutin, *O nedvizhimym*, pp. 505ff.

29. "Raport," 1742, *TsGADA, f.* 18, *d.*, 85, *ch.* 1, *l.* 155.

30. Bulygin, *Monastyrskie*, pp. 202–15.

31. "Doklad Gagarina," 1765, *TsGADA, f.* 18, *d.* 85, *ch.* II, *l.* 237; Borisov, "Krizis," p. 142.

32. "Predlozhenie Shakhovskogo 16 iiulia 1744," *TsGADA, f.* 18, *d.* 85, *ch.* I, *l.* 354.

33. The procurators of the Synod were Iakov Shakhovskoi (1741–1753), Afanasii L'vov (1753–1758), and Aleksei Kozlovskii (1758–1763); procurators of the so-called Economic Chancellery of the Synod included Semen Raevskii (1722–1726) and Ivan Chaplygin (1742–

1744), and of the College of Economy, Platon Musin-Pushkin (1738–1744). "Doklad Aleksei Kozlovskogo," Mar. 25, 1759, *TsGADA, f.* 8, *d.* 47, no. 6, *ll.* 8–9. See Synod officials in E. Amburger, *Geschichte der Behordenorganisation Russlands von Peter dem Grossen bis 1917* (Leiden, 1966), pp. 108–12.

34. Barsov, *Sinodal'nyia*, pp. 200–201.

35. According to a list of monasteries from the early 1740s, categories sometimes overlapped: "Monasteries which have their own revenue collectors and are considered undesignated, nevertheless, after deducting expenditures, must give the remainder to the guberniia chancellery," see *TsGADA, f.* 18, *d.* 85, *ch.* I., *ll.* 89ff., esp. 97; "Zaopredelennymi arkhiereiskimi 10 domami i za 74 monastyrei v votchinakh po svidetel'stvu generaliteta muzheska polu 489,496 dush, 1742 g.," *TsGADA, f.* 18, *d.* 85, *ch.* I., *l.* 155.

36. "Doklad I. Chaplygina," Nov. 30, 1742, *TsGADA, f.* 18, *d.* 85, *ch.* I, *ll.* 145–48.

37. Included in "Doklad," 1762, *TsGADA, f.* 18, *d.* 197, *l.* 279; see also the reports of Shakhovskoi in *TsGADA, f.* 18, *d.* 85, *ch.* I, *ll.* 17–80.

38. E. V. Anisimov, *Podatnaia reforma Petra I, vvedenie podushnoi podati v Rossii, 1719–1728 gg.* (Leningrad, 1982), pp. 41–42.

39. Procurator from 1758 on, Kozlovski described this period of history: "in 1744 the College of Economy was given to the Synod's jurisdiction without in fact it being expressly recommended by ukaz: the procurator and all secular personnel were removed from that administrative institution," "Doklad Kozlovskogo," March 28, 1759, *TsGADA, f.* 18, *d.* 47, *ch.* VI, *ll.* 8–9.

40. *PSZ* 15: 11,481 (*im.*, Mar. 21, 1762), p. 949.

41. The idea comes from the Petrine Ecclesiastical Regulation which had referred to "a new revenue" to be collected "at monasteries" and used on local expenses (*The Spiritual Regulation of Peter the Great*, trans. and ed. A. Muller [Seattle, Wash., 1972]), pp. 77, 81.

42. *PSZ,* 15: 11,481 (*im.*, Mar. 21, 1762), p. 949.

43. I. Smolitsch, *Geschichte der Russischen Kirche 1700–1917* (Leiden, 1964), pp. 352–53.

44. In 1729 Petrine law was reversed in order to allow retired officers to become monks. Shakhovskoi suggested to Elizabeth that a special hospital be constructed in Kazan to house invalids, and an ukaz was enacted to that effect; but no money was found to support such an effort. *Istoriko-statisticheskie svedeniia*, pp. 28–29; *PSZ* 14: 10,790 (Jan. 10, 1758); "O dozvolenii postrigat' v monakhi otstavnykh soldat, otsylaemykh dlia propitaniia v monastyri," June 25, 1729, no. 259; "Protokol Verkhovnago tainago soveta," vol. 7 (January–June 1729); *Sbornik imperatorskogo russkogo istoricheskogo obshchestva* (hereafter *SIRIO*), vol. 94 (1894), pp. 829–30.

45. It may also be that without hope of implementing reform, Elisabeth preferred for the war years to rely on loans, 350,000 rubles, for example, in 1758. "Bumagi Teplova," *TsGADA, f.* 18, *d.* 197, *l.* 303.

46. *Istoriia Senata*, vol. 2, p. 138.

47. On March 28, 1759, Kozlovskii complained to the empress that nothing had been done about the Senate's request, although Peter I had stipulated that the institution should have one. "There was clear reason for the suggestion of the procurator general, Field Marshall [Trubetskoi] to assign Fedor Sazonov as procurator . . . to which the Synod responded on February 5 to the Senate that there cannot be a procurator without your particular order." "Doklad Kozlovskogo," Mar. 28, 1759, *TsGADA, f.* 18, *d.* 47 *ch.* VI, *ll.* 8–9.

48. "Doklad Kozlovskogo," Aug. 8, 1759, *TsGADA, f.* 18, *d.* 47, *ch.* VI, *ll.* 10–11.

49. S. M. Solov'ev, *Istoriia Rossii s drevneishikh vremen*, 15 vols. (Moscow, 1959–65), vol. 12, pp. 494–96; and papers of this commission in *TsGADA, f.* 18, *d.* 158.

50. A. A. Kondrashenkov, "Vosstanie monastyrskikh krest'ian v Isetskoi provintsii v 60-kh gg. XVIII v.," *Uchenye zapiski Kurganskoi ped. instituta* (Kurgan, 1959), pp. 135–36; L. N. Kapterev, *Dubinshchina: Ocherk po istorii vosstaniia dalmatovskikh krest'ian v XVIII veke* (Shadrinsk, 1929).

51. "Kratkii ocherk istorii Viatskogo kraia do otkrytiia v nem namestnichestva," in *Stoletie Viatskoi gubernii* (Moscow, 1880), vol. 1, pp. 51–99, esp. 76–77; A. I. Komissarenko, *Viatskoe krest'ianstvo v 20–60 gg. XVIII v.* (Moscow, 1966), pp. 11–15.

52. Borisov, "Krizis"; Alefirenko, *Krest'ianskoe*, pp. 169ff., villages at Spaso-Iaroslavl' monastery, in Kaliazin, and elsewhere. See the petitions in *TsGADA, f.* 18, *d.* 180, *ll.* 9ff.; and others in *f.* 18, *d.* 158, gathered by the head of the Justice College, Divov.

53. This project from the archives of the Senate's Codification Commission (see Ch. II); see Latkin, *Proekt,* pp. 119–20; see Rubinshtein, "Ulozhennaia komissiia," pp. 230–51.

54. "Doklad Kozlovskogo," Aug. 8, 1759, *TsGADA, f.* 18, *d.* 47, *ch.* VI, *l.* 11.

55. Solov'ev, *Istoriia,* vol. 12, p. 590.

56. See Solov'ev, *Istoriia,* vol. 12, pp. 590ff. He was no doubt an important figure in the history of reform, although his compromises with the Senate show him to have been less than resolute. He claimed in his memoirs to have urged Elizabeth to "fulfill her promised kindness to [the clergy] and find a better way to increase revenues, which belong to the treasury for state expenses; this would preserve revenues from being squandered." Ia. Shakhovskoi, *Zapiski kn. Ia. P. Shakhovskogo, 1705–1777* (St. Petersburg, 1872), pp. viii, 193.

57. On the relationship between war and enlightened reform see *Bulletin of the International Committee of Historical Sciences,* vol. 1 (no. 5, 1928), pp. 601–712; vol. 2 (nos. 34–35, 39, 1937), pp. 2–131, 135–225, 519–37; see also R. Herr, *The Eighteenth-Century Revolution in Spain* (Princeton, N.J., 1958); J. Youings, *The Dissolution of the Monasteries* (London, 1971); J. Bazant, *The Alienation of Church Wealth in Mexico* (Cambridge, 1971).

58. The dating of a report included in *PSZ* on January 4, 1762, reputedly by a special investigatory commission on peasant revolts, is spurious. The report should have been bound with materials for Catherine's reign at the beginning of 1763. The commission found, for example, that the reason for peasant disobedience was that military commands had overstepped their bounds in collecting inventories and taxes, angering the ecclesiastical authorities and provoking still further the peasants. In January 1762, inventories were not being collected nor were military commands yet sent to the provinces to do so. *PSZ* 15: 11,396 (*utv.* Jan. 4, 1762), p. 881.

59. "Raport" Jan. 1, 1762, *TsGADA, f.* 203, *d.* 1, *l.*1. Also Aug. 8, 1759, "Doklad," *TsGADA, f.* 18, *d.* 47, *l.* 16.

60. "Protokol," Jan. 17, 1762, *TsGADA, f.* 248, *d.* 3426, *l.* 53.

61. There are no cabinet papers pertaining to this reform. It is therefore difficult to verify Shtelin's remark that the reform should be attributed to Glebov. "Bumagi o gen. prokuratore A. I. Glebove," pp. 215–16; Solov'ev, *Istoriia,* vol. 13; J. von Staehlin, "Zapiski Shtelina o Petre Tret'em Imperatore Vserossiiskom," *Chteniia v Obshchestve istorii i drevnostei rossiiskikh,* vol. 59 (1866), no. 4, pp. 102–103.

62. *PSZ* 15: 11,441 (*im.,* Feb. 16, 1762), p. 910; Solov'ev, *Istoriia,* vol. 13, p. 18.

63. "Protokol," Feb. 16, 1782, *TsGADA, f.* 248, *kn.* 3420, *ll.* 349–50; *PSZ* 15: 11,481 (*im.,* Mar. 21, 1762), p. 949.

64. "Protokol," Feb. 16, 1762, *TsGADA, f.* 248, *kn.* 3426, *ll.* 349–50.

65. "Protokol," Feb. 19, 1762, *TsGADA, f.* 248, *kn.* 3427, *ll.* 178–93.

66. "I was delighted to write the entire history of the project's origin in the reign of Empress Elizabeth, but that history was removed by the senators." D. V. Volkov, "Pis'mo D. V. Volkova k G. G. Orlovu, Iulia 10-go 1762 g.," *Russkaia starina,* vol. 11 (St. Petersburg, 1874), p. 484.

67. *PSZ* 15: 11,481 (*im.,* Mar. 21, 1762), p. 949.

68. "Protokol," Feb. 19, 1762, *TsGADA, f.* 248, *kn.* 3427, *ll.* 178–93.

69. A crude tax common in Europe to get around the problems of assessment. R. G. Ardant, "Financial Policy and Economic Infrastructure of Modern States and Nations," in *The Formation of National States in Western Europe,* ed. C. Tilly (Princeton, N.J., 1975), pp. 164–242; *PSZ* 15: 11,481 (*im.,* Mar. 21, 1762), p. 949.

70. A precedent was a resolution in 1744 by the Senate, in connection with the general land survey, to rent out the lands and ''otdat' '' land to peasants. *Istoriia Senata,* vol. 2, pp. 137–38.

71. *PSZ* 16: 12,060 (*im.*, Feb. 26, 1764), pp. 549–69.

72. ''Protokol,'' Feb. 19, 1762, *TsGADA, f.* 248, *kn.* 3427, *ll.* 178–93.

73. Ecclesiastical peasants were never considered in the same category with serfs. They could neither be sold nor transferred at the will of ecclesiastical authorities nor could marital bonds be decided by their masters. In the mid-eighteenth century, Shakhovskoi tried to establish regulations for secular supervision of peasants' economic affairs and personal lives, to prevent peasants from marrying outside their native villages. V.I. Semevskii, *Krest'iane v tsarstvovanie im. Ekateriny II* (St. Petersburg, 1903), vol. 1, p. 28; A. A. Kondrashenko, ''Vosstanie monastyrskikh krest'ian v Isetskom provintsii v 60-kh gg. XVIII v.,'' *Uchenye zapiski Kurganskogo pedagogicheskogo instituta* (Kurgan, 1959), p. 138; Barsov, *Sinodal'nyia,* pp. 224–25.

74. ''Ukaz,'' Apr. 27, 1762, *TSGADA, f.* 18, *d.* 198, *ll.* 148–52.

75. *PSZ* 15: 11,481 (*im.*, Mar. 21, 1762), p. 949.

76. ''Ekstrakt o prezhnikh uchrezhdennykh mestakh dlia sborov po sinodal'nomu vedomstvu'' in ''Bumagi Teplova,'' *TsGADA, f.* 18, *d.* 197, *l.* 145; ''Protokol,'' May 30, 1762, *TsGADA, f.* 248, *kn.* 3430, *l.* 490.

77. ''Ukaz,'' Apr. 27, 1762, *TsGADA, f.* 18, *d.* 197, *ll.* 148–49; *PSPR,* vol. 4 (1912), p. 1762.

78. ''Zhurnal prokurorskikh del,'' *TsGADA, f.* 280, *d.* 2050, *ll.*103, 105, 111, 113.

79. A discussion by senators on March 27 focused on the College of Economy, ''which was ordered to take all the above-mentioned ecclesiastical estates with all factories, crafts, industries and revenues under its direction by means of retired officers; all cash revenues, grain and other supplies, as well, cattle of all sorts, mills, fisheries, salt mines, for rent, and all rented land except that which belongs to the peasants. . . . '' ''Protokol,'' Mar. 27, 1762, *TsGADA, f.* 248, *kn.* 3397, *ll.* 144–45.

80. ''Protokol,'' Feb. 16, 1762, *TsGADA, f.* 248, *kn.* 3427, *l.* 193.

81. ''Ekstrakt'' in ''Bumagi Teplova,'' *TsGADA, f.* 18, *d.* 197, *ll.* 232, 236.

82. The reform was probably regulated locally by the voevod chancelleries, as in the following instructions to the Volokolamsk voevod chancellery: ''Proceed with collection of rent, give the 186.50 rubles to the college of economy, and send the ukaz [February 16] to the monastery; rent out the wastelands. . . . Give responsibility for construction at the monastery to peasants' starosty, who previously managed this, under the general direction of the five officers on pension there, with salaries for them and the six invalids in kind, grain and cash, according to payrolls, from the funds of the College of Economy,'' ''Protokol,'' July 18, 1762, *TsGADA, f.* 280, *d.* 2050, *l.* 112; ''Zhurnal,'' *TsGADA, f.* 280, *d.* 2050, *ll,* 111–13, 232, 236.

83. ''Protokol,'' June 17, 1762, *TsGADA, f.* 248, *kn.* 3400, *l.* 490; *f.* 18, *d.* 197, *ll.* 232–36.

84. Its failure to be realized was an excuse for Catherine to start over, Aug. 12, 1762, *PSPR Ekateriny Alekseevny,* vol. 1 (1913), p. 36.

85. *PSZ* 15: 11,498 (*im.*, Apr. 4, 1782), p. 969; Order from the College of Economy, based on Senate and imperial command, ''Zhurnal prokurorskikh del, 25 iiun' 1762 g.,'' *TsGADA, f.* 280, *d.* 7050, *l.* 20.

86. *PSZ* 15: 11,560 (*utv. doklada Senata,* June 1, 1762), p. 1031.

87. ''Ukaz Kollegii Ekonomii'' (following *im.* and *sen.* ukazy) ''Zhurnal prokurorskikh del, 25 iiun' 1762 g.,'' *TsGADA, f.* 280, *d.* 2050, *l.* 20.

88. M. Raeff, ''The Domestic Policies of Peter III and His Overthrow,'' *American Historical Review* (June 1970), p. 1296.

89. Glebov to Volkov, ''Vsepodanneishei raport, 30 maia 1762 g.,'' *TsGADA, f.* 203, *no.* 3, *ll.* 34–35; ''Protokoly,'' June 3, 13, 1762, *TsGADA, f.* 248, *kn.* 3421, *ll.* 6–7, 10, 139; about the uprising.

90. *PSZ* 15: 11,577 (*man.* June 19, 1762), pp. 1045–48.

91. V. A. Bil'basov, *Istoriia Ekateriny Vtoroi*, 2 vols. (Berlin, 1900), vol. 1, p. 426.

92. "March 1760" in *Mémoires et Documents*, no. 27, vol. 9, *AMAE Russie*.

93. "Ukaz Kollegii Ekonomii" to collect one ruble obrok from the land "given to the peasants." July 1, 1762, *TsGADA, f.* 280, *d.* 2050, *l.* 30; see also confirmation of Senate jurisdiction over the College of Economy, July 1, 1762, *PSPR* (1910), no. 4, p. 3.

94. July 20, 1762, *PSPR* (1910), no. 22, p. 20.

95. I. Znamenskii, "Otnoshenie gosudarstvennoi vlasti k tserkvi i dukhovenstvu v tsarstvovanie Ekateriny II," *Chtenie v obshchestve liubitelei dukhovnoi prosveshcheniia* (1874), p. 121.

96. *PSZ* 16: 11,643 (*im.*, Aug. 12, 1762), pp. 51–52.

97. Aug. 13, 1762, *PSPR (1910), no. 38, p. 37.*

98. " . . . and this resulted in the disobedience of bishopric and monastic peasants," Oct. 4, 1762, *PSPR* (1910), no. 47, p. 47.

99. Oct. 4, 1762, *PSPR* (1910), no. 47, p. 47.

100. Oct. 10, 1762, *PSPR* (1910), no. 50, p. 48.

101. *PSZ* 16: 11,643 (*im.* Aug. 12, 1762), pp. 51–52.

102. See the report of the commission on ecclesiastical states, Dec. 10, 1762, *TsGADA, f.* 18, *d.* 47, *ch.* VI., *l.* 233.

103. Ukaz Dec. 1762, *TsGADA, f.* 18, *d.* 197, *ll.* 48–55.

104. "Reestr ot kogo imianno o oslushnosti krest'ian v Sv. Pr. Sinod ot nizheoznachennykh preosviashchennykh arkhiereov i monastyrskikh nastoiatelei proshlogo 1762 goda v raznykh monastyrei i chislei byli predstavleni," *TsGADA, f.* 18, *d.* 47, *ch.* VI, *l.* 229; see also Catherine's manifesto of January 8, 1763, "in many places some backward people exploited the peasants and Our 12 August decree resulted in disturbances, many peasants took part in significant revolts, not wanting to pay the ruble . . . nor work but instead to act in a willful and hostile way . . . " (Jan. 8, 1763, *PSPR* [1910], no. 83, p. 84); the peasants "made false ukazy" about the seizure of land from the monasteries by the peasants (Dec. 10, 1762, *PSPR* [1910], no. 150, p. 149; Dec. 19, 1762, *TsGADA, f. 18, d.* 47, *ch. VI, ll.* 233–34).

105. Nov. 1762, "Bumagi Teplova," *TsGADA. f.* 18, *d.* 197, *ll.* 48–55.

106. Nov. 29, 1762, *PSPR* (1910), no. 70, pp. 68ff.

107. "There must be no quarrels with the secular command over this," *PSPR* (1910), no. 38, p. 37; no. 70, p. 68.

108. 1762, nos. 2 and 7, "Bumagi Teplova," *TsGADA, f.* 18, *d.* 197, *ll.* 40, 44–45 ob.

109. Kondrashenkov, pp. 135–76; L. M. Kapterev, pp. 15–35; I. Z. Kadson, *Pugachevshchina i tserkov'* (Leningrad, 1963), pp. 8–9.

110. She maintained the appearance of support for the Synodal command, as on August 12, "I have no intention of appropriating the lands of the Church," *PSZ* 16: 11,648 (Aug. 12, 1762), p. 52; Aug. 16, 1762, *PSPR* (1910), no. 39, p. 38.

111. Nov. 29, 1762, *PSPR* (1910), no. 76, p. 68.

112. May 12, 1762, *TsGADA, f.* 18, *d.* 85, *ch.* I, *ll.* 477–80.

113. "Raport Kurakina," Feb. 3, 1764," *TsGADA, f.* 18, *d.* 85, *ch.* 2, *ll.* 154–55.

114. Ibid., *l.* 155.

115. *PSZ* 16: 12,060 (*im.*, Feb. 26, 1764), pp. 549–69.

116. He began protest in 1762 by excommunicating peasants who refused to work for the monastery. Catherine ordered his arrest and trial, where he was condemned, defrocked, and exiled. "About the annulment of Arsenii Matseevich's incorrect excommunication of peasants on one votchina of his eparchy," July 24, 1762, *PSPR* (1910), no. 24, p. 21; M. S. Popov, *Arsenii Matseevich i ego delo* (St. Petersburg, 1912); I. Snegirev, "Arsenii Matseevich," *Russkiia dostopamiatnosti* (Moscow, 1862), p. 25. "Donosheniia A. Matseevich Sv. pr. Sinodu," *Biblioteka im M. E. Saltykova-Shchedrina, MSS, f.* 355.

117. Rozanov, *Istoriia*, vol. 1, pp. 328–37; Jan. 27, 1766, *PSPR* (1910), no. 286, p. 327; *Istoriko-statisticheskie svedeniia*, pp. 38–45; Dobronravov, "Sviatoezerskaia pustyn'," *Trud*

Vladimirskoi uchennoi arkhivnoi kommissii, no. 9 (1909), pp. 26–29; G. Dobrynin, *Istinnoe povestvovanie ili zhizn' Gavrila Dobrynina . . . 1752–1823 gg.* (St. Petersburg, 1872), pp. 10ff.

118. "Vedomost' kolikoe chislo . . . izlishnykh protiv shtatov monashestvuiushchikh pokazano. . . . " *TsGADA, f.* 18, *d.* 47, *ch.* VI, *l.* 249; Semevskii, *Krest'iane,* vol. 1, pp. 252ff; Alefirenko, *Krest'ianskoe,* p. 165.

119. Semevskii, *Krest'iane,* vol. 1, p. 252.

120. M. Gorchakov, "Retsentsiia na sochinenie A. Zav'ialova, 'Vopros o tserkovnykh imeniiakh pri imperatritse Ekaterine II' " (St. Petersburg, 1904), pp. 54–55.

121. Dec. 20, 1762, *PSPR* (1910), no. 79, p. 75; *PSZ* 18: 12,060 (*im.,* Feb. 26, 1764), pp. 549–69.

122. *PSZ* 16: 12,060 (*im.,* Feb. 26, 1764), pp. 549–60.

123. A report from 1784, indicating initial assignment of 5,084 officers, and with 1,173 more over two years, a total of 6237; Nov. 4, 1766, "Bumagi Teplova," *TsGADA, f.* 18, *d.* 197, *l.* 112; "Nastavlenie ekonomicheskim pravleniiam," Apr. 4, 1771, pp. 1–14.

124. Got'e, *Oblastnoe,* p. 119; Znamenskii, "Otnoshenie," p. 127.

125. July 15, 1762, *TsGADA, f.* 18, *d.* 85, *ch.* II, *ll.* 172–74.

126. Possibly an exaggeration, since the author was making a case for the sale of economic lands to the nobility. "O ekonomiii monastyrskikh votchinakh," *TsGADA, f.* 18, *d.* 197, *ll.* 212–31.

127. Semevskii, *Krest'iane,* vol. 2, pp. 252ff; and Catherine's stipulation that the minimum plot be 3 desiatiny; "Nastavlenie," pp. 1–14.

128. Alefirenko, *Krest'ianskoe,* pp. 165ff.

129. Borisov, "Krizis," p. 148.

130. Semevskii, *Krest'iane,* vol. 2, p. 269; "Bumagi Teplova, *TsGADA, f.* 18, *d.* 197, *l.* 106.

131. Borisov, "Krizis," p. 148.

132. Semevskii, *Krest'iane,* vol. 2, pp. 260–69.

133. The numbers must nevertheless have roughly matched the percent increase, since the proportion of economic peasants in the population shrank, no doubt due to escape into the merchantry as well as a slide into serfdom. See Augustine, "The Economic Attitudes," pp. 24, 51; M. T. Beliavskii, *Krest'ianskii vopros v Rossii nakanune vosstaniia E. I. Pugacheva* (Moscow, 1985), p. 80.

134. J. H. Hexter, *Reappraisals in History* (New York, 1961), p. 114.

135. See Cracraft, *Church Reform.*

4. National Revenues

1. In 1760, debts reached 8 million rubles. The average annual shortfall of revenues per year was about 1.5 million rubles. S. M. Troitskii, *Finansovaia politika russkogo absoliutizma v XVIII veke* (Moscow, 1966), p. 247; see Table I.

2. The Senate reported that there was no additional money for future campaigns and that an exact estimate of present military expenditures was impossible. It was thought that "expenditures greatly exceed all estimates." A commission established in 1756 to gather information had little success, since even the size of the army was unknown. The Senate reported that cavalry regiments had been created but funds could not be allocated for their maintenance, and since most of the troops had not been paid for the second half of 1761, desertion was massive. "O podnesenii E.I. V-u o vsekh gosudarstvennykh dokhodakh i roskhodakh perechivo vedomstvu," *TsGADA, f.* 248, *kn.* 3383, *l.* 444. "Protokol," Apr. 24, 1762, "Protokoly pravitel'stvuiushego Senata," *Senatskii arkhiv,* vol. 12 (St. Petersburg, 1907), pp. 140–41.

3. *Polnoe sobranie zakonov Rossiiskoi imperii,* 1649–1913, 234 vols. (St. Petersburg, 1830–1916) (hereafter *PSZ*), 15: 11,429 (*sen.,* Jan. 31, 1762), pp. 905–906.

4. "Protokol," May 13, 1762, *Senatskii arkhiv,* vol. 12, p. 149.

5. *PSZ* 15: 11,555 (*im.*, May 29, 1762), p. 1027.

6. "Raport No. 4 ob ukaze 23 maia 1762 g.," *TsGADA, f.* 203, *d.* 1, *l.* 24; *PSZ* 15: 11,548 (*im.*, May 23, 1762), p. 1021.

7. Hicks makes the point about disadvantages of reminting. "To organize a smooth flow of metal through the Mint was not at all simple; the money was liable to be held up, awaiting recoinage, just when it was wanted to be spent" (J. Hicks, *A Theory of Economic History* [London, 1969], p. 89). The Senate estimated that the St. Petersburg minting operation could produce 9,000 rubles a day, and at 260 days a year, 2,360,000 rubles a year. For the entire country, the maximum that could be produced within a year was 4,240,848 rubles. "Protokol," May 3, 1762, *Senatskii arkhiv,* vol. 12, p. 142. To hasten the output of silver and copper, the government requisitioned additional workers from guilds, prisons, and artillery units. *PSZ* 15: 11,532 and 11,533 (*im.*, May 11, 1762), p. 1000–1001.

8. *PSZ* 15: 11,550 (*im.*, May 25, 1762), pp. 1021–1022; 11,581 (*im.*, June 26, 1762), p. 1050.

9. "Protokol," May 6, 1762, *Senatskii arkhiv,* vol. 12, p. 145.

10. Hicks, *A Theory,* p. 13.

11. *PSZ* 15: 11,489 (*im.*, Mar. 28, 1762), pp. 959–60.

12. See objections raised by the Senate, "Protokol," April 18, 22 and May 20, 1762, *Senatskii arkhiv,* vol. 12, pp. 150–67.

13. The use of the word mercantilism is arbitrary. It pertains to a kind of fiscal reasoning and to the assumption that the balance of trade was the key consideration in the wealth of a nation. See the introduction. For a closer study of the complexity of tariff reform movements, see a work on customs reform in France. Tariff reform movement was divided into those who supported protective tariffs and physiocrats who called for the abolition of customs barriers and the reduction of burdens upon the peasantry. See J. F. Bosher, *The Single Duty Project: A Study of the Movement for a French Customs Union in the Eighteenth Century* (London, 1964), pp. 63–83.

14. See Troitskii, *Finansovaia politika,* p. 36.

15. S. L. Kaplan, *Bread, Politics and Political Economy in the Reign of Louis XV,* 2 vols. (The Hague, 1976), vol. 1, pp. 97–98.

16. Osterman advocated the expansion of trade and the elimination of nobles' and merchants' concessions; see Troitskii, *Finansovaia politika,* pp. 52–53.

17. *Istoriia russkoi ekonomicheskoi mysli, epokha feodalizma, chast' pervaia IX–XVIII vv.,* ed. A. I. Pashkov (Moscow, 1955), vol. 1, pt. 1, pp. 411–21.

18. Sukin's "Rassuzhdenie o rossiiskoi kommertsii" of 1760; see Troitskii, *Finansovaia politika,* pp. 90–94, 95–100; V. N. Korzhavin, "Predlozhenie," *AKV,* vol. 24 (Moscow, 1880), pp. 118–19, 123–24.

19. For example, in 1751, Elizabeth allowed foreigners, the ecclesiastical hierarchy, and the upper ranks of the nobility not to pay tariffs on products used for domestic needs; Shuvalov, with his monopoly of production and sale of tallow in the White Sea, had the privilege of not paying tariffs on local tallow and grain. B. B. Kafengauz, *Ocherki vnutrennego rynka Rossii pervoi poloviny XVIII veka (po materialam vnutrennykh tamozhen)* (Moscow, 1958), pp. 26–27.

20. See objections by A. I. Osterman, A. P. Volynskii, V. N. Tatishchev, A. V. Olsuf'iev, D. V. Volkov, I. I. Nepliuev and others. A. E. Presniakov, N. D. Chechulin, *Istoriia Senata za dvesti let v tsarstvovaniakh Elizavety Petrovny i Petra III-go* (St. Petersburg, 1911), vol. 2, pp. 116–28, 289; Troitskii, *Finansovaia politika,* pp. 53, 56–95; Kafengauz, *Ocherki,* p. 27–31; on the salt tax and liquor monopoly, "Raport kollegii arkhivariusa Andreia Liakina o raznykh delakh," May 3, 1762, *TsGADA, f.* 248, *kn.* 3384, *Kamer Kollegii, l.* 215.

21. I. de Madariaga, *Russia in the Age of Catherine the Great* (New Haven, Conn., 1981), p. 470.

22. The decree found the hindrances to trade caused by "false views" about the state's needs, see *PSZ* 15: 11,489 (*im.*, Mar. 28, 1762), p. 961.

23. See the introduction. The proposal on commerce and A. V. Olsuf'ev's attack on monopolies and the restricted sale of salt (December 16, 1761) are examples of the influence of physiocrats. The distinguishing features of physiocracy were an understanding of the importance of an economic as well as fiscal policy, a desire for greater control over the economy, and an encouragement of agriculture. See Troitskii, *Finansovaia politika*, p. 39; *Istoriia Senata*, vol. 2, pp. 289–90.

24. de Madariaga, *Russia*, pp. 455–69.

25. S. M. Troitskii, "Obsuzhdenie voprosa o krest'ianskoi torgovle v komissii o kommertsii v seredine 60-kh godov XVIII v.," *Rossiia v XVIII veke* (Moscow, 1982), pp. 204–18; N. M. Druzhinin, "Prosveshchennyi absoliutizm v Rossii," in *Absoliutizm v Rossii (XVII–XVIII vv.)* (Moscow, 1964), pp. 442–43.

26. Haxthausen to Bernstorff, Jan. 4/15, 1762, *RAD TKUA* 78.

27. "Protokoly," April 18, 22, and May 20, 1762, *Senatskii arkhiv*, vol. 12, pp. 150–67.

28. K. Polanyi, *The Great Transformation* (Boston, 1944), p. 135.

29. Troitskii, "Obsuzhdenie," p. 212.

30. *PSZ* 16: 11,630 (*im.* July 31, 1762), p. 31.

31. The president of the College of Commerce, P. A. Tolstoi, had argued in 1715 that "trade should be free, and monopolies should be denied to everyone." N. V. Kozlova, V. P. Tarlovskaia, "Torgovlia," in *Ocherki russkoi kul'tury XVIII veka* (Moscow, 1985), vol. 1, pp. 227–28; P. Miliukov, *Gosudarstvennoe khoziaistvo Rossii v pervoi chetverti XVIII stoletiia i reforma Petra Velikogo* (St. Petersburg, 1905), pp. 384–93.

32. R. I. Kozintseva, "Russkii eksport sel'khosproduktsii v pervoi polovine XVIII v.," *Materialy po istorii sel'skogo khoziaistva i krest'ianstva* (Moscow, 1981), vol. 9, p. 250.

33. 1727–1731, see Troitskii, *Finansovaia politika*, p. 98.

34. Kozintseva, "Russkii eksport," p. 250.

35. Kozintseva, "Russkii eksport," p. 254; B. N. Mironov, "Eksport russkogo khleba vo vtoroi polovine XVIII–nachale XIX v.," *Istoricheskie zapiski* (Moscow, 1973), vol. 93, p. 155; "Protokoly," April 18, 22, and May 20, 1762, *Senatskii arkhiv*, vol. 12, p. 150.

36. "Protokoly," April 18, 22, and May 20, 1762, *Senatskii arkhiv*, vol. 12, pp. 150–51.

37. D. North and R. Thomas, *The Rise of the Western World: A New Economic History* (Cambridge, 1973), p. 100.

38. J. Appleby, *Economic Thought and Ideology in Seventeenth-Century England* (Princeton, N.J., 1978), p. 54. See also J. Walter and K. Wrightson, "Dearth and the Social Order in Early Modern England," *Past and Present*, 71 (1976), pp. 22–42; E. P. Thompson, "The Moral Economy of the English Crowd in the Eighteenth Century," *Past and Present*, 50 (1971), pp. 76–136.

39. M. Chulkov, *Istoricheskoe opisanie rossiiskoi kommertsii pri vsekh portakh i granitsakh ot drevnikh vremen do nyne nastoiashchego i vsekh preimushchestvennykh uzakonenii po inoi gosudaria imperatora Petra Velikago i nyne blagopoluchnoi tsarstvuiushchei godusaryni imperatritsy Ekateriny Velikoi*, 7 vols. (St. Petersburg, 1781–1788), vol. 4, bk. 5, p. 350; I. M. Kulisher, *Ocherki po istorii tamozhennoi politiki* (St. Petersburg, 1903), pp. 1–10; on Petrine policy see Arcadius Kahan's reinterpretation, in his "Observations on Russia's Foreign Trade," *Slavic Review*, vol. 18, no. 2 (1974), pp. 234–35; and B. N. Mironov, "Eksport russkogo khleba," p. 174.

40. *PSZ* 15: 11,489 (*im.*, Mar. 28, 1762), p. 960.

41. Rubinshtein, "Ulozhennaia komissiia," p. 216; *Istoriia russkoi ekonomicheskoi mysli*, vol. 1, pp. 385–431.

42. S. M. Solov'ev, *Istoriia Rossii s drevneishikh vremen*, 15 vols. (Moscow, 1959–65), vol. 12, pp. 493–94; Troitskii, "Dvorianskie proekty," *Voprosy istorii* (1958), p. 71.

43. M. Ia. Volkov, "Otmena vnutrennikh tamozhen v Rossii," *Istoriia SSSR* (1957), no. 2, pp. 85–86.

44. M. Ia. Volkov, "Tamozhennaia reforma 1753–1757 gg.," *Istoricheskie zapiski* (1962), vol. 71, pp. 134–57; A. Kahan, *The Plow, the Hammer and the Knout: An Economic History of Eighteenth-Century Russia* (Chicago, 1985), p. 238.

45. These were essentially institutions designed to subsidize commerce and put more money into circulation, since there were no provisions for deposits and nobles could be counted on to spend their loans immediately. The banks' only operation was to receive interest on loans. The Nobles' Bank loaned amounts between 500 and 10,000 rubles for three years at 6% on the security of landed estates evaluated by numbers of serfs, each at a value of 10 rubles (against the current market price, 30 rubles). The social position of the borrowers made it difficult for the state to seek repayment of any of these loans. Kahan, *The Plow*, pp. 311–18; de Madariaga, *Russia*, pp. 476–77.

46. K. I. Arsenev, "Istoriko-staatisticheskoe obozrenie monetnogo dela v Rossii," *Zapiski russkogo geograficheskogo obshchestva* (St. Petersburg, 1846) vol. 1, p. 75; I. G. Spasskii, A. I. Iukht, "Finansy, Denezhnoe obrashchenie," in *Ocherki russkoi kul'tury XVIII veka*, vol. 2, p. 118; Troitskii, *Finansovaia politika*, pp. 62–75.

47. The poll tax was frequently not collectible; Troitskii, *Finansovaia politika*, p. 199; S. O. Shmidt, "Proekt P. I. Shuvalova 1754 goda 'O raznykh gosudarstvennoi pol'zy sposobakh,' " *Istoricheskii arkhiv* (Moscow, 1962), vol. 6, pp. 100–18.

48. *Istoriia Senata*, vol. 2, pp. 30–31.

49. Among his critics were D. V. Volkov, I. I. Nepliuev, and N. I. and P. I. Panin. See "Rassuzhdenie o kommertsii" by N. E. Murav'ev (1763), "those who made proposals generally particularly benefited from their proposals" (S. M. Troitskii, "Zapiska senatora N. E. Murav'eva o razvitii kommertsii i putei soobchsheniia v Rossii [60-e gody XVIII v.]," [*Istoricheskaia geografiia Rossii* (Moscow, 1975)], pp. 236–37). For example, according to Shakhovskoi, Shuvalov made "personal use" of his "powerful position" to win exemption from customs on transporting his products, and this was the source of his interest in tariffs; Ia. P. Shakhovskoi, *Zapiski kn. Shakhovskogo* (St. Petersburg, 1887), pp. 136–37; Volkov, "Tamozhenniaia reforma," pp. 134–57; V. A. Bil'basov, *Istoriia Ekateriny Vtoroi*, 2 vols. (St. Petersburg, 1891), vol. 2, pp. 124–25. N. D. Chechulin, *Proekt imperatorskogo soveta v pervyi god tsarstvovaniia Ekateriny II* (St. Petersburg, 1894), pp. 4–8.

50. Karnovich, *Zamechatel'noe bogatstvo*, pp. 265–66.

51. All except 7,000 rubles of the commercial bank's initial reserve of 200,000 was given out between January and December, 1754. S. Ia. Borovoi, *Kredit i banki Rossii (seredina XVII v. do 1861 g.)* (Moscow, 1958), p. 84.

52. E. S. Bak, "Ekonomicheskie vozreniia V. N. Tatishcheva," *Istoricheskie zapiski* (1956), vol. 54, p. 378.

53. Kulisher, *Ocherki po istorii tamozhennoi politiki*, pp. 30ff.; Kn N. Lodyzhenskii, *Istoriia russkogo tamozhennogo tarifa* (St. Petersburg, 1886), pp. 85–91.

54. J. H. Hexter, *Reappraisals in History: New Views on History and Society in Early Modern Europe* (New York, 1961), p. 116.

55. Kahan, *The Plow*, p. 265.

56. Troitskii, *Finansovaia politika*, p. 92.

57. Troitskii, "Zapiska senatora," p. 241.

58. [M. Vorontsov?], "Mémoire sur le commerce," *GBL, f.* 79 *Viazemy, d.* 3, *ll.* 10–11.

59. Kulisher, *Tamozhennoi*, p. 190.

60. M. Roberts, *The Age of Liberty, Sweden, 1719–1772* (Cambridge, 1986), p. 28; A. C. Carter, *The Dutch Republic in Europe in the Seven Years War* (Coral Gables, Fla., 1972).

61. Appleby, *Economic Thought*, p. 72.

62. Troitskii, "Zapiski senatora," p. 244.

63. [M. Vorontsov], "Golland," 1763, *LOII, f.* 36, *d.* 1071, *l.* 350.

64. Report by the chief magistrate of February 28, 1762, that the Evreinovs and others would be sent to Holland "to establish a bureau of commerce and increase trade," "Delo ob otpravlenii v inostr. gosudarstva konsulei o razsmotrenii tarifa i o protchem," *LOII, f.* 36, *d.* 551, *ll.* 246–48; "Protokol," Feb. 28, 1762, *TsGADA, f.* 248, *kn.* 3427, *ll.* 381–82.

65. "Golland," *ll.* 350–51.

66. *PSZ* 15: 11,424 (*sen.*, Jan. 30, 1762), pp. 896–97.

67. Keith to Bute, May 7/18, 1762, *BMAddMSS* 35,493; about the construction of ships and rebuilding of the fleet, *PSZ* 15: 11,458 (*resoliutsiia na doklad Admiralteiskoi kollegii,* Mar. 1, 1762), p. 932.

68. *PSZ* 15: 11,515 (*im.,* Apr. 24, 1762), p. 985.

69. *PSZ* 15: 11,489 (*im.,* Mar. 28, 1762), p. 959.

70. See R. Vorontsov's project on colonization of the south (R. L. Vorontsov, "Proekt," undated, *LOII, f.* 36, *d.* 1067, *ll.* 11–14). Colonization was in fact extensive: the portion of serfs in the Lower Volga region (Saratov, Astrakhan, and Caucasus provinces) increased from 2.29% in 1719 to 38.38% in 1762; V. M. Kabuzan, *Izmeneniia v razmeshchenii naseleniia Rossii v XVIII–pervoi polovine XIX v.* (Moscow, 1971), p. 31.

71. J. Jepson Oddy, *European Commerce showing new and secure Channels of Trade with the Continent of Europe: detailing the Produce, Manufactures, and Commerce, of Russia, Prussia, Sweden, Denmark, and Germany as well as the Trade of the Rivers Elbe, Weser, and Elm with a general view of the Trade, Navigation, Produce, and Manufactures, of the U.K. of Great Britain and Ireland and its Unexplored and Improvable Resources and Interior Wealth* (London, 1805), p. 31.

72. Oddy, *European Commerce,* pp. 81, 140.

73. Kulisher, *Istoriia tamozhennoi politiki,* p. 190.

74. R. L. Vorontsov, report no. 4, June 21, 1762, *LOII, f.* 36, *d.* 1067, *l.* 20.

75. Petition, April 19, 1762, *TsGADA, f.* 248, *kn.* 3384, *ll.* 564–80.

76. "Trade has stopped completely . . . in this premier border city which is a reflection of the glory of the country." D. V. Volkov to I. G. Chernyshev, *LOII, f.* 36, *d.* 550, *ll.* 261–62; Vorontsov, report no. 4, June 21, 1762, *LOII f.* 36, *d.* 1067, *l.* 16; petition by Astrakhan merchants, April 19, 1762, *TsGADA, f.* 248 (*pr. Senata*), *kn.* 3384, *ll.* 550–90.

77. *PSZ* 15: 11,489 (*im.,* Mar. 28, 1762), p. 963; Vorontsov, report no. 4, June 21, 1762, *LOII f.* 36, *d.* 1067, *l.* 24.

78. Volkov to Chernyshev, Dec. 19, 1760, *LOII f.* 36, *d.* 550, *l.* 262; "Mnenie R. I. Vorontsova," June 21, 1762, *LOII, f.* 36, *d.* 1067, *l.* 20.

79. Troitskii, *Finansovaia politika,* pp. 176–77.

80. "Protokoly," April 18, 22, and May 20, 1762, *Senatskii arkhiv,* vol. 12, p. 158.

81. A. Korsak, *Istoriko-statisticheskoe obozrenie torgovykh otnoshenii Rossii s Kitaem* (Kazan', 1857), pp. 43, 58.

82. Kahan, *The Plow,* pp. 232–34.

83. Ibid., pp. 155–56; C. Foust, *Muscovite and Mandarin: Russia's Trade with China and Its Setting, 1727–1805* (Chapel Hill, N.C., 1969), pp. viii and 164; A. K. Korsak, *Istoriko-statisticheskoe obozrenie torgovykh snoshenii Rossii s Kitaem* (Kazan, 1857); M. I. Sladkovskii, *Ocherki ekonomicheskikh otnoshenii SSSR s Kitaem* (Moscow, 1957).

84. "Protokoly," April 18, 22, May 20, 1762, *Senatskii arkhiv,* vol. 12, p. 156.

85. Because of bad harvests in Finland, 1762 was a year of particular shortages in Sweden, and the Swedish government requested that prohibition of grain exports from Russia be lifted. Ekeblad to Posse, Apr. 20, 1762, *RAD DM* 334.

86. Kaplan, *Bread,* vol. 1, p. 132.

87. Decrees of 1713, 1716, 1718, 1723, 1727, and 1735 were concerned with the quality of bracking. These decrees were to be read in churches on Sundays and holidays to impress upon the peasants the seriousness of proper bracking of hemp. Kozintseva, "Russkii eksport," p. 246, n. 69.

88. *PSZ* 15: 11,180 (*sen.,* Jan. 3, 1761), p. 596; see also 15: 11,234 (*sen.,* Apr. 2, 1761), pp. 688–90; 11,361 (*sen.,* Nov. 28, 1761), p. 829.

89. *PSZ* 14: 10,323 (*sen.,* Nov. 18, 1754), pp. 256–57; 10,335 (sen., Dec. 11, 1754), pp. 274–75.

90. Kahan, *The Plow,* p. 169.

91. Rubinshtein, "Ulozhennaia komissiia," p. 218; *Istoriia Senata,* p. 303.

92. "Reestr nakhodiashchimsia v kommisskom arkhive ukazam s 28 fev. 1730 g. po 25 dek. 1761 g., okt. 1760 g.," *LOII, f.* 36, *d.* 381, *ll.* 257–58.

93. According to Rubinshtein, as discussed in chapter 2, this later project should not have been liberal because it belonged to the work of Shakhovskoi, or the second group. The passage undermines either the interpretation or the dating.

94. Part III, chapter XIX first edition, in Latkin, *Proekt,* p. 188.

95. *Istoriia Senata,* vol. 2, p. 116.

96. Troitskii, *Finansovaia politika,* p. 91.

97. *Istoriia Senata,* vol. 2, pp. 116–17.

98. "Ekstrakt," Jan. 5, 1761, *LOII, f.* 36, *d.* 550, *op.* 1, *ll.* 89–101.

99. *Istoriia Senata,* vol. 2, p. 32.

100. The document was marked at the top, "this should be implemented before springtime." "Ekstrakt," Jan. 5, 1761, *LOII, f.* 36, *d.* 550, *ll.* 89–101; cf. Troitskii, *Finansovaia politika,* pp. 96, 177, 182–84.

101. *Istoriia Senata,* vol. 2, p. 291.

102. Member of the ruling Senate.

103. Member of the ruling Senate and presumed author of the 1761 "Mémoire sur le commerce," discussed above.

104. President of the Commerce College, ennobled in Peter III's reign.

105. "Dmitrii Vasilievich Volkov," p. 484.

106. "Doklad," Feb. 8, 1761, *LOII, f.* 36, *d.* 551, *l.* 252.

107. The issues that divided Volkov, Olsuf'iev, and the Vorontsovs from Shuvalov included monopolies, indirect taxes, which the liberals wished to reduce, the issuing of paper money, which Shuvalov resisted, and export tariffs; P. Iu. Trubetskoi to D. V. Volkov, 1761, *TsGADA, f.* 203, *d.* 2, *l.* 1; Feb. 8, 1761, *LOII f.* 36, *d.* 551, *l.* 252; *Istoriia russkoi ekonomicheskoi mysli,* vol. 1, p. 391; Troitskii, *Finansovaia politika,* pp. 70, 96.

108. Volkov to Chernyshev, Dec. 19, 1760, *LOII, f.* 36, *d.* 550, *ll.* 259–65.

109. Volkov to Chernyshev, Dec. 19, 1760, *LOII, f.* 36, *d.* 550, *l.* 260.

110. Ibid., *ll.* 259–65.

111. "The Volkov project is interesting in that we find, so clearly articulated for the first time, one of the demands of the physiocrats—the establishment of economic freedom and the abolition of monopolies and other limitations on trade"; see his *Finansovaia politika,* p. 96.

112. "Ekstrakt o rasprostranenii pol'skogo torgu v Rigu," Jan. 5, 1761, *LOII, f.* 36, *d.* 550, *op.* 1, *l.* 90.

113. "Ekstrakt," Jan. 5, 1761, *LOII, f.* 36, *d.* 550, *ll.* 89–100.

114. The expenses as estimated by the Senate were 30,915.865.82 rubles. This figure excluded recruits. By a recalculation by the Military College, including 13,893,640 expended on recruits, the total was 43,309,842.44 rubles. "Zapiski o summakh izraskhodovannykh v 1756–1759 gg. na zagranichnuiu armiiu vo vremia Prusskoi voiny," *LOII, f.* 36, *d.* 1074, *l.* 185.

115. Troitskii, *Finansovaia politika,* p. 177.

116. Kahan, *The Plow,* p. 320.

117. Taxes on inns, stamped paper, peasant passports, and other taxes dating in some cases to the medieval period; de Madariaga, *Russia,* pp. 480–81.

118. Troitskii, *Finansovaia politika,* p. 206.

119. Troitskii, *Finansovaia politika,* pp. 92, 114–15, 209; *PSZ* 14: 10,234 (*im.,* May 13, 1762), p. 87; V. N. Iakovtsevskii, *Kupecheskii kapital v feodal'nokrepostnoe Rossii* (Moscow, 1953), p. 166.

120. Troitskii, *Finansovaia politika,* p. 209.

121. Shuvalov had suggested minting copper coins at 32 rubles per pud, and reminting silver, devaluating from the 77 to the 72 percent standard; this was discussed in the Senate on October 31, December 21, 1760, April 6, 1761, when Iakov Shakhovskoi finally was able to defeat the measure. Olsuf'ev, however, had it brought back to the Senate, where, as the protocol is written, "the present general procurator [A. I. Glebov], finding no substance to Shakhovskoi's objections, confirmed it." "Protokol," Jan. 7, 1762, *Senatskii arkhiv,* vol. 12, pp. 114–15.

122. Haxthausen to Bernstorff, Dec. 29, 1761/Jan. 9, 1762 (draft), *RAD TKUA* 172; Breteuil to Choiseul, Feb. 1/12, 1762, *AMAE CP Russie* 68.

123. "O podnesenii E. Imp. Velichestvu o vsekh gosudarstvennykh dokhodakh i roskhodakh perechen' vedomstvu," June 1762, *TsGADA, f.* 248, *kn.* 3383, *ll.* 430–44.

124. "There was a secret treasury, a product of the mines of Siberia left by Empress Anne, which Elizabeth made a vow not to touch, and there was a million rubles in ducats left to Peter, found in a cabinet belonging to Elizabeth, of which not much would be left if one paid attention to the fact that the Russian army has not been paid in 5½ months." Breteuil to Choiseul, Feb 1/12, 1762, *AMAE CP Russie* 68; "O dokhodakh," *TsGADA, f.* 248, *kn.* 3383, *ll.* 430–44. The silver was minted into 192,000 rubles by June. June 28, 1762, *TsGADA, f.* 19, *d.* 129, *ll.* 2–79.

125. Troitskii, *Finansovaia politika,* pp. 210–11; "Ukaz Senatu," May 23, 1762, *TsGADA, f.* 1256, *d.* 91, *ch.* 5, *l.* 181.

126. Mar. 4, 1762, *TsGADA, f.* 248 Senata, *kn.* 3428, *ll.* 109–10; June 12, 1762, *TsGADA, f.* 1256, *d.* 91, *ch.* 3, Kommissii o soch. novogo ulozheniia, *l.* 234.

127. "Protokol," Jan. 7, 1762, *Senatskii arkhiv,* vol. 12, p. 114.

128. "Bumagi M. I. Vorontsova," Nov. 20, 22, 1761," *LOII, f.* 36, *d.* 103, *ll.* 188–89, "The King of Prussia has minted a great amount of devaluated currency to the great ruin of his neighbors . . . and they have spred everywhere and in the army. So Sweden was obliged to do the same in Stralsund. . . . " Peter claimed his reform was done in imitation of "neighboring states." May 18, 1762, *TsGADA, f.* 9, *d.* 44, *l.* 2.

129. *PSZ* 15: 11,406 (*im.,* Jan. 17, 1762), pp. 886–87.

130. According to his decree of June 26, "although banks are to serve all of society, we have been informed that money remains in the possession of those who obtain it initially," *PSZ* 15: 11,581 (*im.,* June 26, 1762), p. 1050.

131. In the 1750s, Vorontsov had written to Shuvalov asking for a concession for the export of up to 300,000 chetverty of grain, since "he was very short of money, owing to Baron Wolf of England, 25,000 rubles." M. N. Pokrovskii, *Russkaia istoriia s drevneishikh vremen* (Leningrad, 1924), vol. 3, p. 53. *PSZ* 15: 11,581 (*im.,* June 26, 1762), p. 1050; Borovoi, *Kredit,* pp. 50–52.

132. The banknotes, however, had been approved and ordered—500 notes at 100 rubles' worth apiece, 1,000 at 500 rubles apiece, 4,000 at 100 rubles apiece, 6,000 at 50 rubles apiece, and 3000 at 10 rubles apiece, or 41,500 notes at a total value of two million rubles. May 28, 1762, *TsGADA, f.* 203, *d.* 1, *l.* 78; Sudeikin, pp. 55–56; Borovoi, p. 49.

133. V. Sudeikin, *Gosudarstvennyi bank* (St. Petersburg, 1891), pp. 55–6; "Dmitrii Vasilievich Volkov," pp. 484–86.

134. Troitskii, *Finansovaia politika,* pp. 210–11; Brzhesskii, *Gosudarstvennye dolgi v Rossii* (St. Petersburg, 1884), pp. 47–55; Borovoi, p. 53.

135. June 12, 1762, *TsGADA, f.* 1256, *d.* 91, *ch.* 3, Kommissii o soch. novogo ulozheniia, *l.* 234.

136. Without entirely stabilizing the financial situation, Peter nevertheless managed to achieve revenues sufficient to cover his intended campaign. May 18, 1762, *TsGADA, f.* 9, *d.* 44, *l.* 2; *PSZ* 15: 11,581 (*im.,* June 26, 1762), p. 1050.

137. On May 9, A. I. Glebov wrote two bankers for a loan of 3 to 4 million rubles, which they refused on June 4, claiming that they had no money to lend. Undated report, 1762, *TsGADA, f.* 203 Senata, *d.* 1, *ll.* 11–15; "Protokol," June 14, 1762, *Senatskii arkhiv,* vol. 12, p. 174.

138. N. D. Chechulin, *Ocherki po istorii russkikh finansov v tsarstvovanie Ekateriny II* (St. Petersburg, 1906), p. 326.

139. N. L. Rubinshtein, "Ulozhennaia komissiia 1754–1766 gg. i ee proekt novogo ulozheniia," *Istoricheskie zapiski,* vol. 38 (1951), p. 216.

140. Mironov, "Revoliutsiia," pp. 223–25.

141. Kahan, *The Plow,* pp. 254–58.

142. *PSZ* 15: 11,534 (*utv. dok. senata,* May 13, 1762), p. 1001.

143. *PSZ* 15: 11,489 (*im.,* Mar. 28, 1762), pp. 959–64.

144. *PSZ* 15: 11,489 (*im.*, Mar. 28, 1762), pp. 959–66.

145. *PSZ* 15: 11,489 (*im.*, Mar. 28, 1762) pp. 962–63.

146. The idea was advanced under Peter I. In 1760, it was raised again by the Commerce Commission and, again, on February 7, 1762, when Peter recommended a consulate in the Crimea; Catherine attempted to establish two consulates for the Iranian trade on July 31, 1762. In 1763 the Senate was still deliberating, however. "Protokol," Feb. 7, 1762, *TsGADA, f.* 248, *kn.* 3427, *l.* 59; "Dela o konsulakh," Dec. 10, 1762, *LOII f.*, 36, *d.* 551 *ll* 246–48; Feb. 12, 1762, *ll.* 298–99.

147. "Sekretnoe nastavlenie," *LOII, f.* 36, *d.* 1072, *l.* 238.

148. "Protokol," Jan. 17, 1762, *TsGADA, f.* 248, *kn.* 3426 *l.* 277–79.

149. Some of the wealthiest monopolists were the nobles Peter Shuvalov and Aleksandr Glebov, and the merchants Sava Iakovlev of Iaroslavl' and Lavrentii Gorbylev of St. Petersburg. *PSZ* 14: 10,734 (*sen.*, June 6, 1757), pp. 771–72; Iakovtsevskii, *Kupecheskii kapital*, pp. 159–60.

150. *PSZ* 15: 11,489 (*im.*, Mar. 28, 1762), p. 964.

151. See above, the elimination of Shemiakin's tax concession.

152. *PSZ* 15: 11,424 (*sen.*, Jan. 30, 1762), pp. 896–97.

153. Volkov to A. I. [Shuvalov], June 26, 1762, *TsGADA, f.* 20, *d.* 3, *l.* 1.

154. Ibid.

155. "As stated in His Imperial Highness' decree, there are other goods such as rhubarb, cloth and others which were prohibited because of one-sided views and false thinking about the gains to the treasury, as if that were something separate from the good of the state. . . ." "Protokoly," Apr. 18, 22, May 20, 1762, *Senatskii arkhiv,* vol. 12, p. 155.

156. "Ekstrakt," *LOII, f.* 36, *d.* 550, *l.* 92.

157. "Protokoly," Apr. 18, 22, and May 20, 1762, *Senatskii arkhiv,* vol. 12, p. 163.

158. "Protokoly," Apr. 18, 22, and May 20, 1762, *Senatskii arkhiv,* vol. 12, pp. 150–67.

159. "Protokoly," April 18, 22, May 20, 1762, *Senatskii arkhiv,* vol. 12, p. 156; *Istoriia Senata,* vol. 2, pp. 290–92; Foust, *Muscovite,* p. 284.

160. Troitskii, *Finansovaia politika,* p. 155; D. Baburin, *Ocherki po istorii Manufaktur kollegii* (Moscow, 1939), pp. 140–45; *Sbornik svedenii po istorii i statistiki vneshnei torgovli Rossii,* ed. V. I. Pokrovskii, 2 vols. (St. Petersburg, 1902), vol. 1, p. 128.

161. "Protokoly," Apr. 18, 22, and May 20, 1762, *Senatskii arkhiv,* vol. 12, p. 150.

162. "Protokoly," Apr. 18, 22, and May 20, 1772, *Senatskii arkhiv,* vol. 12, p. 150.

163. "Protokoly," Apr. 18, May 20, 1762, *Senatskii arkhiv,* vol. 12, p. 152.

164. N. L. Rubinshtein, "Ulozhennaia komissiia 1754–1766 gg. i ee proekt novogo ulozheniia 'O sostoianii poddannykh voobshche' (K istorii sotsial'noi polotiki 50-kh—nachala 60-kh godov XVIII v.)," *Istoricheskie zapiski* (Moscow, 1951), vol. 38, pp. 217–51; Troitskii, *Finansovaia politika,* pp. 61–101; his "Dvorianskie proekty sozdaniia 'Tret'ego china,' " *Rossiia v XVIII veke* (Moscow, 1982), p. 206.

165. "Mnenie R. L. Vorontsova," Mar. 1762, *LOII, f.* 36, *d.* 1068, *ll.* 128–29.

166. Note, May 18, 1762, *LOII, f.* 36, *d.* 562, *ll.* 114–17.

167. *PSZ* 15: 11,557 (*im.*, June 1, 1762), pp. 1028–29.

168. *PSZ* 15: 11,558 (*im.*, June 1, 1762), p. 1029.

169. Troitskii, *Finansovaia politika,* pp. 210–11.

170. *PSZ* 16: 11,630 (*im.*, July 31, 1762), pp. 31–32.

171. *PSZ* 17: 12,735 (*sen.*, Sept. 1, 1765), p. 951.

172. "The Catherinian tariffs that gave rise to the cliché about a Catherinian system require close scrutiny. They represented a mixture of a continuity of protection for domestic industry and attempts to get rid of duty payments when they became nominal, rather than effective or real. There is no evidence whatsoever that would permit one to point to instances where domestic industrial interests were sacrificed for the principles of physiocratic or free-market policies." Kahan, *The Plow,* p. 238.

173. P. G. Liubomirov, *Ocherki po istorii russkoi promyshlennosti* (Moscow, 1947), p. 715.

174. S. A. Pokrovskii, *Vneshniaia torgovlia i vneshniaia torgovaia politika Rossii* (Moscow, 1947), p. 153; Kulisher, *Istoriia tamozhennoi politiki*, pp. 212ff.

175. 1762–1765 (unhindered export without tariff), 1766–1774 (prohibited), 1775–76 (unhindered), 1777 (prohibited). "Doklad kommissii o kommertsi," *TsGADA, f.* 19, *d.* 286, *ch.* 3, *l.* 306.

176. Kaplan, *Bread*, vol. 1, p. 255.

177. B. N. Mironov, *Khlebnye tseny v Rossii za dva stoletiia (XVIII–XIX vv.)* (Moscow, 1985), p. 114.

178. I. D. Koval'chenko, "Dynamika urovnia zemledel'cheskogo proizvodstva Rossii v pervoi polovine XIX v.," *Istoriia SSSR* (1959), no. 1, pp. 53–87.

179. N. L. Rubinshtein, *Sel'skoe khoziaistvo Rossii vo vtoroi polovine XVIII v.* (Moscow, 1957), pp. 413–15.

180. B. N. Mironov, "Sel'skoe khoziaistvo Rossii v 60-kh godakh XVIII v.," *Materialy po istorii sel'skogo-khoziaistva i krest'ianstva Rossii* (Moscow, 1980), vol. 9, p. 229.

181. R. I. Kozintseva, *Vneshnetorgovyi oborot arkhangelogorodskoi iarmarki i ee rol' v razvitii vserossiiskogo rynka,"* in *Issledovaniia po istorii feodal'no-krepostnicheskoi Rossii*, ed. S. N. Valk, K. N. Serbina, and A. L. Fraiman (Moscow-Leningrad, 1964), pp. 124–45.

182. Mironov, *Khlebnye tseny*, p. 114.

183. Rubinshtein's estimate, a sixfold increase by the end of the century, failed to calculate for inflation; see N. L. Rubinshtein, "Vneshniaia torgovlia i russkoe kupechestvo," *Istoricheskie Zapiski*, vol. 54 (1955), p. 346; Mironov, *Khlebnye tseny*, pp. 100–103.

184. Mironov, "Sel'skoe khoziaistvo," p. 232.

185. V. M. Kabuzan, *Izmeneniia v razmeshchenii naseleniia Rossii v XVIII-pervoi polovine XIX v.* (Moscow, 1971), pp. 16, 31.

186. Kahan, *The Plow*, pp. 234–35.

187. Kahan, *The Plow*, pp. 163ff.

188. Harvest failure in the 1720s led the government to allow duty-free import of grain to St. Petersburg in 1723 and 1725 and to reduce import duties in 1724. Kozintseva, "Russkii eksport," p. 249.

189. E. Heckscher, *Mercantilism* (London, 1934), vol. 2, p. 12.

190. Troitskii, *Rossiia*, pp. 204–16.

191. Miliukov, *Gosudarstvennoe khoziaistvo*, pp. 271–72.

192. Mironov, "Sel'skoe khoziaistvo," p. 233.

193. *Istoriia Senata*, vol. 2, p. 289; *PSZ* 15: 11,446 (*im.*, Feb. 21, 1762), pp. 918–19; 11,521 (*sen.*, Apr. 26, 1762), pp. 992–93; 11,504 (*sen.*, Apr. 15, 1762), pp. 976–77; Jan. 17, Feb. 7, 1762, *TsGADA, f.* 2, *kn.* 3427, *ll.* 73 and 278–79.

194. Troitskii, *Rossiia*, pp. 207–11.

195. *PSZ* 15: 11,423 (*sen.*, Jan. 23, 1762), p. 895; 11,426 (*sen.*, Jan. 31, 1762), p. 901.

196. "Pravo kupechestva," *Ch.* III, *gl.* XXIII, p. 2, 7, 8, and others, in Latkin, *Proekt*, pp. 188ff.

197. Baburin, pp. 141–55.

198. Ibid., pp. 145–47.

199. Feb. 28, 1762, and enclosures, *TsGADA, f.* 248, *kn.* 3396, *ll.* 52ff; Sept. 28, 1761, *TsGADA, f.* 1257, *op.* 3, *d.* 64, *l.* 70.

200. Sept. 28, 1761, *TsGADA, f.* 1257, *op.* 3, *d.* 64, *l.* 70.

201. Feb. 1, 1762, *TsGADA, f.* 258 Senata, *kn.* 3427, *ll.* 22–23.

202. Feb. 28, 1762, *TsGADA, f.* 248 Senata, *kn.* 3396 (Manufaktur kollegii), *ll.* 52–53; Feb. 28, 1762, *TsGADA, f.* 248, *kn.* 3427, *ll.* 406–407; *PSZ* 15: 11,490 (*sen.*, Mar. 29, 1762), p. 966.

203. E. I. Zaozerskaia, *Rabochaia sila i klassovaia bor'ba na tekstil'nykh manufakturakh v 20–60 gg. XVIII v.* (Moscow, 1960), pp. 303–308.

204. I. D. Nepomiluev, "Kupechestvo v tsarstvovanie Ekateriny II," aftoreferat (Kandidatskaia dissertatsiia, Moscow State University, 1968), pp. 2–3.

205. "This legislation prohibited the further acquisition of serf villages by factories, whether noble or non-noble owned," R. E. Zelnik, "Th.e Peasant and the Factory," *The Peasant in Nineteenth-Century Russia*, ed. W. Vucinich (Stanford, 1968), p. 162; V. I. Semevskii, *Krest'iane v tsarstvovanie Imperatritsy Ekateriny II*, 2 vols. (St. Petersburg, 1881), vol. 1, pp. 394–95.

206. *PSZ* 16: 11,667 (Aug. 8, 1762).

207. Zaozerskaia, *Rabochaia*, pp. 301ff.

208. Jan. 20, 1762, *TsGADA, f.* 248, *kn.* 3426, *l.* 364; Troitskii, *Finansovaia politika*, p. 251; Jan. 22, 1762, *Moskovskie vedomosti*.

209. Liubomirov, *Ocherki*, pp. 251–52; Troitskii, *Finansovaia politika*, p. 251.

210. *PSZ* 15: 11,520 (*sen.*, Apr. 26, 1762), p. 992.

211. Liubomirov, *Ocherki*, pp. 254–62; P. A. Khromov, *Ocherki ekonomiki feodalizma v Rossii* (Moscow, 1957), pp. 179–82; E. I. Zaozerskaia, *Rabochaia*, pp. 310–31.

212. G. S. Islev, *Rol' tekstil'noi promyshlennosti v genezise i razvitii kapitalizma v Rossii 1760–1860* (Leningrad, 1970), pp. 119, 146.

213. N. I. Pavlenko, *Istoriia metallurgii v Rossii XVIII veka* (Moscow. 1962), p. 463; Mavrodin, *Krest'ianskaia voina*, vol. 1, p. 299.

214. Pavlenko, *Istoriia*, p. 463.

215. Mironov, "Khlebnye tseny v Rossii v XVIII v.," pp. 9–11; his *Khlebnye tseny*, pp. 170–71.

216. T. M. Kitanina, *Khlebnaia torgovlia Rossii v 1875–1914 gg. (Ocherki pravitel'stvennoi politiki)* (Leningrad, 1978).

5. Foreign Policy

1. M. L. Vorontsov, "Rassuzhdenie o nyneshnem sostoianii voiuiushchikh derzhav i o sposobakh dlia dostizheniia skol'ko vozmozhno slavnogo, poleznogo i prochego mira 1760 g.," *AKV* (1872), vol. 4, pp. 174–78.

2. Peter III, "Ukaz Kollegii Inostrannykh Del," *TsGADA, f.* 9, *op.*5, *d.* 43, *ll.* 37–38.

3. G. A. Nekrasov, *Russko-shvedskie otnosheniia i politika velikikh derzhav v 1721–1726 gg.* (Moscow, 1964), pp. 171–92.

4. H. Bagger, *Ruslands alliancepolitik efter freden i Nystad. En studie i det slesvigske restitutionssporgsmal indtil 1732* (Copenhagen, 1974).

5. P. Vedel, *Correspondance Ministérielle du Comte J. H. E. Bernstorff 1751–1770* (Copenhagen, 1882), vol. 1, p. ii.

6. It was also agreed that although the Russian throne would not directly pass to a descendent of the dynastic union, a child produced by this marriage might, if invited by a Russian ruler, inherit the Russian throne. P. Schebal'skii, *Politicheskaia Sistema Petra III* (St. Petersburg, 1870), pp. 1–17.

7. "Deductiones und andere Acten die forderung des Staatsarchiv," *Staatsarchiv* in Schleswig, *Best.* 30, *Schrank* I, 25; Shchebal'skii, *Politicheskaia*, pp. 25–26.

8. Caspar von Saldern, Peter's advisor for Holstein affairs, wrote to the Danish merchant Otte, who was in communication with the Danish government, that while Peter was not in principle opposed to an exchange, he had to be sure the counties could be defended, and with its port Kiel was easier to safeguard. If negotiations were to proceed, Saldern explained, there had to be an acknowledgment that both sides should be militarily equal. "The strongest reason is always the best," see Saldern to Otte, Jan. 18, 1763, Korrespondans-Akter vedr. Mageskifter, *RAD Ottes Arkiv*, 35.

9. "Oldenburg and Delmenhorst, which you propose in exchange," he responded to Haxthausen, "are not equal in worth to my Holstein. Do you not think that there is a kind of disgrace in trading a grand duchy for tiny counties?" On May 29, 1761, he told a Danish agent that he would be open to the idea only after the counties were elevated in status. Gregors v. Haxthausen (special envoy to St. Petersburg) to Johan Hartvig Ernst Bernstorff (Danish Foreign Minister), May 29/June 9 and June 1/12, 1761, *RAD TKUA Special Del* 172,

"Note au ministère Impériale de Russie de la part de M. le Grand Duc pour servir de réponse au projet de traité Dannemark," July 27/Aug. 7, 1761, *AMAE CP Russie* 67.

10. Bernstorff to Haxthausen, Sept. 7, 1761, *RAD TKUA Gregors Christian v. Haxthausens gesandtskabs Arkiv* 181, no. 41; Louis Auguste, baron de Breteuil (French ambassador at St. Petersburg) to Etienne François, duc de Choiseul (Secretary of State for Foreign Affairs, in mid-1761 Minister of War and Marine in France), June 17, 1761, *AMAE CP Russie* 67.

11. Bernstorff's instructions to Haxthausen were to "persuade, frappe et inquiète mais ne blesse pas," Vedel, *Correspondance*, vol. 1, pp. 339, 376.

12. Haxthausen to Bernstorff, July 13/24, 1761, *RAD TKUA* 172.

13. Ivan Ivanovich Shuvalov and Mikhail Vorontsov also supported the Grand Duke's claims. Rescript to Baron Korf, July 25/Aug. 5, 1761, *Arkhiv Vneshnei Politiki Rossii* (hereafter *AVPR*), *f*. 53, *op*. 1, *d*. 1, in *RAD;* Haxthausen to Bernstorff, May 26/June 5, 1761, *RAD TKUA* 172.

14. Bernstorff to Haxthausen, Sept. 7, 1761, *RAD TKUA* 181, no. 41.

15. "The Seven Years' War was the way by which Russia made its entry into the great politics of Europe," Vedel, *Correspondance*, vol. 1, p. xii.

16. "The Empress will not force him to negotiate," Haxthausen to Bernstorff, July 8, 1760, "Snosheniia Rossii s Daniei," *AVPR, f*. 36, *d*. 97, *ll*. 80–81. [Response to Haxthausen's declaration], July 25/Aug. 5, 1761, *AVPR, f*. 53, *op*. 1, no. 17 (in *RAD*).

17. On foreign policy in the early years of Catherine's rule, see D. M. Griffiths, "The Rise and Fall of the Northern System: Court Politics and Foreign Policy in the First Half of Catherine II's Reign," *Canadian-American Slavic Studies*, vol. 4, no. 3 (1970), pp. 547–69; H. Scott, "Frederick II, the Ottoman Empire and the Origins of the Russo-Prussian Alliance of April 1764," *European Studies Review*, vol. 7, no. 2 (1977), pp. 153–75; M. Roberts, "Great Britain, Denmark, and Russia, 1763–1770," in *Studies in Diplomatic History: Essays in Memory of D. B. Horn*, eds. R. Hatton, M. S. Anderson (London, 1970), pp. 256–68.

18. Choiseul was Minister of Foreign Affairs, 1758–1761, Minister of War and Marine, 1761–1766, and Minister of War and Foreign Affairs, 1766–1770. See "Mémoire justicatif présenté au Roi par Choiseul en 1765," *Mémoires du Duc de Choiseul, 1719–1785* (Paris, 1904), appendix, p. 383.

19. "The King of Prussia is in a dangerous position and so strong on his own territory that it will cause a new campaign," Haxthausen to Bernstorff, koncept, Sept. 14/25, 1761, *RAD TKUA* 172, no. 39. J. S. Corbett, *England in the Seven Years' War: A Study in Combined Strategy* (London, 1907), vol. 2, pp. 145ff.; W. Dorn, "Frederick the Great and Lord Bute," *Journal of Modern History*, no. 4. (Chicago, 1929), pp. 529–60; P. C. Yorke, *Earl of Hardwicke* (Cambridge, 1910), vol. 3, pp. 262–67; cf. *Semiletniaia voina, Razgrom russkimi voiskami Prussii 1756–1762 gg. Dokumenty* ed. N. Korobkov (Moscow, 1943), p. 14.

20. Breteuil to Choiseul, Jan. 26/Feb. 6, 1761, *AMAE CP Russie* 66.

21. "He had then the whole Austrian Army against him, and was ten German miles distant from his magazines, with bread only for the space of 24 hours for his army, now he is in the midst of his magazines and fortresses, and has to do with a combined army of Austrians and Russians, where it will be difficult to maintain Harmony for any considerable time." Andrew Mitchell (British ambassador to Prussia) to Lord Bute (Secretary of State), Sept. 1, 1761, *PRO SP* 90/78.

22. "Secret," Mitchell to Bute, Nov. 25, 1761, *BMAddMSS* 6809, *folios* 8–9.

23. Mitchell to Bute, Nov. 25, 1761, *BMAddMSS* 6809, *folio* 10.

24. Corbett, *England*, vol. 2, p. 142; Cressaner to Bute, Feb. 16, 1762, *PRO SP* 81/140.

25. Vorontsov, "Rassuzhdenie," pp. 174–78.

26. S. M. Solov'ev, *Istoriia Rossii s drevneishikh vremen*, 15 vols. (Moscow, 1959–65), vol. 12, p. 595.

27. "Without being able to produce very considerable sums" the levies and taxes used to support the war "caused a great murmur among the people. . . . " Haxthausen to

Bernstorff, Sept. 21/Oct. 2, 1761 (draft), *RAD TKUA* 172; capitation on state peasants and additional taxes on salt and spirits amounting to 1,000,000 rubles; Dec. 14, 1761, and Feb. 7, 1762. *Senatskii arkhiv,* vol. 12 (1907), pp. 108–14, 124–25; Breteuil to Choiseul, June 17/28 and July 22/Aug. 2, 1761, *AMAE CP Russie* 67.

28. Haxthausen to Bernstorff, July 6/17, 1761, koncept, *RAD TKUA* 172.

29. "Protokol," Feb. 7, 1762, *Senatskii arkhiv,* vol. 12, p. 126.

30. Haxthausen to Bernstorff, Sept. 21/Oct. 2, 1761, koncept, *RAD TKUA* 172.

31. Haxthausen to Bernstorff, Sept. 14/25, 1761, koncept, *RAD TKUA* 172.

32. Robert Keith (British ambassador to Russia) to Bute, Oct. 5/16, 1761, *PRO SP* 91/68, *folio* 358.

33. Keith to Bute, Oct. 5/16, 1761, *PRO SP* 91/68, *folio* 358.

34. Vorontsov, "Rassuzhdenie," pp. 174–78.

35. "Doklady kantslera grafa M. L. Vorontsova," Jan. 23, 1762, *AKV,* vol. 7, p. 548.

36. Joseph Yorke (British ambassador to Holland) to Bute, Feb. 5, 1762, *PRO SP* 84/495.

37. L. Jay Oliva, *Misalliance: A Study of French Policy in Russia During the Seven Years' War* (New York, 1964).

38. See Shchebal'skii, *Politicheskaia,* pp. 1–6.

39. John Goodricke (British ambassador to Sweden, resident in Copenhagen) to Bute, Jan. 30, 1762, *PRO SP* 75/113, *folios* 8–9, 43–48.

40. "All nations seem to be in the same position," wrote Choiseul, "having made a guarantee to Denmark and being now not able to defend her—France, Austria and England. We are not at all in a condition to help." Choiseul to Breteuil, Mar. 7, 1762, *AMAE CP Russie* 68; Swiss bankers of Berne refused Denmark a loan, even when guaranteed by the French government; see Mathias to Bute, Apr. 13, 1762, *PRO SP* 82/79; Andreas Peter Bernstorff, 1762, *RAD J. H. E. Bernstorffs arkiv.*

41. Choiseul to Louis de Cardavac, Marquis d'Havrincour (French ambassador to Sweden), Jan. 24, 29, 1762, *AMAE CP Suède,* 241, *folios* 232–36.

42. "Neskol'ko neizvestnykh ukazov i pisem imp. Petra III," *Zaria* (Feb. 1871), appendix, pp. 4–5.

43. *Semiletniaia voina,* pp. 809–11.

44. M. L. Vorontsov, "Doklady kantslera grafa M. L. Vorontsova imp. Petru III-mu; doklad 25 dek. 1761 g.," *AKV,* vol. 7, pp. 525–26; Mitchell to Bute, Mar. 13, 1762. *PRO SP* 90/79.

45. "Deklaratsiia 12 fev. 1762 g.," *AVPR f.* 53/ I, *d.* 2 (in *RAD*).

46. Haxthausen to Bernstorff, Feb. 1/12, 1762, *RAD TKUA* 78.

47. *Semiletniaia voina,* pp. 809–10.

48. M. L. Vorontsov, "Doklady," Dec. 25, 27, 1761, Jan. 23, 1762 gg.," *AKV,* vol. 7 (1874), pp. 525–27, 533–47; Breteuil to Choiseul, Feb. 1/12, 1762, *AMAE CP Russie* 68.

49. Vorontsov held no consultations until early February; rumors circulated about his weak health; Baron Posse (ambassador to Russia) to Claes Ekeblad (Chancery President), Feb. 5/16, 1762, *RAS DM* 307; Breteuil to Choiseul, Jan. 14/25, 1762, *AMAE CP Russie* 66; Haxthausen to Bernstorff, Feb. 16/27, 1762, *RAD TKUA 78; Yorke to Bute, Feb. 5, 1762, PRO SP* 84/496; Mitchell to Bute, Jan. 21, 1761, *PRO SP* 90/79; Mercy d'Argenteau to Kaunitz, Jan. 7/18, 11/22, 1762, "Doneseniia grafa Mersi d'Arzhanto Imperatritse Marii Terezii i gos. kantsleru gr. Kaunitzu-Ritbergu, 5-go ianvaria nov. st. 1762 po 24 iiunia nov. st. 1762 g.," *Sbornik imperatorskogo russkogo istoricheskogo obshchestva* (hereafter *SIRIO*), vol. 18 (1876), pp. 46, 67.

50. *PSZ* 15: 11,418 (*im.,* Jan. 28, 1762), pp. 893–94.

51. Peter III to Volkov, Jan. 2, 1762, *TsGADA, f.* 9, no. 43, *l.* 1.

52. Haxthausen to Bernstorff, Feb. 16/27, 1762, *RAD TKUA* 78.

53. Mercy to Kaunitz, Jan. 7/18, 1762, *SIRIO,* vol. 18 (1876), p. 41.

54. Mercy to Kaunitz, Jan. 7/18, 1762, *SIRIO,* vol. 18 (1876), p. 44.

55. Breteuil to Choiseul, Jan. 18/29, 1762, *AMAE CP Russie* 68.

56. "The treaty of commerce between France and Russia is well in progress," Haxthausen to Bernstorff, Mar. 29/Apr. 9, 1762, *RAD TKUA* 79.

57. Breteuil to Choiseul, Jan. 7/18, 1762, *AMAE CP* 68.

58. Choiseul to Breteuil, Jan. 24/Feb. 7, 1762, *AMAE CP Russie* 68.

59. Orders were given to the Danish fleet on the Baltic to stop all neutral ships with provisions to prevent Russians from storing supplies too near Denmark. Goodricke to Bute, July 24, 1762, *PRO SP* 75/113, *folios* 217–18; Bernstorff to Osten [in Warsaw], June 24, 1762, *RAD TKUA* 86; reports from Hamburg, Mar. 12, Apr. 27, and June 18, 1762, *PRO SP* 82/79.

60. Goodricke to Bute, July 24, 1762, *PRO SP* 75/113, *folios* 216–17.

61. Frederick II to Prince George, Mar. 8, 1762, *Schierensee* 705.

62. Peter III, "Ukaz Kollegii Inostrannykh Del," Apr. 6, 1762, *TsGADA, f.* 9, *op.* 5, *d.* 43, *l.* 37).

63. Breteuil to Choiseul, May 3/14, 1762, *AMAE CP Russie* 69.

64. Mar. 6, 1762, *TsGADA, f.* 9, *op.* 5, *d.* 43, *l.* 20.

65. Saldern to Otte, Mar. 8/19, 1762, *RAD TKUA F. V. Ottes arkiv,* Nr. 35; Haxthausen to Bernstorff, May 26/June 6, 1762, *RAD TKUA* 80.

66. Compare Bain, who viewed Peter's foreign policy as inconsistent and irrational, governed by "flights of imagination," R. N. Bain, *Peter III, Emperor of Russia, The Story of a Crisis and a Crime* (Westminster, England, 1902), p. 25.

67. The Austrian interests were still represented by "a strong party" at St. Petersburg, Yorke to Bute, Apr. 6, 1762, *PRO SP* 84/496.

68. S. V. Bakhrushin and S. Skazkin, "Diplomacy," trans. in *Catherine the Great: A Profile,* ed. M. Raeff (New York, 1972), p. 184.

69. "Doklad Petru II-mu M. L. Vorontsova, 23 ian. 1762 g.," *AKV* (1875), vol. 7, pp. 546–47.

70. See Michael Metcalf on the complex process of Sweden's conclusion of a separate peace with Prussia, his *Russia, England and Swedish Party Politics 1762–1766. The Interplay between Great Power Diplomacy and Domestic Politics during Sweden's Age of Liberty* (Stockholm and Totowa, N.J., 1977); M. Roberts, *The Age of Liberty, Sweden, 1719–1772)* (Cambridge, 1986), pp. 42–45; his *British Diplomacy and Swedish Politics, 1758–1773)* (Minnesota/London, 1980/1981). See also T. Säve, *Sveriges deltagande i sjuåriga kriget åren 1757–1762* (Stockholm, 1915), pp. 23ff.

71. Austria first developed a "pacific disposition" in early 1762. Joseph Yorke to Bute, Apr. 30, 1762, *BMAddMSS* 32,937, *folio* 435.

72. Solov'ev, *Istoriia,* vol. 13, p. 42.

73. Breteuil to Choiseul, May 3/24, 1762, *AMAE CP Russie* 69.

74. The armistice was "un peu moins facheuse." Kaunitz was of the same opinion. Breteuil to Choiseul, Jan. 24, Feb. 4, and Choiseul to Breteuil, Jan. 25, 1762, *AMAE CP Russie* 68.

75. *PSZ* 15: 11,516 (*traktat,* Apr. 24, 1762), pp. 987–91.

76. Yorke to Bute, Feb. 5, 1762, *PRO SP* 85/495.

77. Keith, who was close to Peter in the first few months of his reign, reported his "anger" over the Golitzyn dispatch, "arguments" at the table with Prince George about the advisability of a campaign against Denmark. "It is not proper to cross him," Keith wrote. Baron Posse wrote that Peter was "easily angered, . . . and does not accept discussion of anything once his decision is made known." Keith to Bute, Feb. 12/23, 1762, *BMAddMSS* 35,493; Mar. 8/19, 1762, *PRO SP* 91/69; Posse to Ekeblad, Jan. 4/15, 1762, *RAS DM* 306.

78. Keith to Bute, Feb. 12/23, 1762, *BMAddMSS* 35,493.

79. Solov'ev, *Istoriia,* vol. 13, pp. 31–33.

80. Yorke to Bute, Feb. 9, 1762, *PRO SP* 84/495.

81. Volkov claimed to have exerted a moderating influence, and that it was the arrival of Goltz and Brockdorf that produced unrestrained behavior (Solov'ev, *Istoriia,* vol. 13, p. 30). Prince George claimed to have prevented him from placing ten regiments in Pomerania,

arguing that Peter would "provoke a storm in Europe" and anger Frederick. Haxthausen to Bernstorff, Mar. 5/16, 1762, *RAD TKUA* 78.

82. Peter III, "Ukaz Kollegii Inostrannykh Del," Apr. 6, 1762, *TsGADA, f.* 9, *op.* 5, *l.* 37.

83. Solov'ev, *Istoriia,* vol. 13, p. 62.

84. On the success of the Russian military in the eighteenth century, see W. Pintner, "The Burden of Defense in Imperial Russia, 1725–1914," *Russian Review,* vol. 43 (1984), pp. 231–59.

85. Frederick to Goltz, Feb. 7, 1762, *Politische Correspondenz Friedrich's des Grossen,* vol. 21 (Berlin, 1894), pp. 234–35.

86. Keith to Bute, Jan. 19/30, 1762, *PRO SP* 91/69, *folio* 69.

87. "Then Vienna offered financial support for him against Denmark which Peter III disdainfully refused." Keith to Bute, Feb. 12/23, 1762, *BMAddMSS* 35,493; Feb. 28/Mar. 10, 1762, *PRO SP* 91/69.

88. When Mercy and Breteuil requested that they be able to present themselves to Prince George, the latter stalled, sending them back to Peter first. Haxthausen to Bernstorff, Feb. 16/27, 1762, *RAD TKUA* 78.

89. Posse to Ekeblad, Mar. 9/20, 1762, *RAS DM* 307.

90. In late spring, after Maria Theresa had relented, consenting to have her ambassador present his papers first to Prince George Ludwig, Choiseul still resisted. Yorke to Newcastle, May 11, 1762, *BMAddMSS* 32,938, folio 158.

91. Haxthausen to Bernstorff, Mar. 29/Apr. 9, 1762, *RAD TKUA* 79.

92. Yorke to Newcastle, May 11, 1762, *BMAddMSS* 32,938.

93. Breteuil to Choiseul, Feb. 1/12, Apr. 10/21, 1762, *AMAE CP Russie* 68 and 69; Mercy to Kaunitz, Apr. 9/20, 1762, *SIRIO,* vol. 18, p. 273.

94. Haxthausen to Bernstorff, Mar. 29/Apr. 9, 1762, *RAD TKUA* 79.

95. Mercy to Kaunitz, June 18/29, 1762, *SIRIO,* vol. 18 (1876), p. 406; Breteuil was appointed as ambassador after the coup, see Havrincour to Ekeblad, July 4, 1762, *RAS DG* 32.

96. Haxthausen to Bernstorff, May 17/28, 1762, *RAD TKUA* 79.

97. A. Broglie, *Le secret du roi, 1752–1774: Louis XV et ses agents diplomatiques* (Paris, 1957), vol. 1, pp. 11–12.

98. Oliva, *Misalliance,* p. 197.

99. Choiseul, *Mémoires,* p. 391.

100. E. Amburger, *Russland and Schweden 1762–1772* (Berlin, 1943), pp. 30–60.

101. Roberts, *Age of Liberty,* pp. 42–45.

102. Keith to Bute, Jan. 19/30, 1762, *PRO SP* 91/69.

103. The insufficiency of Hat support for the war was perceived and reported to Choiseul. Havrincour wrote, "The small number of true patriots here will make last efforts to oppose a pernicious decision [i.e., for peace—CSL], but one greatly fears that the plurality which decides all will make these efforts of zeal unuseful." Havrincour to Choiseul, Nov. 27, 1761, *AMAE CP Suède* 241, *folio* 119.

104. Peter told Keith that "he would send orders to Osterman to declare publicly for the anti-Gaul party," Keith to Bute, Jan. 19/30, 1762, *PRO SP* 91/69. Haxthausen to Bernstorff, Feb. 19/Mar. 2, 1762, *RAD TKUA* 78; M. Vorontsov, "Voprosy Ekateriny Vtoroi i otvety," *AKV,* vol. 25, pp. 334–39; Keith to Bute, Jan. 19/30, 1762, *BMAddMSS* 35,493; Haxthausen to Bernstorff, Feb. 19/Mar. 2, 1762. *RAD TKUA* 78. See *The Riksdag: A History of the Swedish Parliament,* ed. M. Metcalf (New York, 1987).

105. Haxthausen to Bernstorff, Feb. 19/Mar. 2, 1762, *RAD TKUA* 78; Posse to Ekeblad, Jan. 13/24, 1762, *RAS DM* 307.

106. Posse to Ekeblad, Feb. 15/ 20, May 14/25, 1762 *RAS DM* 307; Haxthausen to Bernstorff, Feb. 19/Mar. 2, 1762, *RAD TKUA* 78.

107. Düben to Peter III, 1762, *RAS Stavsundarkivet Duben,* 0029, 1760–1762.

108. Colonel Ramsay to Christopher Springer [Cap, a fugitive from Sweden resident in London], Mar. 26, 1762, *BMAddMSS* 32,396.

109. Goodricke to Bute, May 4, 1762, *PRO SP* 75/113.

110. Bute's reputation, like Peter's, was due in part to his volte face in foreign policy, mainly the revocation of the Prussian subsidy agreement; see J. S. Corbett, *England*, vol. 2, pp. 145ff. and 287; Dorn, "Frederick," pp. 525–60; see Karl Schweizer, "Lord Bute, Newcastle, Prussia, and the Hague Overtures: A Re-Examination," *Albion: Journal of the Conference on British Studies* (spring 1977), pp. 72–97.

111. Corbett, *England*, vol. 2, p. 142.

112. Schweizer, "Lord Bute."

113. "Money to the New Czarina seems to be very well placed, for she is said to be the Ruling Genius. The Czar is certainly very weak." Hardwicke to Newcastle, *BMAddMSS* 32,934, *folios* 48–49.

114. Wroughton's view of his contacts with "a Lady, who is pleased to honor me with Her protection and confidence in a very particular manner," was "of rendering the thing and my country services by this means, and a time may come when they may be more important." Thomas Wroughton (special envoy to Russia) to Holdernesse, Mar. 6, 1761, *PRO SP* 91/68, *folios* 174–75.

115. Broglie's words, see Oliva, *Misalliance*, p. 109.

116. Keith wrote about Wroughton's friendship "with a great Lady, who they wagered upon in the late change would certainly govern this court and thought it a masterstroke of Politicks to give him the character and send him here." Keith to Mitchell, Feb. 20/Mar. 11, 1762, *BMAddMSS* 6825, *folio* 237.

117. Bute to Keith, Feb. 2, 1762, *BMAddMSS* 6825, *folio* 300.

118. Bute to Keith, Feb. 26, 1762, *BMAddMSS* 35,484.

119. Bute to Newcastle, Feb. 20, 1762, *BMAddMSS* 32,934, *folio* 447.

120. Bute discussed the possibility of making overtures to Austria with Yorke. "Perhaps Austria could be awakened from a dangerous lethargy to a Remembrance and imitation of that glorious Stand, which she formerly made in conjunction with England, against the destructive ambition of the same united powers" (Bute to Yorke, Jan. 12, 1762, *BMAddMSS* 32,933).

121. C. Leonard and K. Schweizer, "Britain, Prussia, Russia and the Golitzyn Letter: A Reassessment," *The Historical Journal* (Cambridge, England), vol. 26, no. 3 (1983), pp. 531–56.

122. Grenville to Mitchell, May 26, 1762, *PRO SP* 90/80.

123. Hardwicke guessed that there would be severe consequences especially with Russia from denying the subsidy, "the predilection and passion, which the new Czar has conceived for the king of Prussia, might make it advisable to give the subsidy for this year," Hardwicke to Bute, Apr. 14, 1762, *Earl*, vol. 3, p. 348. See Leonard and Schweizer, "Britain, Prussia, Russia."

124. Keith to Bute, Dec. 28, 1761/Jan. 8, 1762, *BMAddMSS* 35,493.

125. He inquired again in April; Keith to Bute, Feb. 11/22, 1762, *BMAddMSS* 35,493; Vorontsov, "Konferentsiia," *AKV*, vol. 7, p. 502.

126. On January 23 Vorontsov wrote to Peter that the next stage in commercial negotiations was for England to review the draft that the Russians had proposed. Progress was slow; it was not renewed until 1766. Vorontsov, "Doklad," *AKV*, vol. 7, p. 544; and his "Opisanie sostoianii del vo vremia Gosudaryni Imperatritsy Elizavety Petrovny (soch. v iiule 1762)," *AKV*, vol. 25 (1882), pp. 284–85.

127. Keith to Bute, Mar. 8/19, 1762, *PRO SP* 91/69.

128. Haxthausen to Bernstorff, Feb. 19/Mar. 2, 1762, *RAD TKUA* 78.

129. "The violent partiality which the Emperor at first showed to Mr. Keith, was only the Effect of his being so grossly flattered. . . . The affairs of England here are widely different from what I could wish them. . . . The French party gains ground daily, and Mr. Keith's total want of judgment . . . is not a little the occasion of It." On July 14, after news of Peter's overthrow had reached him, Grenville wrote apologetically, "You are to give the strongest assurances of His Majesty's constant Regard and Friendship to the writer of the note

mentioned in your despatch of the 16th [Catherine], and also with respect to the matter complained of, the King is sending the Earl of Buckinghamshire in Quality of His ambassador to Petersburg, He will have his Instructions for conducting Himself in such a manner as may give satisfaction, and rectify whatever may have been amiss.'' Wroughton to Bute, Mar. 28, 1762, *PRO SP* 88/86, *folio* 212; Grenville to Wroughton, July 14, 1762, *PRO SP* 88/86, *folio* 144.

130. On February 6, Bute had instructed Keith, ''you will do everything in your power towards dissuading him from such a Design (without showing partiality for Denmark over Russia).'' On February 7, he ordered Keith ''to suspend for the present the execution of the Instructions sent to him in His Lordship's Dispatch of yesterday concerning Denmark.'' However, Bute wrote on February 26, ''The King has one apprehension, lest the Zealous affection of the Emperor to the Prussian Cause should hurry him into such measures, as, by encouraging that Prince's ambitions of war-like spirit, may tend to the contrivance of those hostile plans.'' Bute to Keith, Feb. 6, 7, 9, and 26, 1762, *PRO SP* 91/69, *folios* 24, 34–56; Weston to Wroughton, Feb. 7, 1762, *BMAddMSS* 32,934, *folios* 217–19.

131. Keith to Bute, Apr. 5/16, 1762, *PRO SP* 91/69, *folio* 225.

132. Keith to Bute, Apr. 5/16, 1762, *PRO SP* 91/69.

133. Solov'ev, *Istoriia*, vol. 13, p. 63.

134. Hardwicke to Newcastle, Apr. 10, 1762, *BMAddMSS* 32,937, *folios* 18–19.

135. Bute to Keith, Apr. 9, 1762, *PRO SP* 91/69.

136. Hardwicke to Newcastle, Apr. 10, 1762, *BMAddMSS* 32,937.

137. Solov'ev, *Istoriia*, vol. 13, p. 51.

138. Posse to Ekeblad, Apr. 19/30, May 10/21, and May 21/June 1, 1762, *RAS DM* 306.

139. Ekeblad to Posse, Dec. 22, 1761, *RAS DM* 334.

140. Posse to Ekeblad, May 10/21, 1762, *RAS DM* 306.

141. Cooperation with Prussia promised to add new troops and supplies to the depleted Russian forces abroad. Frederick reported that 60,000 Russian troops and 6,000 Prussian troops were anticipated to be sufficient to begin the war. Peter seemed relatively confident. ''We see nothing but preparation for war here.'' Posse to Ekeblad, June 26/July 6, 1762, *RAS DM* 306. Frederick II, ''Mémoires de Frédéric II, Guerre de Sept Ans,'' in *Oeuvres posthumes de Frédéric II, Roi de Prusse* (Berlin, 1788), vol. 2, p. 231.

142. Peter to Korf, May 25/June 5, 1762, *AVPR, f.* 53/1, *d.* 17, *l.* 89 (in *RAD*).

143. Ekeblad to Posse, June 18/29, 1762, *RAS DM* 334.

144. Keith to Bute, Feb. 12/23, 1762, *BMAddMSS* 35,493.

145. P. Shchebal'skii, ''Vopros o kurliandii pri Petri III,'' *Russkii arkhiv* (1865), vol. 4, p. 294.

146. J.-Ch. T. de Laveaux, *Histoire de Pierre III, Empereur de Russie*, 2 vols. (Paris, 1798), vol. 1, pp. 136–38.

147. Peter III, ''Ukaz Kollegii Inostrannykh Del,'' Apr. 6, 1762, *TsGADA, f.* 9, *op.* 5, *d.* 43, *l.* 37.

148. Frederick II to Finckenstein (Minister of State), May 22, 1760, *PC,* vol. 19 (1892), pp. 364–65.

149. Haxthausen to Bernstorff, Mar. 5/16, 1762, *RAD TKUA* 78.

150. Vorontsov. ''Zapiski,'' May 20, 1762, *LOII, f.* 36. *d.* 1072, *l.* 232.

151. Dassow, ''Friedrich,'' p. 53.

152. *Recueil de traités et états de l'Europe*, ed. G. F. Martens (St. Petersburg, 1874), vol. 5, p. 389.

153. G. Elliot to Bute, Apr. 24, 1762, *PRO SP* 88/86; Chechulin, *Vneshniaia*, p. 208; ''Proekt traktata,'' *AKV* vol. 8, p. 563.

154. Peter III, ''Zapiska na pamiat' i dlia ispolneniia grafu Aleksandru Romanovichu Vorontsovu,'' *AKV* (1886), vol. 31, pp. 154–55.

155. Shchebal'skii, ''Vopros o kurliandii,'' pp. 284–94.

156. Haxthausen to Bernstorff, June 10/21, 1762, *RAD TKUA* 80; Solov'ev, *Istoriia*, vol. 13, pp. 169–70.

157. Peter told the delegation, "Upon hearing extent of their oppression, We respond that in the future the Courland nobles' privileges, rights and immunities in the spiritual and temporal will be protected." Under Catherine Biron was reinstated, a resolution that left George Ludwig with Holstein. "Resolution de l'Empereur de Russie aux deputées de la noblesse de Courland," undated. *AMAE MD R* 8; Vorontsov to Bernstorff, Aug. 25/Sept. 5, 1762, *Staatsarkiv Oldenburg*, BII, P 5 Vid. III, no. 3.

158. Haxthausen to Bernstorff, Mar. 12/23, 1762, *RAD TKUA* 78.

159. Haxthausen to Bernstorff, Mar. 5/16, 1762, *RAD TKUA* 78.

160. Haxthausen to Bernstorff, Mar. 12/23, 1762, *RAD TKUA* 78.

161. Haxthausen to Bernstorff, Feb. 27/Mar. 10, 1762, *RAD TKUA* 78.

162. R. E. Jones, "Opposition to War and Expansion in Late Eighteenth Century Russia," *Jahrbücher für Geschichte Osteuropas*, vol. 32 (1984), p. 37.

163. May 31 was the first public announcement that Peter intended to leave with his troops. See Haxthausen to Bernstorff, Mar. 5/16, 1762, *RAD TKUA* 78; 31 May/June 11, 1762, *RAD TKUA* 79; Keith to Bute, May 22/June 2, 1762, *PRO SP* 91/70, *folio* 86; Haxthausen to Bernstorff, Mar. 5/16, 1762, *RAD TKUA* 78.

164. Keith to Grenville, May 27/June 7, 1762, *PRO SP* 91/70, *folio* 90.

165. "Vorontsov says the tsar would be content with some districts of Holstein and the absolute separation of the Ducal part; but he feels the lightest sacrifice would be shameful to Denmark; and this promises but a temporary tranquility, since the government of Denmark would not pass up the only occasion when it is really in a state not to fear Russia to impose its superiority in the Baltic." Breteuil to Choiseul, May 3/24, 1762, *AMAE CP Russie* 68.

166. Haxthausen to Bernstorff, Apr. 29/May 10, 1762, *RAD TKUA* 79.

167. Keith to Grenville, June 26/July 6, 1762, *PRO SP* 91/70, *folio* 33.

168. Haxthausen to Bernstorff, Jan. 11/22, 1762, *RAD TKUA* 78.

169. Saldern believed that there was little real chance of successful negotiations, since Peter had made his ultimatum, the restitution of Schleswig. Mitchell to Grenville, June 27, 1762, *PRO SP* 90/79, *folio* 80.

170. Foreign powers played a part in the coup d'état, Mitchell wrote Bute, "From intercepted letters, both Vienna and Warsaw flatter themselves with hopes of being able to raise Disturbances in Russia by means of the clergy" (Mitchell to Bute, Feb. 23, 1762, *BMAddMSS* 6809, *folio* 59). Choiseul's instructions to Breteuil on February 1 were, if the Emperor joins "our enemies," "you should act together with the imperial ambassador without reserve and with uniform principles" (Choiseul to Breteuil, Feb. 1, 4, 1762, *AMAE CP Russie* 68). A British envoy reported from Warsaw, "Odar said, that the Empress of Russia accepted propositions from all sides. She sent to Breteuil for money which he immediately furnished her with" (Walter Money to Grenville, Aug. 21, 1762, *PRO SP* 88/86, *folio* 202); the Austrian and French ambassadors "are trying to depose Peter III" (Haxthausen to Bernstorff, Apr. 25/May 6, 1762, *RAD TKUA* 79).

171. Haxthausen to Bernstorff, June 10/21, 1762, *RAD TKUA* 80.

172. Choiseul to Breteuil, Jan. 24, 1762, *AMAE CP Russie* 58.

173. Choiseul to Breteuil, Mar. 7, 1762, *AMAE CP Russie* 68.

6. Why the Coup?

1. The author of the manifesto was the scholar and statesman Grigorii Teplov (1711–1779), a leading figure in the coup d'état. G. Helbig, *Russkie izbranniki* (Berlin, 1900), pp. 342–44; *Polnoe sobranie zakonov Rossiiskoi imperii, 1649–1913*, 234 vols. (St. Petersburg, 1830–1916) (hereafter *PSZ*) 15: 11,582 (June 28, 1762).

2. Robert Keith (British ambassador to Russia) to George Grenville (British Secretary of State for Northern Affairs), July 1/12, 1762, *PRO SP* 91/70; published in part in "Diplomaticheskaia perepiska angliiskikh poslov i poslannikov pri russkom dvore," *Sbornik imperatorskogo russkogo istoricheskogo obshchestva* (hereafter *SIRIO*), vol. 12 (1873), p. 9.

3. Laurent Bérenger (French chargé d'affaires at St. Petersburg) to Étienne François de Choiseul (foreign minister in France), July 2/13, 1762, in V. A. Bil'basov, *Istoriia Ekateriny Vtoroi*, 2 vols. (Berlin, 1900), vol. 2, appendix 2, p. 592–93.

4. A few days before the coup, a Lutheran chapel for the Holstein regiments was consecrated at Oranienbaum. Bérenger to Choiseul, July 2/13, 1762, in Bil'basov, *Istoriia*, vol. 2, appendix 2, pp. 592–93.

5. *Osmnadtsatyi vek, Istoricheskii sbornik*, ed. P. Bartenev, 4 vols. (Moscow, 1896), vol. 4, pp. 216–23.

6. Keith to Grenville, July 1/12, 1762, *PRO SP* 91/70.

7. J.-Ch. T. de Laveaux, *Histoire de Pierre III, Empereur de Russie*, 2 vols. (Paris, 1798), vol. 2, p. 164.

8. J. C. Rulhière, *Perevorot 1762*, ed. G. Balitskii (Moscow, 1909), p. 7.

9. Keith to Grenville, July 1/12, 1762 *PRO SP* 91/70.

10. Catherine to Poniatowski, August 2, 1762, *AKV*, vol. 25, pp. 414–17.

11. Béranger to Choiseul, July 2/13, 1762, *AMAE CP Russie* 69; Zapiski pridvornogo bril'iantshchika Poz'e o prebyvanii ego v Rossii 1729–1764 gg." *Russkaia starina*, vol. 1 (1870), p. 219; C. von Saldern, *Histoire de la vie de Pierre III, Empereur de toutes les Russes, présentant sous un aspect impartial, les causes de la révolution arrivée en 1762* (Metz, 1802), pp. 46–47; A. Brückner, *Istoriia Ekateriny Vtoroi*, 3 vols. (St. Petersburg, 1885), vol. 1, p. 126.

12. Haxthausen wrote that discontent among the guards because of Peter's death was directed at the Hetman: "several companies of the Semenovskii and Preobrazhenskii guards . . . marched to the palace . . . crying out for revolt: the Hetman, 'that traitor, made us believe that our Good Emperor was dead, and then proceeded to kill him,' " Gregors von Haxthausen (special envoy to St. Petersburg) to Johan Hartvig Ernst Bernstorff (Danish Foreign Minister), Aug. 2/13, 1762, *RAD TKUA* 80; Brückner, *Istoriia*, vol. 1, p. 126.

13. M. N. Longinov, "Svedeniia ob ofitserakh konnoi gvardii v iiune mesiatse 1762 goda," *Russkii arkhiv*, vol. 5 (1867), pp. 481–86.

14. Catherine to Poniatowski, Aug. 2, 1762, pp. 415.

15. *Skt.-Peterburgskie vedomosti*, Aug. 9, 1762.

16. Prohibition of the sale of vodka; June 29 and July 1, 1762, *TsGADA, f.* 248, *kn.* 3384, *ll.* 392, 433.

17. D. Polivanov, *K vosshestviiu na prestol imperatritsy Ekateriny II: stranichka iz istorii leib-gvardii Izmailovskogo polka, Uchastie polka v Peterburgskom deistvii 28 iiunia 1762 goda* (St. Petersburg, 1913), pp. 7–8; *Perevorot 1762 g.*, pp. 4–5; Thomas Wroughton (special envoy to Russia) to Lord Bute (Secretary of State), July 23/Aug. 3, 1762, *PRO SP* 88/68; "Pokhozhdeniia izvestnykh peterburgskikh deistv," in *Osmnadtsatyi vek*, vol. 2, pp. 631–33.

18. Among the Izmailovstsy, captains, lieutenants, and majors, N. Raevskii, P. Khrushchev, M. Pokhvisnev, A. Raslovlev, P. Golitzyn, M. Lasunskii, P. and I. Gur'ev, I. Obukhov, S. Vsevolodskii, and the cavalry guard, P. Cherkasskii and Ia. Golitzyn, A. Rzhevskii, and forty-three other officers; M. N. Longinov, "Svedeniia ob ofitserakh konnoi gvardii v iiune mesiatse 1762 g.," *Russkii arkhiv* (1867), vol. 5, pp. 481–86; A. A. Vasil'chikov, *Semeistvo Razumovskikh*, 2 vols. (St. Petersburg, 1880), vol. 1, p. 290; S. N. Shubinskii, *Istoricheskie ocherki i rasskazy* (St. Petersburg, 1871), pp. 153–54; *Skt. Peterburgskie vedomosti* (August 9, 1762).

19. B. von Münnich, *"Ebauche" du Gouvernement de l'Empire de Russie* (Geneva, 1989), pp. 129.

20. En route to the cathedral, the procession was joined by "a large part of the Preobrazhenskii and a few of the Semenovskii regiments" and, at the cathedral, by the grenadiers of the Preobrazhenskii, some of the Horse Guards, and the artillery corps; see M. N. Longinov, "Svedenii ob ofitserakh konnoi gvardii v iiune mesiatse 1762 g.," *Russkii arkhiv*, vol. 5 (1867), p. 481; Polivanov, pp. 7–8; G. Helbig, "Primechaniia k knige: russkie izbranniki i sluchainye liudi," *Russkaia starina* (July 1886), pp. 94–95.

21. J. LeDonne, "Outlines of Russian Military Administration 1762–1796: Part II: The High Command," *Geschichte Osteuropas,* vol. 33 (1985), p. 188.

22. Grigorii Orlov, according to Catherine after his death, "was a genius, a brave, decisive and powerful man, but sweet as lamb." *Dnevnik A. V. Khrapovitskogo* (St. Petersburg, 1874), p. 82; Helbig, "Primechaniia," pp. 8–9; A. T. Bolotov, *Zhizn' i prikliucheniia Andreia Bolotova opisannye samim im dlia svoikh potomkov* (Moscow-Leningrad, 1931) [reprinted 1973], vol. 2, p. 93.

23. Bibikov also met Peter Panin in Germany, a friendship by which he later was introduced to Nikita Panin; V. Bibikov, *Zapiski o zhizni i sluzhbe Aleksandra Il'icha Bibikova synom ego Senatorom Bibikovym* (St. Petersburg, 1817), p. 19; *Zapiski Dashkovoi,* p. 58; Helbig, *Izbranniki,* pp. 274, 281–82; Longinov, "Neskol'ko izvestii," pp. 352–54.

24. Catherine to Poniatowski, Aug. 2, 1762, p. 415.

25. Polivanov, pp. 7–8; W. Tooke, *History of Russia,* 2 vols. (London, 1801), vol. 1, pp. 357–58; *Perevorot 1762 g. po neizdannym sobstvenoruchnym zapiskam* (n.p., n.d.), pp. 4–5.

26. Catherine to Poniatowski, Aug. 2, 1762, pp. 417.

27. P. Gilchrist, *A Geniune Letter from Paul Gilchrist, Esp., Merchant at Petersburg, to Mr. Saunders, in London: Giving a particular and circumstantial Account of the Great Revolution in Russia, and the Death of Peter III, the Late Emperor in which that very Extraordinary Affair is set in a true Light* (London, 1762).

28. Bil'basov, *Istoriia,* vol. 2, pp. 40–41; S. M. Solov'ev, *Istoriia Rossii s drevneishikh vremen,* 15 vols. (Moscow, 1959–65), vol. 13, pp. 96.

29. Marc Raeff concluded in an article on Peter III that the senators played a major role in the overthrow. This interpretation is not borne out by evidence from the Senate or elsewhere. Since it seemed obvious from the overwhelming concensus of the literature, Raeff did not actually demonstrate that Peter was an especially arbitrary ruler, that he was attempting to set up a personal regime of favorites, or that the senators wanted him overthrown. I suggest that these assertions have to be proved. M. Raeff, "Overthrow," pp. 1304–1305; C. Leonard, "The Reputation of Peter III," *Russian Review,* vol. 47 (1988), pp. 263–92.

30. He was married to Nikita and Peter Panin's sister. I. I. Nepliuev, *Zapiski, 1693–1773* (St. Petersburg, 1893; republished, Cambridge, Mass., 1974), p. 129.

31. "Reskript," [June 28] 1762, *TsGADA, f.* III Gosarkhiva, *d.* 10; *f.* 248, *kn.* 3431, *ll.* 200ff.

32. Béranger to Choiseul, June 28/July 8, 1762, *AMAE CP Russie* 69.

33. Sent to him by Aleksandr Bressan, his former adjutant and president of the Manufactures College; *Moskovskie vedomosti* (Jan. 22, 1762); Helbig, *Izbranniki,* p. 286.

34. Haxthausen to Bernstorff, May 31/June 11, 1762, *RAD TKUA* 80; Tooke, *History,* vol. 1, p. 355; Frederick II (King of Prussia) to Peter III, May 1, 1762, *PC,* vol. 12, p. 412.

35. Semevskii, "Shest' mesiatsev," *Otechestvennye zapiski,* vol. 173, Section 1 (1867), pp. 160–77.

36. Keith to Andrew Mitchell (British ambassador to Prussia), 2/13 July 1762, *BMAddMSS* 6825 (Mitchell Papers), vol. 22, *folio* 281.

37. Peter had 1,500 troops and 100 cannons. *Perevorot 1762 goda po neizdannym sobstvennoruchym zapiskam im. Ekateriny II* (n.p., n.d.), p. 5.

38. Lukian Ivanovich Talyzin (1714–1767).

39. Tooke, *History,* vol. 1, pp. 248–63; some clarification is provided by a Danish spy at Peterhof, Adriani, who noted that during the last few hours Peter's advisors, unable to decide what to recommend, offered conflicting advice. Possibly this was deliberate, implicating the conspirator Adam Ol'sufiev, who was with Peter at the end; see "Aus dem Munde eines Augenzeugens," Adriani to Bernstorff, Sept. 1762, *RAD Jeresbek Privatarkiv,* Bernstorff, I-II, Breve til J. H. E. Bernstorff fra Forskellige, 1756–1765, Adriani, Gottfried Andreas, v. 1762.

40. *Perevorot 1762,* p. 4.

41. There is no holograph text in Peter's hand, "Reskript," *TsGADA, f.* 3, *d.* 10, *l.* 6.

42. L.-Ph. de Ségur, *Mémoires, ou Souvenirs et anecdotes,* 3 vols. (Paris, 1824–1826), vol. 1, p. 292.

43. Because of the condition of the body, foreign observers concluded that Peter was poisoned.

44. "Many who were dissatisfied by the abdication of Peter III, now will be provoked by his death." Mitchell to Grenville, Aug. 6, 1762, *PRO SP* 90/80; Keith to Grenville, Aug. 9/20, 1762, *PRO SP* 91/70.

45. Bérenger to Choiseul, July 10/23, 1762, in Bil'basov, *Istoriia,* vol. 2, p. 615.

46. "Catherine is not as strong and widely loved as she flatters herself." Haxthausen to Bernstorff, Oct. 3/14, 1762, *RAD TKUA* 80.

47. D. A. Korsakov, "Nekotorye iz storonnikov votsareniia-imp. Ekateriny II-oi (1757–1762)," in *Iz zhizni russkikh deiatelei XVIII veka* (Kazan, 1881), pp. 378–84; *Zapiski Dashkovoi,* p. 13; Buckinghamshire to Grenville, Aug. 9/20, 1762, *PRO SP* 90/70; Haxthausen to Bernstorff, Aug. 2/13, 1762, *RAD TKUA* 80; Béranger to Louis XV (King of France), July 26/Aug. 6, 1763, *AMAE France et Divers États Correspondances secrètes* 536/2.

48. In November, six guards were exiled and two executed for conspiracy, Haxthausen to Bernstorff, Nov. 5/16, 1762, *RAD TKUA* 80.

49. "Obstoiatel'nyi" manifest, July 6, 1762, in *Osmnadsaty vek,* vol. 4, pp. 216–23.

50. Catherine to Poniatowski, Aug. 2, 1762, p. 423.

51. Mercy's report of Mar. 15, 1762, in cypher, "The Empress sent word that if she had the slightest power, then she would preserve the former political system." Mercy to Kaunitz, Mar. 15/27, 1762, *SIRIO,* vol. 18 (1876), p. 235; Wroughton to Bute, enclosing a letter from Catherine for Bute, April 27/May 8, 1761, *PRO SP* 91/69, *folios* 187–88.

52. One source of financial support was the English merchantry at court. She may have been the recipient of funds from other diplomats, including Mercy d'Argenteau, Thomas Wroughton, Aschatz von Asseburg, and Breteuil. Before the death of Empress Elizabeth, there had been a steady stream of money and other assistance from the Danish court. Cash was also distributed by Aleksei Orlov after the coup by his testimony. Shchepkin, p. 676; Bil'basov, *Istoriia,* vol. 1, p. 434; *SP* 88/69; Louis Charles Auguste le Tonnelier, baron de Breteuil (French ambassador to Russia) to Choiseul, Feb. 15/26, 1761, *AMAE CP Russie* 66; Grenville to Wroughton, July 14, 1762, *PRO SP* 88/86; "Description Politique de la Russie, Servant à faire connaître l'État actuel des forces de Souverain, et la richnesses de la Nation, 1767," *AMAE MD* 11/9; "Reflections sur la facilité d'un Révolution en Russie ã la mort de l'impératrice," *AMAE MD* 9/27; Catherine, *Zapiski,* p. 227.

53. Bute sent the envoy Thomas Wroughton to Russia with money for Catherine, whom he remarked to be "the ruling genius." Wroughton had previously been a channel for the correspondence of Catherine with her lover, Prince Poniatowsky of Poland. Haxthausen to Bernstorff, Mar. 5/16, 1762, *RAD TKUA* 78.

54. Baron Posse, the Swedish ambassador, mentions Catherine's plans for "revolution" in mid-January. See Posse to Claes Ekeblad (chancery president), Jan. 18/29, 1762, *RAS DM* 307; Breteuil to Choiseul, Mar. 15/26, 1762, *AMAE CP Russie;* "Catherine is dangerous, but she changes her mind from day to day," "Teplov has been arrested for conspiracy," and others, Haxthausen to Bernstorff, Dec. 29, 1761/Jan. 9, Jan. 8/19, Mar. 5/16, Apr. 19/30, Aprl 25/May 6, June 10/21, 1762, *RAD TKUA* 78, 79; Keith reports on Feb. 15 that the Emperor fears Panin and Shakhovskoi, Breteuil to Choiseul, Feb. 15/26, 1762, *AMAE CP Russie* 68; Keith to Grenville, May 7/18, 1762, *BMAddMSS* 32,438; Yorke to Bute, May 7, 1762, *PRO SP* 84/496.

55. Breteuil to Choiseul, Mar. 30/Apr. 10, 1762, *AMAE CP Russie,* 68; Haxthausen to Bernstorff, Mar. 12/24, May 31/June 11, June 11/22, 1762, *RAD TKUA* 78, 79.

56. "To tell the truth I believe that the Crown of Russia attracted me more than his person. . . . He was sixteen . . . small and infantile, talking of nothing but soldiers and toys. I listened politely and often yawned . . . we never used the language of tenderness." Catherine, *Zapiski,* pp. 58–65, 204–13.

57. Catherine II, *The Correspondence of Catherine the Great When Grand Duchess with Sir Charles Hanbury-Williams and Letters from Count Poniatowski*, ed. and trans. The Earl of Ilchester and Mrs Langford-Brooke (London, 1928), pp. 45, 59, 168. Solov'ev gives an account of a conversation between Ivan Shuvalov and Nikita Panin at this time in which Shuvalov ventured, "Some are inclined to denounce and send into exile both the grand duke, Peter, and his wife, and form a government in the name of their son, Paul Petrovitch." The second plan, wrote Solov'ev, was to send only Peter away, "allowing the mother to remain with her son." Solov'ev, *Istoriia*, vol. 13, p. 81.

58. Catherine II, *Correspondence*, p. 59.

59. Ibid., p. 45.

60. Haxthausen to Bernstorff, May 26/June 6, 1762, *RAD TKUA* 79.

61. Catherine, *Memoirs*, p. 242.

62. Haxthausen to Bernstorff, Dec. 29, 1761/Jan. 11, 1762, Dec. 30, 1761/Jan 10, 1762, Jan. 8/19, 11/21, 1762, *RAD TKUA* 78; Posse to Ekeblad, Jan. 18/29, 1762, *RAS DM* 37; see also Solov'ev, *Istoriia*, vol. 13, pp. 9–10; Mercy to Kaunitz, Jan. 10/21, 1762, *SIRIO*, vol. 18 (1876), pp. 27–33.

63. Yorke to Bute, Feb. 5, 1762, *PRO SP* 85/495.

64. Bil'basov, *Istoriia*, vol. 2, pp. 4–7; Haxthausen to Bernstorff, May 26/June 6, 1762, *RAD TKUA* 79.

65. She concealed her condition by dressing in mourning clothes, Laveaux, *Histoire*, vol. 2, p. 446.

66. Bernstorff to Haxthausen, May 26/June 6, 1762, *RAD TKUA* 80.

67. Haxthausen to Bernstorff, May 31/June 11, 1762, *RAD TKUA* 80.

68. Bil'basov, *Istoriia*, vol. 2, p. 15; *PSZ* 16: 11,584, pp. 3–4.

69. Bil'basov, *Istoriia*, vol. 2, p. 21; Vasil'chikov, *Semeistvo*, vol. 1, p. 290.

70. Panin was associated with Catherine in the 1750s. Catherine spoke of him as her "future Chancellor" as early as 1756. Catherine, *Correspondence*, p. 182; M. D. Polivanov, *K vosshestviiu na prestol imperatritsy Ekateriny II* (St. Petersburg, 1913), p. 8; Bil'basov, *Istoriia*, vol. 2, p. 20. Ransel, *Politics*, p. 62; Raeff, "Overthrow," p. 1302.

71. S. O. Shmidt, "Vnutrenniaia politika Rossii serediny XVIII veka," *Voprosy istorii* (1987), no. 3, p. 45.

72. Peter III's dislike of Bestuzhev was noted in the 1730s, when Bestuzhev took valuable documents from Holstein archives. Animosity increased as a consequence of the intrigues of the 1750s. A. Veidemeier, *Dvor i zamechatel'nye liudi v Rossii v vtoroi polovine XVIII stoletiia* (St. Petersburg, 1846), vol. 1, p. 4.

73. Volkonskii was Bestuzhev's cousin; Nikita Panin, Russian ambassador to Stockholm for twelve years before being appointed to the court, owed his entry into diplomatic circles to his patron, Bestuzhev-Riumin; Admiral Talyzen, who captured the fortress of Kronstadt for Catherine, was also a relative of the former grand chancellor; Solov'ev, *Istoriia*, vol. 13, p. 84; Korsakov, pp. 399–401; Ransel, *Politics*, pp. 4, 22–27.

74. *PSZ* 15: 11,421 (*im.*, Jan. 29, 1762), p. 895.

75. See Nepliuev's explanation of his personal discontent under Peter III, whose behavior, personality, and reforms are not mentioned: "In 1762, after [Peter's] ascent to the throne, general procurator Iakov Petrovich was retired, and I had no hope of anything better; after all the promises, my son got no rewards and was even in disgrace, so I asked the chancellor for retirement, but it was refused. My grandson, at this time in the cavalry, was promoted by Prince George to captain-in-arms at the request of Anna Nikitichna Naryshkina. . . . I suffered. What would become of me and my son? I was at my post every day, but no one . . . listened to my opinion." Nepliuev, *Zapiski*, p. 167.

76. "Accused of speaking too liberally," Haxthausen to Bernstorff, Mar. 17/28, 1762, *RAD TKUA* 79.

77. There was a rumor that he would be removed from the court and sent to Sweden; Haxthausen to Bernstorff, Apr. 5/16, 1762, *RAD TKUA* 79.

78. Solov'ev, *Istoriia*, vol. 13, pp. 9–10; Haxthausen to Bernstorff, Dec. 29, 1761/Jan. 9, 1762, Jan. 8/19, 11/12, 1762, *RAD TKUA* 78.

79. Shakhovskoi was under a court ban for reported open hostility to the emperor; Sievers was under investigation for financial dealings in Livonia; Haxthausen to Bernstorff, Jan. 8/19, 11/22, Mar. 13/24, 1762, *RAD TKUA* 78.

80. Ransel, *Politics*, p. 2.

81. *PSZ* 15: 11,518 (*im.* Apr. 25, 1762), p. 991.

82. At the time of the coup d'état, the guards had just been given their back pay from 1761 and 1762 in copper rubles (43,574 and 26,004 rubles). Apr. 20, 1762, *TsGADA, f.* 248, *kn.* 3383, *ll.* 362–64. Orlov used bribes to help win them over; Helbig, ''Izbranniki,'' *Russkaia starina* (1866), p. 8; Bil'basov, *Istoriia*, vol 1., p. 433.

83. Semevskii, ''Shest','' pp. 160–77.

84. Breteuil to Choiseul, Mar. 15/26, 1762, *AMAE CP Russie* 68; Keith to Grenville, July 2/13, 1762, *BMAddMSS* 35493.

85. ''Bumagi kniazia M. N. Volkonskogo,'' *Russkii arkhiv* (1865), pp. 681–722; ''Ukazy Petra III-go,'' *TsGADA, f.* 9, *op.* 5, *d.* 43, *ll.* 3–5.

86. Saldern told Haxthausen that all of Peter's council opposed the idea of a campaign, that ''war was not in the interests . . . of the Emperor,'' but Peter was ''implacable.'' Haxthausen to Bernstorff, May 21/June 1, 1762, *RAD TKUA* 79; *PSZ* 15: 11,538 (May 18, 1762), p. 1006.

87. Béranger to Choiseul, June 28/July 9, 1762, *AMAE CP Russie* 69.

88. Razumovskii studied abroad, was appointed president of the Academy of Sciences at 18 and in 1750, at 22, Hetman of the Ukraine. He often said that he wished to retire and leave Catherine, for whom he felt great affection, all his lands. Haxthausen to Bernstorff, Nov. 19/30, 1762, *RAD TKUA* 80: Eshevskii, *Sochineniia*, p. 12; Vasil'chikov, *Semeistvo*, vol. 1, p. 290; Shubinskii, *Istoricheskie*, p. 152.

89. Peter to I. Shuvalov, n.d. in *Mémoires de Catherine II*, ed. A. Herzen (London, 1859), pp. 356–57; Haxthausen to Bernstorff, Mar. 5/16, 1762, *RAD TKUA* 78; Vasil'chikov, *Semeistvo*, vol. 1, p. 290; M. Maksimovich, ''O Grigor'e Nikolaeviche Teplove i ego zapiski, 'O neporiadkakh Rossii,'' *Russkaia beseda*, vol. 4 (Moscow, 1857), p. 62.

90. Münnich, *''Ebauche,''* p. 129; Bil'basov, *Istoriia*, vol. 1, p. 433.

91. Solov'ev, *Istoriia*, vol. 13, pp. 100–101.

92. Leonard, ''Reputation.''

93. ''The whole tendency of the eighteenth-century monarchy to regard the Church as an institution of state prepared the way for the reform of the status of all its estates.'' Presniakov, *Istoriia Senata*, vol. 2, p. 139.

94. Dating from Catherine I's testament of 1727, this exclusion was also used as justification for Elizabeth's coup of 1741. Bil'basov, *Istoriia*, vol. 1, p. 30.

95. He consecrated an Orthodox as well as a Lutheran Church at Oranienbaum for his Holstein and Russian regiments. Laveaux, *Histoire*, vol. 1, p. 207; [C. F. Schwan] M. de la Marche, *Histoire et anecdotes de la vie, du regne, du détrônement et de la mort de Pierre III, dernier Empereur de toutes les Russes, écrites en forme de lettres* (London, 1766), p. 203. Catherine wrote elsewhere that Peter sought to ''change the religion'' of the country. Catherine to Poniatowski, Aug. 2, 1762, p. 414.

96. *PSZ*, 15: 11,420 (*im.*, Jan. 29, 1762), pp. 894–95. See his attempt to interfere in ecclesiastical decisions (chapter 3). ''Ukaz nashemu Sinodu, 26 mar. 1762 g.,'' *TsGADA, f.* 18, *d.* 193, *l.* 1. Catherine's criticism and distortion of the intent of his decree on private chapels in *Osmnadtsatyi vek*, p. 218; *PSZ*, 15: 11,460 (Mar. 5, 1762), p. 934; and her confirmation of the decree in *Istoriko-statisticheskaia*, pp. 81–83, 115–16; *Rukovodstvennye dlia pravoslavnogo dukhovenstva ukazy Sv. Pravitel'stvuiushchego Sinoda, 1721–1878* (Moscow, 1879), no. 53, p. 52.

97. Peter I had also prohibited private chapels.

98. Haxthausen to Bernstorff, Nov. 5/16, 1762, *RAD TKUA* 80.

99. Haxthausen to Bernstorff, May 26/June 6, 1762, *RAD TKUA* 79; Vorontsov, "Rassuzhdenie," *AKV*, vol. 4, pp. 174–78.

100. Haxthausen appreciated the discrepancy between Catherine's claims and her first acts. "As soon as she ascended the throne, she condemned all Peter did in her first sovereign acts, but scarcely a month later, she was already changed and revoked many things, beginning to march in his footsteps. Today, she is approximately in the same relation to Vienna and France as Peter III was, if not in action, at least in sentiment, and to Sweden, England and Prussia." Haxthausen to Bernstorff, Nov. 5/16, 1762, *RAD TKUA* 80.

101. Yorke to Bute, Apr. 6, 1762, *PRO SP* 84/495; Haxthausen to Bernstorff, Mar. 12/23, Apr. 19/30, June 10/21, 1762, *RAD TKUA* 78,79.

102. Keith to Bute, May 27/June 7, 1762, *PRO SP* 91/70.

103. Enclosed in Haxthausen to Bernstorff, May 26/June 6, 1762, *RAD TKUA* 79.

104. Haxthausen to Bernstorff, Mar. 5/16, 1762, *RAD TKUA* 78.

105. Catherine to Poniatowski, p. 424.

106. Haxthausen to Bernstorff, Mar. 12/23, 1762, *RAD TKUA* 78.

107. The house of Georg Ludwig, Peter's uncle, was ransacked by the cavalry guard, Catherine to Poniatotowski, p. 417.

108. Compare Raeff, pp. 1304–1305.

109. Nepliuev, *Zapiski*, pp. 166–68.

110. Breteuil to Choiseul, Feb. 14/25, 1762, *AMAE CP Russie* 68.

111. This council met twice a week. *PSZ*, 15: 11,538 (*im.*, May 18, 1762), p. 1006; Haxthausen to Bernstorff, Apr. 29/May 10, 1762, *RAD TKUA* 79.

112. At midcentury, Lomonosov was perhaps the sole literary figure with a sharp sense of national self-consciousness, and he was alone in his unsuccessful effort to replace the Germans at the Academy of Sciences. Ia. Zutis, *Ostzeiskii vopros v XVIII veke* (Riga, 1946), pp. 195–96.

113. Biron was overthrown for other reasons. See the review of the historical literature on Biron and the revolt of November 25, 1741, in Ia. Zutis, *Ostzeiskii*, pp. 184–93.

114. From 1764 to 1796 there were 24 pretenders, most using the name of Peter III. S. M. Troitskii, "Samozvantsy v Rossii XVII-XVIII vekov," *Voprosy istorii*, no. 3 (1969), pp. 134–46; and his "Istoriografiia 'dvortsovykh perevorotov' v Rossii XVIII v.," *Voprosy istorii*, no. 2 (1966), pp. 38–53.

115. The new uniforms and cuirass introduced elements of Prussian style within a variation on Petrine style. Haxthausen to Bernstorff, Mar. 12/23, 1762, *RAD TKUA* 78; Laveaux, *Histoire*, p. 208; J. von Staehlin, "Zapiski Shtelina o Petre Tret'em Imperatore Vserossiiskom," *Chteniia v Obshchestve istorii i drevnostei rossiiskikh*, vol. 59 (1866), no. 4, p. 105.

116. Bartenev, *Osmnadtsatyi vek*, pp. 216–23. This passage is the beginning of Catherine's "comprehensive, careful, and clever use of [the image of the reformer] in her own propagandistic version of the Russian Enlightenment." N. V. Riasanovsky, *The Image of Peter the Great in Russian History and Thought* (New York, 1985), p. 64.

117. "Il voulait casser les gardes," Catherine to Poniatowski, p. 414; Staehlin, "Zapiski," p. 106.

118. Two regiments (Ingermanland and Astrakhan) were placed under guard on the day of the coup. Haxthausen to Bernstorff, Aug. 16/27, 1762, *RAD TKUA* 78.

119. Haxthausen to Bernstorff, May 12/23, 1763, *RAD TKUA* 81.

120. Under Catherine the guard was still feared, "This [Russian] Government have not ventured to put their plan of keeping the Guards at a distance from Petersburg, in execution. . . . those troops cannot be ignorant that they are feared and suspected." John Earl of Buckinghamshire (British ambassador to Russia) to Earl of Halifax (Minister for Northern Affairs), Aug. 5/16, 1763, *SIRIO*, vol. 12 (1873), p. 117.

121. " . . . par rapport meme de la nation, . . . si les Russes m'auraient voulu du mal, ils l'auraient déjà longtemps pu faire, voyant que je ne prends garde à moi, me remettant

toujours à la garde du bon Dieu, . . . que penseraient ces mems Russes de moi, . . . eux qui n'ont jamais souhaité outrement que d'être sous un maitre et pas sous une femme. . . . ''
Peter III to Frederick II, May 15, 1762, *PC,* vol. 21, pp. 509–10.

7. Conclusion

1. S. M. Solov'ev, *Istoriia Rossii s drevneishikh vremen,* 15 vols. (Moscow, 1959–65), vol. 13, pp. 66, 69.

2. R. E. Jones, "Opposition to War and Expansion in Late Eighteenth Century Russia," *Jahrbücher für Geschichte Osteuropas,* vol. 32 (1984), pp. 34–38.

3. V. O. Kliuchevskii, *Kurs russkoi istorii* (vols. 1–4 of his *Sochineniia,* 8 vols. [Moscow, 1955–59]), vol. 4, pp. 353–55.

4. John Le Donne has provided a useful model in his *Absolutism and Ruling Class: The Formation of the Russian Political Order, 1700–1825* (New York, 1991). See also B. Plavsic, "Seventeenth-century Chanceries and Their Staffs," in *Russian Officialdom: The Bureaucratization of Russian Society from the Seventeenth to the Twentieth Century,* ed. W. Pintner and D. Rowney (Chapel Hill, N.C., 1980), pp. 19–46.

5. A. M. Iukht, *Gosudarstvennaia deiatel'nost' V. N. Tatishcheva v 20-kh—nachale 30-kh godov XVIII v.* (Moscow, 1985), pp. 282, 283. Cf. the evolution of law in Prussia. "The authority of law was grounded not on its content but on the will of the unaccountable political commander-in-chief." H. Rosenberg, *Bureaucracy, Aristocracy and Autocracy: The Prussian Experience, 1660–1815* (Boston, 1958), p. 46.

6. Shuvalov's argument to Elizabeth in favor of the compilation of laws shows the attempt to subordinate more closely the imperial will to legal precedent, "In order to break the deadlock of the courts there is no other way, as Your Imperial Majesty has indicated, than to turn to the decrees of your parents and predecessors and to see how these decrees are incompatible with current circumstances, that is, to command the Senate to resolve the discrepancy." Solov'ev, *Istoriia,* vol. 12, pp. 198–99.

7. Shuvalov's policies, for example, were both attacked and defended on the grounds of welfare implications. See Solov'ev, *Istoriia,* vol. 12, pp. 494–96, 587–88.

8. K. Baker, "Science and Politics at the End of the Old Regime," *Inventing the French Revolution: Essays on French Political Culture in the Eighteenth Century* (Cambridge, Mass., 1990), pp. 158–59.

9. M. T. Beliavskii, L. G. Kisliagina, "Obshchestvenno-politicheskaia mysl'," *Ocherki po russkoi istorii XVIII veka* (Moscow, 1988), pt. 3, p. 180.

10. I. T. Pososhkov, V. N. Tatishchev, A. D. Kantemir, A. P. Volynskii. See a review of the literature in Beliavskii, Kisliagina, *Ocherki,* pp. 162–74.

11. Senators and the colleges were to submit weekly reports about the fulfilling of verbal commands. *Polnoe sobranie zakonov Rossiiskoi imperii,* 1649–1913, 234 vols. (St. Petersburg, 1830–1916) (hereafter *PSZ*), 15: 11,411 (*im.,* Jan. 22, 1762), p. 889.

12. Baker, "Science," p. 163.

13. "Pis'ma Ekateriny II-oi k raznym litsam," *18 vek: Istoricheskii sbornik,* ed. P. Bartenev, 4 vols. (Moscow, 1868–1869), vol. 3, p. 390.

14. See works on Russian absolutism, including D. Geyer, "Gesellschaft als staatliche Veranstaltung. Bemerkungen zur Sozialgeschichte der russischen Staatsverwaltung im 18. Jahrhundert," *Jahrbücher für Geschichte Osteuropas,* N.F. vol. 14, no. 1 (1966), pp. 21–50; M. Raeff, "The Well-ordered Police State and the Development of Modernity in Seventeenth- and Eighteenth-Century Europe: An Attempt at a Comparative Approach," *American Historical Review,* vol. 80, no. 5 (Dec. 1975), pp. 1221–43; E. Donnert and P. Hoffman, "Zur Frage der wirtschaftlichen und sozialen Grundlage des Absolutismus in Russland," *Zeitschrift für Geschichtswissenschaft,* vol. 14 (1966), pp. 758–65.

15. This was an enduring goal of Russian foreign policy, as in the "northern system" of alliances Nikita Panin sought to create. D. Ransel, *The Politics of Catherinian Russia* (New Haven, Conn., 1975), pp. 144–50.

16. Recent assessment of the impact of philosophic writings on Catherine and her contemporaries has provided enormous and significant evidence that constitutionalism, serfdom, and social justice in general were not primary political issues, although there is some literature emerging from that era on questions of concern to the philosophes. See Ransel, *Politics;* his "Nikita Panin's Imperial Council Project and the Struggle of Hierarchy Groups at the Court of Catherine II," *Canadian Slavic Studies,* vol. 4, no. 3 (1970), pp. 443–64; D. Griffiths, "Catherine II: The Republican Empress," in *Jahrbücher für Geschichte Osteuropas,* vol. 21 (1973), pp. 323–44; I. de Madariaga, "Catherine and the Serfs: A Reconsideration of Some Problems," *Slavonic and East European Review,* vol. 52 (1974), pp. 34–62; W. Gleason, *Moral Idealists, Bureaucracy, and Catherine the Great* (New Brunswick, N.J., 1981).

BIBLIOGRAPHY

Archival Materials

Denmark (Copenhagen)

Rigsarkivet (RAD)

Tyske Kancellis Udenrigske Afdeling (TKUA) Special Del. Rusland
78–81 Gregors Christian v. Haxthausen (1761–1763) Gesandtskabsrelationer.
171–172 G. C. v. Haxthausens gesandtskabs Arkiv 172. Korrespondance Akter, III, 1761–1766 (Fr. V. OttesArkiv).

Jeresbeck Privatarkiv
Breve til J. H. E. Bernstorff fra Forskellige, 1756–1765, Adriani, Gottfried Andreas, v. 1762.

Stintenburg Privatarkiv
A. P. Bernstorff, Rejse til Paris, 1762.

Wotersen Privatarkiv
Johan Hartwig Ernst Bernstorff (1712–1772).
　　Breve fr Achatz Ferd. v. Asseburg (1755–1771).
　　Breve fra J. F. Bachoff (1752–1770).
　　Breve fra A. v. Osten (1760–1771).

Arkhiv Vneshnei Politiki Rossii (AVPR)
53/I Snoshenii Rossii s Danii.

England

Public Records Office, State Papers: Foreign (PRO SP)
91 Russia, Vols. 68–71.
90 Prussia, Vols. 78–81.
95 Sweden, Vols. 93 and 103.
75 Denmark, Vols. 111–114.
81 Germany, States, Vols. 140–141.
82 Hamburg and Hansa Towns, Vol. 79.
84 Holland, Vols. 495–496.
88 Poland, Vol. 86.
105 Archives of British Legations, Vol. 1.

British Museum, Additional Manuscripts (BMAddMSS)
Cat. no.
6809 Mitchell Papers. Vol. VI. Letters of Sir Andrew Mitchell. Nov. 1761–Dec. 1761.
6823 Mitchell Papers. Vol. XX. Letters from the Undersecretary of State. 1756–1770.
6825 Mitchell Papers. Vol. XXII. Letters from Various Persons. 1757–1762.
6843 Mitchell Papers. Vol. XL. Letters received from the King of Prussia. 1756–1765.
6860 Mitchell Papers. Vol. LVII. Miscellaneous English Correspondence, A–K.

209

35485 Correspondence of Sir Robert Keith, Minister at Saint Petersburg. May 1762–1774.

35493 Correspondence of Sir Robert Keith, Minister at Saint Petersburg. 1762.

32869 Newcastle Papers. Vol. CLXXXIV. General Correspondence. Nov. 11–Dec. 1756

(Including Prince Golitzyn's letters to the Duke of Newcastle, 1756–1762).

32933 Newcastle Papers. Vol. CCXLVII. General Correspondence. January 1–25, 1762.

32934 Newcastle Papers. Vol. CCXLIX. General Correspondence. January 26–February 2, 1762.

32935 Newcastle Papers. Vol. CCXLX. General Correspondence. February 2–March 20, 1762.

32936 Newcastle Papers. Vol. CCLI. General Correspondence. March 21–April 9, 1762.

32937 Newcastle Papers. Vol. CCLII. General Correspondence. April 10–30, 1762.

32938 Newcastle Papers. Vol. CCLIII. General Correspondence. May 1–25, 1762.

32939 Newcastle Papers. Vol. CCLIV. General Correspondence. May 25–June 20, 1762.

32940 Newcastle Papers. Vol. CCLV. General Correspondence. June 21 June–July 20, 1762.

32941 Newcastle Papers. Vol. CCLVI. General Correspondence. July 21–August 25, 1762.

France

Archives du Ministère des Affairs Étrangeres (AMAE)

Correspondance Politique, Russie (CP Russie)
Vols. 65–69. 1760—juli 1762.
Supplement 10. 1758–1762.

Correspondance Politique, Danemark (CP Danemark)
Vols. 146–148. janv. 1761–dec. 1762.

Correspondance Politique, Suède (CP Suède)
Vols. 240–242, janv. 1761–1763.

Mémoires et Documents, Russie (MD Russie)
Vols. V. Document 5. "Mémoire sur la Russie en 1757," par M. le Chevalier d'Édon.
VII. Document 5. "La Commerce de Russie sur la Period de 1728–1787."
IX. Document 2. "Mémoire historique (1748–1750) Concernant les differences de Le Russie et de la Suède depuis la conclusion du Traité de pais de Aix la Chapelle jusqu'à la fin de l'année 1750."
XI. Document 8. "Notice historique sur la Noblesse de Russie." Document 10. "Description politique de la Russie, servant à faire connaître l'État actual des force du Souverain, . . ."
XII. Document "Description politique de la Russie 1767."
XIII. Document 15. "État de l'Empire de Russie," par M. Brunet, 1772.
XVII. Document "Mémoire sur la commerce de la Russie," par M. Legenare, 1784.

Mémoires et Documents, Suède (AMAE MD Suéde)
Vol. XXXII. (1759–1772) Recueil de pieces originales concernant les dépenses de l'ambassade de France en Suède.

Mémoires et Documents, Prusse (AMAE MD Prusse)
Vol. LVIII. Mémoires diverses relatifs aux affaires de Prusse, de 1760 à 1763.

Mémoires et Documents, Angleterre (AMAE MD Angleterre)
Vol. LVIII. Copies de Correspondances echangées entre le duc de Choiseul et le prince Golitzin (1761).

Mémoires et Documents, Autriche (AMAE MD Autriche)
Vol. XL "Mémoires su l'État des Finances Autrichiennes (1762)."

Dossiers Individuels, Personnel (AMAE MD D)
Vol. XI. Baron Breteuil (1760–1783).
Rossignel (Jean-Baptiste Francais) (1749–1821).
Rulhière (Claude Carolman) (1772–1817).

Archives Nationales (AN)

Lettres d'agents divers.
B 7. Vol. 402. Analyse de la correspondance de Petersbourg (1756–1760).

Directoire Executif (Serie AF. III.) Vol. 431
Dossier 2462. "Lettre du Directoire au Ministre de la Police générale, le chargeant d'une enquête pour découvrir l'auteur du vol commis dans un dépot public d'un manuscrit concernant des détailes secrets la dernière révolution de Russe."

Germany
Oldenburg

Staatsarchiv
Depot 2. Gottorper Conseil.
No. 11. Compossessio. Danica. 1762.
Protocola (Conferenz). 1762.
Depot 4. Best. 2. Vedeturs des Geheimen Conseils de Anno 1762.
Depot 4. Best. 4. Depositum Gottorpianum III. Peter, Grossfürst.

Schleswig

Landesarchiv

Arkiv der adligen Güter Schierensee
Familien- und Privatpapiere der Gutsbesitzer Caspar v. Saldern (1752–1771).
703. Nachlassachen und Schulden des ausserordentlichen Kaiserlichen russischen Gesandten in Kopenhagen. N. v. Korff (1740–1768).
704. Schreiben Zar Peters III. an die Gesandten in Kopenhagen und Stockholm, so wie Vollmacht für Saldern zum Berliner Kongress. 1762.

Russia
Moscow

Biblioteka im. V. I. Lenina, rukopisnyi otdel (GBL)

Dissertations
Ageev, A. M. "Reformy 50-kh-60-kh gg. XVIII veka v russkoi artillerii." Leningrad, 1955.
Baranov, N. A. "Krest'iane monastyrskikh votchin nakanune sekuliarizatsii." Moscow, 1954.
Doroshenko, A. P. "Rabochaia sila v 1730–1760-e gody." Moscow. 1964.

Dzhanelidze, D. V. "Iranskii vopros vo vneshnei politike Rossii vtoroi poloviny XVIII veka (1747–1787 gg.) Tbilisi, 1955.

Istomina, E. G. "Novgorodskaia guberniia vo vtoroi polovine XVIII v. (Opyt istoricheskogo-geographicheskogo issledovaniia). Moscow, 1969.

Kozintseva, R.I. "Ocherki vneshnei torgovli i tamozhennoi politiki Rossii pervoi treti XVIII veka." Leningrad, 1963.

fond Panina (222)

XIX (2)Panin, gr, Petr Ivanovich. 1762. Zhurnal sekretnym raportam, ordenam, i soobshcheniiam pisannym v raznye mesta. Nachatom 1762 g. iiulia 5.
1. Raport Saltykovu Petru Semenovichu Fel'dmarshalu ot 1762 iiulia 5.
2. Soobshchenie Baumanu general-maioru ot 1762 g. iiul' 5.
XVII Ekaterina II. Zametki 1766–1767 gg.

fond Viazemy (64)

68/8 Chernyshev, gr. Petr Grigor'evich. Materialy, otnosiashchiesaia k diplomat-icheskoi deiatel'nosti Chernysheva Petra Grigor'evicha, gr. 1732–1762.

69/2 Chernyshev, gr. Petr Grigor'evich. Doneseniia, sviazannye s ego diplomat-icheskoi deiatel'nost'iu, k kantsleru Bestuzhevu-Riuminu, gr. Alekseiu Petrovichu i Vorontsovu, gr. Mikhailu Illarianovichu, Shuvalov, gr. Stepanu Ivanovichu, (Apraksinu) gr. Stepanu Fedorovichu i k dr. 1742–1762.

79/3 (Vorontsov, gr. Mikhail Illarionovich?) Zapiska, "Mémoire sur le commerce de Russie 26 de Juin 1761," ot neustanovlennago litsa.

82/75 Vorontsov, gr. Mikhail Illarionovich, Kantsler. Pis'ma k Chernyshevu, gr. Petru Grigor'evichu 1761 mai-dek.

Tsentral'nyi gosudarstvennyi arkhiv drevnikh aktov. (TsGADA)

fond kabineta Petra III (203)

1   Vnutrennye kollezheskie dela, doklady, reliatsii, raporty, rospisanii i vedo-mosti Petru III ianvar'-iiun'.

2   1762 genv.-iiul'. Pis'ma dukhovnykh, voennykh i statskikh rossiiskikh i inos-trannykh oboego pola . . . k tainomu pri Imperatore Petre III Sekretariu Volkovu o doneseniiakh i proz'bakh khodataistva ego k gosudariu povverennym im delam, . . .

3   Otpuski pisem tainago sekretaria Petra III Dmitriia Volkova raznym litsam 1762, fevral'-iiun'.

5   16 mart, 1762g. Kopiia s reskripta o poluchenii pis'ma ot Generala Livena ot 15 genvaria.

6   Reskript Petra III general-fel 'dtseikhmeisteru Vil'boa o posylke k nemu novago rospisaniia artilerii russkoi armii, nakhodiashcheisia za granitsei. Kopiia 1762g., 9 Fev.

11   Zapiski Braktorfa o peredache del Golshteinskoi kantseliarii tainomu sovet-niku fon Vol'fu, o pokupke u nego v kaznu mednogo zavoda . . . n.d.
17–51 Prosheniia.

fond Senata (248)

531   Reestr reshennym delam 1730 i 1731 kollegii ekonomii.
532   Reestr reshennym delam po kollegii ekonomii s 1734 po 1763 god.
3360–3379   Dela pravitel'stvuiushchego Senata do razdeleniia na departamenty (August 1761).
3383   Dela pravitel'stvuiushchego Senata do razdeleniia na departmenty po ka-mer kollegii (1762).
3396   Dela pravitel'stvuiushchego Senata do razdeleniia na departmenty po man-ufaktur kollegii (1762).
3397   Dela pravitel'stvuiushchego Senata do razdeleniia na departmenty po sol'-ianoi kontor (1762).

3405　　　Dela pravitel'stvuiushchego Senata po iustits kollegii (1762).
3426–3432　　Zhurnaly i protokoly pravitel'stvuiushchego Senata, gen.-iiunia 1762.

fond kollegii Ekonomii (280)
2052–2051　　avg. 1762–1763.

fond kommissii po sochinenii ulozheniia (342)
39–40　　O sostave komissii.
54　　O manufakturakh.
63　　I–II Proekt novogo ulozheniia.
64　　opis' 3 Doklady, mneniia i donosheniia komissii o raznykh predmetakh po gosudarstvennomu upravleniiu.
80　　Reglament po kotoromu postupat' v Sanktpeterburge glavnoi a v Moskve moskovskoi politseimeisterskikh kantseliariiam a v gubernatoram i voevodam Redaktsiia pervaia 1754.
89　　Bank dlia dvorianstva na departamenty po shtats kontoru i revizion kollegii (1762).
91 I–II　　1762 Prospekt i sochineniia komissii; proekty i sochineniia; komissi dlia razsmotreniia grazhdanskikh shtatov; shtaty.

fond gosudarstvennykh uchrezhdenii (370)
21–25　　Dela, kasaiushchikhsia do obrazovaniiu razlichnykh gosudarstvennykh uchrezhdenii, 1762.

fond Vorontsovykh (1261)
16　　Raport Leib gvardii, 1762.
47　　opis' 6 Razsuzhdenie o upadke kursa, chto kak onoi vosstanovit'.
44–56　　Dela kommerts-kollegii.
396　　Protokol o vypolnenie im. imp. ukaza ot 30 sent. 1757 goda o peredache upravleniia monastyrei otstavnym ober i shtab ofitseram i o poriadke vzimaniia i raspredeleniia poluchaemykh s eretikh dereven' dokhodov. Ekstrakt. Ne ranee 1760 g.
378　　Zametki Vorontsova, M. I. o pravakh dvorianstva ''Punkty k razsuzhdeniiu o vol'nosti dvorianstva'' chernovoi avtograf bez data v predelakh 1761–1762 gg.

Razriad III. Dela, otnosiashchiesia do vnutrennoi i vneshnei politiki Rossii
10, 14, 20　　Reskripty o perevorote Petra III.

Razriad IV. Perepiski lits imperatorskoi familii
110, 111, 1762　　Kopii pisem Petra III.

Razriad IX. Kabinet Petra I i ego prodolzhenie
43–44　　Ukazy Petra III.

Razriad XI. Perepiska raznykh lits
318　　Pis'ma I. I. Shuvalova D. Volkovu 1762. g.
751　　Doneseniia gr. I. Vorontsova Imperatoru Petru Tret'emu.
753　　Pis'mo gr. Petra Panina k gr. M. Vorontsovu 23 marta 1762 g.
835, 838, 839　　Bumagi Volkova.

Razriad XVI. Vnutrennee upravlenie
106　　Zapisnyia knigi bumag konferentsii uchrezhdennoi pri Dvore Imperatritsy Elizavety Petrovny 1762 gg. Ch I–III.
141　　Doneseniia v Konferentsiiu iz kantseliarii polkov Leib Gvardii 1757–1761 godov. Moscow, 1964.

St. Petersburg

Biblioteka im. M. E. Saltykova-Shchedrina

Fond Ermitazhnoe sobranie
116   Shcherbatov, Mikhail Mikhailovich, senator, prezident kamer kollegii. Materialy po vladimirskoi gubernii, predstavlennye M. M. Shcherbatovy vo vremiia ego obsledovaniia gubernii. 1785.

Arkhiv Instituta Istorii SSSR, Leningradskoe otdelenie (LOII)

Fond Vorontsovykh (36), opis' 1
91/855   Konferentsii s angliiskimi ministrami 1741–1763 gg.
95/107   Konferentsii s gollandskimi ministrami 1741–1762 gg.
97/108   Konferentsii s danskimi ministrami 1741–1763 gg.
99/656   Konferentsii s prusskimi ministrami 1741–1763 gg.
101/289   Konferentsii s frantsuzskimi ministrami 1741–1763 gg.
103/284   Konferentsii s shvedskimi ministrami 1741–1763 gg.
132/1178   Lettres au chancelier, relations et annexes 1762. g.
379/318   Trudy komissii po sostavleniiu novogo ulozheniia v 2-kh tt. T. I.
380/249   Trudy komissii po sostavleniiu novogo ulozheniia, T. II.
381/736   Reestr nakhodiashchikhsia v komissii o sochinenii proekta novogo ulozheniia (1730–1761 gg.).
382/569   Reestr punktam, otrazhennym v nakazakh deputatam v komissiiu novogo ulozheniia.
427/186   Ekstrakt iz protokolov komissii dlia rassmotreniia novosochinennogo lifliandskogo rytsarskikh i zemskikh prav ulozheniia.
550-1   Dela komissii o kommertsii.
562   O revenom o khlebov.
568   Materialy dlia istorii kommertsii.
596   Raznye instruktsii po tamozhennym dolzhnostiam 1760–1770 gg.
628   Upravlenie finansami voobshche XVIII v.
1060   Mneniia R. L. Vorontsova.
1060   Bumagi R. L. Vorontsova.
1070–77   Bumagi M. L. Vorontsova. I–VIII.
1081–1086   Perepiski Vorontsova, M. L. gr.
1108   Pis'ma kn. D. Golitzyna k gr. M. L. Vorontsovu 1759–1766 gg.

Sweden (Stockholm)

Riksarkivet (RAD)

Diplomatica Muscovitica (DM)
306. Bref till Kanslipresidenten från Baron Posse, July-Dec. 1761.
334. Bref till Baron Posse från Kanslipresidenten (Ekeblad), 1762.

Stavsundsarkivet
Smärre endkilda arkiv.
0029. [Ulrika].

Published Sources

Algarotti, Francesco, comte. *Brieven, behelzende een berigt aangaande den koophandel, de scheepvaart, inkomsten en krigsmagt van Rusland.* Harlingen, 1770.
Asseburg, A. F. Denkwürdigkeiten. Berlin, 1842.

Barsukov, A. P. *Rasskazy iz russkoi istorii 18 v. po arkivnym dokumentam.* St. Petersburg, 1885.

Bartenev, P., ed. *Arkhiv kn. Vorontsova.* 40 vols. Moscow, 1879–1895.

————. *Osmnadtsatyi vek, istoricheskii sbornik.* 4 vols. Moscow, 1896.

Beliavskii, M. T., ed. *Dvorianskaia imperiia 18 veka. Sbornik documentov.* Moscow, 1960.

Bolotov, A. T. *Zhizn' i prikliucheniia Andreia Bolotova: opisannye samim im dlia svoikh potomkov, 1738–1793.* Moscow, 1873.

Boutaric, E. *Correspondance secrete inédite de Louis XV: sur la politique étrangère.* 2 vols. Paris: H. Plon, 1866.

Broglie, Comte de. *Correspondance secrète du Comte de Broglie avec Louis XV (1756–1774).* 2 vols. Paris, 1956–1961.

"Bumagi kn. M. N. Volkonskogo," *Russkii arkhiv,* vol. 3 (1865), pp. 1030–80.

Catherine, Empress of Russia. *Sochineniia imperatritsy Ekateriny II,* vols. 1–12. Ed. R. N. Pypin. St. Petersburg, 1901–1907.

————. *Correspondence of Catherine the Great, when grand duchess, with Sir Charles Hanbury-Williams.* Ed. the Earl of Ilchester. London: Thornton Butterworth Ltd., 1928.

————. *Documents of Catherine the Great.* Ed. W. F. Reddaway. Cambridge: The University Press, 1931.

————. *Mémoires de l'impératrice Catherine II.* Ed. A. Herzen. London, 1859.

————. *Zapiski.* Ed. A. S. Suvorin. St. Petersburg, 1907.

Chebotarev, K. A. *Istoricheskoe i topograficheskoe opisanie gorodov moskovskoi gubernii s ikh uezdami s pribavleniem istoricheskogo svedeniia o nakhodiashchikhsia v Moskve soborakh, monastyriakh i znameniteishikh tserkvakh.* Moscow, 1787.

Choiseul, E. F. duc de. *Mémoires du duc de Choiseul, 1719–1785.* Paris, 1904.

Collyer, A., ed. *Despatches and Correspondence of John, Second Earl of Buckinghamshire, Ambassador to the Court of Catherine II of Russia, 1762–1765.* 2 vols. 1900.

Dashkova, E. R. *Zapiski kn. E. R. Dashkovoi.* London, 1859.

Derzhavin, G. R. *Zapiski, 1743–1812.* St. Petersburg, 1842.

"Diplomaticheskie dokumenty otnosiashchiesia k istorii Rossii 18 v. Doneseniia sekretaria saksonskogo posol'stva pri russkom dvore Petsol'da (ianv. 1742 g. po mar. 1744 g.)," *SIRIO,* vol. 6, pp. 387–506.

"Diplomaticheskaia perepiska angliiskikh poslov i poslannikov pri russkom dvore," *SIRIO,* vol. 12.

"Diplomaticheskie perepiski Ekateriny II, 1762–1766," *SIRIO,* vol. 48.

Dobrynin, G. *Istinnoe povestvovanie ili zhizn' Gavrila Dobrynina (pozhivshego 72 g. 2m. 20 dnei) im samim pisanniia v Moshleve i v Vitebske, 1752–1823.* St. Petersburg, 1872.

"Doneseniia grafa Mersi d'Arzhanto k Imperatritse Marii Terezii 1762 (Ian.–Iiulia)," *SIRIO,* vol. 18.

Engel'gardt, L., "Zapiski," *Russkii vestnik* (1859), kn. 1, pp. 255–78; kn. 2, pp. 619–73.

Frederick II, King of Prussia. *Politische Correspondenz Friedrich's des Grossen.* 46 vols. Berlin, 1879–1939. vols. 19–21.

Gilchrist. *An account of the great revolution in Russia and the death of Peter III.* London, 1762.

Goudar, A. *Mémoires pour servir à l'histoire de Pierre III.* Frankfurt, 1763.

Haxthausen, G. "Doneseniia datskogo poslannika gr. Gakstgauzena o tsarstvovanii Petra III i perevorote 1762 goda," per. N. A. Belevoi, *Russkaia starina* vol. 158 (1914), pp. 539–47; vol. 160 (1914), pp. 70–80; vol. 161 (1915), pp. 274–82; (mar.), pp. 532–47; vol. 162 (1915), pp. 33–39; (mai), pp. 295–98; vol. 164 (1915), pp. 359–63; vol. 169 (1917), pp. 105–15; 160 (okt. 1914), pp. 70–80; (noiab.), pp. 262–83.

Iaroslavl'. *Trudy uchenoi arkhivnoi komissii iaroslavskoi gubernii.* Iaroslavl', 1889–1909.

"Iz dnevnika namestnika Ekebliada, Geteborg, 1762 g.," *Chteniia v Obshchestve istorii i drevnostei rossiiskikh [COIDR],* vol. 112, pp. 1–4.

Khrapovitskii, A. V. *Iz bumag Khrapovitskogo.* St. Petersburg, 1911.

Latkin, V. N. *Proekt novogo ulozheniia sostavlennyi zakonodatel'noi kommissiei 1754–1766 gg.* (*Chast' III 'o sostoianie poddanykh voobshche'*). St. Petersburg, 1893.

Laveaux, J. C. Thiebault. *Histoire de Pierre III.* Vols. 1–3. Paris, 1799.

Lepekhin, I. I. *Dnevnye zapiski puteshestviia doktora i Akademii Nauk ad'junkta Ivana Lepekhina po raznym provintsiiam rossiiskogo gosudarstva.* St. Petersburg, 1771–1805.

Longinov, M. N., "Svedeniia ob ofitserakh konnoi gvardii v iiune mesiatse 1762 goda," *Russkii arkhiv* (1867), pp. 481–86.

Martens, F. *Sobranie traktov i konventsii, zakliuchennykh Rossieiu s inostrannymi derzhavami.* Vols. 1, 5, 9, 13. St. Petersburg, 1874–1902.

Materialy dlia istorii goroda XVII i XVIII stoletii. Borovsk. Moscow, 1888. *Belevsk* Moscow, 1885. *Irkutsk.* Moscow, 1883. *Maloiaroslavets.* Moscow, 1881. *Morotets.* Moscow, 1883. *Pereslav' Zalesk.* Moscow, 1884. *Riazan'.* Moscow, 1884. *Rostov.* Moscow, 1888. *Sibirsk gorod.* Moscow, 1886. *Tobolsk.* Moscow, 1885. *Tula.* Moscow, 1884. *Uglich.* Moscow, 1887. *Ustiug Veliki.* Moscow, 1883. *Zaraisk.* Moscow, 1883.

Materialy dlia istorii dvorian Tverskoi gubernii. Tver', 1912.

Materialy dlia istorii raskola za pervoe vremia ego sushchestvovaniia. Moscow, 1874–85.

Münnich, B. von. *Ébauche pour donner une Idée de la forme du Gouvernement de l'Empire de Russie,* in *"Ébauche" du Gouvernement de l'Empire de Russie.* Riga, 1774; republished Paris: Librairie Droz S. A., 1989.

"Mnenie byvshogo imperatora Petra III-go poslannoe im v Sv. Sinod," *Russkii arkhiv,* 9 (1871), p. 2055.

Moskovskie vedomosti. Moscow, 1750–65.

Nastavlenie ekonomicheskim pravleniiam. St. Petersburg, April 4, 1771.

Nepliuev, I. I. *Zapiski, 1693–1773.* St. Petersburg, 1893; republished Newtonville, Mass.: Oriental Research Partners, 1974.

Nizhegorod. *Deistviia uchenoi arkhivnoi komissii nizhegorodskoi gubernii.* I–XV. Nizhegorod, 1887–1916.

"O memuarakh gertsoga Karla Frederikha, ottsa imp. Petra III," *SIRIO,* vol. 1.

Orenburg. *Trudy orenburgskoi uchenoi arkhivnoi komissii.* Orenburg, 1889–1917.

Pallas, P. S. *Puteshestvie po raznym provintsiiam.* St. Petersburg, 1773–88.

"Perepiski Imperatritsy Ekateriny s Korolem Fridrikhom II," *SIRIO,* vol. 20.

Pis'ma Ekateriny II—A. V. Olsuf'evu, 1763–1783," *Russkii arkhiv,* No. 2 (1863), pp. 391–470.

"Pis'ma Ekateriny II—N.I. Paninu," *COIDR,* vol. 45, pt. 2, pp. 1–160.

"Pis'mo I. I. Shuvalova k kn. G. G. Orlovu," *COIDR,* vol. 40, pt. 2, pp. 169–70.

"Pis'mo kn. E. R. Dashkovoi k imperatritse Ekaterine II," *COIDR,* vol. 15, pt. 2, p. 171.

Poleznoe uveselenie. St. Petersburg, 1762.

Polnoe sobranie postanovlenii i rasporiazhenii po vedomstvu pravoslavnago ispovedaniia tsarstvovaniia Elizavety Petrovny, 1753–1762, vol. 4. St. Petersburg, 1912.

Polnoe sobranie zakonov Rossiiskoi imperii, 1649–1913. 234 vols. St. Petersburg, 1830–1916.

Potemkin, G. *Memoirs.* London, 1813.

"Protokoly konferentsii pri vysochaishem dvore, 1756–1762, 14 mar. 1756–13 mar. 1757." Ed. N. D. Chechulin. *SIRIO,* vol. 136.

Pskov. *Sbornik pskovskoi gubernskoi uchenoi arkhivnoi komissii.* Pskov, 1917.

Recueil des instructions données aux ambassadeurs et ministres de France depuis les traités de Westphalie jusqu'à la Révolution française. Vol. 1. Paris, 1890.

Riazan. *Trudy riazanskoi gubernskoi uchenoi arkhivnoi komissii.* Riazan, 1909–13.

Rudakov, S. A. "D. V. Volkov 1772–1776 gg," *Russkaia starina,* vol. 18 (mar. 1877), p. 576; "1718–1785," vol. 11 (noia. 1874), pp. 478–96; vol. 9 (ian. 1874), pp. 163–74.

Rulhière, C. C. de. *Histoire ou anecdotes sur la révolution de Russie en 1762.* Paris, 1797.

Rukovodstvennye dlia pravoslavnogo dukhovenstva Sv. Pravoslavnogo Sinoda 1721–1878. Moscow, 1879.

Saldern, Caspar von. *Histoire de la vie de Pierre III, Empereur de Russie.* Paris, 1802.

Sankt-Peterburgskie vedomosti. St. Petersburg, 1759–66.

[Schwan, C. F.] M. de la Marche. *Histoire et anecdotes de la vie, du regne, du détrônement et de la mort de Pierre III, dernier Empereur de toutes les Russes, écrites en forme de lettres.* London, 1766.

Semiletniaia voina. Materialy o deistviiakh russkoi armii i flota. Moscow, 1948.

Senatskii arkhiv. Vol. 14. St. Petersburg, 1883–1913.

Shakhovskoi, Ia. P. *Zapiski.* St. Petersburg, 1887.

Sobranie luchshikh sochinenii k rasprostranneniu znaniia k proizvedeniiu udovol'stviia im smeshannaia biblioteka o raznykh fizicheskikh, ekonomicheskikh, takozh do manufactur i do kommertsi prinadlezhashchikh veshchakh. Moscow, 1762.

Staehlin, J. "Zapiski Shtelina ob Imperatore Petre III," *COIDR* (1866), bk. 3, pp. 67–118.

Topograficheskiia izvestiia sluzhashchiia dlia polnogo geograficheskogo opisaniia russkoi imperii. St. Petersburg, 1771–1774.

Topograficheskoe opisanie goroda Kazani i ego uezda. Moscow, 1788. *Iaroslavl'.* Iaroslavl', 1794. *Kaluzhskogo namestnichestva.* Kaluga, 1785. *Kurskogo namestnichestva.* Moscow, 1788. *Khar'kovskogo namestnichestva.* Moscow, 1788. *Voronezhskoi gubernii.* Voronezh, 1800. *Viatka.*

Trudy viatskoi gubernskoi uchenoi arkhivnoi komissii. Viatka, 1905–17.

Trudy vladimirskoi gubernoi uchenoi arkhivnoi komissii. Vladimir, 1899–1918.

Vedel, Peter, ed. *En Brevvexling mellem grev Johan Hartvig Ernst Bernstorff og Hertugen af Choiseul, 1758–66.* Copenhagen, 1871.

Volkov, D. V. "Pis'mo D. V. Volkova k G. G. Orlovu, Iulia 10-go 1762 g.," *Russkaia starina,* vol. 11 (St. Petersburg, 1874), pp. 478–496.

"Vypiska o gosudarstvennykh uchrezhdeniiakh sdelannykh imp. Ekateriny II s 1762 po 1769 god vkliuchitel'no," *SIRIO,* vol. 3, pp. 275–283.

Yorke, C. *Earl of Hardwicke.* Vol. 3. Cambridge, 1913.

Zhukovich, P. N. "Soslovnyi sostav naseleniia zapadnoi Rossii v tsarstvovanie Ekateriny II, 1) Dvorianstvo vostochnoi Belorussii," *Zhurnal ministerstva narodnogo prosvesheniia* (ian. 1915), pp. 76–109.

Zuev, V. F. *Puteshestvennye zapiski V. Zueva ot Skt. Peterburga do Khersona v 1781 i 1782 gg.* St. Petersburg, 1787.

Secondary Works

Absoliutizm v Rossii XVII–XVIII vv. Sbornik statei. Moscow, 1964.

Alefirenko, P. K. *Krest'ianskoe dvizhenie i krest'ianskii vopros v 30-kh-50-kh godakh XVIII veka.* Moscow, 1958.

Aleksandrenko, V. N. *Russkie diplomaticheskie agenty v Londone v XVIII v.* Warsaw, 1897.

Alexander, J. T. "Catherine II, Bubonic Plague, and the Problem of Industry in Moscow," *American Historical Review,* vol. 79 (June 1974), pp. 637–71.

———. *Catherine the Great: Life and Legend.* New York: Oxford University Press, 1989.

Amburger, E. *Geschichte der Behördenorganisation Russlands von Peter dem Grossen bis 1917.* Leiden, 1966.

———. *Russland und Schweden 1762–1772.* Berlin, 1934.

Antonov, A. *Pervyi kadetskii korpus.* St. Petersburg, 1906.

Appleby, J. O, *Economic Thought and Ideology in Seventeenth-Century England,* Princeton: Princeton University Press, 1978.

Augustine, W. "Notes Toward a Portrait of the Eighteenth-Century Russian Nobility, *Canadian-American Slavic Studies,* vol. 4, no. 3 (1970), pp. 373–425.

Bain, R. N. *Peter III, Emperor of Russia: The Story of a Crisis and a Crime.* Westminster, England, 1902.

Balitskii, G. *Perevorot 1762 goda.* Moscow, 1909.

Barsov, T. V. *Sinodal'nyia uchrezhdeniia prezhnego vremeni.* St. Petersburg, 1897.
Barsukov, A. P. "Kniaz' Grigorii Grigorevich Orlov," *Russkii arkhiv,* vol. 10, no. 2 (1873), p. 2073.
Bartlett, R. P., A. G. Cross, and Karen Rasmussen, eds. *Russia and the World of the Eighteenth Century: Proceedings of the Third International Conference organized by the Study Group on Eighteenth-Century Russia and held at Indiana University at Bloomington, USA, September 1984.* Columbus, Ohio: Slavica Publishers, 1986.
Beliavskii, M. T. "Trebovaniia dvorian i perestroika organov upravleniia i suda na mestakh 1775 g," *Nauchnye doklady vysshei shkoly, Istoricheskie nauki,* no. 4 (1960), pp. 125–43.
Berkov, P. N. *Istoriia russkoi zhurnalistiki XVIII veka.* Moscow, 1952.
Beskrovnyi, L. G. *Russkaia armiia i flot v XVIII veka.* Moscow, 1858.
———. *Ocherki voennoi istoriografii Rossii.* Moscow, 1962.
Bil'basov, V. A. *Istoriia Ekateriny Vtoroi,* vols. 1–2. Berlin, 1900.
Blinov, I. *Gubernatory. Istoriko-iuridicheskii ocherk.* St. Petersburg, 1905.
Blum, J. *The End of the Old Order in Rural Europe.* Princeton: Princeton University Press, 1978.
———. *Lord and Peasant in Russia from the Ninth to the Nineteenth Century.* Princeton: Princeton University Press, 1961.
Blum, K. L. *Ein Russischer Staatsmann: Denkwürdigkeiten des Grafen J. J. Sievers.* 3 vols. Leipzig, 1857.
Bochkarev, V. N. "Ekonomicheskii stroi i sotsial'naia struktura nizhegorodskogo kraia v XVIII veka," *Trudy nizhegorodskogo nauchnogo obshchestva po izucheniiu mestnogo kraia, razdel istorii,* vol. 1 (1926).
Bogoslovskii, M. *Byt' i nravy russkogo dvorianstva v pervoi polovine XVII v.* Moscow, 1906.
———. *Istoriia Rossii XVIII veka, 1725–1796.* Moscow, 1915.
Borisov, A. M. "Krizis tserkovnogo i monastyrskogo zemlevladeniia khoziastva v 40-kh i 60-kh godakh XVIII v.," *Istoriia SSSR* (1968), pp. 142–51.
Borovoi, S. Ia. "Banki v Rossii v pervykh desiatiletiiakh sushchestvovaniia," *Sbornik trudov odessogo kreditnoekonomicheskogo instituta,* vol. 1 (Odessa, 1940), pp. 35–49.
———. *Kredit i banki Rossii (seredina XVII v.–1861 g.).* Moscow, 1958.
———. "Voprosy kreditovaniia torgovli i promyshlennosti v ekonomicheskoi politike Rossii XVIII v.," *Istoricheskie zapiski,* vol. 33 (1950), pp. 93–122.
Brennan, J. F. *Enlightened Despotism in Russia: The Reign of Elisabeth 1741–1762.* New York: Peter Lang Publishing, Inc., 1987.
Brückner, A. *Istoriia Ekateriny Vtoroi.* 3 vols. St. Petersburg, 1885.
Bulygin, I. A. "Tserkovnaia reforma Petra I," *Voprosy istorii,* vol. 5 (1974), pp. 79–93.
———. *Monastyrskie krest'iane Rossii v pervoi chetverti XVIII veka.* Moscow, 1977.
Butkov, D. A. *Istoriia finansov SSSR (Finansy rossiiskoi imperii v XVIII i pervoi poloviny XIX stoletii).* Moscow, 1944.
Castera, J. J. *The Life of Catherine II of Russia.* Trans. W. Tooke. London, 1799.
Chechulin, N. D. "Cherty iz zhizni russkikh dvorian v kontse XVIII veka," *Moskovskii nabliudatel'* (1836), pp. 133–45.
———. *Ekaterina II v bor'be za prestol.* Leningrad, 1924.
———. *Russkoe provintsial'noe obshchestvo vo vtoroi polovine XVIII veka.* St. Petersburg, 1896.
———. *Vneshniaia politika Rossii v nachale tsarstvovaniia Ekateriny II, 1762–1774.* St. Petersburg, 1896.
Chulkov, M. *Istoricheskoe opisanie rossiiskoi kommertsii pri vsekh portakh i granitsakh ot drevnikh vremen do nyne nastoiashchego i vsekh preimushchestvennykh uzakonenii po inoi gosudaria imperatora Petra Velikago i nyne blagopoluchnoi tsarstvuiushchei godusaryni imperatritsy Ekateriny Velikoi.* 7 vols. St. Petersburg, 1781–1788.
Confino, M. *Domaines et seigneurs en Russie vers la fin du XVIII siècle: étude de structures agraires et mentalités économiques.* Paris, 1963.

————. *Systèmes agraires et progrès agricole: L'assolement triennal en Russie aux XVIII-XIX siècles.* Paris, 1969.

Corbett, J. *England in the Seven Years' War; A Study in Combined Strategy,* vols. 1–2. London, 1907.

Crummey, R. "Russian Absolutism and the Nobility," *Journal of Modern History,* vol. 49, no. 3 (1977), pp. 456–68.

Dassow, J. von. *Friedrich II. von Preussen und Peter III. von Russland.* Berlin, 1908.

Dirin, P. *Istoriia Leib Gvardii Semenovskogo polka.* St. Petersburg, 1883.

Ditiatin, I. I. *Ustroistvo i upravlenie gorodov Rossii. I. Goroda Rossii v XVIII stoletie.* St. Petersburg, 1875.

Dmitrev, A. *Petr I i tserkov'.* Moscow-Leningrad, 1931.

Dobrotvorskii, N. "Narodnoe predanie ob osvobozhdenii krest'ian iz monastyrskoi nevoli," *Russkii arkhiv,* no. 6 (1887), pp. 483–92.

Dorn, W. L. "Frederick the Great and Lord Bute," *Journal of Modern History,* vol. 1 (1929), pp. 529–60.

Dovnar-Zapolskii, M. V. *Materialy dlia istorii votchinnogo upravleniia v Rossii.* Moscow, 1903–1910.

Dukes, P. *Catherine the Great and the Russian Nobility: A Study Based on the Materials of the Legislative Commission of 1767.* London, 1967.

Ekaterina II. "Bumagi Ekateriny II o monastyrskikh imeniiakh," *Russkii arkhiv,* vol. 3 (1865), p. 479.

Epstein, E. *Les banques de commerce russes.* Paris, 1925.

Eshevskii, S. V. *Sochineniia po russkoi istorii.* Moscow, 1900.

Fagniez, G. "Les antécédents de l'alliance Franco-Russe, 1741–1762," *Revue Hebdomadaire* (1916), pp. 316–38.

Filippov, A. N. *Istoriia Senata v pravlenie Verkhovnogo tainogo sovieta i Kabineta: Chast' I. Senat v pravlenie Verkhovnogo tainogo sovieta.* Iur'ev, 1895.

————. "K voprosu o pervoistochnikakh 'zhalovannoi gramoty dvorianstva.' " *Izvestiia Akademii Nauk SSSR,* vol. 20 (6th series; 1926), pp. 423–44, 479–98.

————. *Pravitel'stvuiushchii senat pri Petre Velikom i ego blizhaishikh preemnikakh (1711–1741).* St. Petersburg, 1911.

Firsov, N. N. "Petr III i Ekaterina II—Pervye gody ee tsarstvovaniia," in *Istoricheskie ocherki i eskizy 1890–1922 gg.,* 2 vols. (Kazan, 1922), vol. 2, pp. 43–98.

————. "Pravitel'stvo i obshchestvo v ikh otnosheniiakh k vneshnei torgovli Rossii v tsarstvovanie Ekateriny II," *Uchenye zapiski kazanskogo universiteta,* vol. 68 (Kazan, 1901), pp. 195–212.

Fleischhacker, H. "Porträt Peters III," *Jahrbücher für Geschichte Osteuropas,* vol. 5 (1957), pp. 127–89.

Florovskii, A. V. "K istorii teksta zhalovannoi gramoty dvorianstvu 1785 g," *Russkii istoricheskii zhurnal,* nos. 3–4 (1917), pp. 186–94.

Florovskii, A. V. *Sostav zakonodatel'noi kommissii 1767 g.* Odessa, 1915.

Forster, R. "The Nobility of Toulouse in the Eighteenth Century, a Social and Economic Study," *John Hopkins University Studies in Historical and Political Sciences* (series 173, no. 1), Baltimore, Md., 1960.

Foust, C. *Muscovite and Mandarin: Russia's Trade with China and Its Setting, 1727–1805.* Chapel Hill: University of North Carolina Press, 1969.

Freeze, G. *The Russian Levites: Parish Clergy in the Eighteenth Century.* Cambridge, Mass: Harvard University Press, 1977.

————. "The Soslovie (Estate) Paradigm and Russian Social History," *American Historical Review,* vol. 91, no. 1 (Feb., 1986), pp. 11–36.

Friis, A. "Bernstorff og Moltke under Krisen 1762. En kritisk undersgelse," *Historick Tidsskrift.* vol. 1 (1918–1920), pp. 317–54.

Friis, A., ed. *Bernstorffske Papirer.* Copenhagen, 1907.

Gattenburg, K. "Vliianie russkogo zakonodatel'stva na proizvoditel'nost' torgovogo bankovago kredita," *Protokoly zasedanii imperatorskogo Khar'kovskogo universiteta*, no. 9 (Khar'kov, 1870), pp. 1–13.

Gerhard, D. *England und der Aufstief Russlands.* Munich, 1933.

Glasenapp, I. *Staat, Gesellschaft und opposition im Zeitalter Katharinas der Grossen.* Munich, 1964.

Gleason, W. *Moral Idealists, Bureaucracy, and Catherine the Great.* New Brunswick, N.J.: Rutgers University Press, 1981.

Golikova, N. B. *Naemnyi trud v gorodakh povolzh'ia v pervoi chetverti XVIII veka.* Moscow, 1965.

Goodwin, A. *The European Nobility in the Eighteenth Century.* London, 1953.

Gorchakov, M. *Monastyrskii prikaz.* St. Petersburg, 1868.

————. *Retsentsiia na sochinenie Zav'ialova "Vopros o tserkovnykh imeniiakh pri imperatritse Ekateriny II."* St. Petersburg, 1904.

Got'e, Iu. V. *Istoriia oblastnogo upravleniia v Rossii ot Petra I do Ekateriny II.* 2 vols. Moscow, 1913, 1941.

————. *Ocherk istorii zemlevladeniia v Rossii.* Sergiev Posad, 1915.

————. "Pervyi nabrosok ekaterinskoi administrativnoi reformy (proekt kn. Ia. P. Shakhovskogo 1763 g.)," *Pone,* no. 90 (1929), pp. 172–80.

Gradovskii, A. D. *Vysshaia administratsiia Rossii XVIII v. i general prokurory.* St. Petersburg, 1866.

Grekov, B. D. "Opyt khoziaistvennykh anket XVIII veka," *Letopis' zaniatii arkheograficheskoi komissii,* vol. 35 (1927–28), pp. 39–104.

Grifffiths, D. "Catherine II: The Republican Empress," *Jahrbücher für Geschichte Osteuropas,* vol. 21 (1973), pp. 323–44.

————. "Russian Court Politics and the Question of an Expansionist Foreign Policy under Catherine II, 1762–1783." Ph.D. diss., Cornell University, 1967.

————. "The Rise and Fall of the Northern System: Court Politics and Foreign Policy in the First Half of Catherine II's Reign," *Canadian-American Slavic Studies,* vol. 4, no. 3 (1970), pp. 547–69.

Grunwald, C. de. *Trois siècles de diplomatie russe.* Paris, 1945.

Gukovskii, G. *Ocherki po istorii russkoi literatury XVIII veka, dvorianskaia fronda v literature 1750kh–1760kh godov.* Moscow, 1936.

Hassel, James. "Implementation of the Russian Table of Ranks during the Eighteenth Century," *Slavic Review,* vol. 29, no. 2 (June 1970), pp. 283–95.

Helbig, G. *Biographie. Peter des Dritten.* Vols. 1–2. Tübingen, 1808.

————. "Primechaniia k knige: russkie izbranniki i sluchainye liudi," *Russkaia starina* (July 1886), pp. 8–9, 74–99.

————. *Russkie izbranniki.* Berlin, 1900.

Hildebrand, K. "Foreign Markets for Swedish Iron in the Eighteenth Century," *Scandinavian Economic History Review,* vol. 6, no. 1 (1958), pp. 3–52.

Horn, A. E. *A History of Banking in All the Leading Nations.* New York, 1896.

Horn, D. B. *Sir Charles Hanbury-Williams and European Diplomacy 1747–1758.* London, 1930.

Humphreys, L. "The Vorontsov family: Russian nobility in a century of change, 1725–1825." Photocopy. Ann Arbor, Mich., 1969.

Iablochkov, M. *Istoriia dvorianskogo sosloviia v Rossii.* St. Petersburg, 1876.

Iakovtsevskii, V. N. *Kupecheskii kapital i feodal'no-krepostnoi Rossii.* Moscow, 1953.

Iavorskii, F. *Petr III, ego durachestva, liubovnyia pokhozhdeniia i konchina.* London, 1896.

Ikonnikov, V. S. "Pavel Koniushkevich, mitropolit Tobol'skii 1758–1768 gg. zametki po povodu novykh o nem materialov," *Russkaia starina,* vol. 73 (March 1892), pp. 697–705.

Islev, G. S. *Rol' tekstil'noi promyshlennosti v genezise i razvitii kapitalizma v Rossii 1760–1860.* Leningrad, 1970.

"Istoricheskie materialy o tserkvakh i selakh XVI-XVIII vv.," *COIDR*, vol. 129, pp. 161–220; vol. 132, pp. 80–161; vol 150, pp. 1–244, 161–284; vol. 167, pp. 1–166; vol. 179, pp. 1–94; vol. 181, pp. 1–80, 95–188; vol. 196, pp. 1–160; vol 238, pp. 123–336; vol 245, pp. 337–80.

Istoricheskoe obozrenie Leib-gvardii Izmailovskogo polka. n.p., n.d.

Istoriko-statisticheskiia svedeniia S.-Peterburgskoi eparkhii. St. Petersburg, 1878.

Ivanow, P. "Zur Frage des 'aufgeklärten Absolutismus' der 60er Jahre des 18. Jahrhunderts in Russland," *Zur Periodisierung des Feudalismus und Kapitalismus in der geschichtlichen Entwicklung der UdSSR*. Edited by K. Wädekin. Berlin, 1952, pp. 208–30.

Jones, Robert E. "Opposition to War and Expansion in Late Eighteenth Century Russia," *Jahrbücher für Geschichte Osteuropas*, vol. 32 (1984), pp. 34–51.

————. *The Emancipation of the Russian Nobility, 1762–1785*. Princeton: Princeton University Press, 1973.

Kabuzan, V. M. *Narodonaselenie Rossii XVIII–pervoi polovine XIX v*. Moscow, 1963.

————. *Izmeneniia v razmeshchenii naseleniia Rossii v XVIII—pervoi polovine XIX v*. Moscow, 1971.

Kafengauz, B. B. *Istoriia khoziaistva Demidovykh v XVII–XIX vv*. I. Moscow-Leningrad, 1949.

————. *Ocherki vnutrennego rynka Rossii pervoi poloviny XVIII veka (po materialam vnutrennikh tamozhen)*. Moscow, 1958.

Kahan, A. "Continuity in Economic Activity and Policy during the post-Petrine Period in Russia," *Journal of Economic History*, vol. 25 (March 1965), pp. 61–85.

————. "The Costs of Westernization in Russia: The Gentry and the Economy in the Eighteenth Century," *Slavic Review*, vol. 25, no. 1 (March 1966), pp. 40–66.

————. "Enterpreneurship in the Early Development of Iron Manufacturing in Russia," *Economic Development and Cultural Change*, vol. 10 (July 1962), pp. 395–422.

————. *The Plow, the Hammer and the Knout: An Economic History of Eighteenth-Century Russia*, with the editorial assistance of R. Hellie. Chicago: University of Chicago Press, 1985.

Kaidanov, N. *Sistematicheskii katalog delam gosudarstvennoi kommerts-kollegii*. St. Petersburg, 1886.

Kalachev, N. *Materialy dlia istorii russkogo dvorianstva*. Vols. 1–2. St. Petersburg, 1885.

Kalashnikov, S. V. *Alfavitnyi ukazatel' deistvuiushchikh i rukovodstvennykh kanonicheskikh postanovlenii Sinoda*. Kharkov', 1896.

Kam, A. "Tsarskaia diplomatiia i bor'ba partii v Shvetsii na iskhode 'ery svobody' (60-e-nachalo 70-kh gg. XVIII v.)," in *Skandinavskii sbornik*, vol. 6 (Tallin, 1963).

Kaplan, H. H. *Russia at the Outbreak of the Seven Years' War*. Berkeley: University of California Press, 1968.

Kapterev, L. M. *Dubinshchina. Ocherk po istorii vosstaniia Dalmatovskikh monastyrskikh krest'ian v XVIII veka*. Mosco, 1929.

Karamzin, N. M. *Karamzin's Memoir on Ancient and Modern Russia*. Trans. and ed. R. Pipes. Cambridge, MA: Harvard University Press, 1959).

Karataev, N. K. *Ocherki po istorii ekonomicheskikh nauk v Rossii XVIII veka*. Moscow, 1960.

Karnovich, E. P. *Zamechatel'nyia bogatstva chastnykh lits v Rossii, ekonomichesko-istoricheskoe izsledovanie*. St. Petersburg, 1874.

Kartashev, A. V. *Ocherki po istorii russkoi tserkvi*. Paris, 1959.

Kaufman, I. I. *K izuchenii o den'gakh i kredite*. Khar'kov, 1868.

Kazanskii, P. *Istoriia pravoslavnogo russkogo monashestva*. Moscow, 1855.

Kellenbenz, H. "The Economic Significance of the Archangel Route (from the late 16th to the late 18th Century)," *Journal of European Economic History*, vol. 2, no. 3 (1973), pp. 541–81.

Kent, H. S. K. *War and Trade in the Northern Seas: Anglo-Scandinavian economic relations in the mid-eighteenth century*. Cambridge: Cambridge University Press, 1973.

Kirchner, W. *Commercial Relations between Russia and Europe, 1400–1800: Collected Essays.* Bloomington: Indiana University Press, 1966.
Kizevetter, A. A. *Posadskaia obshchina v Rossii XVIII st.* Moscow, 1903.
———. *Iz istorii zakonodatel'stva v Rossii.* Paramonov, 1904.
———. *Russkoe obshchestvo v vosemnadtsatom veke.* Rostov-na-Donu, 1904.
———. *Gorodovoe polozhenie Ekateriny II 1785 g.* Moscow, 1909.
———. *Istoricheskie ocherki.* Moscow, 1912.
———. *Mestnoe upravlenie v Rossii IX–XIX st. Istoricheskii ocherk.* Prague, 1917.
Kliuchevskii, V. O. *Istoriia soslovii v Rossii.* Moscow, 1914.
———. "Kurs russkoi istorii," in *Sochineniia,* vols. 4–5 (Moscow, 1957).
Klochkov, M. V. "Rossiia, Avstriia i Prussiia v seredine XVIII v., "*Istoricheskii vestnik,* no. 3 (1915), pp. 839–55.
Klokman, Iu. P. *Ocherki sotsial'no-ekonomicheskoi istorii gorodov severo-zapada Rossii v seredine XVIII v.* Moscow, 1960.
———. *Sotsial'no-ekonomicheskaia istoriia russkogo goroda. Vtoraia polovina XVIII veka.* Moscow, 1967.
Klöse, O. *Die Herzogtümer im Gesamtstaat, 1721–1830.* Kiel, 1960.
Knoppers, J. *Dutch Trade with Russia from the Time of Peter I to Alexander I: A Quantitative Study in Eighteenth Century Shipping.* Montreal: Interuniversity Centre for European Studies, 1976.
Kondrashenkov, A. "Vosstanie monastyrskikh krest'ian v Isetskom provintsii v 60-kh XVIII v.," *Uchenye zapiski kurganskogo pedagogicheskogo instituta* (Kurgan, 1959), pp. 135–76.
Korf, Baron S. A. *Dvorianstvo i ego soslovnoe upravlenie za stoletie 1762–1855 godov.* St. Petersburg, 1906.
Korsakov, D. A. *Iz zhizni russkikh deiatelei XVIII veka.* Kazan, 1891.
Krumm, J. *Der schleswig-holsteinische-dänische Gesamtstaat des 18. Jahrhunderts.* Gluckstadt Augustin, 1934.
Kulisher, I. M. *Ocherk istorii russkoi promyshlennosti.* Petrograd, 1922.
———. *Ocherk istorii russkoi torgovli.* Peterburg, 1928.
A. Kulomzin, "Gosudarstvennye dokhody i raskhody v tsarstvovanie Ekateriny II, 1763–1773," *SIRIO,* vol. 5 (1870), pp. 219–294.
Kurakin, J. A. *Le dix-huitième siècle: des documents historiques en français et en russe.* Moscow, 1904.
Lamanskii, E. I. *Istoricheskii ocherk denezhnago obrashcheniia v Rossii s 1650–1817.* n.p., n.d.
Lariviere, Charles de. *La France et la Russie au XVIIIe siècle.* Paris, 1909.
Le Donne, J. P. *Absolutism and Ruling Class: The Formation of the Russian Political Order, 1700–1825.* New York: Oxford University Press, 1991.
———. *Ruling Russia. Politics and Administration in the Age of Absolutism, 1762–1796.* Princeton: Princeton University Press, 1984.
———. "Police Reform in Russia: A Project of 1762," *Cahiers du Monde russe et soviétique,* vol. 32, no. 2 (Apr.–June 1991), pp. 249–74.
Leonard, C. "The Reputation of Peter III," *Russian Review,* vol. 47 (1988), pp. 263–92.
Liano, A. "Gosudarstvennyi finansovyi kontrol' v tsarskoi Rossii," *Sovetskie finansy,* no. 607 (Moscow, 1945), pp. 31–36.
Liubinetskii, N. A. *Zemlevladenie tserkvei i monastyrei rossiiskoi imperii.* St. Petersburg, 1900.
Liubomirov, P. G. *Ocherki po istorii russkoi promyshlennosti.* Moscow, 1947.
Liutsh, A., et al. *Itogi XVIII veki v Rossii.* Moscow, 1910.
Lodyzhenskii, K. *Istoriia russkogo tamozhennogo tarifa.* St. Petersburg, 1886.
———. *Ocherki po istorii tamozhennoi politiki.* St. Petersburg, 1903.
Longinov, M. N. "Eshche neskol'ko izvestii o pervykh posobnikakh Ekateriny II-i." *Russkii arkhiv,* vol. 8 (1870), pp. 965–69.

Lukin, I. F. "Zhizn' starinnogo russkogo dvorianina," *Russkii arkhiv*, vol. 3, no. 8 (1865).

Luzanov, P. *Shliakhetnyi kadetskii korpus (nyne 1-i kadetskii korpus) pri grafe Minikhe*. St. Petersburg, 1907.

de Madariaga, I. *Russia in the Age of Catherine the Great*. New Haven, Conn.: Yale University Press, 1981.

Maksimov, S. *Rasskazy is istorii starobriadchestva po raskol'nich'im rukopisiam*. St. Petersburg, 1861.

Mediger, W. *Moskaus Weg nach Europa*. Braunschweig, 1952.

Mel'gunov, P. P. *Ocherki po istorii russkoi torgovle IX–XVIII vv.* Moscow, 1905.

——— . *Religiozno-obshchestvennye dvizheniia XVII–XVIII vv. v. Rossii*. Moscow, 1922.

Mel'gunov, S. P. *Moskva i staraia vera*. (*Ocherk iz istorii religiozno-obshchestvennykh dvizhenii na rubezhe XVII–XVIII vv.*). Moscow, 1917.

——— . *Religiozno-obshchestvennye dvizheniia XVII–XVIII vv. v Rossii*. Moscow, 1922.

Metcalf, M. F. *Russia, England and Swedish Party Politics 1762–1766. The Interplay between Great Power Diplomacy and Domestic Politics during Sweden's Age of Liberty*. Totowa, N.J.: Rowan and Littlefield, 1977.

——— , ed. *The Riksdag: A History of the Swedish Parliament*. New York: St. Martin's Press, 1987.

Miakotin, V. A. *Lektsii po russkoi istorii*. St. Petersburg, 1892.

Migulin, P. P. *Nasha bankovaia politika (1729–1902)*. Khar'kov, 1904.

Miliukov, P. N. *Ocherki po istorii russkoi kul'tury*. II. St. Petersburg, 1896–1903.

——— . "Zur Geschichte des russischen Adels," *Arkiv für Sozialwissenschaft und Sozialpolitik*, vol. 41 (1916).

Miliutin, V. *O nedvizhimykh imushchestvakh dukhovenstva v Rossii*. Moscow, 1862.

Milov, L. V. *Issledovanie ob "ekonomicheskikh primechaniiakh" k general'nomu mezhevaniiu (k istorii russkogo krest'ianstva i sel'skogo khoziaistva vtoroi poloviny XVIII v.)*. Moscow, 1965.

Mironov, B. N. "Eksport russkogo khleba vo vtoroi polovine XVIII nachale XIX v.," *Istoricheskie zapiski* (1973), vol. 93, pp. 149–88.

——— . *Khlebnye tseny v Rossii za dva stoletiia (XVIII–XIX vv.)*. Leningrad, 1985.

——— . "O dostovernosti vedomostei o khlebnykh tsenakh XVIII v.," *Vspomogatel'nye istoricheskie distsipliny*. Leningrad, 1969, pp. 249–62.

——— . " 'Revoliutsiia tsen' v Rossii v XVIII veke," *Voprosy istorii*, no. 11 (1973), pp. 49–61.

Morrison, Kerry. "Catherine II's Legislative Commission: An Administrative Interpretation," *Canadian-American Slavic Studies*, vol. 4, no. 3 (1970), pp. 464–84.

Myl'nikov, A. S. *Iskushenie chudom: "Russkii printz," ego ▒prototipy i dvoiniki-samozvantsy*. Leningrad, 1991.

Nadson, I. *Pugachevshchina i tserkov'*. Leningrad, 1963.

Nedosekin, V. I. "Istochniki rosta krupnogo zemlevladeniia na iuge Rossii v XVIII stoletii," *Izvestiia voronezhskogo pedagogicheskogo instituta*, 63 (1967), pp. 252–325.

Neresova, A. "Ekonomicheskoe sostoianie kostromskoi provinstii i moskovskoi gubernii po khoziaistvennym anketam 1760 godov," *Istoricheskie zapiski*, vol. 40 (1953).

Nikol'skii, N. M. *Istoriia russkoi tserkvi*. Moscow, 1937.

Ocherki istorii SSSR: period feodalizma, Rossiia vo vtoroi polovine XVIII v. vol. 3. Moscow, 1956.

Ocherki russkoi kul'tury XVIII veka, vols. 1–3. Moscow, 1985–1988.

Oliva, L. Jay. *Misalliance. A Study of French Policy in Russia During the Seven Years' War*. New York: New York University Press, 1964.

Opisanie dokumentov i del kh. v arkhive Sv. Pravoslavnogo Sinoda. St. Petersburg, 1910.

Oreshkin, V. V. *Vol'noe ekonomicheskoe obshchestvo v Rossii 1765–1917 g*. Moscow, 1963.

Osokin, E. *Vnutrennie tamozhennye poshliny v Rossii*. Kazan', 1850.

Pashkov, I. A. *Istoriia russkoi ekonomicheskoi mysli*. Moscow, 1955.

Pavlenko, N. I. "Sotsial'no-ekonomicheskie potrebnosti russkoi burzhuazii vo vtoroi polovine XVIII veka," *Istoricheskie zapiski*, vol. 69 (1960), pp. 328–44.

——— . "Odvorianivanie russkoi burzhuazii v XVIII v.," *Istoriia SSSR*, vol. 2 (1961), pp. 71–87.

Pavlov, A. *Istoricheskii ocherk sekuliarizatsii tserkovnykh zemel' v Rossii*. Odessa, 1871.

Pavlov-Sil'vanskii, N. P. *Gosudarevy sluzhilye liudi—proiskhozhdenie russkogo dvorianstva*. St. Petersburg, 1898.

——— . *Ocherki po russkoi istorii XVIII–XIX vv.* St. Petersburg, 1910.

Pavlov-Sil'vanskii, N. P. "K voprosu o vneshnikh dolgakh Rossii vo vtoroi polovine XVIII v.," *Problemy genezisa kapitalizma* (Moscow, 1970), pp. 301–33.

Pekarskii, P. *Redaktora, sotrudniki i tsenzura v russkom zhurnale, 1755–1764 godov*. St. Petersburg, 1867.

Peshtich, S. L. *Russkaia istoriografiia XVIII veka*. Vols. 1–3. Leningrad, 1961–1971.

Petrova, V. A. "Politicheskaia bor'ba vokrug senatskoi reformy 1763 goda," *Vestnik leningradskogo universiteta*, ser. 2 (1967), pp. 57–66.

Pintner, W. M., and D. K. Rowney, eds. *Russian Offficialdom: The Bureaucratization of Russian Society from the Seventeenth to the Twentieth Century*. Chapel Hill: University of North Carolina Press, 1980.

Pintner, W. "The Burden of Defense in Imperial Russia, 1725–1914," *Russian Review*, vol. 43 (1984), pp. 231–59.

——— . "The Social Characteristics of the Early Nineteenth-Century Russian Bureaucracy," *Slavic Review*, vol. 39, no. 3 (1970), pp. 429–43.

Pokrovskii, S. A. *Vneshniaia torgovlia i vneshniaia torgovaia politika Rossii*. Moscow, 1947.

Polianskii, F. Ia. *Pervonachal'noe nakoplenie kapitala v Rossii*. Moscow, 1958.

Polivanov, M. D. *K vosshestviiu na prestol imperatritsy Ekateriny II*. St. Petersburg, 1913.

Popov, M. *Arsenii Matseevich i ego delo*. St. Petersburg, 1912.

Popov, V.I. *O Sviateishem Sinode*. St. Petersburg, 1888.

Porai-Koshits, I. A. *Ocherk istorii russkogo dvorianstva ot poloviny IX do konsta XVIII veka*. St. Petersburg, 1874.

Portal, R. "Manufacturiers et classes sociales en Russie au XVIII siècle," *Revue historique*, vol. 201 (1949), pp. 161–85; vol. 202 (1949), pp. 1–23.

Prange, W. "Hans Rantzau auf Ascheberg (1693–1769) im Königlichen Dienst," *Zeitschrift der Gesellschaft für Schleswig-Holstein-Lavenburgische Geschichte*, vol. 64 (1969), pp. 189–229.

Problemy russkogo prosveshcheniia v literature XVIII veka. Moscow-Leningrad, 1961.

Ptukha, M. V. *Ocherki po istorii statistiki v SSSR*. Moscow, 1955.

Pushkarev, I. *Istoriia imperatorskoi Rossiiskoi gvardii*. St. Petersburg, 1844.

Rachlowica, B. *Przewrot w roku 1762*. Warsaw, 1912.

Raeff, M. "The Enlightenment in Russia and Russian Thought in the Enlightenment," *The Eighteenth Century in Russia*. J. G. Garrard, editor. Oxford: Clarendon Press, 1973, pp. 25–47.

——— . *Origins of the Russian Intelligentsia: The Eighteenth-Century Nobility*. New York: Harcourt, Brace & World, 1966.

——— . "The Domestic Policies of Peter III and His Overthrow," *American Historical Review*, vol. 75 (June 1970), pp. 1289–1310.

——— . "The Well-ordered Police State and the Development of Modernity in Seventeenth- and Eighteenth-Century Europe: An Attempt at a Comparative Approach," *American Historical Review*, vol. 80, no. 5 (December 1975), pp. 1221–43.

——— . *The Well-Ordered Police State: Social and Institutional Change through Law in the Germanies and Russia, 1600–1800*. New Haven, Conn.: Yale University Press, 1983.

Rambaud, A. *Russes et Prussiens: Guerre de Sept Ans*. Paris, 1895.

Ransel, D. "The Memoirs of Count Münnich," *Slavic Review,* vol. 30, no. 4 (1971), pp. 843–52.

———. *The Politics of Catherinian Russia.* New Haven, Conn.: Yale University Press, 1975.

———. "Nikita Panin's Imperial Council Project and the Struggle of Hierarchy Groups at the Court of Catherine II," *Canadian Slavic Studies,* vol. 4, no. 3 (1970), pp. 443–64.

Rasmussen, K. "Catherine II and Peter I: The Idea of a Just Monarch, the Evolution of an Attitude in Catherinian Russia." Ph.D. diss., University of California, 1973.

———. "Catherine II and the Image of Peter I," *Slavic Review,* vol. 37, no. 1 (1978), pp. 51–69.

Reddaway, W. F. "Macartney in Russia, 1765–67," *Cambridge Historical Journal,* vol. 3, no. 3 (1931), pp. 260–92.

Remezov, I. S. *Materialy dlia istorii narodnogo prosveshcheniia v Rossii.* St. Petersburg, 1886.

Roberts, M. *The Age of Liberty, Sweden, 1719–1772.* Cambridge: Cambridge University Press, 1986.

———. *British Diplomacy and Swedish Politics, 1758–1773.* Minneapolis: University of Minnesota Press, 1980/1981.

Rogger, H. *National Consciousness in Eighteenth-Century Russia.* Cambridge: Harvard University Press, 1960.

Romanovich-Slavatinskii, A. *Dvorianstvo v Rossii ot nachala XVIII v. do otmeny krepostnogo prava.* Kiev, 1912.

Rostislavov, D. I. *Opyt issledovaniia ob imushchestvakh i dokhodakh nashikh monastyrei.* St. Petersburg, 1876.

Rozanov, N. *Istoriia moskovskago eparkhial'nago upravleniia so vremeni uchrezhdeniia S. Sinoda s 1721–1821.* Moscow, 1870.

Rubinshtein, N. L. "Ulozhennaia komissiia 1754–1766 gg. i ee proekt novogo ulozheniia 'o sostoianii poddannykh voobshche' (k istorii sotsial'noi politiki 50-kh-nachala 60-kh godov XVIII v.)," *Istoricheskie zapiski* (1951), pp. 208–51.

———. "Vneshniaia torgovlia Rossii i russkoe kupechestvo vo vtoroi polovine XVIII v.," *Istoricheskie zapiski,* vol. 4 (1955), pp. 343–61.

———. *Sel'skoe khoziaistvo Rossii vo vtoroi polovine XVIII v.* Moscow, 1957.

Ruffman, K. H. "Russisches Adel als Sendertypus der Europäischen Adelswelt," *Jahrbücher für Geschichte Osteuropas,* vol. 9 (1961), pp. 161–78.

Ryndziunskii, P. G. *Gorodskoe grazhdanstvo doreformennoi Rossii.* Moscow, 1958.

———. "Novye goroda Rossii konsta XVIII v.," *Problemy obshchestvenno-politicheskoi istorii Rossii i slavianskikh stran, sbornik statei k 70-letiiu akademika M. N. Tikhomirova* (Moscow, 1963), pp. 359–70.

Sacke, G. "Adel und Burgertum in der Regierungszeit Katharinas II. von Russland," *Revue belge de philologie et d'histoire,* vol. 17 (1938).

Samsonov, A. M. *Antifeodal'nye vostaniia v Rossii i tserkov'.* Moscow, 1956.

Säve, T. *Sveriges deltagande i sjuåriga kriget åren 1757–1772.* Stockholm, 1915.

Savelov, L. M. *Bibliograficheskii ukazatel' po istorii, geral'dike i rodoslovii rossiiskogo dvorianstva.* Ostrozhok, 1897.

Savluchinskii, P. S. *Russkaia dukhovnaia literatura pervoi poloviny XVIII veka i ee otnoshenie k sovremennost (1700–1762 gg.).* Kiev, 1878.

"Sbornik tserkovno-istoricheskikh i statisticheskikh svedenii o Riazanskoi eparkhii," *COIDR,* vol. 4, pp. 1–108.

Schmidt, K. R. "The Treaty between Great Britain and Russia 1766," *Scando-Slavica,* vol. 1 (1954), pp. 115–34.

Semenov, A. *Izuchenie istoricheskikh svedenii o rossiiskoi vneshnei torgovle i promyshlennosti.* St. Petersburg, 1859.

Semevskii, M. I. *Istoricheskii ocherk.* St. Petersburg, 1859–1862.

————. "Shest' mesiatsev iz russkoi istorii XVIII veka, ocherk tsarstvovaniia imp. Petra III, 1761–1762 goda," *Otechestvennye zapiski*, vol. 173 (1867), pp. 160–94.

————. "Svedeniia ob ofitserakh konnoi gvardii, v iiune mesiatse 1763 goda," *Russkii arkhiv*, vol. 5 (1867), pp. 481–86.

Semevskii, V. I. "Iz istorii obshchestvennykh techenii v Rossii v XVIII i pervoi polovine XIX veka," *Istoricheskoe obozrenie*, vol. 9 (1898), pp. 244–90.

————. "Pravitel'stvo obshchestvo i narod v istorii krest'ianskogo voprosa vo vtoroi polovine XVIII i pervoi polovine XIX veka," in *Velikaia Reforma* (Moscow, 1911), pp. 27–92.

Sh. "Dvorianstvo v Rossii (istoricheskii i obshchestvennyi ocherk)," *Vestnik Evropy*, vol. 22 (Apr. 1887), pp. 539–45.

Shabanova, A. M. "Klassovaia bor'ba krest'ian v votchine Aleksandro-Svirskogo monastyria nakanune sekuliarizatsii (50-kh-nachala 60-kh godov XVIII veka)," *Vestnik leningradskogo gosudarstvennogo universiteta* (1966), pp. 50–60.

Shchebal'skii, P. K. *Politicheskaia sistema Petra III*. Moscow, 1870.

Shchepkin, E. N. *Starinnye pomeshchiki na sluzhbe i doma, iz semeinoi khroniki (1578–1762)*. St. Petersburg, 1890.

Shchepkin, Y. N. *Russko-Avstriiskii soiuz vo vremia semiletnei voiny 1746–1768*. St. Petersburg, 1902.

Shcherbatov, M. M. *O povrezhdenii nravov v Rossii*. London, 1858.

————. "Bumagi," *Russkaia starina*, no. 1 (1870), pp. 28–30.

————. *Sochineniia Shcherbatova*. Vol. 1. Ed. I. P. Khrushchev. St. Petersburg, 1896.

————. *On the Corruption of Morals in Russia*. Ed. and trans. A. Lentin. Cambridge: Cambridge University Press, 1969.

Shirokii, V. F. "Voprosy torgovogo ucheta v zakonodatel'nykh aktakh i literature Rossii XVIII v.," *Trudy leningradskogo instituta sovetskoi torgovli*, no. 3 (1940), pp. 51–87.

Shmelev, G. N., ed. *Akty tsarstvovaniia Ekateriny II*. Moscow, 1907.

Shtrange, M. M. *Demokraticheskaia intelligentsiia Rossii v XVIII veke*. Moscow, 1965.

Shubinskii, S. N. *Istoricheskie ocherki i rasskazy*. St. Petersburg, 1871.

Smolitsch, I. *Russisches Mönchtums Entstehung, Entwicklung, und Wesen*. Wurzburg, 1953.

————. *Geschichte der russischen Kirche, 1700–1917*. Leiden-Cologne, 1964.

Sobranie postanovlenii po chasti raskola. St. Petersburg, 1868.

Solov'ev, I. M. "Shkoly Ekaterininskoi epokhi," *Tri veka* (*Rossiia ot smuty do nashego vremeni*), vol. 4 (Moscow, 1913).

Solov'ev, S. M. *Istoriia Rossii s drevneishikh vremen*, vols. 12–13 (Moscow, 1963).

Sopodovnikov, D. D. *Riazanskie pomeshchiki XVIII v.* Riazan, 1929.

Spasskii, I. G. *Peterburgskii monetnyi dvor ot vozniknoveniia do nachala XIX veka*. Leningrad, 1949.

Stepanov, M. *Finansovye sistemy Anglii, Frantsii i Rossii*. St. Petersburg, 1868.

Storch, H. *Historisch-statische Gemälde des Russischen Reichs*. Leipzig, 1803.

Strumilin, S. G. *Ocherki ekonomicheskoi istorii Rossii*. Moscow, 1960.

Sudeikin, B. *Gosudarstvennyi bank*. St. Petersburg, 1891.

Svatikov, S. *Obshchestvennoe dvizhenie Rossii v 1700–1895*. Rostov na Donu, 1905.

Tankov, A. A. *Istoricheskaia letopis' kurskogo dvorianstva*. Moscow, 1913.

Titov, A. A. *Sviateishii Sinod v pervoi polovine XVIII veka*. Iaroslavl', 1908.

Tolstoi, D. *Istoriia finansovykh uchrezhdenii Rossii so vremeni osnovaniia gosudarstva do konchiny Ekateriny II*. St. Petersburg, 1848.

Tolstoi, D. A. 'Vzgliad na uchebnuiu chast' v Rossii v XVIII stoletii do 1782 goda," *Zapiski imp. AN*, vol. 67 (1883), pp. 1–100.

Tooke, William. *A View of the Russian Empire during the Reign of Catherine II*. London, 1800.

————. *The Life of Catherine*. London, 1801.

Travchetov, N. P. "Svedeniia ob arkhive byvshago Muromskago Dukhovnago Pravleniia," *Trudy vladimirskoi uchenoi arkhivnoi komissii*, vol. 4 (1902), pp. 43–50.

Troitskii, S. M. "Dvorianskie proekty ukrepleniia gosudarstvennykh finansov v seredine XVIII v.," *Voprosy istorii,* no. 2 (1958), pp. 60–75.
——— . *Finansovaia politika russkogo absoliutizma v XVIII v.* Moscow, 1966.
——— . "Istoriografiia 'dvortsovykh perevorotov' v Rossii XVIII v.," *Voprosy istorii* no. 2 (1966), pp. 8–53.
——— . "Materialy perepisi chinovnikov v 1754–1756 gg. kak istochnik po sotsial'no-politicheskoi i kul'turnoi istorii Rossii XVIII v.," *Arkheograficheskii exhegodnik za 1967 g.* (Moscow, 1969), pp. 132–48.
——— . "O nekotorykh istochnikakh po istorii zemlevladeniia v Ingermanlandii v pervoi polovine XVIII v.," *Istochnikovedcheskie problemy istorii narodov Pribaltiki* (Riga, 1970), pp. 11–25.
——— . "O skupke zemel' A. D. Menshikovym, A. V. Makarovym i I. A. i P. A. Musinymi-Pushkinymi," *Voprosy agrarnoi istorii Tsentral i Severo-Zapada RSFSR* (Smolensk, 1972), pp. 85–99.
——— . "Russkie diplomaty v seredine XVIII v.," in *Feodal'naia Rossiia vo vsemirno-istoricheskom protsesse* (Moscow, 1972), pp. 398–406.
——— . *Russkii absoliutizm i dvorianstvo XVIII v.* Moscow, 1974.
Tugan-Baranovskii, M. I. *Russkaia fabrika v proshlom i nastoiashchem.* St. Petersburg, 1907.
Turgenev, A. I. *La cour de Russie il y a cent ans, 1725–1783.* Berlin, 1858.
Tverdokhlebov, V. N. "K voprosu o finansakh Rossii pri preemnikakh Petra," *Trudy finansovo-ekonomicheskogo instituta* (1947), pp. 199–244.
Umrikhina, A. *Polozhenie krest'ian i obostrenie klasskovykh protivorechii v 60-kh godakh XVIII veka v Belgorodskoi gubernii, v pomoshch uchiteliam istorii.* Belgorod, 1969.
Vandal, A. *Louis XV et Elizabeth de Russie.* Paris, 1882.
Veidemeier, A. I. *Dvor i zamechatel'nye liudi v Rossii vo vtoroi polovine XVIII st.* St. Petersburg, 1846.
Veretennikov, V. I. *Iz istorii Tainoi Kantseliarii 1713–1762 gg.* Khar'kov, 1911.
——— . *Ocherki istorii General-prokuratory v Rossii do ekaterininskogo vremeni.* Kharkov, 1915.
Verkhovskii, P. V. *Naselennyia nedvizhimyia imeniia sv. Sinoda, arkhiereiskikh domov i monastyrei pri blizhaishikh preemnikakh Petra Velikogo.* St. Petersburg, 1909.
Vernadskii, G. V. "Manifest Petra III o vol'nosti dvorianskoi i zakonodatel'naia komissiia 1754–1766 gg," *Istoricheskoe obozrenie,* vol. 20 (1915), pp. 51–59.
Veselago, F. *Ocherk istorii Morskogo kadetskogo korpusa, s prilozheniem spiska vospitannikov za 100 let.* St. Petersburg, 1852.
Viskovatov, A. *Kratkaia istoriia pervogo kadetskogo korpusa.* St. Petersburg, 1832.
Vladimirskii-Budanov, M. F. "Gosudarstvo i narodnoe obrazovanie v Rossii XVIII veka (Sistema professional'nogo obrazovaniia ot Petra I do Ekateriny II)," *Vremennik Demidovskogo iuridicheskogo muzeia,* no. 6, ser. 5 (1873), pp. 1–96; no. 7, ser 4, pp. 97–192; no. 8, ser. 4, pp. 193–330.
Volkov, M. Ia. "Tamozhennaia reforma 1753–1757 gg," *Istoricheskie zapiski,* vol. 71 (1962), pp. 134–57.
Waddington, R. *La guerre de sept ans: histoire diplomatique et militaire.* vols 1–4. Paris, 1899–1914.
Wood, J. B. "Social Structure and Social Change among the Nobility of the Election of Bayeux, 1463–1666," Ph.D. diss., Emory University, 1973.
Wortman, R. *The Development of a Russian Legal Consciousness.* Chicago: University of Chicago Press, 1976.
Zagorskii, M. V. "Razbor i opisanie del pravoslavskago dukhovnago pravleniia," *Trudy vladimirskoi uchenoi arkhivnoi komissii* (1902), pp. 1–42.
Zaozerskaia, E. I. *Rabochaia sila i klassovaia bor'ba na tekstil'nykh manufakturakh Rossii v 20–60 gg. XVIII v.* Moscow, 1960.
Zapadov, A. V. *Russkaia zhurnalistika 30-kh-60-kh g. XVIII v.* Moscow, 1957.

Zavialov, A. *Vopros o tserkovnykh imeniiakh pri imperatritse Ekaterine II*. St. Petersburg, 1900.

Zeller, G. *De Louis XIV à 1789*. Paris, 1955.

Zheludkov, V. V. "Krest'ianskaia voina pod rukovodstvom E. I. Pugacheva i podgotovka gubernskoi reformy 1775 g," *Vestnik Leningradskogo Gosudarstvennogo Universiteta* (1963), pp. 56–65.

Znamenskii, I. *Prikhodskoe dukhovenstvo v Rossii so vremeni reformy Petra*. Kazan, 1873.

——— . *Polozhenie dukhovenstva v tsarstvovanie Ekateriny II i Pavla*. Moscow, 1880.

Zorin, V., et al. *Istoriia diplomatii*. Moscow, 1959.

INDEX